Contemporary Studies in Romance Linguistics

Margarita Suñer

Editor

Georgetown University Press, Washington, D.C. 20057

Library of Congress Cataloging in Publication Data

Linguistic Symposium on Romance Linguistics, 7th, Cornell
　　University, 1977.
　　Contemporary Studies in Romance Linguistics.

　　1. Romance languages--Congresses. I. Suñer,
Margarita. II. Title.
PC11.L53　　1977　　　　440　　　78-13028
ISBN 0-87840-044-3

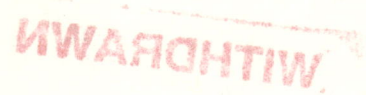

Copyright　© 1978 by Georgetown University
All rights reserved
Printed in the United States of America

International Standard Book Number: 0-87840-044-3

This volume is dedicated to two Cornell professors emeriti who have made outstanding contributions to the field of Romance Linguistics, Frederick B. Agard and Robert A. Hall, Jr.

CONTENTS

Preface   ix

Dwight Bolinger
  Free will and determinism in language:
  Or, who does the choosing, the grammar
  or the speaker?   1

Ivonne A. Bordelois
  Animacy or subjecthood: Clitic movement
  and Romance causatives   18

Michael Canale, Raymond Mougeon, and
Monique Bélanger
  Analogical leveling of the auxiliary
  être in Ontarian French   41

Peter Cannings
  Definiteness and relevance:
  The semantic unity of il y a   62

William W. Cressey
  Absolute neutralization of the phonemic
  glide-versus-vowel contrast in Spanish   90

Carroll N. Davis
  Generative semantic analysis of
  tense in Spanish   106

Jorge M. Guitart
  Aspects of Spanish aspect: A new look
  at the preterit/imperfect distinction   132

Robert A. Hall, Jr.
  Latin and Proto-Romance verb-conjugations   169

Eric P. Hamp
  The British end of the spectrum of Romania   172

Julia Herschensohn
  The predictability of the article
  in French   176

James P. Lantolf
  The variable constraints on mood in
  Puerto Rican-American Spanish   193

Yves-Charles Morin
  Morphological regularization in the
  verbal paradigm of Modern French   218

Ricardo Otheguy
  A semantic analysis of the difference
  between el/la and lo   241

Wayne J. Redenbarger
  Portuguese vowel harmony and the
  'elsewhere condition'   258

Mario Saltarelli
  Sentential clitics and clause reduction
  in Italian   279

Sanford A. Schane
  Syllable versus word boundary in French   302

Albert Valdman
  The 'loi de position' and the direction
  of phonological change in the French
  mid vowel system   316

Barry L. Velleman
  Latinist and universalist models
  in Spanish grammar   330

Stephen Wallace
  What is a Creole? The example of the
  Portuguese language of Tugu, Jakarta,
  Indonesia   340

Stanley Whitley
  Rule reordering in the phonological
  history of Spanish (o sea, ¿tiene el
  idioma un espíritu?)   378

PREFACE

The articles contained in this volume were selected from papers presented at the Seventh Annual Linguistic Symposium on Romance Languages (LSRL-7) held at Cornell University on April 22-24, 1977. As the seventh of a series, this conference reaffirms the status of LSRL as a gathering for specialists in the field of Romance Linguistics. The first symposium was held at the University of Florida in 1971, with subsequent symposia at the University of Illinois, Indiana University, the University of Texas, the University of Michigan, and the Université de Montréal.

The principal goal of the LSRL has been to provide a forum where younger and established scholars alike could contribute to the synchronic and diachronic description of Romance languages in the light of current developments in linguistic theory.

The 20 papers of this collection could be characterized in many ways. One of the simplest would be by language, e.g. Spanish, French, Italian, Portuguese, and Latin; another would be by subfield of endeavor, e.g. syntax, phonology, and semantics. Neither of these characterizations would, however, be particularly enlightening. More interesting is to show how these articles reflect on one of the major trends in the field of linguistics as a whole: that of constraining the power of the theory, of redefining and refining principles and formalisms; thus, by implication, the range of possible grammars is narrowed in the search for the Grammar. Undoubtedly, different approaches to this common aim are possible and indeed several are used in this volume.

A few examples will suffice to illustrate this point. Among the studies concerned primarily with syntax, that by Bolinger argues that no claim of automaticity should be made regarding any fact of syntax until every attempt has been made to discover a meaning for that fact.

Bordelois advocates the syntactic relevance of the feature of animacy and its semantic connotations over subjecthood; this casts doubts on the explanatory power of the Specified Subject Condition. The reader will find it interesting to contrast Bordelois' claim on the existence of a Clitic Movement rule with Saltarelli's hypothesis that such a rule is unnecessary (for Italian), since the placement of clitics--according to him--comes about as a consequence of independently motivated rules of structure reduction. At the same time, these two papers might provide grounds for testing the adequacy of two outgrowths of classical transformational theory, namely, extended standard theory and relational grammar.

Cannings shows that once the linguist 'relativises' the scope of reference to what may be called 'domains of reference', there is no reason to recognize distinct readings of il y a: anomalous readings will be simply discarded due to their 'uninformative' nature.

While Guitart outlines for us what speakers know about the rules that govern the use of the Preterit/Imperfect in Spanish, Davis modifies and extends McCawley's (1971) version of the generative semantics model for tense and applies it to Spanish.

Otheguy provides a semantic analysis--Form-Content Approach--of el/la and lo, where the concept of gender is abandoned in favor of the 'discreteness' hypothesis.

Refinements, refutations, and the undertaking of finding a better and more accurate grammar are not, however, limited to syntactic and semantic studies. In this volume two papers, which deal with different languages, maintain that recent phonological proposals (those of Hooper and Harris, respectively) are not justified. Schane demonstrates the impossibility of stating all phonological rules for French without reference to syntactic boundaries, thus heralding the demise of a strong version of syllable phonology. Redenbarger argues in favor of the specification of Portuguese mid vowels as a contrast in tenseness, since this allows for more naturally stated rules and also eliminates the need for the 'Elsewhere Condition'.

Cressey makes us doubt the generality of Postal's (1968) principle of phonetic-phonological relations, by showing that Spanish is in need of a variable rule which neutralizes any posited systematic phonemic glide-versus-vowel contrast.

Two articles rely on more empirically based data: one on a carefully prepared questionnaire, the other on transcripts of speech in natural context. Lantolf discusses the findings of his questionnaire on the selection of verbal mood in embedded clauses in Spanish, and Canale, Mougeon, and Bélanger report on the variation in the frequency of occurrence in the speech of Franco-Ontarian students, of <u>avoir</u> with some verbs which require the auxiliary <u>être</u> in Standard French.

Many more controversies and points of theoretical interest thread their way throughout the articles. Although space prevents their development here, attentive readers are sure to find discussion of issues which relate to their own research.

In organizing the LSRL-7, I have enjoyed the help and support of many people and want to take this opportunity to thank them all. In addition to those who presented papers at the symposium, my special thanks go to the members of the Selection Committee who gave generously of their time in order to read and judge the 76 abstracts submitted: L. D. King, J. S. Noblitt, F. van Coetsem, and L. R. Waugh. Their sound judgment is evidenced in the quality of the papers in this volume.

Many students provided assistance, especially J. Sternber and M. Howden. K. Molt of the Conference Center provided invaluable help, as did S. Doucett, our secretary. I am also grateful to L. R. Waugh, my coorganizer, for her role in the initial planning of this symposium.

Professors F. B. Agard, R. A. Hall, Jr., L. D. King, and J. S. Noblitt were consulted during the difficult task of selecting and editing the papers for publication and their help is deeply appreciated.

LSRL-7 was sponsored by the Department of Modern Languages and Linguistics and the College of Arts and Sciences of Cornell University. I am grateful both for their support and especially that of Dean H. Levin and Provost D. C. Knapp in providing the funds that made this symposium possible.

FREE WILL AND DETERMINISM IN LANGUAGE:
OR, WHO DOES THE CHOOSING,
THE GRAMMAR OR THE SPEAKER?

DWIGHT BOLINGER
Palo Alto, California

There is a yearning in the human spirit that early sowed the seeds of automation. The mousetrap tells the story: build a better one, and the world will beat a path to your door. Before mousetraps, it was necessary to pay individual attention to the mouse if one wanted to catch him. The trap solved the problem of making the mouse catch himself.

When it comes to the variety of rodents that have to be hunted down, no other science can quite match linguistics. It is very tiring to be a linguist and very natural to long for some labor-saving device that will make it possible, when you bag one rat, to bag one or two more at the same time. The phenomenology is so complex that we are desperate for any means that will reduce the number of entities or at least will make it possible to create a level at which a lower variety becomes a higher unity, and orderly relations can be traced from one level to another.

Our misfortune is that we are not inventors. We cannot improvise a contrivance that will take advantage of something in the behavior of our quarry to make it trap itself. But we can devise our descriptions so that one move in the game is predictable on the basis of another, and once predictable it no longer requires attention for its own sake.

Linguistics is a science of behavior. The things it describes are things that people do, and accordingly, may or may not choose to do. The history of phonology is a record of linguistic attitudes toward the problem of choice. There was a time when every detail of the positions and movements of the speech organs had to be considered in its own right as potentially relevant to the production of an intelligible word or sentence. The better one became as a phonetician and the more delicately the ear was trained, the more unmanageable the profusion of elements became; and the harder it was to believe that speakers could even be aware of all the distinctions, let alone produce them voluntarily. Some of them had to be the automatic result of others, which represented the genuine choices. And that was the genesis of our most famous mousetrap, the phoneme. It captured a whole series of variants and hung them on a very few distinctive features. Whether one says <u>debt</u> or <u>debtor</u>, one chooses to use a single unit of sound, a /t/, that is automatically stop or flap depending on the environment.

There are two ways in which making a choice causes certain other things to happen. If one decides to produce a sentence like <u>Tell me</u> or <u>Take it</u>, one is committed to producing the sound of a /t/. That is determinism from a higher level to a lower. At the same time, one is producing a /t/ sound at the beginning of a sentence and in a word where the /t/ is followed by a full vowel: <u>tell</u>, <u>take</u>. That also has an automatic consequence: the /t/ will be a stop with delayed voicing, not a flap. This is determinism in the context, 'same-level' determinism: something else at the same level as the /t/ makes an automatic selection among the possible varieties of /t/ sounds. The standard term for same-level determinism in phonology is conditioned variation.

We know that the first kind of determinism has to exist in some form. There is always a higher-to-lower order of commandings and obeyings, as part of the way living organisms are built. One decides to go for a walk. That presumably is a free choice. But the act of walking, of putting first one leg forward and then the other, is a consequence of that choice and is generally automatic--it is part of a learned routine, a habit, and becomes conscious only when interfered with. Similarly a speaker who wishes to say the word _tell_ reaches in somewhere and pulls out the routine of sounds that constitutes that word. But about the second kind of determinism we cannot be so sure. Is what happens there an instance of choosing the sound /t/ and then having the neighboring sounds pick out for us the right variety, or is it that we know what the neighboring sounds are going to be, and accordingly choose the right variety to fit that context?

With phonology it makes sense to describe at least some things in automatic terms because it is not really sounds that we are talking about but movements of the speech organs. The human vocal apparatus has certain natural limits. For the most part I am free to move my tongue as I please, but if I clench my teeth one of two things results automatically: either I bite my tongue, or I am unable to stick it out. When one physical movement collides with another, there are predictable effects even when each is chosen voluntarily. If in our description we then set up the predictable effects as entities in their own right, we can class them as automatic and semantically irrelevant variants. Dealing with them as entities is a notational convenience.

But now comes the part that Roman Jakobson calls phonological contraband. The structuralists smuggled phonological techniques into morphology. Our contemporaries have smuggled them into syntax. We hear about 'pronominalization', where pronouns are supposed to spring up under the magic of some process, '_there_-insertion', where an expletive materializes out of nowhere and fills an otherwise empty slot, 'lexical selection', where a word or class of words at one point determines a word or a case form at another point, '_do_-support', whereby an otherwise meaningless auxiliary props up a question or a negation. These are not presented as meaningful signals but as automatic manifestations of something that was already there. It is a curious outcome at a time when syntax was being touted as the creative side of language, the domain of free choice. My contention is that the notion of freedom should not have been surrendered so easily, but rather pushed to the limit: that no claim of automaticity should have been made concerning any fact of syntax before exploring every avenue that might lead to discovering a meaning for it. The fallacy is epitomized in a passage from <u>The sound pattern of English</u>: 'Once the speaker has selected a sentence with a particular syntactic structure and certain lexical items ... the choice of stress contour is not a matter subject to further independent decision' (Chomsky and Halle 1968:25-26). Accent is pictured as a meaningless consequence of decisions at the level of syntax. The fact is that speakers are not only free to make further independent decisions, but do so to convey an indispensable part of their message. The case studies I am going to cite are similar instances of supposed automaticity where meaningful contrasts have been glossed over in order to achieve a neat formulation.

The first case study is one of higher-to-lower determinism in English yes-no questions, the '<u>do</u>-support' case already mentioned. The simplest description lumps together all instances of yes-no questions that invert the subject. To turn the statement <u>John can swallow a goldfish</u> into a question, <u>John</u> and <u>can</u> are inverted: <u>Can John swallow a goldfish?</u> But the statement <u>John swallowed a goldfish</u> no longer allows the inversion <u>*Swallowed John a goldfish?</u>; a <u>did</u> is required: <u>Did John swallow a goldfish?</u> This looks like the pure fabrication of an empty word to make all questions come out the same way regardless of whether the corresponding declarative sentence has an actual auxiliary such as <u>can</u> or <u>should</u>. As a result of choosing to ask a question, the word <u>do</u> automatically pops into its proper place.

This amounts to saying that <u>do</u> has no meaning of its own. Either it has no meaning at all, and is there only to fill an otherwise empty slot, or it has a meaning that merely reflects the construction in which it occurs. Which is right--the naive view that a word is a word, or the clever view that it is nothing? Suppose one asks Do you like it? and receives the reply I do. From the standpoint of communication, I do is a yes answer--do means affirmation. This is hardly surprising in view of the use of do for emphatic affirmation in exchanges like You don't like it.--I do like it! In fact, one might suppose that the simple I do is just a truncated form of I do like it, with the same emphatic do, and that it is not do by itself that carries the affirmation but do as a representative of the full sentence I do like it. But that cannot be right, because the two are not interchangeable. I do is a normal response to Do you like it?; I do like it is not, though it might be used after a moment's hesitation, as if to say, By gosh, it's true! I do like it! So it appears that do by itself is what conveys the affirmation when we say simply I do, and does not get its affirmativeness from the construction in which it occurs.

The same affirmativeness shows up in commands. Shall I leave now? can be answered as readily by Do or Please do as by Yes. And the same affirmative use of do is found in commands that are not in response to a question. If someone comes into a room, it is normal to give the invitation Sit down almost immediately. But if host and guest stand for a time, then it is normal to say Do sit down, with affirmative do in contrast with the prior negation, the not-sitting-down (Bolinger 1977:191-196). In first-person commands, Do let's and Let's do are stereotyped affirmations.

With the affirmativeness of do appearing under so many guises, it would be surprising if questions were the one exception, the one place where all that do accomplishes is to serve as the automatic filler of an otherwise empty slot, triggered by some underlying morpheme called Q. Assuming that yes-no questions are what the name implies, it seems reasonable to suppose that do in questions is a way of calling for an answer that has to do with affirmation or its opposite. The same is true of 'do-support' in negation: if do is an affirmative, the logical way to make a negative is by negating it: don't, doesn't. As for WH questions, they presuppose an affirmation: Why did you hit him? implies 'you did hit him'.

There may be some residue of automaticity here, but do is at least something more than a syntactic reflex.

The second case study concerns a same-level determinism, the supposed process by which a movement transformation results in the insertion of the word it. The sentences To study is hard and It is hard to study presumably represent the same underlying structure. If the subject in the first is moved to the end the result is *Is hard to study, an ungrammatical sequence requiring the addition of it --one more example of a meaningless slot-filler.

But the question is, do the two arrangements really mean the same? If they do, it ought to be possible to use them in the same contexts. Particularly it ought to be possible to use them to answer the same questions. Imagine two friends out taking the night air. The first tells the second that he has to go back because he has an assignment to prepare. The second asks How is it in your room? and the first replies It's hard to study; the place is too noisy. Trading the form of the answer yields nonsense:

 How is it in your room?--*To study is hard; the
   place is too noisy.

Without going through all the motions I am going to make the claim that it is the same word whether it occurs in a sentence like It's hard to study or in one like It's raining or in one like I take it that you don't agree with me, and that in all of them it is a pronoun with an antecedent: it refers to the extant situation, which the hearer is supposed to flesh out with whatever is appropriate under the circumstances. It is hardly strange that a pronoun should have such a function in view of the number of nouns in English that have a similar generality: business, matter, affair, thing—That business of his having cheated says no more than That of his having cheated. The word it is simply the ultimate in generality, and our mistake has been to confuse generality of meaning with lack of meaning. The essential oneness of it is evident in our freedom to make combinations like that of the answer in

>   How was it this afternoon?—It was hot and just about impossible to get anything done.

where 'weather' it and 'extrapositional' it are joined in a single reference to the whole afternoon situation, which was one of heat and futility (see Bolinger 1977:68-89).

So it, like do, is a word in its own right, and not the mechanical, predetermined result of a prior choice.

My third case study I borrow from the work of Erica García on Spanish se. This clitic pronoun has been described in two ways as a same-level bit of determinism. One is the reflexive. Given an underlying Juan vio a Juan with coreferential Juan and Juan, the second Juan automatically switches to se: Juan se vio 'John saw himself'. The other is the indirect object. Given a sentence like Le di el libro 'I gave him (her, you) the book', if the direct object is pronominalized to yield lo the resulting sentence is not *Le lo di but Se lo di—the le 'changes to' se. Traditionally the two processes whereby a se is produced have been regarded as unrelated, and the identity of the result as a coincidence.

García is not willing to swallow the coincidence and has looked for a unitary concept. What meaning could be borne by such a common se? As she words it, 'the l forms (él, le, lo) all share the meaning HIGH DEIXIS, and the s forms (se, sí, su) are all opposed to them in meaning LOW DEIXIS' (García 1975:65). Deixis she defines as 'the force with which the hearer is instructed to seek the referent of the pronoun'. 'HIGH DEIXIS tells him: "Find

the third person referred to!"--an instruction that
is appropriate where the antecedent of the pronoun
is not obvious, or is relatively hard to find, or
should under no circumstances be missed.'

    LOW DEIXIS tells [the hearer]: 'Seek neither
hard nor far for the third person referred to'
--an instruction that is appropriate where the
antecedent is obvious, easy to find, or where
it does not much matter if the referent is
identified or not (as in the case of 'impersonal'
se, which in terms of specific reference, can
perfectly well be left hanging).

    So Spanish se turns out to be like English it--
apparently unrelated uses are only the side effect
of the context. Both are highly abstract words,
with the function of telling the hearer something
to look for. The fact that it is used for weather
is the result of the weather always being with us
--it is the most obvious thing under the circumstances. The fact that se is used for the reflexive results from the antecedent being the most
obvious thing possible, having already been mentioned. Neither is the automatic result of anything.

    My fourth case study I take from D. R. Ladd.
It is a case of supposed higher-to-lower determinism in intonation. Ladd exemplifies with English,
but the same thing could occur in any language that
uses accent for focus. The example he uses is from
Chomsky: John is neither éager to please, nor éasy
to please, nor cértain to please. Chomsky explains:
'In "parallel constructions", in some sense of this
notion that has never been made quite clear, contrastive intonation is necessary' (Chomsky 1971:
205 cited by Ladd 1977:12). In other words, given
the syntactic condition of parallelism, the special
accent emerges automatically. But Ladd argues that
the accent is one of the ways in which we tell that
there is such a thing as parallelism: Chomsky puts
the cart before the horse. The same accent is found

in situations that lack any <u>syntactic</u> parallel, and the accent is then the only clue to the parallelism. For example:

> When was the last time you saw any of your relatives?--My mother called me yesterday--does that count?

If the accent is on <u>mother</u>, the response asks whether <u>parents</u> are to be considered as part of the 'relatives' under discussion. If the accent is on <u>called</u>, it asks whether being called on the telephone counts as some kind of seeing. But if the accent is on both <u>me</u> and <u>mother</u>, the question is about a parallel: does my mother getting in touch with me count the same as my getting in touch with her? Ladd concludes that 'it should be clear that the syntax in no way determines the accent placement; if ... the speaker wants the accent pattern that says "parallel", he uses it' (1977:13).

My fifth case study is the supposed movement transformation that results in '<u>there</u>-insertion'. <u>There</u>, like <u>it</u>, is an extra word thrown in for the sake of the syntax, adding nothing to the meaning. According to one analysis the steps in the transformation are roughly those in

> In front of the carriage rode two men ⟹ There rode two men in front of the carriage ⟹ In front of the carriage there rode two men (see Kuno 1971:361-364).

The initial locative <u>in front of the carriage</u> is moved, but then must be replaced by <u>there</u> to avoid the ungrammatical *<u>Rode two men in front of the carriage</u>. A second movement transformation optionally replaces the locative at the beginning, and <u>there</u> is retained.

This of course implies the claim that the minimal pair <u>In front of the carriage rode two men</u> and <u>In front of the carriage there rode two men</u> involves no difference in meaning. Clearly there is no difference in <u>truth value</u>--but truth value hardly

exhausts the possibilities of linguistic meaning.
Examples like the following show that there does
contrast with its absence:

*As I recall, across the street is a grocery.
As I recall, across the street there's a grocery.
As you can see, across the street is a grocery.
*I can see that across the street is a grocery.
I can see that across the street there's a grocery.

The contrast here is the same as the one noted in
Atkinson (1973) between Vint un homme and Il vint
un homme, in French. The expression without the
particle brings something before our physical
senses--the locative is a kind of stage. The third
example above refers to a visual stage on which
something is actually present. On the other hand,
something recalled is presented to the mind, not to
the eyes. The same is true of factive see that as
against physical see. The function of there is
that of an abstract mental location. There is no
problem in using it with a real locative, because
real locations can be mental when they are remembered or when they are out of sight, or even
when they are within view if we choose to focus on
their presence as informational rather than visual.
The same contrast shows up in the tense of the
verb:

Nearby was a fight in full progress.
??Nearby had been a fight in full progress.
Nearby there had been a fight in full progress.

The action of the perfect tenses is off-stage: the
thread of the narrative--the things we are shown one
by one as they occur--is given by the simple
tenses. Furthermore the contrast shows up in questions versus statements. A statement can be demon-
strative--it can point out that something is somewhere and bring it on stage; but a question has to
be about a fact:

Beside the house were at least a dozen trees.

There were beside the house at least a dozen trees.
*Were beside the house at least a dozen trees?[1]
Were there beside the house at least a dozen trees?

The conclusion is the same as before. When a speaker <u>chooses</u> to present something to the mind, he uses the word <u>there</u> (see Bolinger 1977:90-123). It is not something that is determined by a prior decision to put a locative at the end of the sentence.

My sixth case study comes from the spirit world and could only happen in linguistics. The decision that is supposed to lead to the automatic result does not show up in the actual sentence but stays submerged in the speaker's mind. This kind of thing depends on the theory that there is an underlying structure containing something that produces an effect but remains hidden from view.

The case involves two words that have had a checkered history in linguistics, <u>any</u> and <u>some</u>. Fifteen years ago they were associated with a much cruder kind of determinism. It was supposed that they were suppletive variants, with <u>any</u> triggered automatically by some preceding negative, interrogative, or condition:

I have some raisins.
*I have any raisins.
I don't have any raisins.
Do you have any raisins?
If I had any raisins I'd eat them.

One of the critics of the cruder determinism was Robin Lakoff (1969). She noticed that conditions may show a contrast in meaning:

If you eat some spinach I'll give you ten dollars.
*If you eat any spinach I'll give you ten dollars.
If you eat any candy I'll whip you.
*If you eat some candy I'll whip you.

She felt that something in the underlying structure made the difference--a promise in the first pair, which made <u>some</u> appropriate, and a warning in the second pair, which made <u>any</u> appropriate. Instead of some overt controlling element, we now had an abstract performative verb that first determined whether <u>any</u> or <u>some</u> would be used, and then might or might not be deleted:

> I promise you that if you eat some spinach I'll give you ten dollars. ⟹ If you eat some spinach I'll give you ten dollars.
> I warn you that if you eat any candy I'll whip you. ⟹ If you eat any candy I'll whip you.

This idea is harder to refute because the governing expression does not have to be anywhere in evidence. Nor can one easily claim that it is only a dodge whereby a cause is simply invented to explain an effect. Performatives are a reality, and there are many indications that such abstract verbs as <u>promise</u> and <u>warn</u> have to be reckoned with, as for example in:

> Without mincing words, if you eat any candy I'll whip you.

where the reference is not to your powers of eating candy without mincing words, but to something like 'I warn you with no mincing of words'. If that adverbial expression modifies anything, it has to modify an element that is not physically present. To test the control that <u>warn</u> and <u>promise</u> may or may not exercise it is necessary to bring them back into the sentence. It can then be shown that <u>any</u> and <u>some</u> still operate independently in their own sphere:

> I warn you that if you do something like that I'll whip you.
> I promise you that if you get any good grades at all I'll give you ten dollars.

In the first example the hearer has already given some indication--by word or deed--that he has in mind doing that particular thing. The particularity of it is what leads the speaker to choose <u>something</u> rather than the more inclusive <u>anything</u>. In the second, the speaker has decided to set a low standard—just any reasonably good grades will count; now the reference is inclusive, not particular (see Bolinger 1977:21-36).

As in the other instances, <u>any</u> and <u>some</u> are independent words, used to convey independent meanings.

My last case study is the opposite of the <u>any-some</u> one. With <u>any-some</u> a <u>governing</u> expression was 'there' but out of sight; now it is a <u>governed</u> expression that is felt but not seen. We call this entailment. The sentence <u>I am sorry that you broke your leg</u> entails your having broken it, unlike <u>I hear that you broke your leg</u>, where the speaker may be misinformed. Expressions like <u>be sorry</u>, <u>regret</u> <u>be glad</u>, <u>be surprised</u>, etc. entail the factuality of their complements. 'Fact' is an automatic outcome.

Of course the nature and complexity of meaning is such that it is possible for a verb actually to have 'entailment' as part of its meaning. This is not the case with <u>strike</u>, is almost the case with <u>hit</u>, and is fully the case with <u>dawn on</u>:

   I was worried because it struck me that I was
      being followed (but I found out later that I
      wasn't).
   I was worried because it hit me that I was being
      followed (?but I found out later that I
      wasn't).
   I was worried because it dawned on me that I was
      being followed (*but I found out later that I
      wasn't).

The test of this kind of entailment is that it works in the negative too:

   I wasn't worried because it never dawned on me
      that I was being followed (*and as a matter of
      fact I wasn't).

Whether <u>dawn on</u> is affirmative or negative, it is not used unless the clause following it is viewed as true--this is simply a feature of its meaning. But the majority of verbs waver. This can be seen even with verbs of emotion in the contrast between 'emotions caused' and 'emotions projected'. In all of the following:

> I'm angry that you behaved that way.
> I'm annoyed that you behaved that way.
> I'm hurt that you behaved that way.
> I'm sorry that you behaved that way.

one would probably assume that your behaving that way was a fact. Yet it is easier to add something that questions the fact with <u>annoyed</u> and <u>sorry</u> than it is with <u>angry</u> and <u>hurt</u>:

> *I'm angry that you behaved that way, if you did.
> I'm annoyed that you behaved that way, if you did.
> *I'm hurt that you behaved that way, if you did.
> I'm sorry that you behaved that way, if you did.

<u>Be angry</u> and <u>be hurt</u> express real emotion as a result of something, and if that something has not happened there can be no emotion and the result is a contradiction. But <u>be annoyed</u> and <u>be sorry</u> express an <u>attitude toward</u> something; the emotion is contingent on what can be either a real or a hypothetical fact.

The upshot is that entailment occurs when a speaker intends it to occur. It is not that the speaker chooses a verb for some completely different purpose and then discovers, to his surprise, that he has been caught with an entailment. If he wants to entail he chooses a verb or a context that accomplishes his purpose. A very few verbs, like <u>dawn on</u>, are always appropriate for this--because it is part of their meaning. Most of the time the context takes care of it--if one says <u>He was finally able to open the door</u> we would assume that he opened it, even though being able to do something is no guarantee of doing it (see Bolinger 1976).

If the evidence I have given is sufficient to suggest that all or most cases of supposed determinism in syntax are really false and instead the speaker is exercising two or more choices at the same time, how can we account for the persistence of the fallacy?

Perhaps the main reason is the before-and-after, left-to-right arrangement of the sentence. Coupled with the inveterate tendency of grammars to be expressed in hearer's terms rather than in speaker's, this may explain the apparent predetermination: when <u>you</u> produce a sentence, its elements are given as far as <u>I</u> am concerned--all I can do is interpret it. And though my short-term memory enables me to store a small part of it and process it in a single operation, by and large I am tied down to the sequence of things as you give them to me. This leads to making predictions, and to the illusion of control. If you say, <u>dawn on</u>, I will not wait for the rest of what you say to conclude that there is to be an entailment. As speaker you may have planned both moves in advance, because the pre-coding of a sentence is not necessarily linear; but to me, one element will seem to 'lead to' another.

We might not have been fooled even under these circumstances were it not for another factor, the semantic tenuousness of certain elements. Function words in particular may be very abstract. Without the careful scrutiny of many contexts, it is easy to overlook the meaning of an existential <u>there</u> and to assume that it is merely a grammatical excrescence. Its presence must be accounted for, but that is accomplished by making it depend on elements whose grosser meanings make them easier to grasp. So those three factors--linear arrangement of the sentence, hearer's grammar, and semantic abstractness of supposedly governed elements--are probably the chief causes of the fallacy of determinism. Linearity is in first place and operates even in speaker's grammar to some extent: not all the problems are worked out at the pre-coding stage, and what a speaker has already said may influence what he is about to say.

To claim that syntactic determinism is a fallacy is not to claim free will in a philosophical sense. Looking philosophically at higher-to-lower determinism, we probably have to admit that it does exist in some form. I may be free to choose a meaning, but my language is something of which there are vast stretches that I have simply memorized in the course of my life, and the choice of meaning that I have made probably sets wheels moving over which I have no conscious control. But if A and B are independently meaningful, we must allow for their being independently chosen, without dependence of either on the other but jointly on a higher intention.

The transformational-generative revolution was launched with Chomsky's attack on Skinnerian behaviorism. In place of it we were to have a mentalism that allowed for choices. We got that, but it went only half way. We are still plagued with a 50 percent stimulus-response psychology in syntactic analysis. It is time to complete the revolution.

NOTE

1. <u>Were at least a dozen trees beside the house?</u> is of course a normal sentence, but it is not presentative (the locative is at the end) and it is about a fact.

REFERENCES

Atkinson, James C. 1973. The two forms of subject inversion in Modern French. The Hague: Mouton.
Bolinger, Dwight. 1976. Gradience in entailment. Language Sciences 41.1-13.
Bolinger, Dwight. 1977. Meaning and form. London and New York: Longman.
Chomsky, Noam. 1971. Deep structure, surface structure, and semantic interpretation. In: Semantics: An interdisciplinary reader in

philosophy, linguistics, and psychology. Edited by: Danny Steinberg and Leon Jakobovits. Cambridge: Cambridge University Press.

Chomsky, Noam and Morris Halle. 1968. The sound pattern of English. New York: Harper and Row.

García, Erica. 1975. The role of theory in linguistic analysis. Amsterdam: North Holland.

Kuno, Susumu. 1971. The position of locatives in existential sentences. Linguistic Inquiry 11.334-378.

Ladd, D. R. 1977. Light and shadow: A study of the syntax and semantics of sentence accent in English. To appear in: Cornell Linguistic Contributions, Vol. 2. Leiden: E. J. Brill.

Lakoff, R. T. 1969. Some reasons why there can't be any Some-Any rule. Lg. 45.608-615.

ANIMACY OR SUBJECTHOOD:
CLITIC MOVEMENT AND ROMANCE CAUSATIVES

IVONNE A. BORDELOIS
Rijksuniversiteit, Utrecht

Romance clitics behave like crickets on
a summer night. Nobody knows where they
come from, or when or why they're going
to stop.
        Karl von Frisch in a conversation
        with Vladimir Nabokov

For a theory as interesting as the one that Chomsky has proposed to us, i.e. a theory that strives for nothing less than giving us an appropriate representation of the <u>faculté de langage</u> as it exists in the human mind, the task of limiting the power of human grammars is certainly inescapable. No wonder that over the past few years the thrust of transformationalist debates centered on questions about the number and form of possible universal constraints. My point here is not to contest the validity of the direction of this effort or its feasibility but rather to concentrate on some specific proposals that have been presented within the frame of this challenging project. That is, I understand with Chomsky that, given the distinction between deep structures and superficial structures correlated through transformations, constraints on transformations are needed. Moreover, I hope with him that the task is feasible and promising. This is, I think, a clear and important area of convergence. What I disagree with is the specific type of devices that have been proposed and followed in the recent literature as models for constraints. In particular, I want to focus here on the ability of a particular condition, the Specified Subject Condition, to account in an explanatory way for some complex phenomena involving Causative constructions in Romance languages.

There are a number of well-motivated reasons to consider Causative constructions a crucial area of inquiry and development for syntactic theory within the generative framework. First of all, Causative constructions and movement of clitics within them have long been noticed and described as 'exceptional' and nothing illustrates better the power and cogency of a theory than its ability to reduce exceptional phenomena to typical phenomena following from general, independently justified principles. Second, the increasing bibliography developed during the last years on the matter gives us the opportunity to compare different theories and evaluate them, precisely in terms of the plausibility and generality of the principles assumed to yield a valid explanation for this particular case, and the amount and relevance of the data such principles will cover in a consistent way. I think this is an interesting subject, because of the subtlety of the phenomena involved and the very elaborated proposals they have generated, including frameworks other than transformational theory. It is also, in a way, a necessary one, because theories that claim universality and present devices characterized as would-be-universals deserve and demand a more careful scrutiny than theories that make only particular claims about the soundness or preferability of a given analysis just on grounds of simplicity and completeness, without requiring the presence of specific universals to justify such analysis.

That is, when analyses on Romance data are carried on under the spell of principles assumed to be universal and to reflect innate characteristics of the human mind, we must be particularly careful before

accepting them or crediting them as important or
decisive proofs for the soundness of a theory whose
claims, by the way, are still being largely questioned even within English. In this respect, one
may detect two trends at work within the field. One
purports to show that principles putatively universal will justify or improve our analyses as we
proceed to apply them to languages other than English: this seems to be the strategy adopted by
Kayne and Quicoli. Another possible course of
action will be to look at the variation in the data
of specific languages in order to improve the formulation of the principles themselves, as long as we
consider principles as working hypotheses rather
than given in this particular stage of development of the field. This is the procedure adopted
by Evers in his description of Dutch, for instance,
and by myself with respect to Spanish. Clearly,
the two strategies may not necessarily exclude
each other, and only empirical results will tell
us which principles and analyses are more adequate.
The concrete task I undertake here is to examine
how Romance languages and more specifically how
Causative constructions and Clitic Movement across
Causative constructions in Romance languages may
support Chomsky's contention about the universal
validity of the Specified Subject Condition
(Chomsky 1973, 1975).

In Chomsky's terms, the Specified Subject Condition prevents elements from relating to each other
across a specified subject or its trace. For instance,

(1) *He wants Sally to wash himself

is an impossible sentence because <u>he</u> and <u>himself</u>
relate through a Specified Subject, <u>Sally</u>. (As to
the class of rules that fall under the principle--
Pronominalization, for instance, being excluded--
see Chomsky 1975.) The Specified Subject Condition
(SSC) may block operations even when the subject is
not present, for in this case the trace left by the
removed NP will still be operative. (For numerous

examples of the validity of traces within Romance syntax see Bordelois 1974.)

It is the SSC in conjunction with the trace theory which, according to Chomsky, explains the ungrammaticality of sentences like

(2) *John seems to us to like each other

Assuming this is the deep structure corresponding to (2):

(3) Δ seems to us [John like each other]$_S$

we will have Subject Raising, removing John to an initial position in the matrix sentence. But the trace left by this NP will preclude the linking of each other with us in the resulting string. Graphically then what (1) and (2) illustrate is the following schema:

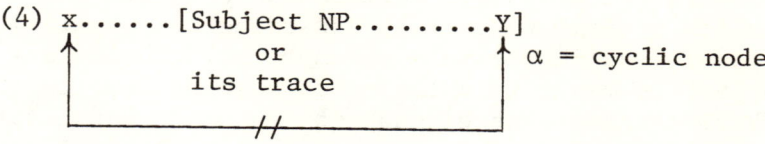

(4) x......[Subject NP.........Y]
　　　　　　　or　　　　　　　　　α = cyclic node
　　　　　　its trace

I think we may accept this analysis provisionally as a starting point for our discussion, a discussion that will center on whether Romance data may confirm the validity of a principle that Chomsky postulates as a plausible candidate for universality in syntax:

If, furthermore, the SSC and the trace theory are part of universal grammar, part of the biologically necessary schematism that determines the essence of human language, the speaker will know all of this [that is, how the SSC will filter out sentences like (2) I.B.] without instruction or even relevant evidence, as appears to be the case. (Chomsky 1975:103)

And also:

. . . SSC may be proposed as a universal principle on the grounds that investigation of English along the lines just reviewed, leads us to postulate this principle as an element of the initial state S_0, a precondition for language learning, a property of the general language faculty, one faculty of the mind. (Chomsky n.d.)

Recent contributions by Kayne (1975) and Quicoli (1977) have been claiming that important empirical support is to be found within Romance Causatives--precisely at the point where they interact with Clitic Movement--to validate the boldness of Chomsky's claim. My contention here will be that, far from validating the SSC, examples from these very constructions show us that a category such as syntactic subjecthood is rather irrelevant as an explanatory device.

My first move will be to propose that there is a possible and plausible formulation of Clitic Movement as a local rule, i.e. excluding an essential variable, which may rule out not only those cases the SSC is meant to exclude but also an important subset of cases where a subsidiary, redundant statement will be needed in case we rely exclusively on the SSC. Secondly, I will enumerate cases where phenomena relating both to Causative constructions and Clitic Movement appear to be restricted in terms of the feature of Animacy for which there is eloquent evidence from French and Spanish. Since this paper reflects research in progress, I am not submitting a set of rules or conditions that incorporate Animacy in a definite formulation. But I think an important step has been taken once we are able to distinguish, within a particularly complex set of phenomena, what is irrelevant and what should not be dismissed in a first approach to the explanation of such phenomena. Switching our attention from Subjecthood to Animacy seems to me a healthy and necessary attitude to improve our understanding of these stimulating problems, and there seems to be enough evidence in the data to validate this new perspective, as I shall now try to show.

with the examination of the syntactic
the rule of Clitic Movement requires.
with Kayne that Clitic Movement is the
relating

le livre à lui
onne le livre

le à Jean
nne à Jean

le à lui
i donne

These examples show that clitic objects are fronted
and attached to the verb of their own sentence.
There are cases where clitics appear to move beyond
the limits of their clause, as in

(11) Je le fais lire à Jean

where two verbs from two different sentences are
left behind by the clitic in its trajectory to the
target position. The material included between the
source location of the clitic and its target has
prompted Kayne to propose the following rule:

(12) NP - V - Y - cl.

The variable Y will cover in (6) the direct object;
in (8) a null context; in (11) a verb, <u>lire</u>.
  It is possible to conceive of a grammar where the
effect this variable has is taken care of by different mechanisms. For instance we might postulate a
Dative Movement operating only on pronominal
datives, of the type we find in German, which would
feed Clitic Movement. If that were the case, then
the variable Y will not be needed in the context of
(6). Still we have to deal with problems concerning prepositional contexts:

(13) Tu lui tombes dessus

where the source

(14) Tu tombes dessus lui

seems to be uncertain: as suggested by M. Ronat (personal communication), the fact that there is no <u>tirer dessus à NP</u> seems to indicate that pronominal datives in French require special treatment, and one could consider a grammar generating them immediately after the verb by the PS rules. Which of the two solutions is to be preferred is an open question. All we want to point out here is that (6) does not legitimate per se the incorporation of an essential variable within the structural description of the rule, a move by no means trivial. For the case where the verb is included, as in (11), we might postulate that in fact Clitic Movement is cyclic (as I have done in Bordelois 1977), and that, therefore, what we have in (11) is a sentence where Clitic Movement has applied twice, once in each cycle. Although admittedly sketchy, these are some plausible ways of questioning the presence of the variable in the structural description of the rule.

But for the purposes of this article, I will accept the presence of the variable Y, in order to evaluate the consequences of a grammar that will control Y through the SSC. Let us examine a sentence like (15):

(15) J'ai laissé Jean lire le livre

According to Quicoli, this sentence relates to the following deep structure:

(16) NP V S

Assume now that <u>le livre</u> is represented by <u>le</u> and that, following the structural description of the rule, we try to apply Clitic Movement to this particular string. The result will be the ungrammatical sentence

(17) *Je l'ai laissé Jean lire

if we allow Y, the variable, to run over <u>Jean lire</u>.
Such an undesirable result is precluded, however,
if we consider that <u>Jean</u> is the specified subject
of the complement sentence. The SSC predictably
filters out the operation of the rule, according to
the following schema:

(18) le.......Jean.......cl

So far, so good. Similar examples may be quoted
from Spanish and Italian which would apparently
confirm the plausibility of this procedure.

Let us examine first the more intriguing case
where a movement may affect the position of the
subject. What happens then? According to the
theory that postulates the convention on traces,
the results will be equally ungrammatical, for the
trace will preserve the blocking effect the subject has. And indeed this seems to be the case:

(19) J'ai laissé l'homme le lire
(20) *L'homme que je l'ai laissé lire s'appelle
      Jean

This is the picture that a theory encompassing both
the Specified Subject Condition and the convention
on traces will give us:

(21)

   wh-word...NP - cl - V...trace of subject NP...cl

The dotted line between V and the rightmost position
of the clitic represents the domain of variable Y,
here obstructed, so to say, by the trace of the
Specified Subject. That is, even in those cases
where the subject may be missing at the surface
structure, the trace it leaves behind won't allow
clitics to move over the higher verb. Before we
accept this explanation, however, we may notice that
these sentences are ungrammatical even when Clitic

Movement does not apply. It is the removal of the
subject that makes them ungrammatical:

   (22) *L'homme que j'ai laissé lire le livre
         s'appelle Jean

French informants will reject this sentence--so
will Spanish, Italian, and Portuguese, as far as I
know. Only the following alternative is acceptable:

   (23) L'homme à qui j'ai laissé lire le livre
         s'appelle Jean

where _à qui_, clearly referring to a dative pattern,
indicates that a different derivation is involved.
Thus this context will not allow us to test the
validity of the claim involving the SSC plus traces.
We can look now for other contexts where other
operations are involved. In fact, Quicoli points
out cases in French where traces of subjects removed
by Clitic Movement will preclude further movement of
object clitics across it, as in

   (24) *Je le le laisserai donner

coming from the unlawful derivation

   (24a) Je le laisserai [t donner le]

where the embedded object clitic may not cross the
trace of the subject represented by _le_. (Notice,
by the way, that Quicoli's analysis involves the
nontrivial claim that clitics may leave traces--
ordinarily, only NP's do, and NP's differ from
clitics in relevant respects.) It is clear, however, that (24) involves an example of infinitival
constructions where the NP interpreted as the
subject of the infinitive is marked as an Accusative, a point which is not obvious in (17), since
case marking differences are manifest only in pronouns in French.

The point I want to show now is that the sequence V - NP - V per se will block Clitic Movement, regardless of the status of the intervening NP.

In order to develop this point I find it necessary to invite the reader to consider the array of possibilities Clitic Movement has beyond the specific realm of Causative constructions. I maintained in my thesis and I strongly hold that progress in syntax is reached through generalizations that cover simplex and complex sentences and, within complex sentences, the whole array of cases a transformation may apply to. That is, if we implement a rule that will cover Causative Movement for Causative constructions leaving out all the other cases where Clitic Movement takes place across clause frontiers, our grammar will be clearly inadequate.

Since Spanish presents a much wider range of data than French with respect to Clitic Movement, it provides a better case to validate the rules of our grammar and the principles of our theory. We are not interested in principles that find their application only in very specific examples of very idiosyncratic constructions, while leaving unexplained an important subset of cases that extend over regular constructions. This is why it is necessary to consider the whole paradigm Spanish offers to us before we claim that our principles have allowed us to reach significant linguistic generalizations.

Here are two cases from Spanish where we may find relevant data for our problem:

(25) Yo enseño a hacer algo a Juan
     I teach John to do something

Juan, in case it is pronominalized, will show up as a Dative le. If the object of the embedded complement is also pronominalized, we will get lo. If both pronominal forms are present, we may get Clitic Movement, as shown in:

(26) Se lo enseño a hacer

(The reader is reminded that the sequence le lo becomes se lo in Spanish, in all cases.) The tree usually related to this sentence may be represented as:

(27)

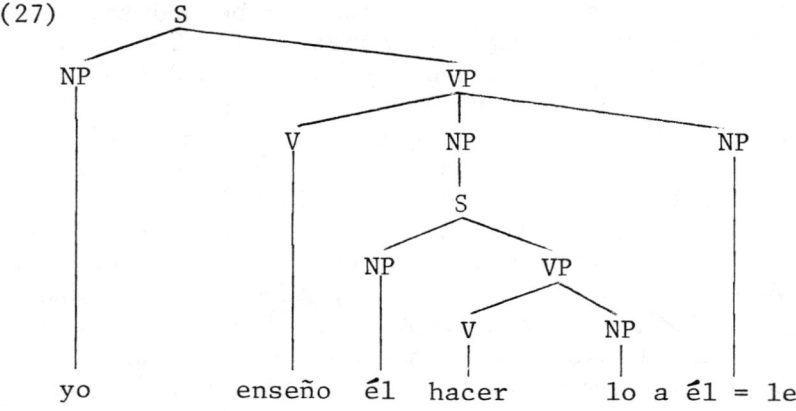

yo   enseño   él   hacer   lo a él = le

The reasons why one should generate the Dative controller at the rightmost position, i.e. after the sentential complement, have been developed in my thesis: to give just one, this is the simplest way of accounting for why the controller never passivizes, as NP's directly generated after the verb do; that is, we may never have:

(28) *El fue enseñado a hacerlo
     He was taught to do it

An illustrative contrast at this point may be found in the verb forzar:

(29) Yo fuerzo a él a hacerlo
     I force him to do it
(30) *Yo se lo fuerzo a hacer

Here the controller is marked as an Accusative, and predictably, it passivizes:

(31) El fue forzado a hacerlo
     He was forced to do it

This is the tree we may hypothesize for this case:

(32)

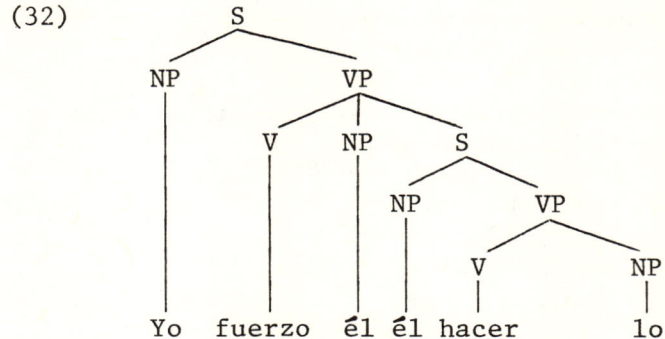

It is interesting to notice that no verb entering this category allows for Clitic Movement. Were we to follow the suggestion made by Quicoli in his article about French Quantifiers, we could perhaps say that Datives and Accusative controllers differ in that the first class of complements exhibit a subject which is thoroughly deleted--and therefore, invulnerable to the Specified Subject Condition, which refers only to NP's, traces or PRO's. In the second case, however, one might assume that <u>forzar</u> requires an interpreted PRO subject, sensitive to the constraint. The distinction, however, appears to be rather artificial. There is no independent evidence that would allow us to predict when a complement will have a deleted subject and when a PRO. In both cases, identity of the embedded subject with an object in the matrix sentence is required:

(33) *Yo enseño a Juan a que Pedro lee
     I teach John for Peter to read
(34) *Yo fuerzo a Juan a que Pedro lea
     I force John for Peter to read

In this respect, it is worth noticing that both verbs differ from a verb like <u>querer</u>, where subjects may differ:

(35) Yo quiero leer
    I want to read
(36) Yo quiero que tú leas
    I want you to read

Querer, however, behaves like enseñar in that it allows for Clitic Movement:

(37) Yo quiero leerlo
    I want to read it
(38) Yo lo quiero leer
    I it want to read

There is, furthermore, an interesting similarity between querer and enseñar, as shown in the following tree:

(39)

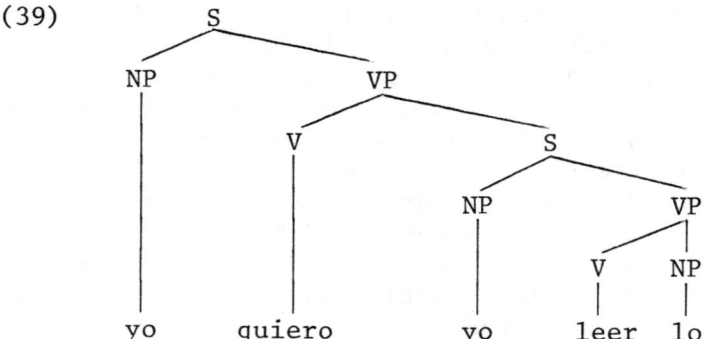

If we compare (39) and (27) we may see that after deletion we are left with a string of contiguous verbs. This is not the case for (34), forzar, where the matrix controller disrupts the continuity of the verbal chain. It is natural to assume that, rather than tacit differences in the status of the missing subject, these overt structural differences are responsible for the failure of Clitic Movement in the case of forzar and for its operation in querer, enseñar. Further confirmation may be drawn from the fact that, in case we intrapose the Dative controller in enseñar, a permissible move, as witnessed in:

(40) Yo enseño a Juan a hacerlo

then Clitic Movement becomes impossible:

(41) *Lo enseño a Juan a hacer

Clearly, nobody would claim that an interpreted subject is blocking Clitic Movement in (41) while a deleted subject is allowing for it in (26) from (27). There is a limit to the inconsistencies our grammars may admit, and this must be one. If we are to preserve the explanatory power of our theory, we should not proliferate the number and types of tacit symbols in deep structures just to duplicate the irregularities we find in surface structure. A phlogiston theory will help linguistics as little as it helped chemistry.

Notice that a theory incorporating the SSC would read as a coincidence, the fact that only in cases where verbs are contiguous in surface structure will clitics move: the correlation between the derived structures of <u>querer</u> and <u>enseñar</u> and the possibility of Clitic Movement for both of them, while <u>forzar</u>, structurally different, precludes the transformation, is totally missed. Furthermore, (41) will require presumably an independent constraint, a constraint which must rule out the sequence <u>V NP V</u>, where NP is clearly an object, not a subject. The fact that two independent constraints are needed to eliminate sequences which are structurally homogeneous reveals an undesirable amount of redundancy in our grammar. A system that forces us to miss generalizations and incorporate redundancies instead may not be the preferred one.[1]

The general point of this section has been to emphasize that rather than relying on the adequacy of a general constraint to reduce the power of a given variable, we may construct a better grammar if we question, to begin with, the legitimacy of the variable and rewrite the Clitic Movement rule essentially as a cyclic, local, iterative rule, presumably of the form:

(42) V - cl
      ↑_____|

It seems to me that the difficulties that this formulation may encounter are not so grave as those stemming from the formulation involving an essential variable constrained by the SSC, in that the regularities and symmetries in the system of complementation seem to be better reflected once we adopt the restrictive version of the rule I am proposing here.

What we may infer from these examples is the almost trivial conclusion that for all of these cases:

(43) *Lo dejo a Juan hacer
(44) *Lo enseño a Juan a hacer
(45) *Lo fuerzo a Juan a hacer

one and the very same cause is blocking the movement of clitics, namely, the presence of V-NP-V, and the subjecthood or objecthood of NP is perfectly irrelevant in this case: any NP will do, as long as it intervenes between V and V.

One interesting property of the verb <u>laisser</u>, <u>dejar</u>, in French and Spanish (but not in Italian, where it follows the pattern of <u>fare</u>) is its ability to enter both the <u>forzar</u> and the <u>enseñar</u> pattern. That is, basically, the subject of the embedded complement may show up either as an Accusative or as a Dative:

(46) Je le lui ai laissé lire
         Sub.
(47) Yo se lo dejo leer
        Sub.
(48) Je le laisse le lire
        Sub.
(49) Yo lo dejo leerlo
        Sub.

An interesting observation is that the variation is permitted only when the embedded object is

[-Animate]. In case the embedded verb requires an Animate object, we find only the pattern where the subject shows up as an Accusative:

(50) Je le laisse lui parler
(51) Je le laisse l'embrasser
(52) Lo dejo hablarle
(53) Lo dejo abrazarla
(54) *Je le lui laisse parler
(55) *Je le lui laisse embrasser
(56) *Se lo dejo hablar
(57) *Se la dejo abrazar

Similar facts are to be found when subjects and objects are expressed through NP's:

(58) J'ai laissé Jean parler à Marie
(59) J'ai laissé Jean embrasser Marie
(60) Dejé a Juan hablar a María
(61) Dejé a Juan abrazar a María
(62) *J'ai laissé parler à Marie à Jean
(63) *J'ai laissé embrasser Marie à Jean
(64) *Dejé hablar a María a Juan
(65) *Dejé abrazar a María a Juan

The sentences above appear to show that whether Accusative or Dative, embedded objects exhibiting the feature of Animacy do not cooccur with embedded subjects marked as Dative. And whenever there is no Dative marking on the subject, there is no chance for Clitic Movement to operate. According to Kayne--and Quicoli follows a similar, although not identical, line of argument here--the reason why (54) is ungrammatical is a violation of the SSC. If we assume that within the embedded complement of _laisser_ there is a sentence where the verb is raised and attracted to the higher verb _laisser_ via Faire Inversion, we will have a derived string:

(66) J'ai laissé parler le lui

But in case Clitic Movement applies to this structure, _lui_ will not be able to cross over the embedded subject *le*--even though it is not perfectly clear what mechanisms will preserve the subjecthood of *le* once it is positioned after the verb and turned into an Accusative. Therefore, we expect (54) to be ungrammatical, and our expectations and predictions turnout to be right.

Rather than criticizing particular points in this analysis, I would rather try to question its scope. For neither Quicoli nor Kayne tells us why (55) is also bad, even though in this case Faire Inversion is supposed to involve both the embedded verb plus the direct object, leaving behind the embedded subject, which one should expect to show up as a Dative. We might consider instead that the operations leading to the positioning and marking of the embedded subject as a Dative depend crucially on the presence of an embedded [-Animate] subject: this might explain simultaneously (50) and (51), as compared to (54) and (55). Again, it appears as if appealing to the SSC leads us to miss a generalization, instead of gaining insight. Notice that when the embedded complement has a sole reflexive object, the subject may not appear as a Dative either. This may suggest that reflexives may not carry a [-Animate] marking. Relevant examples may be:

(61) Je l'ai laissé se baigner
(62) *Je lui ai laissé se baigner
(63) Lo dejé bañarse
(64) *Le dejé bañarse

(I am excluding here, of course, the dialect of Spanish where the distinction between *le* dative and *lo* accusative is eliminated in favor of *le*.)

Alternative solutions do not seem to help us here. For instance, the Clause Union theory, as proposed by Aïssen and Perlmutter, tells us that Clitic Movement requires as a previous input the collapsing of the double sentential structure into a single one where clitics move to the initial verb as they move to their own verb in simplex sentences. But the Clause Union theory leaves

unexplained the same questions that the SSC failed
to answer: why is it that verbs of the type forzar
are never submitted to Clause Union? (Aïssen and
Perlmutter do not give the structural description
of the rule, since their framework defines operations over relational dimensions--such as object,
subject--rather than in terms of syntactic positions.) Why is it that the presence of an Animate
object appears to preclude Clause Union within
Causative constructions? (Italian is exceptional
in this sense.) Notice, by the way, that a similar
phenomenon appears to restrict Clitic Movement in
verbs of the enseñar type. Thus, Marta Luján (1976)
notes the following contrast (permitir takes, as
enseñar, a Dative controller):

(65) Te permitieron comerla
     Te la permitieron comer
     To you it they permitted to eat
(66) Te permitieron saludarla
     *Te la permitieron saludar
     To you her they permitted to greet

These examples show that the embedded object of
permitir, if Animate, will not be removed via
Clitic Movement. There is probably a generalization to be formulated here, which may collapse
both the Causative case and the permitir case. At
this point, however, I am not yet able to express
it, although I am certain that the notion of
Animacy will be crucially involved in the restrictions we need to state.
   This seems to be a rather general situation.
George and Toman (1976) report that in Czech, for
instance, it is impossible to cliticize an embedded
object across clause frontiers when it is a
[+Animate] NP, and it is also unavailable for
Passivization and Relativization in this context,
while [-Animate] NP's feed all these rules in the
same environment.
   A similar situation seems to involve the unresolved contrast--first noted by Kayne--in English:

(67) They are letting honey drip on each other's feet
(68) *They are letting Bill slap on each other's face

In general, what we observe here is that Animates resist the operation of certain rules that apply freely to [-Animate] NP's or pronouns. We have only delimited the area where these phenomena appear to be relevant, but many questions remain to be answered. For instance [+Animate] clitics move obligatorily in simplex sentences and also in complex sentences other than the type illustrated in (65) and (66):

(69) Te la presento
   I introduce her to you
(70) Te la quiero presentar
   To you her I want to introduce

Thus, it is not immediately obvious how to define and circumscribe the cases where Animacy becomes relevant as a blocking effect. Other possible questions concern the metaphorical status of the feature [+Animate], and whether distinctions between [+Human] and [-Human] also may play a distinctive role, across different languages and dialects within them. The fact that the relevant verb is Agentive or non-Agentive may also interact with these phenomena, in particular when the non-Agentive verb may take both [-Animate] and [+Animate] objects. In such cases, the restriction on Animates may be dispensed with:

(71) Te la hice conocer
   To you her I made know
   I had you know her

A theoretical question that may have interesting consequences is whether the restrictions on Animacy have to be incorporated at the level of rules or rather at the level of conditions on rules. Certainly, work in this direction will be likely to contribute some insights to the problem of the autonomy of syntax.

Another important theoretical question is how general the distinction is: even within Romance languages there are important exceptions. In Italian, for instance, we may find:

(72) Gliela faccio uccidere
     To him her I make kill
     I have him kill her

whose equivalents are not available in general in French or Spanish. This may illustrate a tendency to eliminate rules that refer to features like Animacy--a trend that perhaps represents the nature of the syntactic component itself. This type of distinction lies below the level appropriate to constituents: features are only parts of full symbols. Therefore, a distinction of this type is ignored in favor of simpler and larger statements of rules, where all NP's, regardless of their feature composition, are referred to as equivalent as long as they share the same general distribution in syntax. If this is the case, then Italian might be considered perhaps a pioneer among Romance languages, in the sense that it appears as if in Italian the relevance of Animacy is being sacrificed to a progress in the simplification of certain syntactic rules. However sketchy, I think these remarks are clear enough to allow us to perceive the general direction of the process. I expect also that diachronic studies adequately oriented will contribute to our understanding of these very stimulating problems.

A last theoretical question we may ask is the following: why has the syntactic relevance of this feature taken so long to be noticed? The answer may simply be: because our present framework does not make us expect it. I mean that generally rules and constraints on rules have been stated in terms of symbols or configurations of symbols, rather than in terms of features like Animacy, which clearly enters strict selectional

restrictions and has direct semantic connotations.
But a theory where features of this type are finally
admitted as pertinent for the delimitation of syntactic phenomena might be, after all, not stronger
than needed, and more illuminating than a theory
that discards any interaction of these levels a
priori.

Principles and formalisms we need, but the question is: what principles? And how natural are the
analyses that support them? And how really solid
the evidence they rest on? The examination of the
SSC appears to show us that we should be cautious
before we claim any significant approximation to
the domain of innateness. I expect to have shown
that in this particular case a more restrictive
version of the rule of Clitic Movement may reach a
larger generalization over a more extended set of
facts than those examined by Quicoli and Kayne. At
the same time, I have been concerned with a type of
phenomena where Animacy seems to play decisively a
restrictive role, although we still have to explore
which are the better devices to capture the relevance of this feature. This is, I think, an area
where our research may fulfill more demanding expectations. Grammars that collect principles in
order to become more restrictive are just as un-
interesting as grammars that collect data in order
to become broader. What we need are devices and
principles that receive confirmation from different
contexts within the same component and from different languages for the same type of phenomena. In
no other way may universality be reached.

I hope that in the future the work of Romance
linguists will clarify, through adequate formalisms
and data, the interaction of features and syntax so
richly represented in our languages. There is no
doubt in my mind that such a task, if successful,
may represent a major step towards the promised
land of human grammars.

NOTES

I am thankful to M. de Boer, A. Evers, F. Heny, D. Napoli, H. van Riemsdijk, M. Ronat, and J. Schroten for helpful discussions. Errors are my own responsibility.
   1. It is perhaps important to notice that not all VV sequences are available for Clitic Movement. Thus a verb like <u>lamentar</u> (regret) will not allow it:
   (i) Lamento haberlo hecho
   (ii) *Lo lamento haber hecho
       It I regret having done
This is so for reasons I consider to be semantic (for a different view, see M. Luján). What should be clear is that the sequence VV is a necessary, not a sufficient condition for Clitic Movement--while V NP V will always block the rule.

REFERENCES

Aïssen, Judith, and David Perlmutter. To appear. Clause reduction in Spanish. Proceedings of the Second Annual Meeting of the Berkeley Linguistic Society.
Bordelois, Ivonne. 1974. The grammar of Spanish causative complements. Unpublished doctoral dissertation. M.I.T.
Bordelois, Ivonne. 1976. On traces of specified subject in Romance languages. In: Green ideas blown up. Papers from the Amsterdam Colloquium on Trace Theory. Edited by H. van Riemsdijk. Amsterdam.
Bordelois, Ivonne. 1977. Pour une grammaire universelle: Montée de clitiques et condition de frontière en espangnol et en français. Communication to the Linguistic Colloquium of Vincennes, Paris. January.
Chomsky, Noam. Undated. On cognitive structures and their development. Royaumont.
Chomsky, Noam. 1973. Conditions on transformations. In: A Festschrift for Morris Halle. Edited by S. Anderson and P. Kiparsky. New York: Holt, Rinehart and Winston.

Chomsky, Noam. 1976. Reflections on language. New York: Pantheon.
Evers, Arnold. 1977. The transformation cycle in Dutch and German. Bloomington: Indiana Linguistics Club.
George, Leland, and Jindrich Toman. 1976. Czech clitics in universal grammar. In: Papers from the Twelfth Regional Meeting, CLS.
Kayne, Richard. 1975. French syntax: The transformational cycle. Cambridge: MIT Press.
Luján, Marta. 1976. La enclisis y el modo en los complementos verbales del español. Presented at the VI Linguistic Symposium on Romance Languages, Université de Montréal. April.
Quicoli, Carlos. 1976. Conditions on clitic movement in Portuguese. Linguistic Analysis 2.3.
Quicoli, Carlos. 1976. Conditions on quantifier movement in French. Linguistic Inquiry 7.4.
Quicoli, Carlos. Forthcoming. Clitic movement in French causatives.
Radford, Andrew. 1976. On the nature of clitic promotion in Italian. Linacre College, Oxford. Mimeograph.
Roldán, Mercedes. 1974. Constraints on clitic insertion in Spanish. In: Linguistic studies in Romance languages. Edited by R. Campbell, M. Goldin, and M. Wang. Washington, D.C.: Georgetown University Press.

ANALOGICAL LEVELING OF THE
AUXILIARY ÊTRE IN ONTARIAN FRENCH

MICHAEL CANALE, RAYMOND MOUGEON, AND
MONIQUE BÉLANGER
Centre for Franco-Ontarian Studies

0. Introduction. This paper reports on the analogical leveling of the distinction between verbs requiring the auxiliary *être* and those requiring the auxiliary *avoir* (E-verbs and A-verbs respectively in our discussion) in *passé composé* and *plus-que-parfait* constructions in Ontarian French. In contrast to Standard French, Ontarian French tends to conjugate the small subset of E-verbs (e.g. the intransitives *aller* 'go', *venir* 'come', etc. and all reflexive (or pronominal) verbs, such as *se souvenir* 'remember', *se laver* 'wash oneself', etc.) with *avoir* in all composed tenses of the active voice. However, not all E-verbs show the same frequency of regularization in our data. We propose to examine variation in the frequency of occurrence of *avoir* with a number of E-verbs based on the spontaneous speech of Franco-Ontarian students in Grades 2, 5, 9, 10, and 12 at French schools in three Ontarian communities. In particular, we shall examine the possible influence of a number of linguistic factors on the leveling process at work in the auxiliary system of Ontarian French.

1. Historical background. Various aspects of the use of the auxiliaries *avoir* and *être*

throughout the history of French have been discussed in a number of reference works (cf. Benveniste 1966, Brunot and Bruneau 1969, Elcock 1960, Grevisse 1969). The essential points—some quite controversial—can be summarized as follows.
There was only one auxiliary in Latin, *esse*, which was used to form certain tenses in the passive voice. In Postclassical Latin, as composed tense (analytic) forms tended to co-exist with and eventually replace noncomposed (synthetic) forms, a sentence such as (1a) could be interpreted as in either (1b) or (1c):

(1a) Mihi amatus es.
(1b) 'You are/were loved by me.'
(1c) 'I loved you.'

Note that the optional reference to past time (the perfect) in (1a) could be expressed unambiguously as in (2).

(2) Mihi amatus fuisti.
  'You were loved by me.'

The possibility of distinguishing the present and perfect tenses as in (1a) and (2) suggests that the construction passive participle + *esse* could also be interpreted as verbal adjective + copula (cf. Modern French *Elle est sortie maintenant* 'She is out now').

The potential confusion between active perfect (1c) and passive perfect (1b) readings of transitive verbs in the passive participle + *esse* construction seems to have existed in written Latin until the time of the Christian writers (about the 5th Century A.D.). By this stage the analytic construction *habere* + passive (past) participle had come to express the active perfect or pluperfect of transitive verbs (3).[1] The example is from Elcock (1960:50).

(3) ... ubi ipsi castra posita habebant (A.D. 415?)
  '... where they had placed ...'

ANALOGICAL LEVELING OF THE AUXILIARY ÊTRE / 43

The passive participle + <u>esse</u> construction continued to express the passive perfect/present of transitive verbs and, in addition, was extended to express the (active) perfect of intransitive verbs (4a) and reflexives (4b). We are not sure if all intransitives were affected by this development or if it was limited, say, to intransitives expressing movement.[2]

(4a) In Romam venitus sum.
    'I came into Rome.'
(4b) Me sum levatus.
    'I arose.'

Of particular interest for our purposes is the tendency in the Romance languages to form all composed tenses in the active voice (i.e. for transitive, intransitive, and reflexive verbs alike) with the <u>habere</u> + passive (past) participle construction. This tendency fleshed out in Spanish and Portuguese,[3] and in Old and Middle French one finds that intransitives and reflexives, although they could still be conjugated with <u>être</u>, were frequently conjugated with <u>avoir</u>. Furthermore, the past participle form of certain intransitives (e.g. <u>entrer</u>, <u>partir</u>, <u>sortir</u>, <u>tomber</u>) could be used in an adjectival manner with the copula to express the state resulting from a past action. Thus, in earlier varieties of French one finds distinctions as in (5).

(5a) Maintenant Jean est parti.
    'John is gone now.'
(5b) Hier Jean était parti.
    'Yesterday John was gone.'
(5c) Hier Jean a parti.
    'Yesterday John left.'

We have not been able to determine whether the Latin construction passive participle + <u>esse</u> could be interpreted as verbal adjective + copula for intransitive verbs in Vulgar Latin, and thus are not sure if (5a,b) are simply reflexes of earlier forms in the history of French.

In (Modern) Standard French, the construction
être + past participle is used to form tenses in
the passive voice for all transitive verbs (6a) and
the composed tenses of the active voice for all reflexives (6b) and a small subset of the intransitive verbs (6c)--viz. certain verbs of motion, such
as aller, arriver, descendre, entrer, monter, partir,
passer, retourner, sortir, tomber, venir, and their
various composed forms (e.g. redescendre, parvenir,
etc.); and certain verbs expressing a state or
change of state, such as décéder, mourir, naître,
rester. In addition, the past participle of certain intransitive verbs may be used adjectivally
with être (6d).

(6a) René est/était aimé.
 'René is/was loved.'
(6b) Marie s'est lavée les mains.
 'Mary washed her hands.'
(6c) Je suis allé/resté à Ottawa.
 'I went to/stayed in Ottawa.'
(6d) Hélène est encore partie.
 'Helen is still gone.'

The construction avoir + past participle serves to
form the composed tenses of the active voice for
the verbs avoir (7a) and être (7b), for all transitive verbs (7c) and for all intransitives except
the E-verbs (7d).

(7a) Ils ont eu un accident hier.
 'They had an accident yesterday.'
(7b) L'année dernière j'ai été malade pendant
  deux jours.
 'Last year I was sick for two days.'
(7c) Paul a vu une pièce de Tremblay.
 'Paul saw a play by Tremblay.'
(7d) On a diné tôt ce soir.
 'We ate dinner early tonight.'

It is not clear why the tendency to form composed
tenses with avoir in the active voice is not fully
realized in Standard French. Although Grevisse

(1969:650) claims that the conjugation of reflexive verbs with être (e.g. Je me suis levé 'I arose') was generalized under the influence of the copula + adjective construction (e.g. Je suis levé 'I am up'), the motivation and evidence for such a generalization are not clear to us. It may be that in the case of both the reflexives and the E-verbs, the use of the auxiliary être in composed tenses was standardized by prescriptive grammarians at the Modern French stage (perhaps for the reasons discussed in footnote 3). One still finds reflexives and E-verbs conjugated with avoir in popular (European) French and in various French patois (cf. Frei 1971, Guiraud 1968).

2. Methodology. The data on the use of the auxiliaries avoir and être in Ontarian French were gathered in tape-recorded interviews conducted with students enrolled in Grades 2, 5, 9, 12 at French language schools in the cities of Welland and Sudbury and in Grades 2, 5, 9, 10 at French language schools in the township of Rayside/Azilda (near Sudbury). The interviews were semi-directed and designed to elicit informal speech from the subjects. There was a total of 23 students in Grade 2, 20 in Grade 5, 114 in Grade 9/10,[4] and 13 in Grade 12. At each grade level, subjects were selected so as to assure a fairly equal number of males and females as well as an equal representation of socioeconomic groups (working, middle, and professional classes).

All instances of E-verbs in the passé composé and plus-que-parfait were examined. Adjectival uses of the past participle of the intransitive verbs (e.g. Marie est sortie maintenant 'Mary is out now') were not counted. Such cases were usually distinguishable from passé composé and plus-que-parfait forms with the help of contextual cues identifying the time of the event, etc. (cf. Sankoff and Thibault 1977 for a discussion of several such cues). Ambiguous cases due to lack of such contextual cues and cases where we were unable to distinguish the second and third person singular forms of _avoir_ and _être_ in the present tense (e.g. _tu as_ ~ _tu es_, _on a_ ~ _on est_) were discarded. Also omitted from analysis were those verbs for which there were less than five composed past tense forms at all grade levels.

3. Results. A summary of our findings is represented in Figure 1. Since the initial indication is that the use of the auxiliaries _avoir_ and _être_ varies from verb to verb and from one age group to another, we shall briefly discuss the findings in light of these two factors and then focus on the historical processes that seem to be at work.

On the whole, the Grade 2 students show a stronger tendency to conjugate the E-verbs in Figure 1 with _avoir_ than do the Grade 5 and the secondary school students. Such a tendency is not unexpected if one acknowledges the existence of the acquisition strategy of 'overgeneralization' as concerns young (first or second) language learners (cf. Brown 1973, Dulay and Burt 1974, Grégoire 1947). The verbs _tomber_, _rentrer_, _rester_, _sortir_ would appear to be conjugated categorically with _avoir_, the verbs _venir_ and _arriver_ show strong tendencies in this direction, and the verbs _partir_, _revenir_, _aller_ and the reflexives show relatively weaker tendencies to be conjugated with _avoir_.

The use of the auxiliaries _avoir_ and _être_ by the Grade 5 students resembles that of the Grade 2 students. Once again, _tomber_, _rentrer_, _sortir_ are most often conjugated with _avoir_, the verbs _rester_, _venir_, _arriver_ have the next highest percentages of _avoir_ (all over 50 percent), and _partir_, _revenir_, _aller_ and the reflexives show percentages of _avoir_ use of less than 50 percent.

Finally, we note that the secondary school students tend to use _avoir_ less frequently with the E-verbs listed than do the elementary school students. As to the pattern of _avoir_ use for this group, only the percentages of _avoir_ found for the reflexives and _partir_ appear to be inconsistent with the findings for the elementary school groups.

In summary then, the overall tendency is for both the elementary and secondary school students to conjugate tomber, rentrer, rester, sortir most often with avoir, the verbs venir and arriver less consistently with avoir, and the verbs partir, revenir, aller and the reflexives more often with être. A general ranking of these verbs according to their tendency to be conjugated with avoir or être is suggested by their list order in Figure 1.

4. Discussion. We noted above (cf. section 1) the tendency in Romance to level the distinction between E-verbs and A-verbs. Furthermore, we suggested that this process may have been braked in Modern French due to the intervention of prescriptive grammarians. It is our impression that in Ontario, where the level of exposure to Standard French has, until recently, been relatively low (cf. Mougeon and Canale 1977 for further details), the exigencies of normative grammars have had little impact on the informal speech of Franco-Ontarians. Thus, analogical leveling of the E-verb/A-verb distinction may be assumed to be an active process in Ontarian French. Below we would like to discuss several factors that, according to our findings, may account for the variation in the use of avoir and être: (i) the existence of lexical counterparts (homophones of the E-verbs) that must be conjugated with avoir; (ii) the acceptability of the adjectival use of each E-verb with the copula (e.g. as in Maintenant elle est partie 'Now she is gone'); (iii) the relative frequency of each E-verb; and (iv) the morphological properties of certain E-verbs.

It is worth pointing out that we have examined the possible role of other linguistic factors (e.g. the influence of the form of the grammatical subject on the use of avoir) and sociolinguistic factors (e.g. socioeconomic status, language dominance) in this leveling process. However, our findings in these areas are at present either incomplete or inconclusive and must be relegated to a future report. The reader may consult Thibault and Sankoff (1975)

Figure 1. Non-standard usage of the auxiliary avoir in the speech of the Grade 2, 5, and 9/10/12 students.

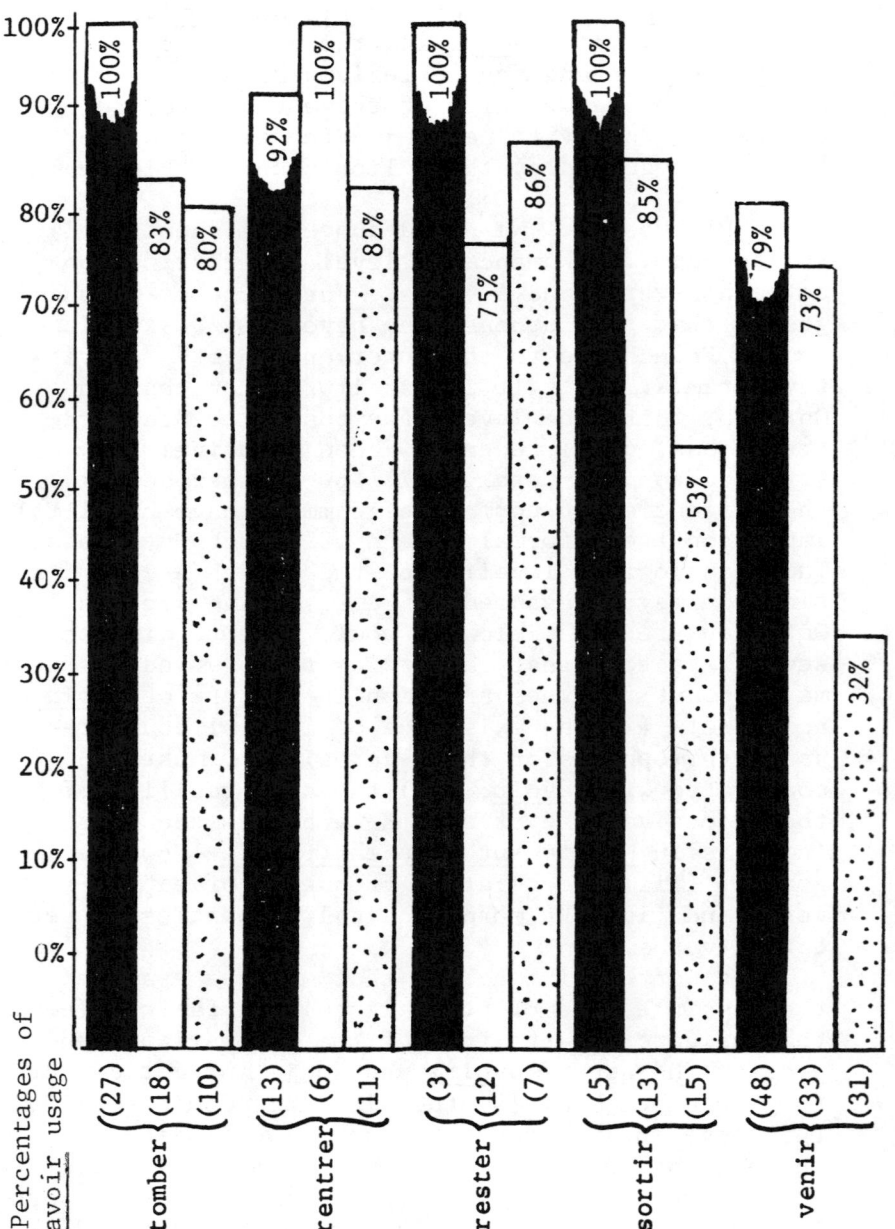

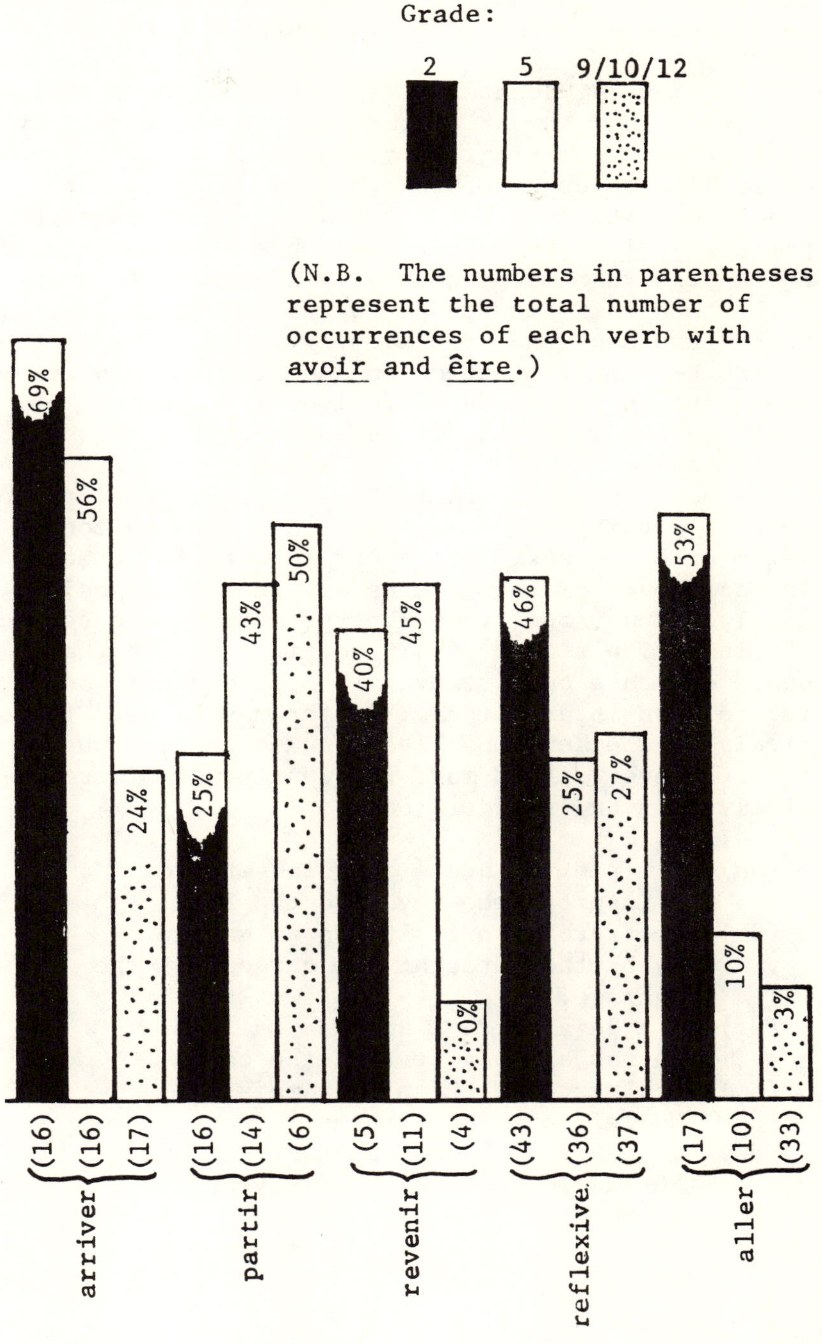

ANALOGICAL LEVELING OF THE AUXILIARY ÊTRE / 49

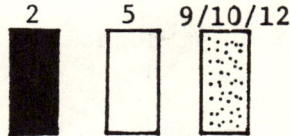

Grade:
2   5   9/10/12

(N.B. The numbers in parentheses represent the total number of occurrences of each verb with avoir and être.)

and Sankoff and Thibault (1977) for a discussion of
the role of such factors in the variable use of the
auxiliaries <u>avoir</u> and <u>être</u> in Montreal French.

4.1. Lexical counterparts. It seems reasonable
to assume that the obligatory use of the auxiliary
<u>avoir</u> with a verb that is a homophone of an E-verb
could lead to or reinforce the use of <u>avoir</u> with
the E-verb itself. The rationale is that once the
pattern <u>avoir</u> + past participle has been introduced
for a verb that is phonetically identical to an E-
verb, then this pattern can be easily generalized
on the basis of phonetic identity. To maintain the
A-verb/E-verb distinction in such cases would require one to ignore phonetic identity and rely on
semantic and syntactic differences of the verbs
concerned.

Of the E-verbs listed in Figure 1, <u>rentrer</u>, <u>rester</u>,
<u>sortir</u>, <u>partir</u> have homophones that must be conju-
gated with the auxiliary <u>avoir</u> in Ontarian French.
In fact, each of these verbs may be used transitively. Thus, one finds <u>rentrer</u> used in the sense
of 'insert, put into' (8a), <u>sortir</u> taken in the
sense of 'take out, remove' (8b), and <u>partir</u> serv-
ing to mean 'start' (8c). <u>Rester</u> may be used transitively in the sense of 'leave something somewhere'
(8d); however, it is more frequently used intransi-
tively to mean 'reside' (8e).

(8a) J'ai rentré la clé dans la serrure.
 'I inserted the key into the lock.'
(8b) Mon frère a sorti l'auto du garage.
 'My brother brought the car out of the
  garage.'
(8c) Il a déjà parti l'auto.
 'He has already started the car.'
(8d) On a resté le chien à la maison.
 'We left our dog at home.'
(8e) Elle a resté à Wawa pendant six ans.
 'She lived in Wawa for six years.'

Thus the existence of lexical counterparts conjugated with _avoir_ could account for the overall high percentages of _avoir_ usage with _rentrer_, _rester_, _sortir_ and the lower percentages for _revenir_, _aller_ and the reflexives.⁵ However, this factor does not appear to account for the high percentages of _avoir_ use found for _tomber_, _venir_, _arriver_ and the relatively low percentage for _partir_. We have no immediate explanation for our findings concerning _venir_ and _arriver_. Although _tomber_ is not used transitively in modern Ontarian French (according to our data and consultants), it is possible that _tomber_ could have been used in this way at an earlier stage of Canadian French. This possibility is suggested by the claim in _Le Robert_ that the transitive use of _tomber_ was frequent at earlier stages of French. Furthermore, _partir_ is perhaps not used productively in its transitive sense: we did not find any occurrences of its transitive use in our data.

4.2. Adjectival use. Sankoff and Thibault (1977) suggest, with reservation, that use of _avoir_ to form the composed past tenses of the active voice could be most expected with just those verbs that can be used adjectivally. In this way the composed past forms could be easily distinguished from the copula + adjective construction (cf. Benveniste 1966:204-205 for the original discussion). Also, given this line of reasoning, one would expect verbs that cannot be easily adjectivized (e.g. reflexives, _aller_, _venir_) to continue to be conjugated with _être_.⁶

Of the E-verbs we have discussed, those listed in (9) seem to us to be acceptable when used adjectivally with the copula.

(9) Marie est $\begin{Bmatrix} \text{sortie} \\ \text{partie} \\ \text{arrivée} \\ \text{rentrée} \\ \text{revenue} \\ \text{tombée} \end{Bmatrix}$ maintenant

'Mary is out now', etc.

However, the adjectival use of <u>aller</u>, <u>rester</u>, <u>venir</u> and the reflexives (10) does not seem to us to be acceptable in Ontarian and Standard French.

(10) *Marie $\begin{Bmatrix} \text{est restée} \\ \text{est venue} \\ \text{est allée} \\ \text{s'est lavée} \\ \text{etc.} \end{Bmatrix}$ maintenant

*'Mary is stayed now', etc.

Thus, ability or inability to be used adjectivally with the copula does seem to correlate with the percentage of <u>avoir</u> or <u>être</u> use in the case of <u>aller</u>, <u>arriver</u>, <u>rentrer</u>, <u>sortir</u>, <u>tomber</u> and the reflexives. However, this factor alone would not account for the high frequency of <u>avoir</u> with <u>rester</u> and <u>venir</u> nor the high frequency of <u>être</u> with <u>partir</u> and <u>revenir</u>. Although Sankoff and Thibault (1977) prefer this factor to the lexical counterparts one to account for their findings on the use of the auxiliaries <u>avoir</u> and <u>être</u> in Montreal French, our own findings are better accounted for by appealing to both of these factors rather than selecting one to the exclusion of the other.[7]

For example, the relatively frequent use of <u>avoir</u> with <u>arriver</u>, could be related to the ability of <u>arriver</u> to be used adjectivally but not to its lack of lexical counterparts conjugated with <u>avoir</u>. On the other hand, the fact that <u>rester</u> is conjugated most often with <u>avoir</u> and <u>revenir</u> most often with <u>être</u> can be accounted for in terms of the lexical counterparts factor but not in terms of the acceptability of <u>revenu</u> and the unacceptability of <u>resté</u> as adjectives.

4.3. Frequency. It has often been observed that analogical leveling tends to affect infrequent items before frequent ones, ceteris paribus (cf. Hooper 1976 and Martinet 1969:115ff., among others). In terms of the leveling process we have been examining, one could hypothesize that infrequent

E-verbs will tend to be conjugated more often with avoir than will frequent E-verbs.

The E-verbs listed in Figure 1 occurred in the passé composé or plus-que-parfait forms in our data with the following frequency: reflexives (116), venir (112), tomber (65), aller (60), arriver (39), partir (36), sortir (33), rentrer (30), rester (22), revenir (20). Unfortunately, we have been unable to find a frequency dictionary of Canadian French with which to compare our findings. Frequency dictionaries of European French (for example, Juilland, Brodin, and Davidovitch 1970) do not rank reflexives as a single category, but do rank venir and aller among the most frequent verbs. Much lower in frequency are, in relative order, rester, arriver, revenir, partir, sortir, tomber, rentrer.[8]

Although little can be said with any certainty about the relation between frequency and use of avoir for most of these verbs, a few verbs are worth commenting on. If one assumes that retention of idiosyncratic features (e.g. conjugation with être) is more likely to occur in forms that are used frequently than in those used infrequently, then one might ask why venir should tend to be conjugated with avoir in our data. Similarly, one wonders why revenir should be conjugated most often with être, given that it occurs relatively less frequently than venir in the frequency counts we have mentioned. However, the fact that the reflexive verbs and aller are normally conjugated with être in our data may indicate some influence of frequency on the leveling process.

4.4. Morphological properties. In discussions of morphological and phonological change, it has been pointed out that morphologically derived forms often seem to be regularized more easily than non-derived ones. For example in English, a non-derived form such as cast continues to surface as cast in the past tense whereas a morphologically derived form such as broadcast or forecast tends to show a regularized past tense in -ed, i.e.

broadcasted, forecasted (cf. Kiparsky 1973 for discussion).

It is not clear that this factor does or should play a role in the leveling process we are examining. However, the reflexive verbs, inasmuch as certain of them may be morphologically derived (e.g. lever 'raise' > se lever 'arise'), nonetheless do not appear to be as easily affected by this leveling process as do other non-derived verbs (tomber, venir, etc.). Similarly, the fact that revenir is conjugated much less frequently with avoir than is venir suggests that a morphologically derived form may be less easily affected by such leveling processes than a non-derived one. We find this an interesting possibility and look forward to further research on this aspect of morphosyntactic change.

4.5. Summary. The main points of our discussion in this section are summarized in Table 1. The rank order of the E-verbs according to their percentage of occurrence with avoir (cf. Figure 1) is given in the column 'verb'. The plus sign (+) indicates that a given verb has the property in question, a minus sign (-) that it does not, and the combination of plus and minus (±) that its status is undecided (based on our comments above).

5. Conclusion. The leveling process in the Franco-Ontarian auxiliary system seems to have its roots in the tendency in early Romance to form the composed tenses of all verbs with habere in the active voice and esse in the passive. We hypothesize that due mainly to the intervention of prescriptive grammarians at the Modern French stage, the reflexives and certain intransitive verbs must be conjugated with the auxiliary être in Standard French. However, due in part to the Franco-Ontarians' lack of exposure to Standard French (until quite recently), the leveling process in the auxiliary system appears to have had a measurable impact on the use of the auxiliaries avoir and être in Ontarian French. It is our understanding

Table 1. Summary correlation of the rank order of E-verbs with four of their linguistic properties.

Verb	Mean% of avoir usage*	Lexical counterpart with avoir	Adjectival use	Highly frequent	Morphologically derived
tomber	91%	±	+	–	–
rentrer	90%	+	+	–	±[9]
rester	82%	+	–	–	–
sortir	73%	+	+	–	–
venir	64%	–	–	+	–
arriver	49%	–	+	–	–
partir	36%	±	+	–	–
revenir	35%	–	+	–	+
reflexives	34%	–	–	+	+
aller	18%	–	–	+	–

*The mean percentage of avoir usage was computed on the basis of the combined raw scores obtained for each verb.

that other relatively isolated varieties of French have been undergoing this same leveling process.

Our present findings indicate that no single linguistic factor can account for the variable use of avoir and être with the E-verbs we have examined. Rather, factors such as the existence of lexical counterparts to the E-verbs, which are conjugated exclusively with avoir, acceptability of the adjectival use of each E-verb with the copula, the relative frequency and the morphological properties of these verbs may all contribute in some way to the spread or restriction of this morphosyntactic change.

Two further points should be kept in mind. First, the factors we have discussed are not sufficient to account for all of our findings. For instance, the relatively high frequency of occurrence of avoir with venir does not seem to follow from any of these four factors; in fact, the behavior of venir clearly goes against the tendencies of the other E-verbs with respect to lexical counterparts and adjectival use.[10] This suggests that at least one other factor --still unknown to us--can condition the use of the auxiliaries avoir and être. Second, it is not clear from our findings whether such factors can be said to compete with or reinforce one another. Consider, for example, the use of avoir with tomber and rester. Although avoir is used most frequently with both verbs, tomber can be used adjectivally but has a lexical counterpart that must be conjugated with avoir in Ontarian French; on the other hand, rester cannot be used adjectivally but does have a lexical counterpart conjugated exclusively with avoir. We cannot conclude that these two factors compete with one another in this case, since both tomber and rester appear to be relatively infrequent verbs, another factor that might explain the tendency to conjugate them with avoir. Thus, in the present paper we must leave unanswered questions such as these, in addition to the interesting and more ambitious question of how the various aspects of this leveling process are to be handled in a theory of grammar or grammar change.

NOTES

The research reported on in this paper was funded in part by grants from the Ontario Ministry of Education and the Ontario Institute for Studies in Education. We are grateful for this support. We also wish to thank Jean-Yves Morin and Jim Martin for useful discussion of some of the ideas presented here.

1. According to Elcock (1960) and Nicolau (1936), the development of habere as an auxiliary is most likely based on the earlier and frequent use of habere as a main verb indicating possession. Thus, Elcock (1960:108-109) points out that Plautus and Cicero used habere as a main verb and the passive participle as an adjective as in (i)

(i) Habeo cultellum comparatum.
'I have a bought knife.'

Additional examples may be found in Grandgent (1907:54-55). Nicolau (1936:30) goes on to claim that the Old French structure in (ii) represents an intermediate stage in the development of the auxiliary avoir.

(ii) J'ai des lettres lues.
'I have read the letters.'

See Benveniste (1966) and Kuryłowicz (1931) for discussion of an alternative hypothesis on the origin of the auxiliary habere/avoir.

2. The use of esse with intransitive verbs of motion may have been influenced by the frequent use of the impersonal passive forms of such verbs in Classical Latin; thus, ventum est 'one came', itum est 'one went' may have provided the pattern for venitus sum 'I came', etc. in Vulgar Latin. Grandgent (1907:55) cites P. Thielmann's 'Habere mit dem Part. Perf. Pass.' in Archiv fur lateinische Lexicographie und Grammatik, Vol. II (Leipzig) for further discussion.

3. Tenere 'hold, keep' rather than habere has come to be used as an auxiliary in Portuguese (cf. Elcock 1960:109) and according to Nicolau (1936: 28), in certain Italian dialects as well.

4. A total of 100 students enrolled in Grades 9 and 10 at the French secondary school in Rayside have been grouped with the Grade 9 sample. See Lamérand and Ross 1974 for further details on the students from Rayside.

5. Note that the conjugation of certain reflexives with _avoir_ or _être_ may be influenced by this same factor. Thus, an E-verb such as _se lever_ 'arise' may also be said to have a lexical counterpart (though not homophone) that is conjugated exclusively with _avoir_ in the active voice, i.e. _lever_ 'raise'. Furthermore, certain reflexives may be used transitively as in _Je me suis coupé la main_ 'I cut my hand'; _Je me suis acheté un livre_ 'I bought myself a book'. To date we have not found any convincing evidence to suggest that transitivity or existence of a lexical counterpart conjugated with _avoir_ plays any role in the use of _avoir_ and _être_ with reflexives.

6. One wonders then why intransitives such as _courir_ 'run', _marcher_ 'walk', etc.--which can never be used adjectivally--are conjugated with _avoir_ and not with _être_.

7. Sankoff and Thibault (1977) report the percentage of _avoir_ use for the following verbs: _demeurer_ (96%), _changer_ (95%), _passer_ (90%), _rester_ (78%), _rentrer_ (74%), _tomber_ (72%), _déménager_ (70%) _monter_ (68%), _sortir_ (67%), _descendre_ (50%), _retourner_ (46%), _partir_ (36%), _arriver_ (9%), _venir_ (7%), _revenir_ (6.5%) _entrer_ (6%), _aller_ (0.7%). It is not at all clear to us why Sankoff and Thibault favor the adjectivization factor over the lexical counterparts factor (cf. 4.1 above) in interpreting their results.

8. In our own frequency count, transitive uses of _sortir_, _rentrer_ and _rester_ were not included. Nor were uses of _rester_ in the sense of 'reside'. Juilland, Brodin and Davidovitch (1970) do not distinguish these various uses in their own frequency counts. We should note that although transitive uses of _sortir_, _rentrer_, _rester_, _partir_ were very infrequent in our data (less than three occurrences for each such use), a larger body of data might

reveal an interesting relationship between frequency of the transitive use of these verbs and frequency of <u>avoir</u> with their intransitive counterparts. Similarly, the fact that <u>rester</u> was found in our data to be used in the sense of 'reside' in 17 cases (and conjugated with <u>avoir</u> in each case) and in the sense of 'remain' in 22 cases may account for the relatively high percentage of <u>avoir</u> use with <u>rester</u> in the latter sense (see Figure 1).

9. It is not clear that there is any synchronic morphological rule relating the forms <u>entrer</u> and <u>rentrer</u> in Ontarian French. Furthermore, the form <u>rentrer</u> seems to have taken over the meaning of <u>entrer</u> to the extent that <u>entrer</u> was seldom encountered (a total of six cases) in our data (cf. similar findings in Sankoff and Thibault 1977). For further discussion of the morpheme <u>re-</u> in Ontarian French, see Canale, Mougeon, and Bélanger 1977.

10. The fact that use of <u>avoir</u> with E-verbs is a feature of popular European French, for example, leads us to reject structural borrowing from English as a source for the use of <u>avoir</u> in Ontarian French. However, we cannot rule out the role of English in reinforcing or accelerating the leveling process. For discussion of other features of Franco-Ontarian students' French and English in terms of intra- and inter-language simplification, see Canale, Mougeon, Bélanger, and Ituen (1977), Mougeon, Bélanger, Canale, and Ituen (1977), and Mougeon, Canale, and Carroll (1977).

REFERENCES

Benveniste, E. 1966. Problèmes de linguistique générale I. Paris: Gallimard.
Brown, R. 1973. A first language: The early stages. Cambridge, Mass.: Harvard University Press.
Brunot, F., and C. Bruneau. 1969. Précis de grammaire historique de la langue française. 5th edition. Paris: Masson et Cie.

Canale, M., R. Mougeon, and M. Bélanger. 1977.
Analytical alternates to the morpheme re- in
Ontarian French. Toronto: Ontario Institute for
Studies in Education. (Mimeograph)

Canale, M., R. Mougeon, M. Bélanger, and S. Ituen.
1977. Aspects de l'usage de la préposition pour
en français ontarien: Interférence et/ou surgénéralisation? Working Papers on Bilingualism
12.61-78.

Dulay, H. C., and M. K. Burt. 1974. You can't learn
without goofing. In: Error analysis. Edited by
J. C. Richards. London: Longman Group Ltd.
95-123.

Elcock, W. D. 1960. The Romance languages. London:
Faber Ltd.

Frei, H. 1971. La grammaire des fautes. Geneva:
Slatkine Reprints.

Grandgent, C. H. 1907. An introduction to Vulgar
Latin. Boston: McGrath-Sherrill Press.

Grégoire, A. 1947. L'apprentissage du langage II.
Paris: Société d'Edition 'Les Belles Lettres'.

Grevisse, M. 1969. Le bon usage. Gembloux,
Belgium: Duculot.

Guiraud, P. 1968. Patois et dialectes français.
Paris: Presses universitaires de France.

Hooper, J. B. 1976. Word frequency in lexical
diffusion and the source of morphophonological
change. In: Proceedings of the Second International Conference on Historical Linguistics.
Edited by: W. M. Christie, Jr. Amsterdam:
North Holland.

Juilland, A., D. Brodin, and C. Davidovitch. 1970.
Frequency dictionary of French words. The Hague:
Mouton.

Kiparsky, P. 1973. Productivity in phonology.
In: Issues in phonological theory. Edited by
M. Kenstowitz and C. Kisseberth. The Hague:
Mouton.

Kuryłowicz, J. 1931. Les temps composés en roman.
Prace Filologiczne 15.448-53.

Lamérand, R., and Y. Ross. 1974. Projet F1A2:
Rapport intérimaire. Toronto: OISE. (Mimeograph)

Martinet, A. 1969. Le français sans fard. Paris: Presses universitaires de France.

Mougeon, R., M. Bélanger, M. Canale, and S. Ituen. 1977. L'usage de la préposition sur en franco-ontarien. Montreal Working Papers in Linguistics 8.

Mougeon, R., and M. Canale. 1977. Minority language schooling in English Canada: The case of the Franco-Ontarians. Toronto: OISE. (Mimeograph). To appear in: Canada's visible minorities: Selected dimensions in their education. Edited by V. D'Oyley.

Mougeon, R., M. Canale, and S. Carroll. 1977. Acquisition of English prepositions by monolingual and bilingual (French/English) Ontarian students. Toronto: OISE. (Mimeograph). To appear in: Proceedings of the Sixth Annual University of Wisconsin-Milwaukee Linguistics Symposium: Language acquisition. Edited by F. Eckman and A. Hastings.

Nicolau, M. 1936. Remarques sur les origines des formes périphrastiques passives et actives des langues romanes. Bulletin Linguistique. Bucharest. 4.15-30.

Sankoff, G., and P. Thibault. 1977. L'alternance entre les auxiliaires avoir et être en français parlé à Montréal. Département d'anthropologie, Université de Montréal. (Mimeograph)

Thibault, P., and G. Sankoff. 1975. L'alternance entre les auxiliaires avoir et être dans le français parlé à Montréal. Montréal: Département d'anthropologie, Université de Montréal. (Mimeograph)

DEFINITENESS AND RELEVANCE:
THE SEMANTIC UNITY OF IL Y A

PETER CANNINGS
Indiana University

Whilst flying under the colours of the French 'existential' il y a, this paper is not so much concerned with il y a itself, but with what follows it, and, more particularly with the contribution of the 'definiteness' of the terms it introduces to the particular reading assigned to the sentences it occurs in. My intention is to outline a framework within which problems involving what one might call 'syntactic definiteness' may be approached in a way more suited to the problems of 'ordinary language' than the logical models which linguists have taken, perhaps a little uncritically, from philosophers and logicians. The basic point to be made is that whereas for the purposes of logic one might find it convenient to ignore questions of 'contextual' relevance, it is necessary for the linguist to 'relativise' the scope of reference to what may be called 'domains of relevance' in order to account for the facts. Once this is recognized, the problem of linguistically relevant 'definiteness' may be characterised in a fairly precise and simple manner. Whilst the solution is tentative, and leaves many questions unanswered, it has, I believe, the virtue of enabling one to approach this, and other 'presuppositional' phenomena in more orderly fashion.

The central problem we are attempting to account for is the following: why is (1), in contrast with (2), not construed as a statement asserting the existence of Santa Claus?

(1) Il y a le Père Noël
(2) Il y a un Père Noël

We have two sentences differing only in the 'definiteness' of the determiner preceding the noun, each with a quite distinct prevalent reading. There are, essentially, three readings available for sentences of the form il y a NP--an 'ontological' reading, a 'presence' reading, and a 'specificational' reading, as illustrated in the following examples:[1]

(3) Je viens d'apprendre qu'il y a un Père Noël
    On m'a appris cela en classe de philosophie
(4) Tiens! Il y a un Père Noël. Je ne m'attendais pas à en voir dans un endroit pareil
(5) Qu'est-ce que tu vois dans mon dessin?
    Il y a un Père Noël, mais à part ça je n'y vois pas grand'chose

Thus (3) is taken as an ontological statement which may roughly be paraphrased as 'there is such a thing as a Santa Claus', (4) is equivalent to 'there is a Santa Claus here', and (5) specifies the value of a previously announced variable. On the latter reading, the focal term is asserted to be an instance of a previously enunciated type. Following Higgins' (1973, 1977) account of copulative sentences, I term these 'specificational' items on the grounds that un Père Noël may be seen as being 'entered' into the list of x que je vois dans le dessin. (1), however, is interpreted on the lines of (4) and (5), and a reading corresponding to (3) is uniformly rejected by speakers.

A similar problem arises in English with the there is NP construction which has been studied quite extensively in the generative literature (cf. in particular Milsark (1974), Jenkins (1975), Ross (1973, 1974), and the references contained therein),

with the difference that the 'presence' reading is
unnatural with 'definites' in much the same way as
the ontological reading is (see Cannings (to appear)
for some discussion on this). The specificational
reading of existential sentences in English has not
received much attention in the literature, although
the 'definiteness' restrictions on the existential
readings of there is have been analysed in some detail (Postal 1966, Milsark 1974, and Ross 1974).
These authors have seen the deviance of the English
equivalent of our (1) as a grammatical fact, in the
broad sense of the term--that is, as either a syntactic (Postal) or a semantic (Milsark) incompatibility. Here I will apply the logic of these approaches to the problem at hand, and argue that the
oddness of (1) is due not to the violation of a rule
of grammar, but to the fact that it is merely a
platitudinous statement, and thus violates only the
principle whereby one assumes that speakers in making statements are intending to inform (cf. Grice
1968). The analysis proposed corrects a crucial
defect in the analyses quoted--namely, that they
fail to take into account the 'relativity' of reference.

As far as il y a is concerned, there is (except
in more formal styles) no restriction on the
definiteness of NPs occurring in presentational
sentences (type 4) as is shown in the following
examples:

(6) Tiens! Il y a $\begin{Bmatrix} \text{mon père} \\ \text{Pierre} \\ \text{le Père Noël} \end{Bmatrix}$.
    Je ne savais pas qu'il allait venir.

We shall, however, for the moment cast aside any
discussion of this interpretation, and first of
all devote our attention exclusively to the
specificational and ontological readings. Returning to example (1), whilst the specificational reading is perfectly acceptable, speakers reject the
ontological reading:

(7) Qu'est-ce que tu vois dans ce dessin?
--Il y a le Père Noël (des sapins, des gens qui jouent au loto ...)[2]
(8) ?L'analyse ontologique de Tel Quel démontre de façon très claire qu'il y a le Père Noël

(1) therefore, or so it would seem, requires the interpretation whereby <u>le Père Noël</u> is the item on a list whose heading has already been announced, and does not allow an 'ontological instantiation' reading. There is, however, an obvious sense in which an ontological statement constitutes the enumeration of part of the ingredients list of the world, and I shall attempt here to provide an explanation for this common-sense observation. After considering the conditions which must hold for this reading to obtain, and after a critical review of the equation of these conditions with either morphological or semantic definiteness, an explicit formulation is proposed which accounts for the facts observed in a simple and natural manner.

A first hypothesis one might entertain to account for the lack of an ontological reading for (1) is that it is the morphological definiteness of <u>le Père Noël</u> which blocks such readings: that is, that the rule which interprets such sentences as 'existential' is sensitive to the feature [-DEFINITE].[3] This gains some initial plausibility, given the lack of an ontological reading for sentences like the following:

(9) ?Ontologiquement parlant, il y a $\begin{Bmatrix} \text{le livre} \\ \text{ce livre} \\ \text{mon livre} \\ \text{Paul} \\ \text{lui} \\ \text{moi-(même)} \end{Bmatrix}$

Such an analysis is proposed for English in Postal (1966), and under this view the rule of <u>There</u>-insertion has appended to it a condition that it apply only to NPs which are marked [-DEFINITE] (cf. e.g. Burt 1971). Other rules of grammar (the 'fronting' involved in sentences like <u>Bad as Benny is</u>, <u>he always finds time to smile</u>, for example (see Postal)) are, under a similar view sensitive to the [+DEFINITE] status of the subject NP. For French, the feature value [+DEFINITE] has been assumed to be appropriate for the constraining of Dislocations (Gross 1968, Langacker 1972) on the basis of data like the following:

(10) #Un garçon, il est myope
(11) #Des chevaux, ils courent dans le pré

(12) $\left\{\begin{array}{l}\text{Le garçon}\\ \text{Ce garçon}\\ \text{Paul}\\ \text{Mon garçon}\\ \text{Lui}\end{array}\right\}$, il est myope

(13) $\left\{\begin{array}{l}\text{Les}\\ \text{Ces}\\ \text{Mes}\end{array}\right\}$ chevaux, ils courent dans le pré

The essence of the feature analysis position is that there exist syntactic contexts which 'select' NPs which are either [+ or - DEFINITE], and that the feature motivated as a classificatory device to distinguish <u>un</u> from <u>le</u> may be used as the basis for the expression of such restrictions. Thus, morphological definiteness, and 'syntactic' definiteness coalesce. As far as I am aware, no one has ever taken this analysis too seriously--counterexamples are well known--but no one to my knowledge has ever attempted to seek out a more adequate explanation, despite the inherent circularity of the definition of definiteness, noted only by Milsark. More careful analysis reveals that this position is completely untenable (see Cannings to appear), and principally for the following reasons: Firstly, there are many [-DEFINITE] NPs which may be dislocated (left or right)[4] provided a 'non-specific' interpretation is possible, in the sense that it occurs in a referentially opaque context (Quine 1960; see also Hall-Partee 1972) or is 'generic':

(14) Un enfant, ça sait des choses, quand-même

(15) Ç'a tendance à être fantaisiste, un linguiste
(16) Des cas pareils, j'en vois tous les jours
(17) J'en avais trois à l'époque, d'articles
(18) Il faut savoir bien la tenir, une grenouille australienne
(19) Un cygne, il suffit qu'il soit perçu comme tel
(20) Des allumettes, j'en ai cherché partout
(21) J'en veux pas, de cadeaux

Secondly, there are many morphological definites which may occur with ontological interpretations in sentences of the form il y a NP:

(22) Selon l'ontologie grecque, il y a les choses suivantes--les dieux, les hommes, et les Jeux Olympiques
(23) Il y a de nouveau l'ontologie d'antan
(24) Il y a le seul et unique pouvoir qui est dispensé par les dieux
(25) Il y a le feu, l'air et le vent
(26) Il y a, comme il y a toujours eu, la nécessité primordiale de se nourrir
(27) Il y a le fait que les hommes sont egoïstes
(28) Il y a l'ultime sanction qu'est la mort

All of the above may be interpreted as ontological statements, yet all the focal NPs are [+DEFINITE]. I shall return to these examples.

Thirdly, there are cases of NPs with [+DEFINITE] morphology which are unacceptable in dislocations, and notably cataphoric and self-referential expressions:[5]

(29) #Celui-ci, il est beau: Pierre
(30) #Le troisieme word de ce NP, $\{\begin{smallmatrix}il\\ce\end{smallmatrix}\}$ n'est pas français
(31) #Mon exemple 31, il est bizarre
(32) #Le mot suivant, c'est un pronom
(33) #Le mot 'frasard', je l'ai inventé en construisant cet exemple

Thus (30) (whilst true) is deviant if <u>ce NP</u> refers
to the dislocated NP as a whole, and <u>the latter</u> thus
to <u>word</u>, (32) if <u>le mot suivant</u> refers to <u>c'</u>, and so
forth. It is important to note that despite the con-
volution of such examples, it is the fact of dis-
locating the NP which produces the deviancy, since
the simple sentences to which they are in some way
related are all acceptable. All, moreover, are presumably true.6

Fourthly, there are cases of [-DEFINITE] NPs which
are, for reasons to be discussed later, extremely
marked for the specificational reading, and are not
construed as statements of ontological instantiation:

(34) Il y a un doigt
(35) Il y a un oncle
(36) Il y a une fourmi
(37) Il y a une cigarette

From these examples, it is clear that the feature
[DEFINITE] does not delineate natural classes with
respect to the ontological interpretation of sentences containing <u>il y a</u>. The feature analysis is
both too weak and too strong, even when one restricts one's attention to quite simple cases involving those determiners for which the feature is
clearly motivated on a morphological level.

Finally, there are determiners whose morphologically based definiteness is non-transparent, which
must be considered both [+DEFINITE] and [-DEFINITE]
(i.e. unmarked for this feature) since they may
occur in both of the criterial contexts we are discussing:

(38) Il y a pas mal de licornes
(39) Pas mal de licornes, on a du mal à les
     classer
(40) Il y a 789 candidats
(41) 789 candidats, ça fait beaucoup

Given the inadequacy of the [DEFINITE] analysis,
even for the simple cases it was intended for, and
the additional fact that a given value for the

feature is not uniquely specifiable for other determiners, there seems little point in retaining it as a serious candidate for the expression of 'definiteness' restrictions. Whilst it is important not to trivialise the complexity of the dislocation examples (especially in terms of the pronoun selection), it seems quite clear that no such morphologically based feature is likely to shed much light on the matter.

Milsark (1974), whilst rejecting this morphologically based characterisation on the definiteness restriction on the English existential, formulates a semantic account involving the quantificational properties of determiners which also categorically excludes definite descriptions. Milsark's account requires that the determiner of the NP whose existence is being asserted be interpretable as a statement of the cardinality (in the sense of Chomsky 1975) of the set denoted by the head N. Following Chomsky's (1975) characterisation of the definite article as involving universal quantification, sentences like <u>there is the Loch Ness Monster</u> may not be interpreted existentially, since 'universal' is not a statement of cardinality. Pressures of space forbid us examining this account in more detail (see Cannings to appear), but the following summarises the relevant aspects of the Chomsky-Milsark account, as far as the problem at hand is concerned. Chomsky assumes, following Russell (1905), that uniqueness is the essential attribute of the definite article, and, furthermore that the relevant notion of uniqueness is semantic. However, the uniqueness analysis suffers from the defect that it cannot naturally account for plurals (unless the iota operator is allowed to quantify classes as well as individuals). This defect may be corrected, and the essentials of Russell's analysis maintained if the iota operator is replaced by the universal quantifier ($\forall$), and the singular-plural distinction may be conveyed by a statement of the cardinality of the set. Thus, <u>le garçon</u> would translate as $\underline{\forall\ x\ (garçon,x)C = 1}$ the set of 'everything which is a boy, having cardinality 1', and les garçons as $\forall x\ (\text{garçon}, x) C = \text{plural}$ 'the set of everything which is a boy, having cardinality plural'. Milsark's rule of interpretation of there is NP has as its output a statement of the form 'there exists (an) x having the cardinality of Q' where Q is the reading of the determiner of the NP. The reading of the definite article being $\forall$, the resultant reading is ill-formed since 'universal' is not a statement of cardinality. A sentence like our (1) is thus deviant in the same way as the logical formula $*_\exists \forall x$ is an ill-formed formula. Milsark's formulation thus subsumes morphological definites in toto by virtue of the semantic spelling of the being a special case of the more general ban on what Milsark calls 'quantificational' determiners. As it stands, this analysis therefore makes the same predictions with respect to morphological definites as the feature analysis.

Milsark does briefly discuss a number of 'definite' counterexamples, but considers these 'crypto-indefinites', that is, NPs having overtly definite morphology, but whose definiteness in a semantic sense is 'somewhat open to question'. The following are French equivalents of such 'crypto-indefinites':

(42) Il n'y a pas eu la moindre protestation
(43) Il n'y a pas eu la réaction habituelle
(44) Il y a les mêmes objections que la dernière fois

Under this view, the presence of the definite article must be conditioned by factors distinct from those responsible for inducing 'normal' cases of definiteness. If one follows the logic of this approach to the problem at hand, the following hypothesis suggests itself: the definiteness restriction on existential interpretations is sensitive to the semantic import of the definite article, and the recalcitrant morphologically definite examples are instances of a 'dephasing' of semantic and morphological definiteness. If one could motivate a distinction between, for instance, base-inserted and transformationally derived definite articles, such an hypothesis might be viable.

However, the statement that such NPs are somehow spurious cases of semantic definiteness is a curious one, given Milsark's espousal of uniqueness. Examples (42) and (44) at least are quite compatible with Russell's account. Thus, <u>le même x</u> is of necessity unique, since no two objects constitute 'the same thing'; they can only be instances of the same thing-type, in which case it is this that is unique. Superlatives are by definition unique, since, given any set of objects displaying a given property, only one may possess this property to an extent greater than that of all the other members of the set. Superlatives thus guarantee uniqueness by their meaning alone, and are in fact the principal justification for considering uniqueness (as against, for instance, anaphoricity) as the fundamental attribute of the definite article. Similar remarks may be made in connection with our examples (22)-(28). Facts are unique by virtue of their 'names' being specified in the <u>que S</u> which follows <u>le fait</u> (notice <u>le fait que S</u> may not be restrictively modified qua their uniqueness), (27), and similar remarks hold for (26). In (22), the 'warrantry' for the definite article is the following list, and (24) is particularly recalcitrant to any 'crypto-indefinite' analysis. Consider the cases of 'locational' <u>il y a</u>, which Milsark (for English) also considers existential, in example (45): these examples show that the more 'delicate' the description (and thus the more plausible their uniqueness), the more acceptable the sentence becomes.

(45) Il y a $\begin{Bmatrix} \text{l'homme} \\ \text{l'homme au chapeau rouge} \\ \text{le plus grand homme que j'aie jamais vu} \\ \text{le seul homme qui soit susceptible de vous aider} \end{Bmatrix}$

dans le jardin.

Notice, furthermore, that such sentences do not, under normal intonation, have specificational readings. Thus uniqueness is in no way antipathic to non-specificational sentences in general, and ontological statements in particular. We are therefore caught in an interesting paradox--the very motivation for the [DEFINITE] analysis of the restriction on 'ontological' readings of sentences containing il y a must surely be the hope that the 'natural' basis of the restriction may be derived from the semantic distinction formally marked by un vs. le. This is in fact carried over into the semantic account proposed by Milsark. Now the cornerstone notion in philosophical and linguistic discussions of the definite article has been uniqueness, yet the very examples which pose problems for this analysis seem to be the paradigm examples one would wish to adduce in favour of such an analysis of the definite article. We may thus conclude at this point that neither syntactic, nor semantic definiteness (at least insofar as it is expressed by uniqueness) is responsible for blocking the ontological interpretation of (1). The examples we have given suggest, moreover, that the problem is not one of form, but of interpretation.

A third corner of the definiteness hat to which one might turn is the notion that definite descriptions in some way 'presuppose' the existence of their referents (Strawson 1950, 1952). One might thus see (1) as simultaneously asserting and presupposing the existence of Santa Claus, and take this to be the reason for the lack of an ontological reading. This, I believe, is closer to the mark. Two observations are relevant here, however. Firstly, unless the relevant notion of presupposition is elucidated, such an account has no explanatory value, given the controversy surrounding the notion in general (see Kempson 1975, Wilson 1975), and the fact that neither the presuppositional approach, nor the entailment approach advocated by Kempson and Wilson, satisfactorily explains the non-parallel behaviour of subject and nonsubject positions first noted by Strawson. Analogous to

this is the fact that depending on which approach
one chooses within presuppositional accounts,
different predictions will be derived (see Wilson
1975). Thus, until the relevant notion of presupposition is analysed, this is by no means an
explanation. Secondly, under this conception there
is no reason for the ontological reading for (1) to
be blocked--simultaneously presupposing what one is
asserting does not result in either a syntactically
or semantically deviant sentence, but merely in one
which appears pointless, since it is uninformative,
in much the same way as (46) is:

(46) Si je regrette d'être venu, alors je suis
venu

Under this conception, a sentence like (47) should
be necessarily true, yet platitudinous, in much the
same way as (46) is:

(47) Si le Père Noël existe, alors il y a le
Père Noël

If such an analysis is essentially correct, then
this entails that previous attempts at character-
ising the definiteness restriction fail because the
anomaly of (1) has been erroneously assumed to be a
grammatical fact. In the rest of this paper, I
shall argue that there is abundant evidence for the
correctness of this claim, and propose an analysis
which captures this fact and at the same time does
not leave unanalysed the relevant notion of presupposition.

Let us first consider the 'uniqueness' conveyed
by the definite article. For this discussion I
shall use (arbitrarily) Chomsky's formulation of
definiteness, although I believe there are reasons
for considering uniqueness a pragmatic condition on
the 'delicacy' of definite descriptions (see
Cannings to appear, Kempson 1975)[7] and not a truth-
based notion. The particular formulation given for
the definite article is, I believe, irrelevant for the
point I am about to make. Consider a sentence like
(48):

(48) Le tigre n'aime pas le lion
(49) ∀x, ∀y (tigre,x)(lion,y) - aimer x,y

The semantic representation in (49), as it stands, is equivalent to a 'generic' statement, and, strictly speaking reads as something like 'this kind of animal does not like that kind of animal'. This is, I believe, carried over from the fact that in logic one is not normally concerned with the 'domain of interpretation' of statements, since the laws of valid inference with which logic is concerned are intended to hold whatever domain of interpretation is considered. Included in a domain of interpretation (roughly speaking 'universe of discourse') is a domain of individuals which may be referred to. Now, for the example we are considering it is necessary to derive other readings besides the generic statement in (49). Both animals may be specific beasts. For instance--assuming I have a pet tiger and a pet lion called Clarence and Charles respectively--(48) may mean, within a domain of interpretation narrower than the 'universe', that 'Clarence n'aime pas Charles'. Deriving this interpretation is not unduly problematic, since one may consider the domain of interpretation 'vague', and that the particular (specific vs. generic) interpretation is only determinable contextually, i.e. in pragmatics or discourse theory. However, there is obviously a third reading of (48) under which one term may be interpreted generically, and the other specifically: namely, 'Clarence doesn't like that kind of animal'. This involves <u>le tigre</u> and <u>le lion</u> belonging to distinct 'domains of individuals': the tiger to a linguistically or situationally determinable domain, and the lion to a more 'universal' domain of 'ideal' objects almost. Now there is no way for this latter interpretation to be derived from (49) as it stands--the problem is essentially that of 'relativising' the scope of the quantifiers to 'distinct domains'. Thus, what we need is something like 'the tiger (in my household) doesn't like the lion (in the world of 'ideals')'. We can incorporate this into our semantics by saying that uniqueness holds relative to an arbitrary domain of individuals, D_x. Thus, we can refine (49) in the following manner:

(50) $\forall x \ \varepsilon \ D_i \ \forall x \ \varepsilon \ D_j$ (tigre,x)(lion,y) - aimer x,y.

We need further to express in the rules of interpretation that D_i may or may not equal D_j, and, more importantly, to state a 'vocabulary' of 'possible domains'. Before turning to these problems, let us consider further the notion of 'domain of interpretation' for sentences. Consider the following example:

(51) Est-ce que la grenouille est carnivore?

If I walked up to someone on the street and asked him this question, he would probably assume I was referring to the frog as a species, and therefore that I was asking a question about what holds 'generically'. One may consider that he is interpreting the domain of interpretation of the sentence to be (roughly) the universe. However, if, for instance, the person I approach has in his arms a child, and I am proffering forth a leg of chicken, there is every chance that (51) will be interpreted as a (particularly uncomplimentary) remark on the physical appearance of the child. In other words, the sentence is interpreted as being relevant to the specific situation in which he, I, and the baby are part of the 'cast of characters' or domain of individuals. This can be seen as a function of pragmatic principles on the lines developed by Grice (1968). Let us say that the hearer is seeking to interpret the 'domain of relevance' to which the sentence pertains. This involves in part interpreting the domain of individuals over which the definiteness operator ranges: in example (51), on the first interpretation, the domain of individuals is in some sense 'universal', whilst on the second, it is 'people in the situation'. Similarly, the sentence is being used to initiate a discourse 'about' the 'universe' or the situation, respectively. A third possibility for the domain of individuals is 'terms mentioned in the discourse', as exemplified in (52):

(52) Un homme et une femme sont rentrés.
L'homme a enlevé son manteau.

Here, the description operator is interpreted as ranging over the set of individuals contained in the discourse. Besides a domain of individuals, we may consider that the domain of relevance contains time and place coordinates, and, moreover, that it is these which are responsible for 'genericity' and the like. Consider, for example, (53):

(53) Un castor fait des barrages

Even excluding the 'progressive' reading, <u>un castor</u> may be interpreted either generically or specifically, as shown by the following contextualisations:

(54) J'ai appris en classe de philo
qu'un castor fait des barrages
(55) Qu'est-ce qui se passe dans le nouveau film de Warhol?--Un castor fait des barrages
(56) Tout au long du 3^e Acte, un castor fait des barrages

One may consider this to be a scope vagueness of the domain of relevance to which the sentence is 'paired'--this I shall refer to henceforth as 'W' --rather than as an ambiguity between an existential and a universal quantification. In the absence of any cues in the sentence, there is no way of determining whether (53) is a statement about the 'world in general' or refers to some more restricted domain of relevance. If W pertains to the 'universe', then the sentence will be interpreted generically; if it pertains to some narrower domain, then un castor will be interpreted specifically. Under this conception all such sentences are 'generic in W_x'. The scope of W will be in part determinable from temporal and locational cues when present. Let us thus suppose that every sentence generated by the grammar is 'paired' to a domain of relevance W_x, and apply the previous analysis to sentences containing il y a.

Let us give the following rule of interpretation for il y a NP:

    Rule 1. il y a NP
                Term x, having the reading of NP exists relative to W_x, the domain of relevance to which the S is paired.

This we may further specify by stating that x is asserted to be a member of the domain of individuals in W:

    Rule 1'. il y a NP
                Term x, having the reading of NP belongs to D_W · $x \in D_W$.

Let us furthermore express the interpretation of le on the lines suggested above:

    Rule 2. le N(X)
                Everything in some domain of relevance having the reading N(X) $\forall x \in D_j(Px)$
                (where P is the reading of N(X))

The following restriction on 'definiteness' follows from the preceding formulation:

DEFINITENESS RESTRICTION (Pragmatic)
Given Grice's maxim of Quantity.
$D_j \neq D_W$, or the sentence is uninformative

Thus, (1), with W interpreted as 'universal' is interpreted as (57):

    (57) $\forall x \in D_W$ (Père Noël,x)$x \in D_W$

Similarly, if D_j, the domain of individuals which binds le is included in D_w, a platitudinous reading will likewise be derived. Thus, example (58) will be excluded for essentially the same reason (as an ontological statement):

(58) Il y a l'exemple 57

L'exemple (57), by virtue of belonging (in the context of this paper) to a textually determined domain, of necessity included in the 'universal' domain, is not interpreted as having its ontological existence asserted. Thus, this analysis asserts that there is in fact no grammatical restriction at all; if $D_j \leq D_w$, then the sentence is merely uninformative, and any 'bizarreness' is predictable from Grice's (1968) maxim of Quantity (roughly 'be informative'), which we assume to be independently necessitated in pragmatic theory.

Thus, this analysis predicts that when one interprets sentences with il y a NP in isolation, one will seek to pair them to domains of relevance which do not subsume the domain of individuals D_j to which we might deduce that the definiteness of the focal term is bound. The essential problem is that, given the almost total absence of contextual clues, such a sentence could be inserted into infinitely many discourse contexts. Furthermore, in the absence of any explicit 'warrantry' for the definite article (i.e. the vagueness of D_j), we naturally interpret this domain as 'maximal'--i.e. with Santa Claus as our legendary benefactor at Christmas time. In a real sense, this is equivalent to a 'generic' reading--the only difference between le Père Noël and, say, le cheval, is that our encyclopaedic knowledge tells us that the former, but not the latter, is a unit class (has only one member). We have two major alternatives: either the presence of Santa Claus is being called to our attention (i.e. W is the 'situation'), or some highly restricted, previously delineated domain has been opened, into which Santa Claus is being entered as a member. This entry into the linguistically specified domain of individuals results in the specificational reading. All that is happening is that since we are left relatively clueless as to what the scope of D_W might be, and since we know that if it is the 'universe', then the sentence constitutes a platitudinous statement, we deduce via our pragmatic competence that the linguistic context has delimited a more restricted domain of relevance. French differs from English in allowing the 'situational' middle ground in its il y a existential. We return to the terms we have introduced below, but we must first argue that the predictions made by this analysis are correct, and demonstrate how the 'counterexamples' given above are accounted for in this framework.

Firstly, this analysis predicts that if the platitudinous nature of the statement is explicitly signalled within the sentences, or if a 'counter-to-fact' ontology is envisioned, then such sentences should be, in the first case, more acceptable, and in the second, both acceptable, and informative. This is indeed the case:

(59) Heureusement qu'il y a le Père Noël!
Sans lui, les fêtes seraient insupportables.
(60) N'oublie pas qu'il y a le Père Noël!
(61) Il y a le Père Noël, après tout
(62) La plupart des ontologies sont fautives en ce qu'elles oublient, presque toutes qu'il y a le Père Noël
(63) Il n'y a plus que le Père Noël
(64) S'il n'y avait pas le Père Noël, il n'y aurait plus d'ontologie
(65) S'il n'y avait pas les licornes, il n'y aurait plus de philosophie
(66) S'il n'y avait pas le roi de France, ma théorie serait parfaite
(67) S'il n'y avait pas Lacan, il y aurait un espace de mort entre l'ontologisé et l'ontologisant

It is worth noting that the versions with or without the definite article are not equivalent:

(68) S'il n'y avait pas $\begin{Bmatrix} \text{(a) Chomsky} \\ \text{(b) un Chomsky} \end{Bmatrix}$, il n'y aurait pas de grammaire générative.

(68a) suggests that if Chomsky did not exist, then generative grammar would not exist either, and even if there existed someone other than Chomsky who had led the same life as he had through the late 50s, there would still be no generative grammar. (68b), on the other hand, can clearly be true if one can conceive of Chomsky's role having been accomplished by another person. Similarly, (69) uttered by me is necessarily true whilst there are circumstances in which (70) could be false (e.g. if I changed my name tomorrow):

(69) S'il n'y avait pas Peter Cannings, je n'existerais pas
(70) S'il n'y avait pas un Peter Cannings, je n'existerais pas

Basically, one is stuck with one's extension, but not with one's irreplaceability. These examples show that the indefinite <u>un Père Noël</u> in no way suppletes a putative 'hole in the paradigm'. The following examples are particularly clear:

(71) Zut alors! Il n'y a plus $\begin{Bmatrix} \text{de linguistique} \\ \text{une linguistique} \\ \text{la linguistique} \end{Bmatrix}$
J'en ai marre que le Bureau Central change tous les jours l'ontologie.

One important fact which has not been recognised in the literature is that the syntax following the postcopular NP is irrelevant to the unacceptability of definites in such sentences (compare Ross 1973, 1974): if what follows imposes a 'broad scope' interpretation of the domain of relevance to which the sentence is paired, then the sentence is just as good or bad as an 'ontological' sentence with <u>il y a</u>:

(72) Il y a le Père Noël
(73) Il y a le Père Noël dans ce monde
(74) Il y a le Père Noël qui existe
(75) Il y a le Père Noël à inclure dans la liste des choses qui existent
(76) Qu'existe-t-il dans ce monde?--Il y a le Père Noël
(77) Il y a le Père Noël comme être existant

The postcopular phrase gives clues as to the scope of W, and if, as we predict, this is forced to contain the universal domain of individuals, then the sentence shares the oddity of (1) (repeated as (72)). Similarly odd sentences may be constructed where the domain is smaller than the universe:

(78) Il y a la voiture dans le garage
(79) Il y a moi qui suis là
(80) Qui est ici?
    --Il y a moi

If <u>la voiture</u> and <u>le garage</u> are both 'situationally' bound (as when said by someone in his own home) (78) is odd unless said as a reminder, or to someone who perhaps does not know I use the garage to keep my car in. (79) is odd if <u>là</u> is the place where I am, since it is quite obvious to anyone who can see me that I am here. To obtain a non-platitudinous reading, one might interpret <u>là</u> as 'at that point in life' or some such. (80) is similarly uninformative unless <u>ici</u> is interpreted as somewhere distinct from where the two speakers are standing (e.g. a place on a photo etc.). Thus the 'uninformative' remarks apply across the board. We have thus shown that there is no reason to recognise distinct readings for existential and specificational <u>il y a</u>, or any other <u>il y a</u> for that matter (except perhaps the 'temporal' use, which seems to require a special statement). There are still a number of important questions to be answered, to which we return later, but let us first consider the 'counterexamples' of (14)-(41), and how they are accounted for by the analysis we have proposed. The point at issue is

that, for one reason or another, the statements
made by the [+DEFINITE] examples are not construed
as platitudinous, and that the [-DEFINITE] examples
are all instances of count nouns. Thus, les choses
suivantes has definite morphology since the list
which immediately follows constitutes the relevant
'warrantry' for their uniqueness: the domain of
individuals may be considered to be that linguistically specified, but it is not part of the
priorly constituted domain. (23) switches time
references, so is informative since obviously the
universal domain of individuals may change with
time. (26) benefits from a similar comparison of
times. (25) may be construed as informative by
what it omits--since everyone assumes that more
things than these exist, it is equivalent to something like a statement to the effect that any less
reductionist ontologies are overcluttered (although
the sentence is still technically platitudinous).
In (26) and (27), the head NPs act to all intents
and purposes as cataphora, as has already been
noted. The [-DEFINITE] counterexamples are all
instances of members of classes which we assume
have many members--it takes a large stretch of the
imagination to envisage a world in which only one
of each item would exist. Thus, in exactly the
same way as le Père Noël these sentences are interpreted situationally or specificationally. In the
case of endangered species, such sentences become
more plausible as ontological statements:

(81) Il y a un linguiste paninien
(82) Il y a une baleine blanche

The un, moreover, is interpreted as a statement of
the cardinality of the relevant classes. To re-
capitulate, we have suggested that incorporating
a 'relativisation' of definiteness operators (and
in fact all other quantifiers) with respect to
'domains of relevance' allows a simple characterisation of the definiteness restriction in question,
and, I believe, of definiteness restrictions in
general. The rest of this paper will be devoted

to some rather speculative remarks on the substantive content of such domains, and on their more general application.

First, let's examine the domains of individuals. There is, I believe, some merit in attempting to restrict these to three in number. The 'universe', which should not be confused with the real world, is rather the domain of things we can talk about. This is similar to what Kuno (1973) calls the 'permanent registry'. The 'situation' is the immediate non-linguistic context which includes the participants in the discourse and whatever trappings we may assume 'belong' to them (e.g. cars, houses, etc.). The 'discourse domain' consists of all terms which have been explicitly mentioned in the discourse, plus what may either be considered an 'open set', or perhaps an individual variable into which specificational terms may be entered. In other words, through the language we may define a 'cast of characters' through a discourse, but at any point offer an open set into which new characters may be introduced (or old characters resituated). A metaphor may illustrate things here. A discourse is like a play: it has its cast of characters, but at the same time it is self-constituting and an open entity. Rather like an ever dilating, roving aperture, it may introduce new terms, recall old ones, etc. Just as in a play, once a character has appeared once on stage, but left, there is no need for him to reintroduce himself when he steps back on stage. He is thereafter a member of the discourse domain of individuals. A character in a play may refer to the sun, since it belongs to the universal domain, or may refer to my wife, since in our culture this can receive 'situational' warrantry. The 'open set' is rather like the notion of an open-ended play-- perhaps like the lights being dimmed, a spotlight being lit, and a member of the audience being allowed to 'step into' the cast of characters. Now these remarks are quite traditional, and I believe it would be of some interest to try and constrain domains of individuals to these. This, I believe, entails abandoning uniqueness as a semantic notion.

The alternative would appear to be allowing a domain of individuals to be any arbitrary set of individuals, especially if, as I believe is correct, the analysis of definiteness should also account for pronouns. Quine's remarks (Quine 1948) are particularly suggestive on this topic. The problem is that otherwise sentences like (83) must be characterised as technically false, which is clearly counterintuitive:

(83) He shot him

(As pointed out to me by Roger Higgins, there can be no appeal here to a principle of disjoint reference, since this should follow from the analysis.) An approach to the definite article which seems worth investigation is that it is essentially a pronoun, thus a 'constant term' bound to a domain of relevance--with the description functioning as a means of identifying the particular constant term to which it refers. Given this function of the description, the uniqueness requirement seems to follow automatically. It seems worthwhile to point out this line of investigation, since it seems to me to be the one which allows the more constrained theory of relevance.

The greater problem is the domain of relevance to which the sentence is paired, although I think some remarks can be made which enable at least a preliminary insight into what these might be, and how they are linguistically relevant. We have in our discussion implied that <u>il y a</u> always enters terms into the domain of individuals in W. This is clearly not so--it merely happens to be the case when there is no specification within the sentence. More precisely, one may say that <u>il y a</u> locates terms with respect to a part of the domain of relevance--this may or may not be the domain of individuals. It may be a point in time, or in space, be it physical, 'psychological' or whatever. The following examples are representative, and are well known:

(84) Il y a ta mère au téléphone
(85) Il y a des chevaux dans la cour
(86) Il y avait des colonies à cette époque

One may see W as a kind of 'map'. _Il y a_ may specify points on the map ('existential' readings), locate terms at various points on the map, relocate them, etc. As the discourse progresses, the area covered may be extended or narrowed down. One interesting phenomenon which may be accounted for in this way is the restriction on the _par_ phrase of the passive in terms of definiteness. It has been noted many times that the less 'thematic' a term, the more susceptible it is to occur in the _par_-phrase of a passive. Let us propose the following restriction on _par_-phrases:

Rule 3. _par_ NP
 Term referred to by NP is not in W_x.

This accounts for the fact that such NPs may not normally be discourse anaphoric. But consider the case where NP is a pronoun, and thus of necessity discourse anaphoric. Rule 3 entails that W_x to which the sentence is paired not contain term y to which the PRO refers. This therefore entails that the discourse has moved to another point on the map as it were, and is switching directions. It is only in this way that the 'cast of characters' may be erased. Now this is precisely what is noted in Cannings and Moody (in press) with respect to the _faire_-causative with _par_. The two sentences (87) and (88) were compared:

(87) On a fait construire une villa au Corbusier, puis on lui a fait construire une piscine
(88) On a fait construire une villa par le Corbusier, puis on a fait construire une piscine par lui

The distinction was stated to be a difference in 'deictic orientation' at the level of discourse. Whilst (87) implies a 'unity' between the two 'constructions', (88) implies that the villa and the pool were built at different times, or different places, or on different contracts, etc. This may be seen as a function of 'domains of relevance'—if the object of <u>par</u> may not already occur in W, but has clearly been linguistically specified already, then the W paired to each conjunct must be 'different' (with respect to time or place), whereas in (87) it is the same for both. It seems, moreover, that most of the implications of faire-<u>par</u> as compared with faire-<u>a</u> may be seen to follow from a statement in terms of domains of relevance. Now such examples clearly show that sentence-domains (Ws) are much more complex and varied than what we have termed domains of individuals. This to me makes the simple three-domain approach to the latter the more realistic and constrained of the two. Whilst these remarks have been speculative, it is obvious that the questions raised are of crucial importance. Thus, to conclude, let me summarise the proposal.

(1) Let all sentences of the grammar be paired to a domain of relevance W, which has (at least) a time-specification slot, a place-specification slot, a domain of individuals, and a domain of propositions.

$$W = (time_x\ place_y\ D_i P_j)$$

(2) Let definiteness operators be 'bound' to domains of individuals $D_{universe}$ $D_{situation}$ $D_{discourse}$, where $D_{discourse}$ contains constant terms, and possibly variable terms, or the open set ($D_{discourse}(x, y \ldots n; u_x)$ where u_x is the variable term.

(3) Let elements of W be 'copied in' on the basis of specifications contained in the sentence.

The analysis is highly programmatic, yet it seems to me that the success with which the 'definiteness' restriction is accounted for warrants its careful consideration. Finally, a speculation. On the basis of the above, it seems highly plausible that 'strong' presuppositional phenomena may be accounted for in terms of 'belonging to D_i or P_j'. If, as suggested, the analysis proposed captures the idea that one cannot simultaneously assert the existence of what one presupposes to exist, and since this is expressed as being 'contained in D_w', then presupposition might be characterised in this way. This I leave for further research.

NOTES

*This paper has benefited much from comments and suggestions by Robert Franklin. Ruth Kempson and Roger Higgins have much influenced my thoughts on 'definiteness', and I gratefully acknowledge their contributions. The necessity of relativising the scope of uniqueness was noted independently by Higgins (semantics class 1975). All the aforementioned are, of course, in no way responsible for the errors that remain.

1. This is an extension of the term as used by Higgins (1973). It is perhaps closer to Akmajian's original definition (Akmajian 1970).
2. Such examples are more natural if the list contains more than one member.
3. I assume that no movement transformation is involved. See Kayne (1975).
4. The restrictions are, however, different. See Cannings (in preparation).
5. I am grateful to Robert Champigny for discussions on the topic of self-referential expressions. (30) is based on an example of his invention.
6. It is interesting to note that if Dislocations were transformationally derived, then in the case of (32) the truth value of the sentence would change. The base S is false, the left-dislocated example is true, and the right-dislocated example of unspecifiable truth value if the NP <u>le mot suivant</u> is cataphoric. Hirschbühler (1975) argues quite convincingly that Left Dislocation is not a transformation.
7. Ducrot (1973) contains an interesting discussion of descriptions which bears on this point.

REFERENCES

Akmajian, Adrian. 1970. Aspects of the grammar of focus in English. Unpublished doctoral dissertation. MIT.
Burt, Marina. 1971. From deep to surface structure. New York: Harper and Row.
Cannings, Peter. To appear. Remarks on the status of 'definiteness'. IULC.
Cannings, Peter. In preparation. Dislocations: What goes where?
Cannings, Peter, and Marvin Moody. In press. A semantic approach to causation in French. In: Actes du 5e Symposium des Langues Romanes. Edited by Y-Ch. Morin.
Chomsky, Noam. 1975. Questions of form and interpretation. Linguistic Analysis 1.1.
Ducrot, Oswald. 1973. Dire et ne pas dire. Hermann.
Grice, H. P. 1968. Logic and conversation. Unpublished mimeograph. Partially reproduced in: Syntax and semantics 3. Edited by Cole and Morgan. New York: Academic Press.
Gross, Maurice. 1968. Grammaire transformationnelle du Français. Larousse.
Hall-Partee, Barbara. 1972. Opacity, coreference, and pronouns. In: Semantics of natural language. Edited by Harman and Davidson. Reidel.
Higgins, Roger. 1973. The pseudo-cleft construction in English. Unpublished doctoral dissertation. MIT.
Higgins, Roger. 1977. The pseudo-cleft construction in English [slightly augmented version of Higgins 1973]. IULC.
Hirschbühler, Paul. 1975. The source of lefthand NPs in French. Linguistic Inquiry 6.1.
Jenkins, Lyle. 1975. The English existential. May Niemeyer.
Kayne, Richard. 1975. French syntax: The transformational cycle. Cambridge, Mass.: MIT Press.
Kempson, Ruth. 1975. Presupposition and the delimitation of semantics. Cambridge University Press.

Kuno, Susumo. 1973. The structure of the Japanese language. Cambridge, Mass.: MIT Press.
Langacker, Ronald. 1972. French interrogatives revisited. In: Generative studies in the Romance languages. Edited by Casagrande and Saciuk. Newbury House.
Milsark, Gary. 1974. Existential sentences in English. IULC.
Postal, Paul. 1966. On so-called pronouns in English. In: Modern studies in English. Edited by Reibel and Schane. Englewood Cliffs, N.J.: Prentice-Hall.
Quine, Willard. 1960. Word and object. Cambridge, Mass.: MIT Press.
Quine, Willard. 1948. On what there is. In: From a logical point of view. Cambridge, Mass.: MIT Press.
Ross, John. 1973. A fake NP squish. In: New ways of analyzing variation in English. Edited by Bailey and Shuy. Washington, D.C.: Georgetown University Press.
Ross, John. 1974. There, there, there, there ... In: Papers from the 10th Regional Meeting of the Chicago Linguistic Society. Edited by La Galy et al.
Russell, Bertrand. 1905. On denoting. In: Semantics. Edited by Zabeeh et al. Chicago: University of Chicago Press.
Strawson. 1950. On referring. In: Semantics. Edited by Zabeeh et al. Chicago: University of Chicago Press.
Strawson. 1952. Introduction to logical theory. Methuen.
Wilson, Deirdre. 1975. Presuppositions and non-truth-conditional semantics. Academic Press.

ABSOLUTE NEUTRALIZATION OF THE PHONEMIC GLIDE-VERSUS-VOWEL CONTRAST IN SPANISH

WILLIAM W. CRESSEY
Georgetown University

1. Phonetic-phonological relations. An important assertion about phonological descriptions was made in Postal (1968:56). This is the assertion that, for the vast majority of cases, the same distinctions which are needed to specify the phonetic differences between segments also serve for the specification of the phonological properties of those same segments. Thus, when it is found to be the case that a set of segments behaves in a certain way (e.g. is subject to a particular rule), it is usually the case that the particular set of segments in question can be defined with reference to one or more phonetic features. Most linguists recognize that this correlation is not universally maintainable, and therefore most linguists consider valid the use of abstract diacritic features which are devoid of phonetic content, and which serve to specify phonological properties which do not seem to be correlatable to phonetic properties. In addition, some linguists permit the absolute neutralization of a phonetic feature during the course of a derivation as an additional method of handling exceptions to Postal's general principle.
The purpose of this paper is to discuss a case in the phonological system of Spanish which appears to

require the kind of separation of phonetic structure and phonological structure which has been called 'absolute neutralization'. Specifically, I shall claim that although a glide-versus-vowel distinction exists at an abstract level of representation (systematic phonemic level), and another glide-versus-vowel distinction exists at the phonetic level, the two distinctions cannot be related to each other in a straightforward manner. The problem which I shall discuss can be summarized as follows: There is a variable rule which accounts for the formation of many glides in Spanish. Recent investigations suggest that this variable rule applies to all nonconsonantal segments, without regard to their phonemic status (vowel or glide), which means that the rule, in effect, neutralizes any phonemic glide-versus-vowel contrasts which may have been posited. Although the research which has been done to date does not allow the formulation of statistically accurate variable rules, I shall suggest the linguistic factors which I believe to be relevant to the variable glide formation rule, and I shall present data which casts serious doubt upon the phonetic-phonological integrity of the analysis which I set forth in Cressey (1974).

2. Two glide formation rules. In Cressey (1974), I claimed that there are two glide formation rules in Spanish: a marking convention and a variable rule, and thus that there are two quite distinct types of glide in Spanish. For ease of reference, I shall call these two types of glides 'marking convention glides' and 'variable glides'. The marking convention in question applies to lexical representations which contain sequences of nonconsonantal segments, one of which is high and not marked for the feature [syllabic]. The marking convention thus generates glides at the systematic phonemic level. The marking convention also applies (as a linking rule)[1] to the high nonconsonantal segments generated by the diphthongization rule. Thus the derivation of *bien* is as shown in Figure 1.

Figure 1. Derivation of <u>bien</u>.

b e n [+D]	underlying form
b é n	stress assignment
b ié n	diphthongization
[bjén]	linking application of marking convention

Since all variable glides are derived from vowel phonemes, and since some marking convention glides are glides at the systematic phonemic level, the phonemic glide-versus-vowel contrast is established. In Cressey (1974), I presented some evidence in favor of these two different derivations of glides, and additional evidence is presented in Harris (1976). This evidence is examined in detail in Section 4, but first a dialect phenomenon which has added to the confusion must be cleared up.

3. Glide-y versus fricative-y dialects. In Mexico, Central America, the Caribbean, and the coastal areas of Venezuela and Colombia, the y of words such as <u>yate</u>, <u>yema</u>, <u>yegua</u>, <u>mayo</u>, etc. is normally pronounced more or less like y in English, thus: [jate] [jema] [jeǧwa] [majo]. However, in the rest of the Spanish-speaking world, this segment is pronounced as an obstruent, and involves considerable friction, thus: [yate] [yema] [yeǧwa] [mayo]. There are other dialect differences in the pronunciation of this segment, and of orthographic <u>ll</u>, but they do not concern us here. The crucial distinction is between a phonetic obstruent and a phonetic glide. This dialect difference is relevant to the present discussion for the following reason: In the glide-y dialects, the distinction between what I am calling marking convention glides and variable glides is less evident. The distinction must be maintained in all dialects, but it is easier to illustrate in the fricative-y dialects,

and thus the pronunciations cited in the sections which follow are those of the fricative-y dialects.

4. Why two types of glide must be maintained. In Cressey (1974) and in Harris (1976), it has been shown that the marking convention glides and the variable glides differ in three important ways.

4.1. Variation versus nonvariation. In Cressey (1974), I showed that some glides are in variation with vowels. Thus __guión__ 'hyphen' can be pronounced either as [gi-ón] (with two syllables) or [gjón] (one syllable). Other glides, I claimed, are not in variation. I claimed, for example, that __bien__ is always [bjén] and never *[bi-én].[2]

4.2. Susceptibility to syllable-initial obstruentization. In fricative-y dialects, some glides, but not all, become obstruents if they are syllable-initial. This is discussed in Harris (1976). His examples are __hierba__ and __hiena__. The derivations of these two words are given in Figure 2.

Figure 2. Derivations of __yerba__ and __hiena__.

e⎤ r b a +D⎦	i e n a	underlying forms
é	é	stress assignment
jé		diphthongization
yé		obstruentization
	j	glide formation
[yérβa]	[jéna]	

The crucial point is that although the initial segment of __hierba__ is sometimes pronounced as an obstruent, the syllable initial segment of __hiena__ never is. Harris cites these examples in his argument that the variable rule of glide formation

cannot be a part of the process of diphthongization.
He claims, as his derivation (Figure 2) illustrates,
that diphthongization is a single rule which converts /ó/ to [wé] and /é/ to [jé]. As shown in
Figure 1, my own treatment of diphthongization is
slightly different; however, I agree with Harris on
the point which is crucial to the present discus-
sion--the variable glide of hiena and the glide
which occurs as an intermediate step in the derivation of hierba must be two distinct types of
glide.[3]

4.3. Glide formation rules and stress assignment.
The third reason why there must be two types of
glide has to do with the interaction between glide
formation rules and stress assignment. In Harris
(1969), it was pointed out that the variable glide
formation rule must follow stress assignment, in
order to handle such pairs as [país] vs. [pajsáno];
[baúl] vs. [bawléro], in which the i's and u's become glides when they are not stressed. However,
some other glides must already be glides when stress
assignment applies. Figure 3 shows relevant parts
of the conjugations of the verbs ampliar and cambiar. As pointed out in Harris (1969), the stem-
final segment of ampliar must be a vowel at the
point in the derivation when stress assignment applies, whereas the stem-final segment of cambiar
must be a glide.[4]

Figure 3. Present tense of ampliar and cambiar.

[amplío]	[kámbjo]
[amplías]	[kámbjas]
[amplía]	[kámbja]
[ampljámos]	[kambjámos]
[amplían]	[kámbjan]

4.4. Summary. To summarize, then, we have three
reasons why there must be two types of glide in
Spanish: different status with regard to variation,
different status with regard to obstruentization,
and different status with regard to stress

assignment. Naturally, we would be most confident of this argument if the three reasons for the distinction could be shown to coincide with respect to all segments under analysis; that is, if it could be shown that marking convention glides (e.g. puedo, bien, hierba, cambiar) are, in all cases, formed before stress assignment, always undergo obstruentization if syllable initial, and never occur in variation with vowels, and if, conversely, it could be shown that variable glides are never formed before stress assignment, never undergo obstruentization, and are always in variation with vowels.

Naturally, there are many instances in which these confluences have no empirical value, and are therefore not testable (e.g. any glide which is not syllable initial is not testable with regard to obstruentization). The best we can hope for, therefore, is a situation in which there are no contradictions among these three criteria. This brings us to the problem to which this paper is addressed.

5. The problem. The difficulty in the analysis of glides lies in the fact that there do, in fact, exist contradictions between two of the criteria discussed in Section 4. Specifically, it appears that some of the glides which must be formed before stress assignment occur in variation with vowels, although according to the analysis presented thus far, they should not. For example, native speakers accept variant pronunciations of the verbs of the cambiar type. Thus both [kámbjo] and [kámbio] are accepted as valid pronunciations. However, in the previous section, it was shown that this stem must be represented with a systematic phonemic glide.

Furthermore, the adjective amplio 'large' which derives from the same stem as ampliar has exactly the same variants as does cambio.[5]

It would seem obvious that all forms which are subject to this variation should undergo one and the same variable rule to account for these phonetic glide-versus-vowel variants. However, this leaves us with a difficulty concerning the systematic phonemic representation of the glide segment in <u>cambiar</u>. If <u>cambiar</u> is to be represented with a systematic phonemic glide, how can this segment undergo a rule which converts it from a vowel to a glide? I propose a new analysis of the phonetic glide-versus-vowel contrast in Section 5.3, but first I should like to discuss the phonetic data and the phonological analysis in further detail, in order to ascertain that there is no way around this difficulty.

5.1. Physical data. Obtaining reliable data concerning the acceptability of variant pronunciations of the words in question is not an easy matter. It appears that, for many speakers, the so-called 'variable' glide formation rule is very nearly absolute insofar as it applies to a high unstressed vowel which is adjacent to another vowel within the same word. As a consequence, one is forced to rely, for the most part, on data as to which pronunciations are accepted by native speakers rather than recorded data actually containing the variant pronunciations. As mentioned earlier, native speakers do accept pronunciations such as [kam-bi-o] which should contain a marking convention glide. In questioning native speakers, I first thought that at least the glides resulting from application of the diphthongization rule were exempt from the difficulty which I am discussing. That is, I thought that these segments never appeared as vowels, even in slow highly monitored speech. However, a closer examination reveals that the application of the rule to words such as <u>pienso</u>, <u>bien</u>, <u>prefiero</u>, etc. is close to absolute because the environment is one which maximally favors application of the rule, with stress on the following vowel. However, when stress is removed to another syllable by cyclical application of the stress rule, as in <u>dieciseis</u>, <u>diecisiete</u> (see Figure 4), there is considerably more potential for a vowel pronunciation of a segment which is the result of diphthongization. The segment in question is the <u>i</u> of <u>diez</u>, which is derived by diphthongization (cf. decena, décimo), and which can be pronounced as a vowel in highly monitored speech when the word diez appears in compounds such as dieciseis, diecisiete.

Figure 4. Derivation of dieciseis.

$\begin{bmatrix} \text{[d e s] i [s e i s]} \\ \text{+D} \end{bmatrix}$		underlying form
é	é	stress assignment
jé		diphthongization
e		stress cycle rule*
	j	glide formation
[djesiséis]		

*'Erase all stresses except the rightmost.'

Figures 5 and 6 are spectograms derived from the words dieciseis and diecisiete as pronounced on a laboratory tape intended for beginning students of Spanish.[6] In each case, the i of diez appears as a straight line, with vowel characteristics, rather than as a glide. Furthermore, in the case of dieciseis, the i appears to be longer than the e which immediately follows, and when this tape is listened to, it appears that the i bears secondary stress.[7]

From this data, and other research which I have done, it appears that there is a variable rule of glide formation which applies to all nonconsonantal segments and accounts for the phonetic glide-versus-vowel variants, and which is totally independent of any abstract glide-versus-vowel distinctions which may be needed for the reasons discussed earlier. The factors which favor glide formation are as follows: height of the segment in question, and stress on the following segment.[8] The factors which tend to inhibit glide formation are the presence of word boundary between the two nonconsonantal

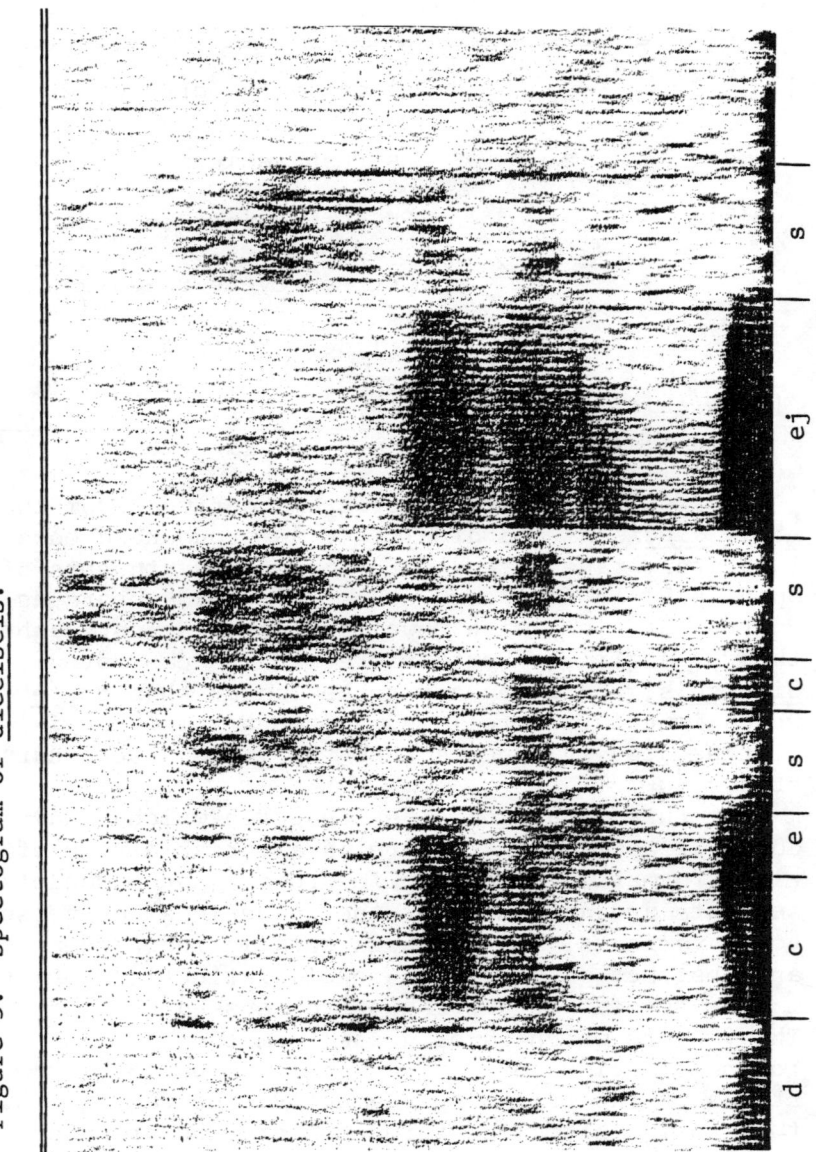

Figure 5. Spectogram of dieciseis.

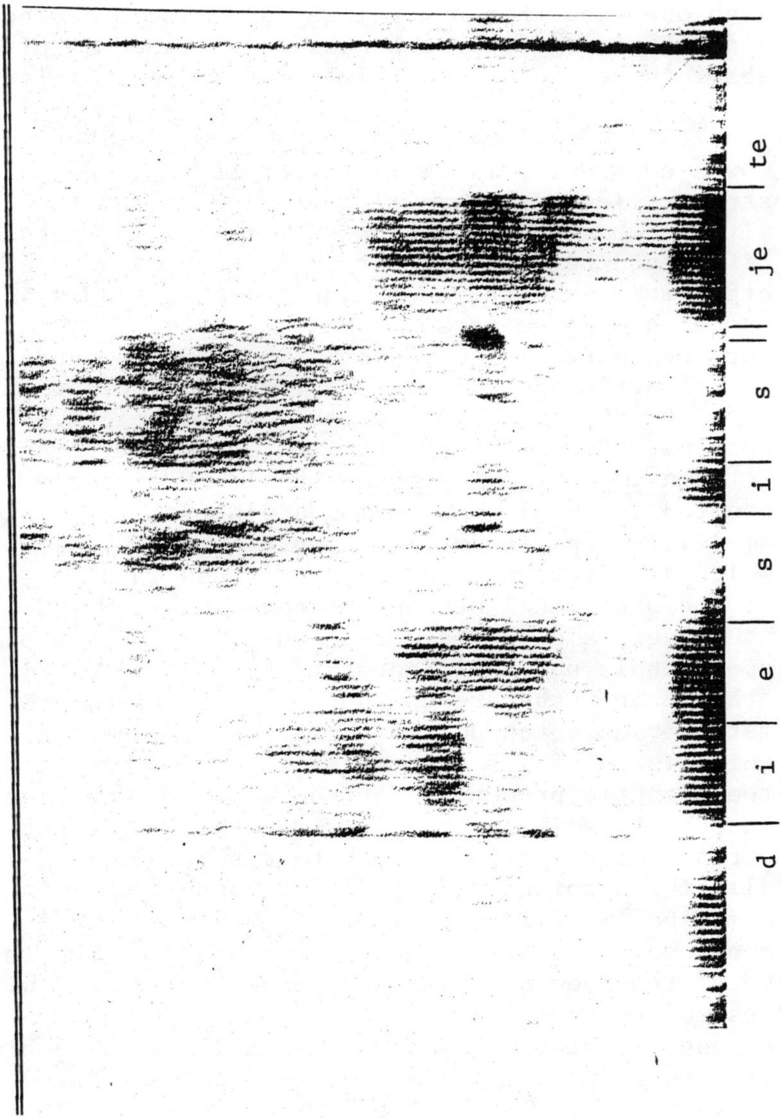

ABSOLUTE NEUTRALIZATION / 99

Figure 6. Spectogram of <u>diecisiete.</u>

segments, and a syllable onset which already has two consonantal segments (as in the case of ampliar).

Let us now return to the phonological analysis and examine our alternatives. There seem to be but two: (1) we can deny that any abstract glide-versus-vowel contrast exists, or (2) we can establish one, and then neutralize it as suggested herein. Since the first approach would avoid the use of an absolute neutralization, let us examine it first.[9]

5.2. The validity of the phonemic glide-versus-vowel contrast. If we deny that there is any abstract glide-versus-vowel contrast, we are faced with the task of accounting for the stress pattern difference between ampliar and cambiar via some other means. Perhaps we might claim that Harris' use of the glide-versus-vowel contrast for this purpose is really a diacritic in disguise, and that the phonemic analysis is created only for the purpose of getting the stress to come out right.[10] Perhaps we might argue that the stress differences between ampliar and cambiar should best be accounted for by in fact using a diacritic, for example, by applying Harris' own diacritic [+X], which triggers antepenultimate stress in nouns, to the stem-final segment of cambiar.[11]

However, a closer examination shows that this approach is not satisfactory. Lexical categories other than verbs are characterized by a penultimate versus antepenultimate stress distinction which is not fully predictable by reference to the phonetic properties of the words in question. There are semifinal vowels which fail to accept stress regardless of their other features (i.e. all five Spanish vowels show up unstressed in semifinal position): sábana, número, música, monótono, rótulo. However, when one examines the verb stems which would have to be marked [+X] with respect to the final segment in order to be stressed 'antepenultimately' as in cámbio, cámbias, etc., one finds that only high vowels ever need to be so marked. To adopt the analysis suggested in

this section would be to claim that it is simply a
lexical accident of Spanish that only verb stems
which end in a high vowel have the stress pattern
of cambiar. Harris' analysis, thus, has an explanatory value that is lacking in the proposed analysis
in terms of the diacritic [+X].

Furthermore, all treatments of Spanish stress going back to the Real Academia's (1885) rules for
placement of the orthographic accent mark, have
treated forms such as amplío (rather than cambio)
as the ones which must somehow be specially marked.
The Academy accomplishes the required marking by
placing a written accent over the i of amplío, and
this accent mark has the function of preventing the
formation of a diphthong. In other words, the
Academy is saying that the formation of a diphthong
(as occurs in cambio) is the more normal case.

The Academy's viewpoint concerning cambio versus
amplío is easily translated into markedness notation. As explained in Cressey (1974), the i of
cambio is specified as a glide by a marking convention, the relevant part of which is given as
Figure 7. The i of amplío is marked [m syllabic]
in the lexicon, and is thus specified as a vowel
by the same marking convention.

Figure 7. Glide formation marking convention.

$$[u \text{ syllabic}] \longrightarrow [-\text{syllabic}] / \left[\underline{}\atop +\text{high}\right] V$$

From this discussion, it is seen that Harris'
analysis of these verbs in terms of a glide-versus-
vowel contrast is well motivated, and not a diacritic in disguise. The stress patterns are a
logical and natural consequence of the [±syllabic]
distinction.

5.3. Neutralization of the glide-versus-vowel
contrast. In the light of these two conclusions
(that a phonemic glide-versus-vowel contrast is
well motivated, and that a variable glide formation

rule applies to all nonconsonantal segments), there
seems to be no alternative to absolute neutralization of a phonetic feature. One might propose a
completely ad hoc rule ([-consonantal] --->
[+syllabic]) which applies after one is finished
'using' the phonemic contrast and which returns all
nonconsonantal segments to vowels, thus preparing
them for the variable rule of glide formation. However, since this rule is totally unmotivated, it
seems that a preferable solution would be to incorporate the neutralization into the variable rule
itself by allowing it to apply to all nonconsonantal
segments, specifying them as either vowels or
glides, and specifying the linguistic factors which
favor each output.

I therefore propose the rule given as Figure 8.
The notation is generally that of variable rules.
The large angled brackets enclose hierarchies of
factors with those factors which tend to favor glide
formation at the top. The two possible outputs of
the rule ([-syllabic] and [+syllabic]) are also included in large angled brackets. This is a new notation designed to implement my proposal that this
variable rule accomplishes an absolute neutralization. The interpretation of this new notation is
as follows: The factors nearest the top of the
environment section of the rule favor the choice
at the top of the output part ([-syllabic], a
glide). The factors near the bottom of the

Figure 8. Glide formation variable rule.

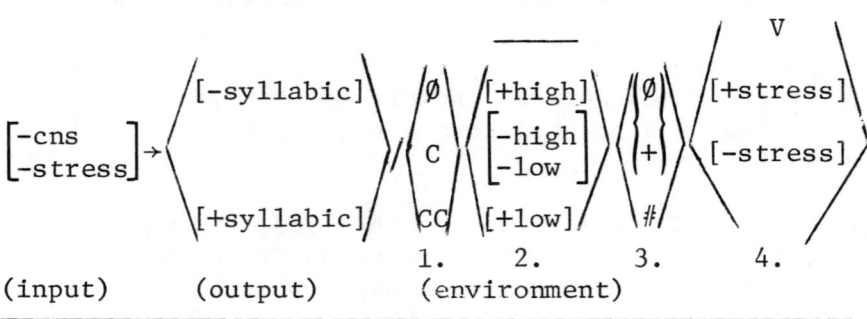

hierarchies in the environment part of the rule favor the other choice ([+syllabic], a vowel).

In conclusion, glide-versus-vowel distinctions are seen to exist both at the phonemic level and at the phonetic level, but in between the two levels, it is necessary to neutralize this distinction completely. This aspect of the analysis of Spanish constitutes an exception to the general principle of phonetic-phonological relations enunciated by Postal.

NOTES

1. The term 'linking rule' is adapted from Chomsky and Halle (1968). In more recent terms, it would seem appropriate to consider that marking conventions function as 'everywhere rules'. This assumption would automatically yield the desired results without the need for additional conventions such as 'linking'.
2. In Cressey (1974), many glides were classified as nonvarying which do, in fact, vary. For example, radio can be pronounced either [ra-ɖi-o] or [ra-ɖjo], contrary to the claim made in Cressey (1974).
3. In these derivations, the two types of glide are kept distinct by virtue of rule ordering. The obstruentization rule applies before the variable glide formation rule and thus obstruentization can never apply to the output of glide formation. This is an interesting example of the natural consequences of rule ordering, and a good illustration of the fact that rule ordering forms a part of a natural theory of phonological systems.
4. Stress is assigned to the penultimate vowel of these verb forms. Cambiar can be considered regular with regard to the stress rule only if the i is represented as a glide at the point in the derivation when the stress rule applies.
5. Actually, it seems that the i of cambio has a slightly higher tendency to become a glide than does the i of amplio. However, this is not related to the phonemic status of the two segments. Rather,

it is the result of the different syllable onsets. The *i* of *amplio* is preceded by two consonants in the same syllable, whereas the *i* of *cambio* is preceded by only one.

6. Admittedly this is a very highly monitored speech style. However, it is, I submit, exactly the style which one should examine if one seeks an instance of nonapplication of a variable rule.

7. This fact, in itself, constitutes an additional problem in the analysis of this word. It is easy to see how the *e* of *diez* might bear secondary stress, by reduction of the primary stress originally assigned to it. However, the *i* of *diez* can only bear secondary stress if we assume that secondary stress is assigned to the finished word by some principle which operates independently of the stress cycle.

8. The discussion presented here, and the rules themselves are based only on glides which precede the vowel nucleus of the syllable. The rules should be re-expressed as mirror image rules in a formal treatment.

9. This suggestion implies that absolute neutralization should be avoided in phonological analyses.

10. Harris (1977) has levied a similar charge against Schwartz-Norman and Sanders (1976) regarding the use of this same feature [syllabic] as a means of specifying application versus nonapplication of a proposed monophthongization rule.

11. The proposal has already been made by Schane (1976) that the diacritic [+X] be applied to verbs as well as nonverbs.

REFERENCES

Chomsky, N., and M. Halle. 1968. The sound pattern of English. New York: Harper and Row.
Cressey, W. 1974. Spanish glides revisited. In: 1974 Colloquium on Spanish and Portuguese Linguistics. Edited by Milán et al. Washington, D.C.: Georgetown University Press.
Harris, J. 1969. Spanish phonology. Cambridge, Mass.: The MIT Press.

Harris, J. 1976. Remarks on diphthongization. Bloomington: The Indiana University Linguistics Club.

Harris, J. 1977. A rejoinder to 'Vocalic variations in Spanish'. Unpublished MS.

Postal, P. 1968. Aspects of phonological theory. New York: Harper and Row.

Schane, Sanford. 1974. Truncation and stress in Spanish. In: Current studies in Romance linguistics. Edited by Luján and Hensey. Washington, D.C.: Georgetown University Press.

Schwartz-Norman, L., and G. Sanders. 1976. Vocalic variations in Spanish. In: Minnesota Working Papers in Linguistics and the Philosophy of Language. Edited by Hutchinson. Minneapolis: The University of Minnesota Linguistics Program.

GENERATIVE SEMANTIC ANALYSIS
OF TENSE IN SPANISH

CARROLL N. DAVIS
Georgetown University

1. Introduction. In this paper, I propose a modified and extended version of McCawley's (1971) generative semantic (GS) model for tense and apply it to Spanish. A general treatment of Spanish tense illustrates theoretical reasons for preferring the revised model. Empirical support is found in explanations which the proposed analysis permits for (1) the analysis of simple present and present progressive in Spanish and (2) the contrast of ser and estar in certain circumstances.

2. Spanish tense. The GS model connects surface forms and underlying representations corresponding to meaning. Therefore, it is useful to begin with a summary of the forms and meanings comprising the Spanish tense system. Table 1 outlines the inventory of tensed verb forms in Spanish. Table 2 summarizes the range of meanings denoting time reference in Spanish and the tense forms which convey them. For clarification, the meanings in Table 2 are rendered in linear diagrams.
The Spanish verb system is morphologically richer than that of English. Compared to two categories, present and past tense, marked in English, Spanish has seven inflectional paradigms for verbs, commonly

known as present, preterite, imperfect, future, conditional, present subjunctive, and imperfect subjunctive forms. As in English, the intersection of the categories 'perfect' and 'progressive' defines four classes, which, in turn, intersect with the seven inflectional categories. This results in 28 possible surface forms.[1]

Not all meanings associated with Spanish tense forms are concerned with time reference. It is interesting that Spanish uses verb morphology to express meanings represented in English by modal auxiliaries and periphrastic expressions. These include mood and indication of probability. The present analysis is concerned with tense, time reference, and their logical structure, however, some other meanings are dropped from consideration. The subjunctives will not be discussed. Neither will nontemporal meanings of the future, the conditional, and their related paradigms, although these may correspond to the majority of occurrences of these forms.

Also, the difference between the instantaneous/completed and unrestrictive meanings of tenses, which distinguishes the preterite and the imperfect, apparently brings in considerations of verbal aspect which are interesting and worthwhile, but not under investigation here. For the purpose of this discussion, the unnatural assumption is made that Spanish has only one past tense form, which is represented by the imperfect.

3. GS analysis of tense

3.1. Generative semantics. This paper assumes the GS model advocated by McCawley (1967, 1968) and described by Franz (1974). In particular, the following assumptions are relevant to the arguments presented here.

In the GS model well-formed sentences are derived from logical structures (hereafter LSs) composed of minimal semantic units and representing the literal meanings of sentences (as opposed to conveyed meanings of sentences in context, which I assume to be

Table 1. Spanish tense forms.

Nonprogressive		Progressive	
Nonperfect	Perfect	Nonperfect	Perfect
1. Simple present: canta	8. Present perfect: ha cantado	15. Present progressive: está cantando	22. Present perfect progressive: ha estado cantando
2. Simple preterite: cantó	9. Preterite perfect: hubo cantado	16. Preterite progressive: estuvo cantando	23. Preterite perfect progressive: hubo estado cantando
3. Simple imperfect: cantaba	10. Pluperfect: había cantado	17. Imperfect progressive: estaba cantando	24. Pluperfect progressive: había estado cantando

4. Simple future: cantará
5. Simple conditional: cantaría
6. Present subjunctive: cante
7. Imperfect subjunctive: cantara (cantase)

11. Future perfect: habrá cantado
12. Conditional perfect: habría cantado
13. Present subjunctive perfect: haya cantado
14. Pluperfect subjunctive: hubiera (hubiese) cantado

18. Future progressive: estará cantando
19. Conditional progressive: estaría cantando
20. Present subjunctive progressive: esté cantando
21. Imperfect subjunctive progressive: estuviera (estuviese) cantando

25. Future perfect progressive: habrá estado cantando
26. Conditional perfect progressive: habría estado cantando
27. Present subjunctive perfect progressive: haya estado cantando
28. Pluperfect subjunctive progressive: hubiera (hubiese) estado cantando

Table 2. Spanish time reference.

Simple tenses refer to a point in time, present (NOW), past (NOW⁻), or future (NOW⁺); perfect tenses to the interval between some point and a related time in its past; progressives to a 'temporal frame' focused around some point. Conditionals may convey future reference from past viewpoint. Perfect progressives may be interpreted as projecting progressive time framing onto perfective intervals.

Description	Associated form(s)	Scheme
Instantaneous Present	Simple present	—NOW—
Unrestrictive Present	Simple present	←NOW→
Instantaneous/Completed Past [a]	Simple preterite, simple present	—NOW⁻— NOW
Unrestrictive Past	Simple imperfect, simple present	←NOW⁻→ NOW

Instantaneous Future	────┼────────✕──── NOW^- NOW^+	Simple future, simple present
Unrestrictive Future	────┼────────↕──── NOW^- NOW^+	Simple future, simple present
Instantaneous Future of Past	────┼────────✕──── NOW^- $(NOW^-)^+$	Simple conditional
Unrestrictive Future of Past	────┼────────↕──── NOW^- $(NOW^-)^+$	Simple conditional
Present Perfect	────┼⌒⌒⌒⌒⌒┼──── NOW^- interval NOW	Present perfect, simple present
Past Perfect	────┼⌒⌒⌒⌒⌒┼──── $(NOW^-)^-$ interval NOW^-	Pluperfect, preterite perfect, simple imperfect

Description	Associated form(s)	Scheme
Future Perfect	Future perfect, present perfect, simple future	$(NOW^+)^-$ ⌒interval⌒ NOW^+
Future Perfect of Past	Conditional perfect, simple conditional	$((NOW^-)^+)^-$ ⌒interval⌒ $(NOW^-)^+$
Present Progressive	Present progressive, simple present	⌒framing⌒ NOW
Past Progressive	Imperfect progressive, simple imperfect	NOW^- ⌒framing⌒ NOW
Future Progressive	Future progressive, simple future	NOW^- ⌒framing⌒ NOW^+
Future Progressive of Past	Conditional progressive, simple conditional	NOW^- $(NOW^-)^+$ ⌒framing⌒

GENERATIVE SEMANTIC ANALYSIS OF TENSE / 113

Present Perfect Progressive	Present perfect progressive, present perfect	⟵——interval——⟶ [NOW⁻ — framing NOW]
Past Perfect Progressive	Pluperfect progressive, pluperfect	⟵——interval——⟶ [(NOW⁻) — framing NOW⁻]
Future Perfect Progressive	Future perfect progressive, future perfect	⟵——interval——⟶ [(NOW⁻) — framing NOW⁺]
Future Perfect Progressive of Past	Conditional perfect progressive, conditional perfect	⟵——interval——⟶ [((NOW⁻)⁺) — framing (NOW⁻)⁺]

ᵃInstantaneous and Completed Past may be consolidated because a 'point' in past time may range from a single instant to a considerable stretch of time, as shown in (i)–(ii).

(i) Entramos en la sala.
    'We went into the room.'
(ii) Tres años vivimos en Madrid.
    'We lived in Madrid for three years.'

the subject matter of pragmatics). Logical structures include two terminal categories, corresponding to logical predicates (verbs) and arguments (noun phrases). The only branching category in LS is the sentence (S). Sentences may fill argument positions and, indeed, must do so in all but the most deeply embedded sentence of an underlying structure, since S is the only branching node.

Surface structures are derived from underlying LSs by an ordered set of transformational rules. These include a Predicate Raising transformation (hereafter PR), which applies optionally and cyclically. PR adjoins the predicate of an embedded sentence to the predicate of the matrix sentence in which it is embedded. Thus, PR has the function of combining simple, or 'atomic', predicates into complex terms, which may or may not have corresponding surface forms in the lexicon.

The GS model necessarily assumes a lexical insertion process of considerable power, since it must replace the complexes of semantic predicates which PR produces with appropriate lexical forms. Lexical insertion is performed at various places throughout the derivation of a sentence, rather than at any discrete level such as Chomskian deep structure. Specifically, lexical insertion occurs whenever the processing of a unit prior to surface structure has been completed.

The combination of optional PR and lexical insertion as just described produces an effect which I will call the Principle of Survival. The Principle of Survival is, simply, that, if predicates on successive sentence levels in LS are not combined into complex terms by Predicate Raising, then each surfaces with its own individual lexical form. One consequence of this principle is that different surface structures may be derived from the same logical structure due to the application or non-application of PR on different sentence cycles. For example, (1) shows the LS and partial derivation of <u>Ivan heated the soup</u>. PR applies here wherever possible, producing the complex semantic term CAUSE + COME ABOUT + HOT.

(1) CAUSE(Ivan, COME ABOUT(HOT(soup)))
    Logical structure
    CAUSE(Ivan, COME ABOUT+HOT(soup))
    PR (Cycle 2)
    CAUSE+COME ABOUT+HOT(Ivan, soup)
    PR (Cycle 3)

This matches the lexical entry <u>heat</u> and is replaced by it. No PR on any cycle yields <u>Ivan caused it to come about that the soup was hot</u>. PR on the second cycle but not on the third leads to <u>Ivan caused the soup to heat</u>. PR on the third cycle but not on the second results in <u>Ivan made the soup hot</u>. The Principle of Survival will be important in discussion later on.

3.2. McCawley's (1971) model. McCawley (1971) proposes an analysis of tense for English under the GS model. Many of McCawley's claims are assumed here to be generally applicable to an analysis of tense in Spanish, as well.

Tenses are represented in LS by one-place predicates which take sentential arguments exclusively. Tense is the most inclusive predicate in underlying structure, taking all the rest of LS as its sentential argument. McCawley proposes two atomic tense predicates, namely, PRESENT and PAST.[2]

Tense predicates may take as their sentential arguments phrase markers which already have tense predicates as their topmost verbs. In fact, McCawley argues that perfect forms are derived from underlying structures in which PAST is embedded under another predicate. The perfect auxiliary <u>have</u> (<u>haber</u> in Spanish) is the surface reflex of an embedded predicate PAST in LS. The present perfect forms derive from structures in which PAST is embedded under PRESENT. Past perfect derives from PAST embedded under another PAST predicate. An important corollary established by this analysis is that the relative positions of predicates on successive sentence levels in LS are regarded as semantically significant.

Two proposals of McCawley's analysis, however, are rejected here. The first is the Tense Replacement rule (hereafter TR) by which McCawley accounts for the conversion of embedded PAST into auxiliary have (haber). TR performs three functions. (1) It converts any embedded PAST into have. (2) It deletes PRESENT in all instances where it is embedded under another predicate. (3) In cases where an entire past perfect construction is embedded under yet another predicate (for example, a modal auxiliary in English) and the first part of TR consequently produces a sequence of two auxiliaries have, TR deletes one of the have's. The second of McCawley's claims which I reject is that progressive forms are derived from LSs containing an aspectual predicate BE and that the progressive auxiliary be (estar in Spanish) is the surface reflex of this underlying BE.

McCawley's analysis, accepting TR and derivation of progressives from structures containing BE, will hereafter be referred to as the Tense Replacement (TR) model. It defines logical structures and partial derivations for a subset of the Spanish tense system (corresponding to the English forms accounted for by McCawley) as shown in (2)-(9).

(2) Present:
PRESENT(CANT(X))   'X canta.'
PRESENT+CANT(X)   PR

(3) Past:
PAST(CANT(X))   'X cantaba.'
PAST+CANT(X)   PR

(4) Present perfect:
PRESENT(PAST(CANT(X)))   'X ha cantado.'
PRESENT(hab(CANT(X)))   TR
PRESENT+hab(CANT(X))   PR

(5) Past perfect:
PAST(PAST(CANT(X)))   'X había cantado.'
PAST(hab(CANT(X)))   TR
PAST+hab(CANT(X))   PR

(6) Present progressive:
PRESENT(BE(CANT(X)))   'X está cantando.'
PRESENT+BE(CANT(X))   PR

(7) Past progressive:
PAST(BE(CANT(X)))   'X estaba cantando.'
PAST+BE(CANT(X))   PR

(8) Present perfect progressive:
PRESENT(PAST(BE(CANT(X))))   'X ha estado cantando.'
PRESENT(hab(BE(CANT(X))))   TR
PRESENT+hab(BE(CANT(X)))   PR

(9) Past perfect progressive:
PAST(PAST(BE(CANT(X))))   'X había estado cantando.'
PAST(hab(BE(CANT(X))))   TR
PAST+hab(BE(CANT(X)))   PR

3.3. *Criticism.* Certain asymmetries may be observed in the TR model and the analysis which it permits. First, TR applies differently with respect to the two tense predicates accepted so far. On the one hand, it functions with the same ultimate effect on both in one regard, namely, deletion. An embedded PAST predicate, however, has the possibility of being transmuted to <u>haber</u>, in which form it can survive to appear on the surface. PRESENT is allotted no comparable survival form and is assumed to delete inescapably when embedded in LS.

Second, the distribution of the two tense predicates in LS is likewise imbalanced. PAST can occur as a lone tense predicate; it can embed under PRESENT; it can embed under PAST. PRESENT can appear as a lone tense predicate; but it cannot embed under another tense predicate, whether PAST or PRESENT.

Actually, these last circumstances are not impossible, just vacuous under the TR analysis. McCawley's account predicts only deletion for embedded instances of PRESENT, so they can never be reflected in surface structure. This is because PRESENT has no survival form analogous to <u>haber</u> in the case of PAST, due to the formulation of TR.

Thus, the two anomalies in the TR model turn out to be sides of the same coin.

3.4. The lexical insertion model. An alternative analysis is proposed which eliminates these irregularities and which replaces the two claims of McCawley's that I rejected earlier.

First, the grammar needs no such rule as Tense Replacement. The conversion of underlying PAST into haber can be accomplished by mechanisms independently motivated in the GS grammar, namely, those underlying the Principle of Survival. Recall that PR is an optional rule. Where PR is possible but is not applied, it is natural for the predicates onto which raising has failed to apply to be represented on the surface by separate lexical forms. It is obvious that embedded PAST predicates which surface as perfect haber have not been amalgamated into complex configurations by PR. It follows that they should be replaced individually by lexical forms corresponding to them on the surface. A natural explanation, then, is that auxiliary haber is simply the lexical form inserted for PAST when a derivation allows it to surface in atomic form. It is precisely the fact that it has not been raised which results in the replacement of embedded PAST by the perfect auxiliary. Further duties which McCawley attributes to TR may be dispatched by a Tense Deletion rule, which is conditioned by the compositions of predicate configurations derived by PR. Tense Deletion is discussed more fully later on.

Second, progressive forms should be derived not from an underlying aspectual BE as supposed by McCawley, but rather from LSs in which PRESENT is embedded under tense predicate. The progressive auxiliary estar can be derived from PRESENT by the Principle of Survival, the same as haber from PAST. That is, estar is the lexical form which normally replaces PRESENT when the latter is not consolidated with other predicates by PR. This analysis has the virtue of paralleling the derivation of haber from an embedded PAST in LS. It also

provides surface correspondents for underlying
PRESENT over PRESENT, namely, the present progressive form, and for underlying PAST over PRESENT,
namely, the past progressive and perfect progressive forms. Thus, the proposed revision provides a
simpler and more general account for the progressive
than the TR analysis.

Moreover, this analysis is consonant with the
meaning described for the progressive by Leech
(1971:17), i.e. that of a 'temporal frame'. 'That
is, within the flow of time, there is some point of
reference from which the temporary eventuality indicated by the verb can be seen as stretching into the
future and into the past.' In other words, the
stretch of time within which an event is going on
(in other words, the 'present' of that event) is
framed off against another time background. This
is plausibly represented in semantic structure by
the embedding of PRESENT under another tense predicate. The Present Progressive may, then, be interpreted as a present-within-the-present, and the
Past Progressive as a present-within-the-past. The
Perfect Progressives correspond to a 'present'
framed off somewhere within a past interval defined
by two related points in time.

The analysis proposed here, which accounts for
perfect and progressive auxiliaries by lexical insertion and derives progressives from LSs with embedded PRESENT, will hereafter be referred to as
the Lexical Insertion (LI) model. The LI model provides the same accounts of the simple present and
past tenses as in (2)-(3). The LSs and partial
derivations which the LI account defines for the
remaining tenses of Spanish are shown in (10)-(23).

(10) Future:
FUTURE(CANT(X))   'X cantará.'
FUTURE+CANT(X)   PR (Cycle 2)

(11) Future of past (conditional):
PAST(FUTURE(CANT(X)))   'X cantaría.'
PAST(FUTURE+CANT(X))   PR (Cycle 2)
PAST+FUTURE+CANT(X)   PR (Cycle 3)

(12) Present perfect:
PRESENT(PAST(CANT(X)))   'X ha cantado.'
PRESENT(hab(CANT(X)))   No PR (Cycle 2) + LI
PRESENT+hab(CANT(X))   PR (Cycle 3)

(13) Past perfect:
PAST(PAST(CANT(X)))   'X había cantado.'
PAST(hab(CANT(X)))   No PR (Cycle 2) + LI
PAST+hab(CANT(X))   PR (Cycle 3)

(14) Future perfect:
FUTURE(PAST(CANT(X)))   'X habrá cantado.'
FUTURE(hab(CANT(X)))   No PR (Cycle 2) + LI
FUTURE+hab(CANT(X))   PR (Cycle 3)

(15) Future perfect of past (conditional perfect):
PAST(FUTURE(PAST(CANT(X))))   'X habría cantado.'
PAST(FUTURE(hab(CANT(X))))   No PR (Cycle 2) + LI
PAST(FUTURE+hab(CANT(X)))   PR (Cycle 3)
PAST+FUTURE+hab(CANT(X))   PR (Cycle 4)

(16) Present progressive:
PRESENT(PRESENT(CANT(X)))   'X está cantando.'
PRESENT(est(CANT(X)))   No PR (Cycle 2) + LI
PRESENT+est(CANT(X))   PR (Cycle 3)

(17) Past progressive:
PAST(PRESENT(CANT(X)))   'X estaba cantando.'
PAST(est(CANT(X)))   No PR (Cycle 2) + LI
PAST+est(CANT(X))   PR (Cycle 3)

(18) Future progressive:
FUTURE(PRESENT(CANT(X)))   'X estará cantando.'
FUTURE(est(CANT(X)))   No PR (Cycle 2) + LI
FUTURE+est(CANT(X))   PR (Cycle 3)

(19) Future progressive of past (conditional
     progressive):
PAST(FUTURE(PRESENT(CANT(X))))   'X estaría cantando.'
PAST(FUTURE(est(CANT(X))))   No PR (Cycle 2) + LI
PAST(FUTURE+est(CANT(X)))   PR (Cycle 3)
PAST+FUTURE+est(CANT(X))   PR (Cycle 4)

(20) Present perfect progressive:
PRESENT(PAST(PRESENT(CANT(X))))   'X ha estado cantando.'
PRESENT(PAST(est(CANT(X))))   No PR (Cycle 2) + LI
PRESENT(hab(est(CANT(X))))   No PR (Cycle 3) + LI
PRESENT+hab(est(CANT(X)))   PR (Cycle 4)

(21) Past perfect progressive:
PAST(PAST(PRESENT(CANT(X))))   'X había estado cantando.'
PAST(PAST(est(CANT(X))))   No PR (Cycle 2) + LI
PAST(hab(est(CANT(X))))   No PR (Cycle 3) + LI
PAST+hab(est(CANT(X)))   PR (Cycle 4)

(22) Future perfect progressive:
FUTURE(PAST(PRESENT(CANT(X))))   'X habrá estado cantando.'
FUTURE(PAST(est(CANT(X))))   No PR (Cycle 2) + LI
FUTURE(hab(est(CANT(X))))   No PR (Cycle 2) + LI
FUTURE+hab(est(CANT(X)))   PR (Cycle 4)

(23) Future perfect progressive of past (conditional perfect progressive):
PAST(FUT(PAST(PRES(CANT(X)))))   'X habría estado cantando.'
PAST(FUT(PAST(est(CANT(X)))))   No PR (Cycle 2) + LI
PAST(FUT(hab(est(CANT(X)))))   No PR (Cycle 3) + LI
PAST(FUT+hab(est(CANT(X))))   PR (Cycle 4)
PAST+FUT+hab(est(CANT(X)))   PR (Cycle 5)

3.5. Discussion. How 'no Predicate Raising' motivates a stage in derivation may require explanation at this point. Lexical insertion occurs in the GS model at any point where processing of a term prior to surface structure has been completed. When the opportunity for PR to raise a subordinate verb onto an also-embedded tense predicate passes without application of the rule, preparation of the tense predicate for its surface realization is essentially finished. A separate lexical item must be inserted for it due to the Principle of Survival. Applications of PR on subsequent cycles cannot change this. Therefore, failure of PR to apply on an embedded PRESENT's cycle is sufficient to trigger lexical insertion of <u>estar</u>; failure of PR to apply on an embedded PAST predicate's cycle is sufficient to motivate insertion of <u>haber</u>.

The present analysis has had to go beyond McCawley's account in one feature not mentioned so far. An atomic predicate FUTURE has been posited in the LSs of future, conditional, and related forms. The conditional, in its time reference usage, is represented underlyingly by FUTURE embedded under PAST. This structure is consonant with the meaning Future of Past which the form conveys and exploits the assumption that relative positions of predicates in LS are semantically productive. To maximize the comparison with McCawley's English analysis and to provide a base for evaluating the proposed LI model, the present study will concentrate on structures and derivatives involving PAST and PRESENT. Therefore, FUTURE will not be discussed further here, though such a discussion on another occasion seems worthwhile. It is not obvious that the behavior of FUTURE is like that of the predicates PAST and PRESENT used so far. In particular, this analysis assumes that FUTURE has the ability to fuse with another tense predicate, PAST, in the derivation of a separate inflectional form, the conditional.[3] Also, the distribution of FUTURE in LSs is asymmetrical. FUTURE may appear as lone tense predicate; it may stand over both PAST and PRESENT underlyingly; but it may stand beneath only PAST, not PRESENT. No reason for this uneven distribution is apparent at this time.

4. Two problems. So far, reasons for preferring the LI model are largely theoretical. The revised model uses fewer atomic predicates to represent tenses semantically and makes more efficient use of their possible combinations. It gives PAST and PRESENT symmetrical distributions in LSs. It derives well-formed surface structures without a Tense Replacement rule, requiring only the strong lexical insertion capability already needed in generative semantics. The LI model, therefore, supplies simpler analyses than the TR account and makes more comprehensive use of generalizations. These grounds for preference, however, are matters of formal esthetics. Empirical evidence for the LI approach has not yet been given. That is, it has not been demonstrated

yet that the LI model explains something which the
TR model cannot.
  Also, so far, no particular advantage has been
shown to have derived from extending the GS analysis of tense to include Spanish. All discussion
using Spanish data so far could just as well have
been based on English examples.
  Both of these needs, i.e. empirical proof for
the superiority of the LI model and demonstration
of unique relevance of Spanish data to the discussion at hand, are answered by the treatment the LI
model allows for two classical problems arising in
the comparison of Spanish and English. One is the
distribution of the Present Progressive meaning
over the simple present and present progressive
forms in Spanish. The other is the distinction between the copula _ser_ and _estar_ in certain circumstances.

4.1. Simple present and present progressive in
Spanish. English maintains a fairly clear division
of the meanings of the simple present and present
progressive tenses. The present usually associates
a state, event, or action with the present without
restricting its relevance to past and future; the
present progressive denotes an event going on in
an interval of time (its 'present') framed off
against the unrestricted present. Table 1 shows
that Spanish also associates these meanings with
these respective forms, but not in such a dichoto-
mous fashion. The Spanish simple present may denote
the Unrestricted Present; but it may also express
the latter meaning, that of Event Going on at the
Present Time.
  If simple present and present progressive forms
in Spanish may express the same meaning, that
associated with the present progressive so far, it
follows that both must be derivable from the same
LS, that assigned to the Present Progressive. The
derivation of the surface present progressive has
been demonstrated. It remains to be seen how
derivation of the simple present from the same
underlying structure can be justified.

Since deriving the surface progressive entails nonapplication of optional PR on the embedded predicate PRESENT's cycle, a reasonable course in the current problem might be to consider what would happen if PR did apply. The result would be that shown in (24).

(24) PRESENT(PRESENT(CANT(X))) Logical structure
   PRESENT(PRESENT+CANT(X)) PR (Cycle 2)
   PRESENT+PRESENT+CANT(X)   PR (Cycle 3)

Two identical tense predicates end up in the same semantic configuration. It is proposed that a rule of Tense Deletion (TD) removes one of the duplicate tenses prior to lexical insertion. On the one hand, TD may be narrowly explained as a kind of degemination rule in semantics, parallel to degemination rules discussed for syntax and phonology.

On the other hand, Tense Deletion may be generalizable to broader circumstances in English. Hoffman (1966) observes that simple past, present perfect, and past perfect tenses in English are neutralized as <u>have</u> after modal auxiliaries, as illustrated in (25)-(27).

(25a) John came at noon.
(25b) John may have come at noon.
(26a) John has come by now.
(26b) John may have come by now.
(27a) John had come by then.
(27b) John may have come by then.

All of these have PAST in their LSs; and the LI model explains how PAST changes into <u>have</u>. But some mechanism is needed to eliminate additional tense predicates, PRESENT and PAST, from present perfect and past perfect structures, respectively, under modal auxiliaries. If these tense predicates are adjoined to the modal auxiliaries by PR, then a rule resembling TD might have the desired effect. Therefore, there is independent motivation for a rule which deletes tenses from complex predicate configurations and is conditioned by the composition of those configurations.

Consequently, the derivations of present progressive and simple forms from the same semantic structure may be explained as (28) and (29), respectively.

(28) Present progressive:
PRESENT(PRESENT(CANT(X)))   'X está cantando.'
PRESENT(est(CANT(X)))   No PR (Cycle 2) + LI
PRESENT+est(CANT(X))   PR (Cycle 3)

(29) Simple present:
PRESENT(PRESENT(CANT(X)))   'X canta.'
PRESENT(PRESENT+CANT(X))   PR (Cycle 2)
PRESENT+PRESENT+CANT(X)   PR (Cycle 3)
PRESENT+CANT(X)   TD (Cycle 3)

Note that lexical insertion of <u>estar</u> in (29) is blocked by application of PR in the second cycle.

This analysis is compatible with the findings in Klein (1976) of a quantitative study of the same phenomenon in the speech of New York City Spanish-English bilinguals. Klein examines whether the use of simple present for ongoing events by native Spanish-speakers who have lived a long time in New York has been affected by contact with the more prestigious English pattern. She reasons that such an influence would be reflected in the quantity of simple present versus present progressive forms produced by speakers in natural speech. The study finds that the quantity of simple present used by these speakers is significantly less than that used by a control group of speakers who have been in New York a comparatively short time. Moreover, the report discerns circumstances in which speakers are more likely to use progressive forms than in others. Thus, the quantity of simple present and present progressive forms produced is subject to conditioning by linguistic and sociolinguistic factors. Such variable facts of language may be expressed by variable rules in the grammar. In the LI analysis given above, the quantity of simple present or present progressive forms expressing the Present Progressive depends on the application or nonapplication of PR in the derivations of individual utterances. The variable alternation of simple and progressive forms may, then, be related to rule operation in the LI analysis. The Predicate Raising rule, formerly described as optional, now seems to be more properly considered variable. McCawley's TR model derives simple present and present progressive forms from quite different underlying structures, with that of the progressive including aspectual BE. There is no simple way the TR model can explain the variable use of simple and progressive forms with the Present Progressive meaning in Spanish.

4.2. _Ser_ and _estar_. Not all the differences between the uses of _ser_ and _estar_ can or will be addressed here. The LI analysis is useful, however, in explaining the distinction between the two in one set of circumstances where they stand in direct contrast.

Both _ser_ and _estar_ may appear as copula before adjective complements, as illustrated by (30)-(31).

(30) Connie es hermosa (siempre).
 'Connie is beautiful (always).'
(31) Connie está hermosa (hoy).
 'Connie is (=looks) beautiful (today).'

In (30) _ser_ is used to express that a state or condition is an inherent attribute of the subject: Connie is beautiful by nature. The use of _estar_ in (31) associates the predicated state or condition with a limited frame of time reference centered in the present. It has the effect of a comment, rather than an attribution: Connie is beautiful now, whether or not she is so at any other time. The meaning difference between the two copula is perhaps made clearer by an example cited by Aid (1976). _Gazpacho_ is a Spanish soup which is characteristically served cold. Therefore, it is perfectly natural for a native Spanish-speaker to say (32).

(32) El gazpacho es frío.
    'Gazpacho is cold.'

Yet, upon taking a taste of the soup on a particular occasion, it would be unnatural to say anything but (33).

(33) Ay, está frío.
    'Hey, it's cold.'

Ser would be inappropriate in this context. *Estar* sets the condition denoted by a stative predicate precisely within the context of a present situation set off separate from the background of the unrestricted present. The problems arise at this point of what the logical structures associated with these contrasting meanings are and of why *estar* rather than *ser* is required for the 'comment' expression.

The 'comment' meaning just described for the complement structure with *estar* closely resembles that associated with progressive tenses, that is, that of a 'temporal frame'. On the other hand, the time reference associated with (30) and (32) is clearly the Unrestrictive Present. It is natural to derive the latter from a simple present LS. Proposed underlying structures for stative sentences with *ser* and *estar* are, then, as shown in (34)-(35).

(34) PRESENT(FRIO(gazpacho)) → 'El gazpacho es frío.'
(35) PRESENT(PRESENT(FRIO(gazpacho))) → 'El gazpacho está frío.'

In the derivation of (34), PR applies on the tense predicate's cycle. It is proposed here that FRIO is one of a number of stative predicates which are satisfactory as logical predicates, but not as unaccompanied lexical verbs. Therefore, when lexical insertion occurs, a form of *ser* is added to such a predicate if it has a tense attached to it. Consequently, the derivation of (34) is as shown in (36).

(36) PRESENT(FRIO(gazpacho))   'El gazpacho es frío.'
    PRESENT+FRIO(gazpacho)   PR (Cycle 2)
    PRESENT+ser frío (gazpacho) Lexical Insertion

In the derivation of comment sentences, PR does
not apply on the embedded PRESENT's cycle, it is
assumed here. Consequently, the embedded PRESENT
surfaces as a form of *estar* for the same reasons
as in the derivation of progressive forms. The
derivation of (35) proceeds as shown in (37).

(37)
PRESENT(PRES(FRIO(gazpacho)))   'El gazpacho está frío.'
PRESENT(est(FRIO(gazpacho)))   No PR (Cycle 2) + LI
PRESENT+est(FRIO(gazpacho))   PR (Cycle 3)

Lexical insertion does not add *ser* to the predicate
in (37), (1) because it is already accompanied by
estar and (2) because it does not have a tense
attached.

There remains the problem of why a present participle ending -*ndo* does not appear on the following
predicate, as it does in progressive tense forms.
Lakoff (1966) cites the absence of progressive forms
as an identifier for stative verbs. He says that
stative verbs cannot accept the progressive. Perhaps Lakoff's claim is properly relevant only to
surface structure, and not to semantic structure.
It may be the nature of stative predicates which
specifically cancels the presence of progressive
markings which are motivated by underlying LS.
This argument claims that the grammar makes a significant distinction between stative and nonstative
verbs; but justifications for this division have
been discussed elsewhere.

This analysis has the advantage of relating similarities in meaning to similarities in form. It
explains the resemblance in meaning between progressives and *estar* comments in terms of like underlying structures. Common principles are shown to
underlie the fact that *estar* is the form required
for both, which fact no longer need be treated as

mere coincidence. These advantages are not available to the TR model.

5. Conclusion and future problems. It is noteworthy that these two problems should support the LI analysis. They are recurrent issues and perennial trouble sources for translators and English speakers learning Spanish. This analysis of Spanish tense is also interesting because (1) it demonstrates the application of McCawley's general, if not specific, approach outside English and (2) it proves the need for the proposed revisions in McCawley's model.

Obviously, many noteworthy topics have been dealt with summarily or not at all here. For instance, discussion of the atomic predicate FUTURE has been minimal. English must use this predicate in LS, since it plainly can express the meaning of future time. But where Spanish marks future tense morphologically, English derives modal auxiliaries from underlying FUTURE. Further investigation is indicated into the different surface expressions Spanish, English, and other languages find for similar logical tense structures. This may bring added insight into the derivational relations between surface categories and underlying semantics.

The analyses of the perfect and the progressive presented here also expose a pitfall for generative semanticists. Commonly, these are regarded as matters of aspect, not tense. The corresponding auxiliaries have and be have been posited elsewhere as simple predicates in themselves (cf. Ross 1969). The present analysis relates the perfect and the progressive to complex logical structures involving only tense predicates. Although GS studies the derivation of sentences from a semantic base, work to date, including this study, has concentrated more on derivation and less on semantics. Some atomic predicates may have been adopted too easily. The semantics of tense and aspect requires more careful study before the logical atoms of tense and aspect can be discussed with confidence.

Whenever possible in this study, language-particular phenomena have been consigned to the derivation of surface structures by transformations and lexical insertion, which is where idiosyncrasies should be expected to arise. Conscious effort has been made to simplify and generalize the units and constructions of logical structure, since, presumably, these should most nearly represent language universals. The validity of these proposals must be tested against data from the analyses of tense in many languages. Such a body of applied research is prerequisite to the development of an adequate semantically based universal grammar.

NOTES

I am grateful to Larry King, Donna Jo Napoli, and Walter A. Cook for their helpful comments, suggestions, and criticisms. Any errors are of course my own responsibility.

1. The preterite perfect, preterite progressive, and all the perfect progressive forms may be considered marginal in normal discourse; but native speakers have insisted to me that they are possible forms.
2. I adopt the convention in this paper of writing names of logical predicates in all uppercase letters. Names of meanings are written with uppercase initials. Names of surface forms are written in lowercase except where orthography demands otherwise.
3. Such an analysis, incidentally, is harmonious with the possible intuition that the morphological marking for conditionals resembles a 'fusion' of the endings for future and imperfect forms.

REFERENCES

Aid, Frances M. 1976. Semantics in Spanish language curricula. In: Georgetown University Round Table on Languages and Linguistics 1976. Edited by Clea Rameh. Washington, D.C.: Georgetown University Press.

Fillmore, Charles J., and D. Terence Langendoen,
  eds. 1971. Studies in linguistic semantics.
  New York: Holt, Rinehart and Winston, Inc.
Franz, Donald G. 1974. Generative semantics: An
  introduction. Bloomington: Indiana University
  Linguistics Club.
Hoffman, T. Ronald. 1966. Past tense replacement
  and the modal system. In: Mathematical linguistics and automatic translation. Edited by A.
  Oettinger. Clearwater, Virginia, NSF-17 (1966).
Klein, Flora. 1976. A quantitative study of syntactic interference in the speech of U.S. Spanish-English bilinguals. Paper presented at NWAVE-5,
  Georgetown University, Washington, D.C.
Lakoff, George. 1966. Stative adjectives and
  verbs in English. In: Harvard Computational
  Laboratory report NSF-17.
Leech, Geoffrey N. 1971. Meaning and the English
  verb. London: Longmans, Ltd.
McCawley, James D. 1967. Meaning and the description of language. In: Grammar and meaning 5.99-120.
McCawley, James D. 1968. Lexical insertion in a
  transformational grammar without deep structure.
  CLS 4.71-80.
McCawley, James D. 1971. Tense and time reference
  in English. In Fillmore and Langendoen, 96-113.
Ross, John Robert. 1969. Auxiliaries as main
  verbs. Journal of Philosophical Linguistics
  1(1).77-102.

ASPECTS OF SPANISH ASPECT:
A NEW LOOK AT THE
PRETERIT/IMPERFECT DISTINCTION

JORGE M. GUITART
State University of New York at Buffalo

This study[1] is an attempt to outline what the Spanish speaker knows about the uses of the Preterit and Imperfect forms (henceforth referred to as PRET and IMP), usually identified in the literature as signaling perfective and imperfective aspect respectively.

My intent is not directly pedagogical, but I hope that it may serve eventually to aid students of Spanish as a second language in acquiring such a knowledge. In fact, the study was largely motivated by an analysis of the errors made by my American students when they thought they were applying faithfully the rules laid down in their textbooks.

In developing the views presented here, I have benefited greatly from the observations made by the Venezuelan grammarian Andrés Bello more than a century ago, which have reached us through successive editions of his justly famous <u>Gramática de la lengua castellana</u> (see Bello and Cuervo 1970). I have also profited considerably from observations made by Samuel Gili y Gaya (1961) and Dwight Bolinger (1963). I would like to regard my analysis as an attempt to integrate and expand on the insightful formulations of these noted grammarians.

1. What do we talk about? In discussing the PRET/IMP distinction, Hispanic linguists seem to have concentrated primarily on the uses of the forms for speaking of past occurrences or happenings. For instance, Bull (1965) is largely concerned with the reporting of what he calls 'events', meaning actually things that happened or were happening--what Comrie (1976) calls 'dynamic situations'. Speakers, however, report other things for which the label 'happening' would be inappropriate. These are the situations that Comrie terms 'static', or simply 'states'. Comrie (1976:49) provides the following distinction:

> With a state, unless something happens to change that state, then the state will continue ... With a dynamic situation, on the other hand, the situation will only continue if it is continually subject to a new input of energy.

There are certain situations or experiences that we do not normally call states but which are not occurrences either. In this category fall perceived 'properties' or 'qualities' of beings or things. For instance, the utterances My name is Julio and Two and two are four are not normally thought of as referring to a state. On the other hand they are indeed static situations. By 'state' I mean here a static situation, whether it is a property or quality of a being or thing or the condition it is in.

All situations, whether static or dynamic, 'take place', they occupy a space of time, have duration. But the distinction between an occurrence--or something that happens--and a state--or something that is in effect--has important consequences for the interpretation of Spanish simple past predicates, as will become evident in the course of the discussion.

2. Type of states. The static situations that Spanish speakers talk about may be conveniently

divided into the following categories and subcategories (examples are given):

I. Identity:
   a. Individual:
      Me llamo Blas 'My name is Blas'
      Soy el dueño 'I am the owner'
   b. Class:
      Soy anarquista 'I am an anarchist'
      Soy diabético 'I am a diabetic'

II. Existence:
   Hay gente que pasa hambre
   'There are people who go hungry'

III. Location:
   Hay mucha gente aquí
   'There are a lot of people here'
   El está aquí 'He is here'

IV. Condition:
   Estoy enfermo 'I am sick'
   El radio está roto 'The radio is broken'

V. Having:
   a. Knowledge:
      Conozco a su hermano 'I know your brother'
   b. Ownership:
      Tengo dinero 'I have money'
   c. An intellectual, sensorial, or emotional frame of mind:
      Ella cree en Dios 'She believes in God'
      Me siento bien 'I feel fine'
      Me gusta Mahler 'I like Mahler'
   d. A potential:
      Puedo ir 'I can go'
      Puede estallar 'It may explode'
   e. An obligation:
      Tengo que irme 'I have to leave'
      Tiene que caer 'It has to fall'
   f. A relationship:
      Tengo dos hijos 'I have two children'

3. Classes of occurrences. I will classify occurrences in a manner similar to the way Bull (1965) classifies 'events', but using what I believe are more mnemonic labels. Occurrences can be either 'completive' or 'extendable'. A completive occurrence (cf. Bull's 'cyclic event') can be described as follows: (1) it is not thought of as happening 'totally' until it is completed and (2) once it is completed, it is over. <u>Me senté</u> 'I sat down', <u>Abrí la puerta</u> 'I opened the door', and <u>El tren pasó por la estación</u> 'The train went by the station' refer to completive occurrences. Not until the caboose has gone by has the train gone by, but once the caboose goes by, the train's passing is over. An extendable occurrence (cf. Bull's 'noncyclic event'), in contrast, is one that is thought of as taking place the moment it starts and of continuing for some time afterwards. Once it takes place, it can be extended, thus the label. The phrases <u>Caminar por el parque</u> 'to stroll in the park', <u>Mirar por la ventana</u> 'to look out the window', and <u>Ver televisión</u> 'to watch television' refer to extendable occurrences.

For Bull the classification of occurrences into cyclic and noncyclic is essential for understanding the uses of PRET and IMP, and the pedagogical strategies that his analysis has inspired call for making the learner aware of such a distinction. The textbook <u>Communicating in Spanish</u> (henceforth referred to as CIS), by Lamadrid, Bull, and Briscoe (1974), contains a very explicit formulation of Bull's theory of the uses of PRET and IMP (developed in Bull 1960, 1965). This formulation can be seen to coincide essentially with the formulations commonly found in discussions of aspectual distinctions in Spanish which state that PRET refers to either the beginning or the end of an event or to the whole event, while IMP refers only to the middle, or the event in progress. In CIS the formulation is specifically summarized for learners as follows:

At a point in the past the Imperfect states that
any event was in progress. The Preterit states
that a cyclic event reached its termination and
took place. In contrast, the Preterit may say
either that a noncyclic event began (and may or
may not have come to an end) or that the whole
event took place before the moment of speaking.
(CIS:252)

This statement is inaccurate in several respects,
as I will now attempt to show.

4. Occurrences and the IMP/PRET distinction.
Let us accept for the sake of discussion that any
occurrence we talk about has a beginning (B), a
middle (M), and an end (E). Let us accept also for
the time being that IMP always states that an occurrence was in progress. Let us then concentrate on
the statements made about PRET in the cited paragraph from CIS.
In my opinion Statement (1) is an inaccurate
characterization of what the speaker knows:

(1) 'The Preterit states that a cyclic event
reached its termination and took place'
(CIS:252).

Suppose a newspaper reports the following completive (cyclic) occurrence:

(2) El tren presidencial pasó por la terminal
de Buffalo 'The presidential train went by
the Buffalo terminal'

If (1) be true, what (2) reports is, essentially,
that the caboose of the presidential train went by
the station and therefore the passing of the train
took place. It is clear, however, that (3) and
(4) do not 'refer' to the same occurrence:

(3) El tren presidencial pasó por la terminal
'The presidential train went by the terminal'

(4) El furgón de cola del tren presidencial pasó
    por la terminal
    'The caboose of the presidential train went
    by the terminal'

Of course, if the occurrence reported in (3) took place, then the occurrence reported in (4) took place, and vice versa. That is to say, I can make the (trivial) logical statement (5):

(5) 'The train went by if and only if the caboose went by.'

But (2) obviously does not refer exclusively to the passing of the caboose, and so it would seem that PRET is stating something other than the termination of the cycle.

If PRET does not focus exclusively on E, does it focus then on the whole occurrence, i.e. on B, M, and E? This question is relevant only if we see IMP as 'excluding' some portions of the occurrence, i.e. if we regard IMP as meaning 'already started and not yet completed'. But IMP does not mean that, as is evident in the nonsynonymity of (6) and (7):

(6) En ese momento ya había pasado la locomotora
    pero todavía no había pasado el furgón de
    cola
    'At that point the engine had already gone
    by but the caboose had not yet gone by'
(7) En ese momento pasaba el tren
    'At that point the train was going by'

So far as completive (cyclic) occurrences are concerned, the contrast between PRET and IMP is not 'having reached termination versus not having reached termination' because PRET does not mean 'termination reached' and IMP does not mean 'termination not reached'. PRET actually means that the occurrence is anterior in time to the moment of speaking, and that is all it means. 'Termination reached' can be inferred from the completive nature of the occurrence. That is to say, if I state that

the passing of the train occurred in the past, then
anybody who cares to do so can say that the train
is not going by anymore, because our knowledge of
the way trains behave includes the fact that once
a particular train goes by a station, that same
train does not keep on going by. I will postpone
until later the definition of what IMP means.

Using Bull's own terminology, we can then make
the following statement with respect to the use of
PRET in talking about completive occurrences:

(8) The Preterit states that a cyclic event took
place, from which it can be inferred (trivially) that it reached termination.

As regards the use of PRET in speaking about extendable occurrences (noncyclic events), I would
like to show that (9) is not a correct characterization of what the speaker knows:

(9) 'The Preterit may say either that a noncyclic event began (and may or may not have
come to an end) or that the whole event took
place before the moment of speaking' (CIS:
252)

Let us first consider the second part of (9), or
the claim that PRET refers sometimes to the whole
event. In CIS:251 the students are offered the
following example:

(10) Ayer el presidente habló por televisión
'The president spoke on television yesterday'

and they are told that in (10) <u>habló</u> '(he) spoke'
tells that 'the entire event took place yesterday'.
Consider now the following example:

(11) El presidente habló por televisión esa noche
'The president spoke on television that
evening'

Presumably <u>habló</u> would tell that the entire event took place that evening. But what does <u>habló</u> tell in (12)?

(12) El presidente habló por televisión esa noche
 y a la mañana siguiente todavía seguía
 hablando por televisión
  'The president spoke on television that
   evening, and he was still speaking on
   television the morning after'

Obviously PRET is not telling that the entire event took place that evening, for that would contradict the rest of (12); (12), however, is well formed.

Actually all that (11) is saying is that the president spoke on television that evening, and all that (10) is saying is that he spoke on television yesterday. Since <u>hablar por televisión</u> is extendable (noncyclic), the possibility is not ruled out in (10) that the president may still be talking this morning. Of course the normal interpretation of (10) is that the president's speech finished yesterday but that is due to the presence of the word <u>ayer</u>, not to the use of PRET. In (13), for instance,

(13) Ayer el presidente hablaba por televisión
   y ...
  'Yesterday the president was speaking on
   television and ...'

there is no reason to suppose that the President's speech continued until the next day and every reason to suppose that it ended yesterday.

Therefore it is not the PRET that states that an extendable (noncyclic) occurrence occurred entirely within a certain period of time, but rather the co-occurrence of a simple past form with the word or expression referring to that period of time.

Let us now consider the claim made by Bull that PRET is initiative in noncyclic event predicates. In CIS:283 it is stated explicitly that in (14) <u>oyeron</u> 'they heard' means 'they began to hear':

(14) Entraron en la casa y después oyeron los
animales
'They went in the house and afterwards
they heard the animals'

If that were true, then (15) and (16) would be synonymous:

(15) Dijo adiós y corrió hacia el avión
'He said goodbye and ran toward the plane'
(16) Dijo adiós y echó a correr hacia el avión
'He said goodbye and took off running toward
the plane'

But it can be shown that they are not synonymous. Compare the following:

(17) Dijo adiós y corrió lentamente hacia el avión
'He said goodbye and ran slowly toward the
plane'
(18) *Dijo adiós y echó lentamente a correr hacia
el avión
*'He said goodbye and slowly took off
running toward the plane'

The expression <u>echar a correr</u> 'to take off running' is clearly initiative: it refers to the sudden movement that characterizes the start of running, the shifting to the mode of running. In contrast with (18), (19) is well formed:

(19) Dijo adiós y echó rápidamente a correr hacia
el avión
'He said goodbye and swiftly took off running
toward the plane'

Since <u>echar a correr</u> is incompatible with <u>lentamente</u> 'slowly', it is obvious that in (17) <u>corrió</u> does not include <u>echó a correr</u> 'he took off running'. Consequently in (17) <u>corrió</u> does not refer to B, i.e. <u>corrió</u> is not initiative.

But what does PRET refer to, then? Certainly not to E: we do not know from (16) whether he ran all

the way or switched to walking or stopped. All
that is left is M, but if PRET refers to M, then
such a reference is irrelevant to the PRET/IMP
distinction, since IMP also refers to M and only
to M. That is to say, either PRET does not refer
to any particular part of an extendable (noncyclic)
occurrence or looking at those parts has no bearing
on deciding whether PRET or IMP should be used in a
certain context.

What is the contrast then between (20) and (21)?

(20) El hombre corrió hacia el avión
'The man ran toward the plane'
(21) El hombre corría hacia el avión
'The man was running toward the plane'

In (20) corrió expresses simply that the act of
running toward the plane took place at a time
anterior to the moment of speaking, without specifying which portions of such an act were witnessed.
Corría in (21) expresses that at a certain time
anterior to the moment of speaking, the act of
running toward the plane was taking place. The
experience described in corrió is not specifically
associated with any stretch of past time, while the
experience described in corría is always associated
with a particular stretch of past time, specifically
that in which at least one other experience took
place or was taking place. And this association
is expressed by referring to the other experience
as well, within the same verbal context. In other
words, every time we use IMP in referring to a
specific occurrence we always mention at least one
other experience or situation that took place or
was taking place within the same stretch of time.
A sentence like (21) would not normally be uttered
in isolation or within a context where it is clear
that other situations mentioned do not cooccur at
all with the act of running. For instance, the use
of corría is anomalous in (22):

(22) *Corría hacia el avión y se ajustó el
cinturón de seguridad

'He was running toward the plane and he adjusted his seatbelt'

The meaning of IMP can then be stated as follows:

(23) IMP tells that an occurrence was taking place at a time before the moment of speaking in which some other situation took place or was taking place.

I say 'some other situation' and not simply 'some other occurrence' because states may be involved, too. I shall return to the uses of IMP further on.

Returning to PRET in extendable (noncyclic) occurrence predicates, if all that it means is that the occurrence took place before the moment of speaking, there is no difference between that and what it means in completive (cyclic) occurrence predicates (cf. (8)). We can then formulate the following statement:

(24) PRET states that an occurrence took place before the moment of speaking.

This is, of course, the traditional view held by Bello, Gili y Gaya, and many others. Whether or not one can say that the occurrence took place totally at a time anterior to the moment of speaking depends of course on the nature of the occurrence. Completive occurrences that took place lie wholly in the past. Extendable occurrences may or may not be going on still. Since the contrast between PRET and IMP does not depend on what portions of the experience the speaker 'intends' to include or exclude--as I believe I have shown--the use of the forms follows the same criteria regardless of the type of occurrence one is telling about. That is to say, the contrast between PRET and IMP is the same in speaking of completive (cyclic) occurrences as it is in speaking of extendable (noncyclic) occurrences.

But even though Bull's notion that PRET is terminative in cyclic occurrence predicates and initiative in noncyclic occurrence predicates is incorrect, still the distinction between cyclic and noncyclic--or between completive and extendable can be a useful pedagogical tool.

Bull's distinction has probably done much to dispel the notion that PRET is only for things that are 'over and done with'--a statement that has not entirely disappeared from textbooks. On the other hand Bull's insistence on the initiative quality of noncyclic predicates has not contributed to dispelling the equally erroneous notion that anything that is 'continuative' calls for IMP. For instance, in wanting to say 'I looked at her and told her I loved her' students have used *<u>La miraba</u> instead of <u>La miré</u> for 'I looked at her', explaining that IMP is needed because 'when you told her, you were still looking'. In cases like this it is useful to point out to the students that certain occurrences--extendable ones--keep on occurring once they occur-- you do not stop looking the minute you are looking.

A definite shortcoming of many pedagogical treatments of the PRET/IMP contrast is their failure to distinguish clearly between dynamic situations and static ones. It is to the latter that we now turn.

5. States and the IMP/PRET distinction. Consider the contrast between (25) and (26):

(25) Pedro era comunista 'Pedro was a communist'
(26) Pedro fue comunista 'Pedro was a communist'

They do receive the same translation in English, which is perhaps a learning problem for the English-speaking. <u>Era</u> tells that at a certain point in the past and coinciding with some other situation (which would be mentioned in a larger context), Pedro was a communist. The meaning of IMP in speaking of a specific state is then essentially the same as in speaking of a specific occurrence. <u>Fue</u> tells that Pedro was a communist in the past and that now he is not. The meaning of PRET then is not the same in speaking of states as it is in speaking of occurrences, for in the latter case nothing is said

about the present. In speaking of an extendable
occurrence, for instance, I never tell by using
PRET that it is no longer occurring.

The fact that a stative predicate in the PRET
tells that the state is no longer in effect does
not mean that PRET is basically terminative. For
instance, (27) and (28) do not mean the same
thing:

(27) Él estuvo preocupado 'He was worried'
(28) Él dejó de estar preocupado 'He stopped being
worried'

Rather, PRET refers also to the time that the state
was in effect, as shown in the fact that, in (29),
(a) and (b) are roughly equivalent:

(29a) Él tenía dinero y ya no tiene
'He had money and now he doesn't'
(29b) Él tuvo dinero 'He had money'

What I have said so far applies to stative predicates that are adverbially unmodified. Certain
adverbial expressions change radically the meaning
of stative predicates, as we shall see further on.

6. State-egressive predicates. In the foregoing
examples of stative predicates in the PRET we are
told that a state came to an end but no reference
is made to how it ended. This is true of many
stative predicates. There are other stative predicates, however, that make specific reference to the
occurrence that constituted the end of a state.
Consider the contrast between (a) and (b) in the
following pairs:

(30a) El libro costó $4
'The book cost $4' [It was bought for $4]
(30b) El libro costaba $4
'The book cost $4' [It was for sale for $4]
(31a) Tuve que ir al aeropuerto
'I had to go the airport' [I went]

(31b) Tenía que ir al aeropuerto
'I had to go the airport' [I had not gone yet]

In (30a), until the transaction was completed the book cost $4. In (31a), on the way to the airport, I still had the obligation of going. The point is that the state that comes to an end when the purchasing of the book is completed or when I get to the airport is in effect 'until then'. Therefore the (a) predicates (in the PRET) refer at the same time to a static situation and to a dynamic situation in which such a static situation came to an end. In contrast the (b) predicates (in the IMP) refer only to the state as it was in effect.

Some might say that <u>costó</u> in (30a) refers only to an occurrence--the act of purchasing the book for $4--since, for instance, (32) and (33) might seem to be synonymous:

(32) El auto costó $5,000 'The car cost $5,000'
(33) Compraron el auto por $5,000
      'They bought the car for $5,000'

But they are really not synonymous, as seen in the following contrast:

(34) El auto costaba $6,000 pero lo compraron por $5,000
      'The car cost $6,000 but they bought it for $5,000'
(35) ?El auto costaba $6,000 pero costó $5,000
      '?The car cost $6,000 but it cost $5,000'

While (34) clearly tells of a bargain, (35) is odd. The reason is that the normal interpretation of <u>Costó $5,000</u> is 'It was for sale for $5,000 and was bought for $5,000'. Hence (35) contains the contradiction 'It was for sale for $6,000 but was for sale for $5,000'.

I will call 'state-egressive' or simply 'egressive' those PRET predicates which refer inseparably to a state and to the occurrence that brought it to an end, and will call 'pre-egressive' the associated

predicates in the IMP which refer only to the state.
The latter name does not indicate of course that the
state must necessarily come to an end, only that it
is expected to do so. The $4 book may never sell
but the expectation is that it will.

7. State-ingressive predicates. Certain stative
predicates in the PRET are the mirror image of the
state-egressive ones. They can be called 'state-
ingressive' or simply 'ingressive' and they refer to
an occurrence in which a state comes fully into effect. Their associated 'post-ingressive' predicates
in the IMP refer simply to the state and are no different in meaning from other stative predicates in
the IMP. Three very common verbs that can enter
into ingressive predicates are <u>gustar</u> 'to like',
<u>saber</u> 'to know', and <u>conocer</u> 'to know, be acquainted
with'. (Many other verbs which like <u>gustar</u> denote
an emotional frame of mind--e.g. <u>molestar</u> 'to
bother', <u>aterrar</u> 'to frighten', <u>complacer</u> 'to please',
etc.--can also enter into ingressive predicates.)

Consider the contrasts in meaning between the (a)
predicates in the PRET and the (b) predicates in the
IMP in the following:

(36a) Me gustó el lugar y decidí quedarme
      'I liked (came to like) the place and
        decided to stay'
(36b) Me gustaba el lugar y decidí quedarme
      'I (already) liked the place and decided
        to stay'
(37a) Conocí a todo el mundo 'I met everyone'
(37b) Conocía a todo el mundo 'I knew everyone'
(38a) Supe lo sucedido
      'I learned (came to know) what had happened'
(38b) Sabía lo sucedido
      'I knew what had happened'

In Bull's theory <u>me gustó</u>, <u>supe</u>, and <u>conocí</u> are
regarded as referring to the initiation of non-
cyclic events (see Bull 1965:170; CIS:251, 8).
It is obvious, however, that (39) and (40) do not
mean the same thing:

(39) Empezó a gustarme aquel cuadro
    'I began to like that painting'
(40) Me gustó aquel cuadro
    'I liked that painting'

Ingressive predicates do not refer to the beginning phase of a state but rather to its coming fully into effect. This is supported by the fact that you can say (41) but cannot say (42):

(41) Lentamente empezó a gustarme aquel cuadro
    'I slowly began to like that painting'
(42) *Lentamente me gustó aquel cuadro
    '*I slowly liked that painting'

Similarly one cannot say *Lentamente supe la verdad '*I slowly learned the truth' or Lentamente lo conocí '*I slowly met (came to know) him'. Once you like something you like it, once you come to know someone or something, you know him, her, or it. The occurrence--reacting in the case of gustó, meeting in the case of conocí, learning in the case of supe--is inseparable from the state--liking in the case of gustó, knowing in both conocí and supe. Because states are extendable unless otherwise specified, gustó means 'liked and continued to like', and supe and conocí mean 'I came to know and continued to know'.

At this point it is useful to introduce a distinction between 'monomial predicates', or those that refer solely to an occurrence or solely to a state, and 'binomial predicates', or those that refer inseparably to a state and an occurrence. Both ingressive and egressive predicates are of course binomial predicates, while their associated post-ingressive and pre-egressive predicates are monomial.

7.1. BE-ingressive predicates. Perhaps of great interest are the ingressive predicates entered into by the two verbs, ser and estar. In the case of ser, reference is to the acquisition of a certain characteristic on the part of the subject and in the case of estar to the subject being in a certain

state or condition in which it was not before.
Consider the following examples:

(43) Velázquez fue el primero en utilizar esa
     técnica
     'Velazquez was the first one to use that
     technique'
(44) La cena estuvo lista y nos llamaron a comer
     'Dinner was ready and they called us to eat'
     [Dinner was not ready before]

As is the case in all ingressive predicates, (43) and (44) convey the notion of a change of state taking place. Like all ingressive predicates they refer to a new state (whereas egressive predicates, which also convey the notion of a change of state, refer to an old state and its ceasing to be). In this they differ from monomial ser/estar predicates, which refer to an old state and to the fact it is no longer in effect, without referring to the change (cf. (26) and (27)). I call predicates like (43) and (44) 'BE-ingressive'.

Perhaps of interest also are the BE-ingressive predicates that refer to subjective perceptions, where '[Subject] was' is really equivalent to 'I perceived [Subject] to be'. Examples follow.

(45) Fue una experiencia inolvidable
     'It was an unforgettable experience'
(46) La fiesta estuvo muy divertida
     'The party was great fun'

Of course (45) does not mean 'it was an unforgettable experience and is no longer so', nor does (46) mean 'the party was great fun and is not great fun anymore'. Rather, (45) conveys the notion that I perceived a certain experience as being of the unforgettable kind and continued to perceive it as such. And (46) tells that I perceived the party as being great fun and continued to perceive it as such. BE-ingressive predicates that refer to subjective perceptions are actually very similar in meaning to other ingressive predicates that refer

to the acquisition of feelings. For instance, in
(47), (a) and (b) are quite close in meaning if
not equivalent:

(47a) El viaje fue muy placentero
      'The trip was very pleasing'
(47b) Nos gustó mucho el viaje
      'We liked the trip very much'

8. The case of quedar(se) and other 'time-
partitioning' verbs. Of interest also are those
ingressive predicates entered into by the verb
quedar and its reflexive associate quedarse which
are similar to BE-ingressive predicates. In certain other (noningressive) predicates quedar(se)
refers to an old state--one already in effect--as
in (48):

(48) La puerta estaba abierta y así se quedó
     'The door was open and it stayed that way'

But in the following examples quedar(se) in the
PRET refers to a new state:

(49a) La sesión quedó abierta
      'The meeting was called to order'
(49b) Luis quedó como tutor de sus sobrinos
      'Luis was appointed the guardian of his
       nephews'
(49c) Irma se quedó dormida viendo televisión
      'Irma fell asleep watching television'

Of course the meeting had not been called to order
before, Luis was not the guardian before, and Irma
was not asleep before.
   The verb quedar(se) has a property that is manifested both in (48) and in the examples in (49):
it in effect divides all time into a 'before' and
an 'after'. In (48) and (49) quedar(se) has
entered into what I call 'time-partitioning' predicates. Notice, however, that whereas in (49) the
notion conveyed is 'a state that was not in effect
before was in effect after' (i.e. it is a new

state), the notion conveyed in (48) is 'a state
that was in effect before was in effect after'.
That is to say, in the context (50):

(50) /OLD STATE _____

<u>quedar(se)</u> means 'to stay' while in the absence of
such a context it means 'to become'.
  The time dividing property of the PRET forms of
<u>quedar(se)</u> in (51) is shared by the PRET forms of
<u>permanecer</u> 'to remain', <u>continuar</u> 'to continue',
and <u>seguir</u> 'to continue'. (Continuar and seguir
have different selectional restrictions, as will be
apparent below.) These verbs are frequently used
in contexts where one wishes to specify that, even
though a certain subject ceased being in a certain
state, a certain other subject did remain in that
state, as in the examples in (51) and (52):

(51) Yo entré pero ellos { se quedaron / continuaron / siguieron / permanecieron } fuera

'I came in but they { stayed / continued to stay / continued to be / remained } outside'

(52) Ella se durmió pero yo { me quedé / continué / seguí / permanecí } despierto

'She went to sleep but I { stayed / continued to stay / continued to be / remained } awake'

<u>Quedar(se)</u> also figures in contrasts in which one
subject gets to be in a new state but another sub-
ject does not, with <u>continuar</u>, <u>seguir</u>, and <u>permanecer</u>
excluded from the same context, as in the examples in
(53):

(53a) La explosión no dañó la oficina pero el
 laboratorio quedó destruido
 'The explosion did not damage the office
 but the lab was destroyed'
(53b) A ella no le pasó nada pero él se quedó
 ciego
 'Nothing happened to her but he lost his
 sight'

There is a very important difference between
<u>quedarse</u> and the other three verbs in (51) and (52).
The latter effect a partition of time while at the
same time expressing continuation. But <u>quedarse</u>
does not express continuation: all it tells is that
the state was in effect in the 'after' period. Moreover, the other verbs, <u>continuar</u>, <u>seguir</u>, and <u>permanecer</u> may express continuation without conveying
time partition (by being in the IMP). These two
differences, crucial to the rules that govern the
use of PRET and IMP, are evident in the following
example:

(54) El niño se durmió pero la niña {continuaba / *se quedaba}
 despierta tres horas más
 tarde
 'The boy fell asleep but the girl {was still / *stayed} awake three hours later'

Either <u>permanecía</u> or <u>seguía</u> may be substituted
for <u>continuaba</u> in (54) without any change in grammaticality; both would receive the same translation
in English. Of course these verbs are not interchangeable (the difference is of no interest to us
here) but they all express continuation.

9. Stative predicates and adverbial modifications. The time partitioning effect, intrinsic to
<u>quedar(se)</u> and other verbs, can be achieved by the
use of adverbial expressions that refer to the
beginning of a new period (and, by implication, to
the end of an old one), e.g. <u>desde ese día</u> 'from
that day on', <u>a partir de entonces</u> 'from then on',
<u>desde aquel momento</u> 'from that moment on', etc.

The use of these expressions has the curious effect of having monomial stative predicates refer to a state that came into effect rather than to one that has come to an end. Compare:

(55a) Ellos fueron enemigos
  'They were enemies' [and now they are not]
(55b) Desde aquel día fueron enemigos
  'From that day on, they were enemies'
  [They became enemies]
(56a) Ellos estuvieron peleados
  'They were not on speaking terms' [but now they are]
(56b) Desde aquel momento estuvieron peleados
  'From that moment on they were not on speaking terms' [but they had been before]

Such adverbial expressions have also the effect of turning any egressive predicate into an ingressive one, as in (57):

(57) Desde aquel día tuvo que venir más temprano
  'From that day on he had to come in earlier'

which tells that the obligation to come in earlier was imposed on him. A similar inversion occurs in (58):

(58) Desde aquella fecha costó un dineral ir a España
  'From that date on it cost a mint to go to Spain'

which tells that a higher price went into effect. In passing, I would like to mention that based on examples such as (57) and (58), some Spanish textbooks state that PRET is for focusing on the beginning of 'an event'. It is clear that the focusing here is being accomplished by the use of adverbial phrases, not by the use of PRET.

Exactly the reverse of the inversion just described occurs when a normally ingressive predicate is modified by an adverbial expression that refers to the end of a period (and, by implication, to the beginning of a new one). The result is an egressive predicate, as in (59):

(59) Me gustó ese cuadro hasta aquel día
   'I liked that painting until that day'

which tells both that I had a favorable feeling toward the painting and that my feeling changed. Again, focusing on the end is accomplished by the adverbial expression, not by the use of PRET, as some texts say.

10. Persistive predicates. Not all binomial predicates are either ingressive or egressive. Consider, for example, the following contrasts:

(60a) Podía quedarme en el mejor hotel
   'I could stay at the best hotel'
(60b) Pude quedarme en el mejor hotel
   'I was able to stay at the best hotel'
(61a) No quería ir al cine
   'I didn't want to go to the movies'
(61b) No quise ir al cine
   'I refused to go to the movies'

It should be clear that (60b) and (61b) are binomial but are not ingressive. The fact that I was able to stay at the hotel—a dynamic situation—presupposes I had the potential to do so—a static quality. My refusal to go to the movies—a dynamic situation—presupposes I did not feel like going—an emotional state. But (60b) and (61b) are not egressive either: once I was lodged at the hotel my privilege to stay did not end; once I refused to go to the movies, I still did not want to go. Predicates such as these can be called 'persistive'. They refer to an occurrence that is the manifestation of a certain state that does not come to an end upon being manifested.

In contrast, the corresponding IMP predicates—e.g. (60a) and (61a)—refer only to the existing state.

11. The PRET/IMP contrast in single-instance stative predicates. What I have said so far applies to the uses of PRET and IMP in speaking of single instances of situations (whether dynamic or static or having both dynamic and static characteristics) as opposed to their uses in speaking of situations that entered our experience at different times in the past, which we will discuss further below.

The contrast between PRET and IMP in predicates referring to single instances of static situations or states can perhaps be summarized as follows:

(62i) IMP tells that a state was in effect at a time before the moment of speaking in which some other situation took place or was taking place

(62ii) Depending on the meaning of the verb and the context in which it appears, PRET may tell either (a) that a state was in effect before the moment of speaking and is not in effect at the moment of speaking (IMP says nothing about the moment of speaking), or (b) that a change of state took place-- either a new state came into effect or a state that was in effect came to an end (IMP cannot tell of such a change), or (c) that a continuing state was manifested without coming to an end (IMP cannot tell of such a manifestation), or (d) that a new period began and a state was in effect that was in effect before (IMP cannot tell of a state being in effect on both sides of a time partition).

12. The meaning of IMP in single instance predicates. When one compares the statements made in (23) and (62i) regarding the meaning of IMP in telling of occurrences and states respectively, one is struck by their similarity. We repeat them here as (63) and (64):

(63) IMP tells that an occurrence was taking place at a time before the moment of speaking

in which some other situation took place or
was taking place,
(64) IMP tells that a state was in effect at a
time before the moment of speaking in which
some other situation took place or was taking place.

It is obvious that IMP means the same thing in all single situation predicates: the duration of the situation being spoken of by using IMP coincided at some point anterior to the moment of speaking with the duration of some other situation. The co-occurring quality of IMP is a well-known fact. Bello had a name for IMP that is quite descriptive of its function in single situation predicates. He called it <u>copretérito</u> 'copreterit'. Another noted nineteenth-century grammarian, Vicente Salvá, called it <u>pretérito coexistente</u> 'coexistent preterit' (cf. Suárez 1957). In its recent outline of the next edition of its grammar, the Real Academia (1973) uses both terms to describe this function of IMP, though still preferring the label <u>Pretérito Imperfecto</u> 'Imperfect Preterit' to refer to the forms.

To say--as Bull says--that IMP states that any event was in progress does not adequately describe its function in single situation predicates. For one thing, what is in progress, for instance, in the situations spoken about in (65)?

(65) El hombre estaba muerto 'The man was dead'
No teníamos dinero 'We didn't have money'
El concierto era gratis
'The concert was free'
La viuda se llamaba Elsa
'The widow's name was Elsa'

The crucial function of IMP in single situation predicates is not really to look at the middle portion of an occurrence or state but to talk about situations that cooccurred at some point. The use of IMP for establishing the background of narrations is well known. So strong is the sense of cooccurrence in the IMP that it is used stylistically to stress the relationship between two situations that took place within the same period of time, even though their duration did not coincide at any point. Such is the case in (66):

(66) Llegamos a Washington el 22 por la mañana. Esa misma tarde asesinaban a Kennedy en Dallas. La noticia nos dejó anonadados
'We arrived in Washington the morning of the 22nd. That very afternoon they killed Kennedy in Dallas. The news left us in a state of shock'

The use of IMP in (66)--actually optional or stylistic--stresses the fact that our arrival in Washington and Kennedy's assassination took place on the same day, even though the two situations did not coincide at any point in their duration.

13. Recurrences and PRET/IMP distinction. As is well known, the IMP/PRET contrast is used in speaking of a situation that entered our experience at different times in the past. This is what is normally referred to as speaking about a 'series'. Since in my mind the term 'series' can refer to a set of dissimilar actions, I prefer the term 'recurrence' to describe such a situation.

The use of IMP and PRET in speaking of a situation experienced at different times in the past can be stated as follows:

(67) In speaking of situations that entered our experience at different times in the past, IMP identifies a situation as something that recurred, while PRET refers to a set of instances of such a situation.

An example of this contrast is provided in (68):

(68a) Blas nunca faltaba a clase
'Blas never missed class/used to never miss class/would never miss class'

(68b) Blas nunca faltó a clase
'Blas never missed class'

While (68a) tells of Blas's good habit, (68b) tells of his perfect attendance record. When I say that IMP identifies a situation as something that recurred, as a recurrence, I mean to say that the situation, having entered the speaker's experience before, was expected to enter the speaker's experience again, and this expectation existed before the moment of speaking. 'Previous repetition' and 'expectation of subsequent instances' are the components of a recurrence. PRET actually does not refer to a recurrence but to a collection of instances of the same situation. There is no expectation of subsequent instances and no direct reference to the iterative quality of the situation (though its iterative quality can be trivially inferred from the context, i.e. if I say that Blas never missed class, I of course mean he was present at more than one class). The point is that when it comes to iterative situations, IMP and PRET are not two different ways of looking at the same set of situations. In fact IMP is not looking at such a set at all. It does not refer to any particular instance of a situation but rather to 'qualities' a certain situation had, those qualities being precisely that it had occurred before more than once and that it was expected to occur again. I can say that (69a) is a synonym of (68a), and that (69b) is a synonym of (68b):

(69a) Blas tenía la costumbre de no faltar nunca a clase
'Blas had the habit of never missing class'
(69b) Blas vino a todas las clases
'Blas came to every class'

It is obvious that (69a) does not refer to Blas's attending any class in particular, whereas (69b) does. It is equally obvious that (69b) does not refer to a habit of Blas's. The two sentences are talking about different things.

The contrast between PRET and IMP is not 'including the last case of the series' versus 'not including the last case'. In the first place IMP does not refer to any case. Secondly, PRET does not necessarily include the last case, let alone every case. The fact that (68b) includes not only the last case but every case is an outcome of the context provided by the word <u>nunca</u> 'never'. Of course (70) is not possible:

(70) *Blas nunca faltó a clase en el verano, pero un día faltó
'Blas never missed class in the summer (came to every class), but one day he missed class'

However, (71) is perfectly normal:

(71) Blas sí fue a clase en el verano pero el ultimo día no estaba
'Blas did go to class in the summer but he was not there the last day'

In short one can say that, even though PRET and IMP are used in speaking of situations that entered our experience at different times in the past, PRET is actually used for speaking collectively of a number of instances of a given situation, while IMP is used for speaking of a given situation as being a recurrence.

Because a situation that involves both dynamic and static characteristics can be seen to recur, binomial predicates, which are always in the PRET when they refer to single situations, are in the IMP when they refer to a recurring situation. The examples in (72) are all references to recurring situations, one single instance of which would instead be referred to in the PRET:

(72a) El almuerzo costaba menos que la cena
'Lunch was cheaper than dinner' [at any given time]

(72b) A los turistas que llegaban, el lugar les
gustaba instantáneamente
'Arriving tourists liked the place instantly' [Different arriving tourists.]
(72c) Se quedaba desvelado cuando tomaba café
'He would be up all night whenever he drank coffee'
(72d) Por la noche podíamos estudiar allí
'At night we were able to study there'

The examples in (72) illustrate the fact that reference to a recurrence does not have to be overtly marked as such, i.e. it does not have to be modified by an expression such as cada vez que 'each time that'. Use of IMP is sufficient. The examples in (72) serve also to illustrate the fact that recurrences in English can be unmarked completely, with the context telling that I am not referring to a single situation. In contrast, in Spanish, recurrences are at least marked by the use of IMP.

Notice, however, that even though (b) and (c) in (72) are not ambiguous, for they can only refer to a recurrence, (a) and (d) can mean either a recurrence or one single static situation. Within a larger context, though, the ambiguity will disappear if there is a clear indication that there was no time overlapping at all between situations. For instance, (73) can only be a recurrence, for it is obvious that the two occurrences mentioned do not coincide at any point in time:

(73) Ella abría y cerraba los ojos
'She would open and close her eyes'

This is so because in speaking of single situations IMP always indicate simultaneity or overlapping between at least two situations, the one referred to in the IMP and at least one other-- also mentioned--which is spoken of in the IMP in case of simultaneity and in the PRET in case of overlapping, as shown in (74):

(74a) Cuando salía ella, entraba yo
   'When she was coming out, I was going in'
   (simultaneity)
(74b) Cuando salía ella, entré yo
   'When she was coming out, I went in'
   (overlapping)

Sentence (74b) is not ambiguous: it cannot refer to a recurrence since in speaking of recurrences we are not interested at all in particular instances. But (74a) is still ambiguous. It would not be so, however, within a larger context that contained a single situation seen to cooccur with both occurrences, as in (75):

(75) Cuando salía ella, entraba yo y chocamos
   'When she was coming out, I was going in, and we collided'

again because in speaking of recurrences we are not interested in instances, so that (75) would be unambiguously interpreted as a reference to a single situation.

Consider now the following interesting phenomenon. Sentence (76) is not ambiguous: it can only refer to a recurrence:

(76) Cuando salía ella, entraba yo y nos saludábamos
   'She would be coming out and I would be going in, and we would greet each other'

Obviously, the greetings are not simultaneous with the coming and going; for if it were so, then simultaneity would not suffice to have an IMP predicate be interpreted as a single situation. But it does suffice, as shown by the fact that (74a) can be interpreted as a reference to a single situation. Therefore in (76) the greetings are subsequent to the coming and going. On the other hand, since the coming and going had not terminated, the greetings overlap both. That is to say, in (76) we have a situation that overlaps other situations and is referred to in the IMP, and yet it is not interpreted as telling about a single situation, but rather as telling about a recurrence.

Notice, however, that the greetings are not overlapping any subsequent situation. And here is the crux of the matter; for in order for an IMP predicate to be interpreted as a reference to a single situation, the situation referred to--if it is not simultaneous with some other situation--must be overlapping a subsequent situation. Or, in other words, that the situation referred to in the IMP must be either simultaneous with another situation or must have started before another with which it overlaps.

Since in (76) the last predicate in the IMP refers to an occurrence that is neither simultaneous with another situation nor overlapping with a subsequent one, it cannot be a reference to a single situation. Therefore, it is a reference to a recurrence; and if it is, then the others logically are, too.

14. Recalling situations versus recalling predications. Bello observes that IMP is used for speaking of 'eternal truths' and offers as an example the sentence in (77):

(77) Copérnico probó que la tierra giraba
    alrededor del sol
     'Copernicus proved that the earth rotated
     around the sun'

Bello mentions that *gira* 'it rotates' could be tolerated in that context; but he points out that in that case 'we would not see within Copernicus's mind the eternal rotation of the earth, as called for by the sense' (see Bello and Cuervo 1970:221). I take Bello to mean that we would not see Copernicus asserting mentally (78):

(78) La tierra gira alrededor del sol
     'The earth rotates around the sun'

If that is what Bello meant, my agreement with him is total. I will elaborate on this further on.

For Bello, a sentence like (77) shows the 'co-preterit' function of IMP: the earth's rotation is anterior to Copernicus's proof, in the same manner that raining is anterior to my coming in (79):

(79) Cuando vine, llovía
    'When I came it was raining'

There are, however, sentences such as (80):

(80) Son las tres y él me dijo que venía a las cinco
    'It's three and he said he was coming at five'

Obviously his coming is posterior to his telling me. Of course, <u>venía</u> 'he was coming' can be replaced by <u>vendría</u> 'he would come' which is indeed posterior to his telling me; and this is quite in consonance with Bello's theory. <u>Vendría</u> for him is a <u>pos-pretérito</u> 'post-preterit' form, referring to something that is posterior to a past situation. The use of <u>venía</u> in (80) is normal, it is the past of present tense <u>viene</u> 'he comes' used in a future sense, in the same way that <u>vendría</u> is the past of the future form <u>vendrá</u> 'he will come'. In addition <u>había venido</u> 'he had come'--the pluperfect--is the past of PRET <u>vino</u> 'he came'.

These relationships are exploited in so-called indirect discourse. For instance if someone says (81a), what he said is reported as (81b):

(81a) Ayer fui pobre, hoy soy pobre y mañana seré pobre
    'I was poor yesterday, am poor today, and will be poor tomorrow'
(81b) Dijo que ayer había sido pobre, hoy era pobre y mañana sería pobre
    'He said he had been poor yesterday, was poor today, and would be poor tomorrow'

It seems to me, however, that the relationship between IMP and PRET is different in (79) than it is in (77) or (80). In (79) I am establishing a relationship between two occurrences, but in (77) and (80) I am relating an occurrence to something else. In (77) and (80) I am not actually telling about an occurrence, but 'telling about telling about one', i.e. I am reporting a 'predication' (a true-false statement) not a situation.

This difference becomes clear in the case of performatives, or speech acts that do what they say and say what they do at the same time. One such act is <u>Protesto</u> 'I protest'. If you say 'I protest' you are saying what you are doing and doing what you are saying. What happens when a performative is recalled? If it is recalled as an occurrence, PRET is used; but if it is recalled as a predication, IMP is used instead. Suppose that as a reaction to some unreasonable demand, I say <u>Protesto</u>. I can later be asked either of two questions about my reaction and they could be answered as follows:

(82a) ¿Qué hiciste? 'What did you do?'
(82a') Protesté 'I protested'
(82b) ¿Qué dijiste? 'What did you say?'
(82b') (Dije) que protestaba 'I said I protested'

The parentheses in <u>dije</u> indicates its optional character. It is normal to give as answer the truncated form <u>que protestaba</u> 'that I protested'.

It is obvious that the relationship between <u>dije</u> and <u>protestaba</u> in (82b) is the same as the relationship between <u>dijo</u> and <u>venía</u> in (80). In both cases I am talking about what someone said; but the use of IMP cannot be explained by appealing to temporal relationships in the case of the performative since <u>dije</u> and <u>protestaba</u> are simultaneous. (Some observant student might argue with the teacher that both should be in the IMP, given their simultaneity.) Therefore the function of IMP in (82b) must be 'other' than expressing the anteriority or posteriority of a situation with respect to an utterance made about that situation. What could that function be? Actually <u>Dije que protestaba</u> 'I said I protested' and <u>Dijo que venía a las cinco</u> 'He said he was coming at five' have something in common in addition to reporting utterances: they report something that is either true or false. I may have been lying when I said <u>Protesto</u> but I wanted my audience to think that I was protesting and that is why I said it. Therefore, when I said <u>Protesto</u> it was like saying '<u>Protesto</u> is true'. <u>Protesto</u> was an assertion. In <u>dije que protestaba</u> I am speaking about that assertion. In the case of <u>Dijo que venía a las cinco</u> I can say the speaker is speaking about the assertion <u>Vengo a las cinco</u> 'I'm coming at five', which was made--or could have been made--by another person.

Does it not make sense, then, to say that in (77) I am speaking about Copernicus's assertion--i.e. (78)--or an assertion that could have been made by Copernicus?

I would like to propose that the function of IMP in (77), (80), and (82b) is to speak of assertions that were made or could have been made using the Present tense. I would describe as follows the relationship between the form of an assertion and the form that is used to speak about it:

(83) Assertions made in the Present tense or the IMP are spoken about in the IMP, while assertions made in the PRET are spoken about in the Pluperfect

Suppose I receive a piece of information via someone's assertion--let me call it A--and I believe A is true. I may choose to do any or all of these three things with respect to A: (1) tell another person about it, (2) tell somebody else that I know it, (3) comment upon it. In Spanish I can do (1), (2), and (3) by subordinating the original assertion--after making certain changes--to a predicate that will indicate precisely which of those three things I am doing with respect to A. This is illustrated in (84):

(84a) Doing (1): $\begin{Bmatrix} \text{Dice} \\ \text{Anuncia} \\ \text{Informa} \\ \text{etc.} \end{Bmatrix}$ que A

'$\begin{Bmatrix} \text{He says} \\ \text{He announces} \\ \text{He informs} \\ \text{etc.} \end{Bmatrix}$ that A'

(84b) Doing (2) $\begin{Bmatrix} \text{Sé} \\ \text{Me doy cuenta} \\ \text{Estoy consciente de} \end{Bmatrix}$ que A

'$\begin{Bmatrix} \text{I know} \\ \text{I realize} \\ \text{I am aware} \end{Bmatrix}$ that A'

(84c) Doing (3) $\begin{Bmatrix} \text{Es fantástico} \\ \text{Me gusta} \\ \text{Encuentro mal} \end{Bmatrix}$ que A

'$\begin{Bmatrix} \text{It's fantastic} \\ \text{I like it} \\ \text{I find it objectionable} \end{Bmatrix}$ that A'

I am not interested here in (84c) since PRET and IMP do not appear in the corresponding past sentences (the subordinate takes the subjunctive). In past predicates of the type shown in (84a) and (84b), the use of the forms in the subordinate clause is as described in (83). This is illustrated in (85), where A represents the original assertion that was made or could have been made:

(85a) Dijo que tenía que esperar
'He said I had to wait'
A = Tiene que esperar 'You have to wait'
(85b) Anunciaron que se había muerto el dictador
'They announced the dictator had died'
A = Se murió el dictador 'The dictator died'
(85c) Oye, Julio, pensé que eras más listo
'Listen, Julio, I thought you were smarter'
A = Julio es más listo 'Julio is smarter'
(85d) Me di cuenta de que no había pan
'I realized there was no bread'
A = No hay pan 'There is no bread'

(85e) No sabía que había habido una huelga
'I didn't know there had been a strike'
A = Hubo una huelga 'There was a strike'

Notice that in the past there is the added possibility of telling that one did not know A, as is the case in (85e).

Consider (85c). I probably never had the exact thought 'Julio is smarter' but I am telling Julio that I did. I am telling him the equivalent of (86):

(86) Oye, Julio, yo pensé: 'Julio es más listo'
'Listen, Julio, I thought: "Julio is smarter"'

The point is that even though I may have never uttered, or thought, or heard someone utter, any of the assertions above, I speak 'as if I had'. When I say (85d) I speak as if I had said or thought, looking at an empty bread box, No hay pan 'There is no bread'.

Curiously, dreams are usually reported as if they consisted of a number of mental assertions, a phenomenon that warrants, perhaps, further investigation. In telling dreams, forms that would usually be in the PRET in a narrative, appear in the IMP, as in the following sample:

(87) Soñé que entraban el Murciélago y Robin y
se sentaban a comer con nosotros
'I dreamed Batman and Robin came in and sat down to eat with us'

Sometimes telling about assertions occur in independent clauses. For instance, a newspaper reporter may write (88), recalling the performative in (89):

(88) Quedaba abierta la sesión
'They called the meeting to order'
(89) Queda abierta la sesión
'The meeting will now come to order'

15. What does the speaker know? It should be obvious from the preceding that the rules that govern the use of PRET and IMP are different in at least four areas of discourse: (1) when speaking of dynamic situations, (2) when speaking of static situations or of situations combining both dynamic and static characteristics, (3) when speaking of situations that entered our experience at different times in the past, and (4) when speaking of assertions (real or imaginary) instead of situations. It seems to me that any serious attempt at making explicit those rules, either for the purpose of adequately characterizing the competence of the speaker or for the ulterior purpose of having nonnatives acquire them must consider those four areas separately.

NOTE

1. I would like to thank Houghton Mifflin Company for their permission to quote from <u>Communicating in Spanish</u> (Copyright Houghton Mifflin Company 1974), and Cambridge University for their permission to quote from <u>Aspect</u> (Copyright Cambridge University Press 1976). I am indebted to Henry J. Richards and Kathleen N. March for their comments on various versions of this work. I thank also Dwight L. Bolinger and Maryellen Garcia for comments that reached me too late but from which I will undoubtedly profit in my future work. I am grateful to my wife, Sarah D. Guitart, and to David Lagmanovich for valuable stylistic suggestions. I am solely responsible for all errors.

REFERENCES

Bello, Andrés, and Rufino J. Cuervo. 1970. Gramática de la lengua castellana. Octava edición. Buenos Aires: Editorial Sopena Argentina.
Bolinger, Dwight L. 1963. Reference and inference: Inceptiveness in the Spanish Preterite. Hispania 46.128-135.

Bull, William E. 1960. Time, tense, and the verb. Berkeley and Los Angeles: University of California Press.
Bull, William E. 1965. Spanish for teachers: Applied linguistics. New York: The Ronald Press Company.
Comrie, Bernard. 1976. Aspect. London and New York: Cambridge University Press.
Gili y Gaya, Samuel. 1961. Curso superior de sintaxis española. Barcelona: Biblograf.
Lamadrid, Enrique, William E. Bull, and Laurel E. Briscoe. 1974. Communicating in Spanish. Boston: Houghton Mifflin Company.
Real Academia Española. 1973. Esbozo de una nueva gramática de la lengua española. Madrid: Espasa-Calpe, S.A.
Suárez, Marcos Fidel. 1957 [1881]. Estudios gramaticales, 46 [under the editorship of Miguel Antonio Caro]. Bogotá.

LATIN AND PROTO-ROMANCE VERB-CONJUGATIONS

ROBERT A. HALL, Jr.
Cornell University

In virtually all Latin school and reference grammars (such as those of Allen and Greenough or Hale and Buck), the conjugations of the Latin verb are presented as shown in Table 1. The criteria for this traditional classification are (1) the first person singular present indicative of the verb (which was the normal citation-form) and (2) the relation of this form to the infinitive. Note that, in this classification, a verb with a short /a/ in the infinitive, such as /dare/ 'to give' or /stare/ 'to stand', is treated as an 'irregular' verb of the first conjugation and lumped together with 'regulars' like /kanta·re/ 'to sing'. Similarly, a verb like /fakere/ 'to do' is treated as 'irregular' in the third conjugation because its first person singular /fakio·/ is like /au̯dio·/, but its infinitive is in /-ere/ as is that of /u̯e·ndere/. Verbs of the /fakio·/ type are also considered 'irregular' because they show an /i/ in other forms where the 'regular' /-ere/ verbs have simply /e·/: thus, in the imperfect, /fakie·bam/ 'I was doing' vs. /u̯ende·bam/ 'I was selling'.

This traditional classification is unsatisfactory from several points of view, especially because it is based on the relation of two individual verb-forms to each other, rather than on that of an entire set of forms and the stem on which they are

Table 1. Traditional conjugations of Latin verbs.

Conjugation	Pres. 1 sg.	Infinitive
I Reg.	kanto·	kanta·re 'to sing'
Irreg.	do·	dare 'to give'
II	ualeo·	uale·re 'to be well'
III Reg.	ue·ndo·	ue·ndere 'to sell'
Irreg.	fakio·	fakere 'to do'
IV	audio·	audi·re 'to hear'
Irreg.	possum	posse 'to be able'

based to the root of the verb. As a result, some verbs (such as /dare/ and /kanta·re/) are classed together when they belong apart, and others are treated as 'irregular' when they can be seen to be regular as soon as certain morphophonemic alternations are taken into account. Both for the description of Latin itself, and for our understanding of the development of the Romance verb-conjugations, it is desirable to view the subclasses of the Latin verb as determined by the relation of the root to the stem, as manifested in the choice of stem-vowel, shown in Table 2. We still recognize four conjugations, but with a clearly more regular patterning than in the traditional arrangement. There are three stem-vowels /a i e/, each occurring both long and short, and zero. The root of /fakere/ is thus seen to be /faki-/, with short /i/ which is automatically replaced by /e/ before inflectional /r/.

For Proto-Romance we must reconstruct, on the basis of later developments, a simpler conjugation-system, with only three stem-vowels /a i e/. The distinction between long and short /a·/ and /a/ had, as is well known, not been replaced in Romance by a corresponding contrast between tense and lax. Similarly, in verb-morphology, the contrast between tense and lax /i/ and /e/ was not kept, so that we have the system shown in Table 3. The only distinction between /e/ and /ê/ appears in the infinitive, so that we must set up subclasses IIIa and IIIb for, say, /ualê^re/ as opposed to /u̯ê^ndere/.

Table 2. Latin verb-conjugations according to stem-vowels.

Conjugation	Stem-vowel	Root	Stem	Infinitive
Ia	a·	kant-	kanta·-	kanta·re
Ib	a	d-	da-	dare
IIa	i·	aud-	audi·-	audi·re
IIb	i	fak-	faki-	*faki-re → fake-re
IIIa	e·	u̯al-	u̯ale·-	u̯ale·re
IIIb	e	u̯e·nd-	u̯e·nde-	u̯e·ndere
IV	—	pot-	pot-	*pot-se → pos-se

Table 3. Proto-Romance conjugations.

Conjugation	Stem-vowel	Root	Stem	Infinitive
I	a	kant- d-	kanta- da-	kantáre dáre
II	î	aud-	audî-	audîre
IIIa	ê	u̯al-	u̯alê-	u̯alêre
	e	u̯e^nd-	u̯e^nde-	u̯é^ndere

Interestingly, although verb-stems with zero stem-vowel appear in the conjugation-systems of various Romance languages, this phenomenon appears in different individual forms, so that we cannot reconstruct any one specific verb-stem with zero stem-vowel for Proto-Romance.

The reclassification proposed here will, I believe, be useful for a better understanding of the verb-morphology of Latin, reconstructed Proto-Romance, and later developments in the Romance languages.

THE BRITISH END
OF THE SPECTRUM OF ROMANIA

ERIC P. HAMP
University of Chicago

The purpose of this little paper is to invite attention to two aspects of interaction between Romance and Celtic studies. One aspect inheres in the fact that work in the Western reaches of Romania may at times profit in more than a casual way from a knowledge of Celtic scholarship, and that Celtic linguistics can certainly ill afford to pass up opportunities for suggestive lines of enquiry to be found in the neighboring Romance scholarship. The other aspect consists in the fact that westernmost Romance dialects are quite simply geographic neighbors of British Celtic; that historically they occupy adjacent portions of the ancient range of northwesternmost Latin speech. We should, therefore, not be surprised to find deeply embedded features linking both sides of the Manche in a Sprachbund.

The word for 'black' in the British Celtic languages (Welsh, Cornish, and Breton) must surely go back to a pre-form *dŭbo-, or more likely *dŭbu-; the Irish and Scottish Gaelic forms, as well as other considerations, assure this. The problem lies in the fact that the observed form du shows a vowel u [ü] (> modern North Welsh [ɨ], South Welsh [i]) instead of [u] (Welsh orthographic w), as one might expect; the Welsh word for 'water',

for instance, is dwfr [duvr] ~ dŵr [duːr] < dubro-
(see Hamp 1972:233-237). It should perhaps be
noted overtly that it proves impossible to explain
this vowel quality by the loss in earlier Welsh
and Breton of the spirant in final position that
resulted from original *b.

Kenneth Jackson (1953:277) states that British
dŭbo- or dŭbu- gave Primitive Welsh Cornish Breton
dŭb (which then yielded also Primitive Welsh dæb-⸚,
Old Welsh dəb-⸚). Then, says Jackson, in the 7th-
9th centuries ŭ > ü independently in Welsh, Cornish, and Breton when next to ƀ.

Now it may very well be that the final result
shows up distinctively only in the separate languages. But surely we must suppose that the preparatory phonetics, the allophonics, were already
developing in Common British. This must date the
true change several centuries earlier, to a time
of close connection with Roman speech. As I also
imply, we must seek, too, the basis for seeing this
change as a regularity, provoked and shaped by
natural phonetic conditions.

First, we must see the development proposed as
applying in an open syllable. Hence it did not
overtake such forms as Welsh dwfr, dwfn, or Annwfn.
The general development must have been of the form
British ŭ > [X]/___β.¹ The question we must
answer, then, is what most plausibly was X?

A possible output in such an open syllable would
be a diphthong tending in articulation toward the
position of [β]; schematically, it would be of the
form [Vu̯<]. Such a diphthong would then have fallen
in with old *ou, although I agree with Jackson
(1953:277, footnote 2) in rejecting Loth's earlier
suggestion of an original ablauting pre-form
*doubo-; the latter is both unparalleled and unmotivated. But another possibility would be an
intervening [o̦], dissimilated in opening from the
[β]. The quality of this [o̦] would have been similar to that which rendered Latin ō; on the latter
see Jackson (1953:§19).

In fact, the second possibility looks much the
more likely on several grounds. The development

we are considering is probably too late for the
diphthongization envisioned; that is, such early
diphthongs would already have monophthongized.
Moreover, it would fit well with the Latin contact
chronology just suggested. This assumption also
accords well with the slender piece of documentary
evidence (Jackson 1953:275-276) which we possess in
Dove. Finally, it is easy to explain a reduction
to dəb-́ from a monophthong, but not so easy from a
diphthong.

We, therefore, suppose that [ǫ̆] and [ǭ] merged
as one quality, just as occurred in Italian for [ĕ̦]
and [ē̦]. Now the graphic history of [o̦] is well
known for the relevant period: the outcome of
Latin ō (Rufawn < Rōmānus) and Celtic ou au (budd,
Alun) alike are said to be graphic u͡ for the 4th
century. Jackson (1953:306) attributes length to
this vocalism, but actually the quality is sufficient for distinctiveness; e.g. NVDENTE CIL vii
139, and (6th century) NVDI CIIC 515, NV(D)INTI
CIIC 359. By this time old ū was [ü] (cūpa > cib,
musc'lus > misgl), and Latin ū, moreover, usually
gave Jackson's u͡ (1953:302; diēs Lūnae > Llun).
Therefore, it makes better sense to revise Jackson's tables of vowel development along lines
(though on a different theoretical basis today)
that I have outlined for the surface phonetics in
the Bulletin of the Board of Celtic Studies (1956).

We may claim then that in late Latin ū any length
could have been redundant, and the distinctive feature was really tenseness. The British Celtic evidence is of no insignificant value in leading to a
clear perception of this feature.

We are now in a position to reconstruct the
series:

dubu-	> dubu-	> dǫbu-	> dub̭(u)	> mid 6th	düb̭
	cubitus	cob̭id*	cub̭id	century	cüb̭id
	humilis	ob̭il-	ub̭il		üb̭il

It is now seen that this opening of ŭ is reminiscent
in phonetics and in chronology of a similar development in French:

ursu	> *ǫrsǫ	> 11th–12th century	urs
*tǒttu	tǫt		tut
dub(i)tare	dǫter		duter
tǒrmentum	tǫrmẽnt		turmãnt

Apparently the later closing of [ǫ] to [u] was earlier in the western French dialects; see for example Pope 91§184. This development and its chronology should be inspected in relation to the Breton evidence. It is noteworthy that under certain conditions Breton has closed vowels corresponding to Welsh o to [u]. Here again we have a seeming point of Celtic-Romance contact with shared developments.

NOTE

1. Beta here may stand for any (voiced) labial.

REFERENCES

Bulletin of the Board of Celtic Studies. 1956. 17.30–36.
Hamp, Eric P. 1972. Studies in linguistics in honor of George L. Trager.
Jackson, Kenneth. 1953. Language and history in early Britain. Edinburgh.

THE PREDICTABILITY OF THE ARTICLE IN FRENCH

JULIA HERSCHENSOHN
Cornell University

Arbitrary choice rather than predictability characterizes both traditional and transformational accounts of articles in French. In this paper I propose a more adequate analysis which predicts article distribution by making selection dependent on the same conditions as pronominalization, that is, coreference and type/token relations. According to syntactic and semantic characteristics, articles can be categorized as marked (definite) or unmarked (indefinite for count nouns and partitive for mass nouns), and can have one of two functions, generic or existential.

Traditional French grammars divide articles into three classes, definite (le, la, les), indefinite (un, une, des), and partitive (du, de la). Grevisse (1961:246) points out that 'the partitive article can be linked, by its form, to the definite article, and by its meaning, to the indefinite article'. He considers the partitive a variety of indefinite article. Wartburg and Zumthor (1958) distinguish the three categories as follows: definite--the noun is known to both speaker and addressee; indefinite--the noun is known only to the speaker; partitive--an indeterminate quantity of a divisible whole. Wagner and Pinchon (1962) indicate that choice among the three possible forms of the article depends on variables they call 'extension' (species or individual), 'precision' (definite or indefinite), and 'form' (count or mass). None of these grammars is exhaustive in describing the categories of articles, and only the last even suggests the functions that articles may fulfill.

Two possible transformational accounts of articles are the subcategorization of Dubois and Dubois-Charlier (1970), and the transformational of Baker (1973).[1] The first treatment makes article choice the selection of one of two features proposed by the phrase structure re-write rules.

> The category of the article can be rewritten either under the form of the subcategory Definite (...) or under the form of the subcategory non-Definite. These two subcategories are not defined on the basis of semantic criteria, but only as two symbols representing specific rewrite rules. (Dubois and Dubois-Charlier 1970:45-46)

The choice between definite and indefinite is based on the feature matrix of the noun, and is thus arbitrary, since there is no means for assigning the definite feature to the noun in the first place. Partitive is derived by preceding [+Def] nouns by the preposition *de*. This analysis is unable to describe the correct distribution of definite and indefinite articles in French, much less to explain that distribution.

Baker proposes that all indefinite NPs in English derive from a noun with an existential sentence embedded under it. Definiteness is introduced by a rule which applies 'whenever there is an occurrence of an identical noun (with identical reference) in an existential occurring previously in the discourse or else in the same tree' (Baker 1973:16). His argument could apply to French, and would give the following underlying structure for sentence (1).

(1) Une petite fille est entrée, et la fille a demandé à boire.
   'A little girl came in, and the girl asked for a drink.'

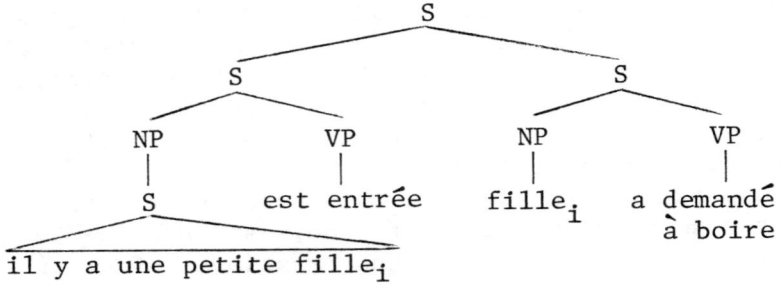

The second occurrence of <u>fille</u> would be realized as definite by Baker's rules. The semantic distinctions Baker draws are significant, and point up the similarity of definitization to pronominalization; however, his analysis is inadequate for at least two reasons. First, there is no syntactic justification for an existential sentence underlying every indefinite NP; such a proposal is based only on the semantic notion of assertion of existence. Second, his proposal must be limited to referential NPs, and even then cannot account for all instances of definite and indefinite. He is forced to suggest that 'there will have to be other rules in the grammar which have the effect of introducing the feature of definiteness' (Baker 1973:17). This suggestion violates the recoverability condition, since the various sources of definite articles would be absolutely neutralized in surface structure.

An adequate description of articles in French must first take into account the two axes of function and markedness, and then clarify the regularities of the marking system. I distinguish the generic from the existential function; the latter can be defined by two subfeatures, referential and nonreferential.[2] These classifications are based on semantic and syntactic behavior which will be described. Referential NPs are specific, that is, they have actual referents; these are the NPs that Baker would generate with existential sentences.[3] Referential NPs are usually unmarked (indefinite) in discourse initial appearance because their existence is asserted; repeated referential NPs are marked (definite) because their existence is

presupposed. However, even discourse initial NPs
may have definite articles if they are marked either
anaphorically or deictically. Nouns which exist
within the universe of 'givens' (that is, within the
immediate or extended context of the speaker) are
thus marked: 'la chaise là-bas', 'la lune', 'le
monsieur que j'ai vu' ('that chair', 'the moon',
'the man I saw'). Within this universe also are
found nouns whose existence is presupposed by other
semantic and syntactic information in the discourse,
for example, trees when the existence of a forest
has already been established.[4]

The relationship of definite and indefinite referential NPs illustrates the similarity between pronominalization and article selection. Referential NPs require articles which change from unmarked (existence asserted) to marked (existence presupposed) under the same conditions as normal 'token' pronominalization.

(2) Six chevaux tiraient un coche. Il/le coche
    arrive au château.
    'Six horses drew a coach. It/the coach
    arrives at the castle.'
(3) Il y avait du vin sur la table. Jean l'a bu./
    Jean a bu le vin.
    'There was wine on the table. John drank it/
    the wine.'

Nonreferential NPs, which have no specific referent
require the unmarked article under conditions parallel to 'type' pronominalization.[5]

(4) J'aimerais avoir une Deux-chevaux. Mon père
    m'en achetera une./ Mon père m'achetera une
    Deux-chevaux.
    'I would like to have a car. My father will
    buy me one/ a car.'

Because nonreferential articles are identical to
unmarked referential, the NPs they modify are perceived as opaque, for their referent is not obvious.[6] It is the reference status of the NP which

determines the pronoun or article form that its
repetition will take (that is, type or token).
Within the nonreferential group are found non-
specific indefinites (as in (4)) and quantified
mass nouns (which manifest only type repetition
as in (5)).

>(5) J'aimerais avoir beaucoup d'argent. Mon
>   père m'en donnera beaucoup./ Mon père me
>   donnera beaucoup d'argent.
>   'I would like to have a lot of money. My
>   father will give me a lot of it/of money.'
>   *Mon père me le donnera beaucoup./ *Mon père
>   me donnera beaucoup l'argent.
>   'My father will give me it/the money a lot.'

Negated unmarked nouns are always nonreferential
since the negation essentially denies their existence.

>(6) Je n'ai pas bu de vin./ Je n'en ai pas bu.
>   'I didn't drink any wine./ I didn't drink
>   any.' 'There was no wine such that I drank
>   it.'

For marked nouns negation does not deny the existence of the noun, but has a broader scope, including
the verb or the whole sentence.[7]

>(7) Je n'ai pas bu le vin./ Je ne l'ai pas bu.
>   'I didn't drink the wine/it.' 'There was
>   wine, but I didn't drink it.'

The analysis I propose does not distinguish a
class of partitive nouns, but rather sees the
partitive as the class of unmarked mass nouns.[8]
However, other analyses, e.g. Dubois and Dubois-
Charlier, propose a derivation of partitives from
a partitive preposition de plus the definite
article.[9] Such a derivation is supported by the
morphological form of the partitive article and by
the use of a 'partitive' de independent of the
following article, as in (8) and (9).

(8) Je n'ai pas mangé de la tarte qui était sur la table.
    'I didn't eat any of the pie that was on the table.'
(9) J'ai mangé de cette tarte.
    'I ate some of this pie.'

This hypothesis requires that unmarked mass nouns be preceded by partitive _de_ + definite article to give the correct partitive article (_du_, _de la_). This is neither semantically nor syntactically motivated: partitive nouns are semantically related to indefinite nouns by their characteristic of assertion of existence, a characteristic manifested in the shared syntactic behavior shown in sentences (2) and (3). The partitive _de_ which shows up with marked nouns in sentences (8) and (9) is not the _de_ which appears in the unmarked mass articles, since the homophonous forms of (10) and (11) behave differently when negated in (8) and (12) respectively.

(10) J'ai mangé de la tarte qui était sur la table. (marked)
     'I ate some of the pie that was on the table.'
(11) J'ai mangé de la tarte. (unmarked)
     'I ate some pie.'
(12) Je n'ai pas mangé de/*de la tarte. (unmarked)
     'I didn't eat any pie.'

Furthermore, the unmarked mass articles behave differently with quantifiers.

(13) J'ai mangé beaucoup de/*de la tarte. (unmarked)
     'I ate a lot of pie.'
(14) J'ai mangé beaucoup de la tarte qui était sur la table. (marked)
     'I ate a lot of the pie that was on the table.'

The existence of a partitive _de_ which can be used with marked referential NPs does not necessitate the derivation of unmarked mass noun articles from

that partitive _de_. Partitive _de_, like any other
preposition, can precede the marked referential
article to give _de_ + definite article (or other
determiner); the behavior of unmarked mass articles
(whose differentiation from marked ones is neutralized in certain environments, such as in (10)-(11))
is quite distinct and predictable.

An investigation of the interaction of quantifiers and negatives with unmarked articles clari-
fies the distinction between marked and unmarked,
and delineates the necessary underlying structure
of the articles as well as the modifications they
undergo in certain environments. The unmarked
article under quantification or negation is almost
always nonreferential, since the referent is never
clearly delimited (cf. (5)-(6)). The exception is
the unmarked plural (that is, count nouns) which
frequently has a referent, even under quantification.

(15) J'aimerais avoir plusieurs livres. Mon
père me donnera les livres./ Mon père me
les donnera.
'I would like to have several books. My
father will give me the books/them.'

The behavior of the adverbial pronoun _en_ demands
the existence of _de_ in the underlying form of unmarked articles (cf. (4)-(6)). Kayne (1975:30)
says 'the _de_ phrases must be analyzed as _de_ +
articleless NP'. The proposal of underlying _de_ is
further supported by the behavior of quantified
(including negated or 'zero quantified') NPs which
show nothing but _de_ in article position (cf. (12)-
(13)), and by the appearance of _de_ with postposed
NPs coreferent with _en_.

(16) J'en ai trois, de soeurs.
'I have three (of them), sisters.'

Three possible treatments of this phenomenon can be
proposed. The first is that of Kayne, who suggests
_de_ + bare NP after quantifiers. While this approach

can correctly predict pronominalization to en and postposition of de NP (as in (16)), it denies any underlying similarity between the en in (16) and that in (4) or (17). (17) could in fact correspond to sentence (9) or (10) or (11), because en can replace almost any NP preceded by de.

(17) J'en ai mangé.
'I ate some of it.'

The second treatment would have the same underlying article for quantified and unquantified unmarked articles, and produce de by means of some deletion rule. This could be formulated to change du, de la, des to de after any quantifier or negation. Postposition could apply after this to correctly predict (16). This approach acknowledges a single underlying representation for unmarked mass noun articles, but proposes an ad hoc adjustment in the environment of quantification.

The third treatment, which would correctly predict the data and also maintain the uniformity of the underlying article, is supported by independent evidence. Certain verbs (avoir besoin, avoir envie, se passer) require de before a following object or infinitive.

(18) Je peux me passer de la tarte qui est sur la table.
'I can go without the pie that is on the table.'

When the noun has an unmarked reading, however, only de appears.

(19) Je peux me passer de tarte.
'I can go without pie.'

The simplest analysis reduces de + du/de la/des to de:

(20) du/de la/des --> ∅ / de ___.

This rule can be applied to quantified nouns by assuming that quantifiers are accompanied by <u>de</u> in underlying representation. Figure (21) compares the underlying trees of (13) according to the three treatments outlined.

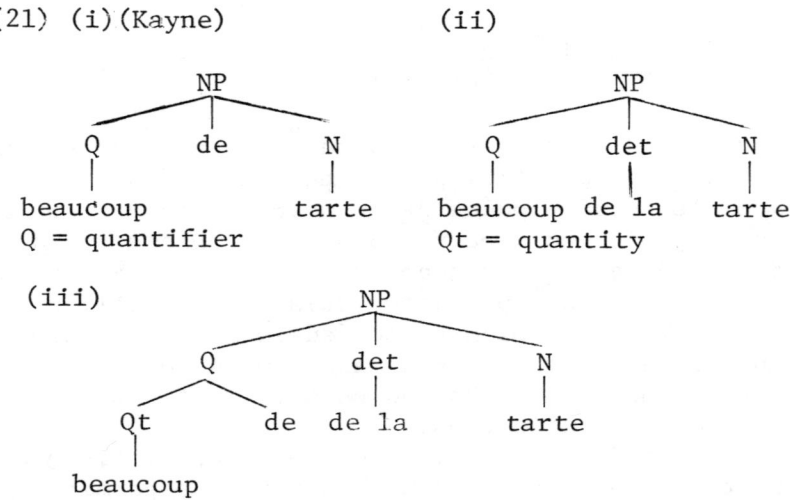

(21) (i)(Kayne)   (ii)

beaucoup   tarte   beaucoup de la tarte
Q = quantifier   Qt = quantity

(iii)

Qt de de la tarte

beaucoup

The structure proposed in (21iii) is supported by quantifiers of measure (<u>un litre de</u>, <u>50 grammes de</u>, etc.) and other quantifiers (<u>beaucoup de</u>, <u>peu de</u>, <u>assez de</u>, etc.).[10] The <u>de</u> reduction rule (20) applies to NPs preceded by <u>de</u> from any source: in (19) <u>me passer de de la tarte</u> becomes <u>me passer de tarte</u>; in (13) <u>beaucoup de de la tarte</u> becomes <u>beaucoup de tarte</u>.

There are two groups of quantifiers which seem to pose a problem to this analysis, negatives and plural quantifiers. To correctly predict negative sentences such as (6), it is necessary to propose a zero quantification (under Qt) accompanied by <u>de</u>. This is not as arbitrary as it seems, for the negative of unmarked NPs particularly focuses on their nonexistence. It is necessary to semantically mark the scope of negation specifically on the non-referential unmarked NP rather than on the whole sentence, so the underlying structure of (21iii) represents the syntactic correlate of the semantic reading. As for plural quantifiers (<u>plusieurs</u>, <u>quelques</u> and numbers), they pose a problem inasmuch as they show no surface <u>de</u> (except when their coreferent NP is postposed as in (16)). This fact could be handled by a very limited rule deleting <u>de</u> after <u>plusieurs</u>, <u>quelques</u>, and numbers, a rule which would apply after postposition. The plural quantifiers are the only ones which are consistently [+referential], whereas quantification usually entails nonreferentiality.[11]

A consequence of the proposal of this underlying structure is that the unmarked singular article, <u>un/une</u>, must be generated in quantifier position and followed by the unmarked plural article <u>des</u> in the determiner slot, since <u>un/une</u> are numbers. Perlmutter proposes this for English, pointing out that <u>a/an</u> is a reduced unstressed form of <u>one</u>. The evidence for this argument in French is even stronger, since the indefinite article and number <u>one</u> are identical in that language; moreover, it has been shown that syntactic evidence supports such a proposal, since <u>un/une</u> do indeed act like other numbers with respect to repetition and pronominalization, and since the determiner <u>des</u> provides a source for <u>en</u>. Perlmutter (1970:246) concludes by saying 'Within this framework, there is no motivation for an Article node in either deep or surface structure'.

In French there is motivation for a determiner node in surface structure, since the presence of a determiner is required with every noun, and since that determiner may or may not be an article (which may or may not be predictable). Moreover, the difference between sentences (8)/(12) and (13)/(14) is accounted for by the underlying structure proposed in (21iii) which is the input for the <u>de</u> reduction rule (20). There is no evidence to suggest that the structure proposed in (21) evolves at some intermediate point between deep and surface structure. Emonds' structure preserving hypothesis would necessitate the inclusion of a determiner node in the deep structure. The form that the determiner takes does depend on features of the noun: it can be [±generic], and if it is [-generic], it can be [±referential]. But these features alone cannot predict the correct article, so a system which would copy noun features onto the article node is inadequate. Rather, articles can be predicted only by considering three factors: the aforementioned features, coreference relations, and the markedness of the article.

While the existential function subordinates markedness to the syntactic exigencies of the noun modified, the generic function exploits the semantic difference between marked and unmarked articles. Indeed, this difference, characterized as <u>cinétisme</u> (kineticism) by Guillaume (1964), is the primary criterion for generic article selection.

(22) L'ours est un gros animal.
 'The bear is a large animal.'
(23) Un ours est un gros animal.
 'A bear is a large animal.'

Guillaume describes the article system as a binary dynamism whose two poles are the particular, represented by the indefinite article, and the general, represented by the definite article. While both articles can have a generic use, they are distinguished by different kinetic values: the definite article describes a universal class of nouns, and thereby implies the general, the plural. On the other hand Guillaume says, 'In the case when generalization is demanded of the article <u>un</u>, the result is a mitigated generalization, kinetically inflected on the side of the particular' (1964:151). The indefinite article thus gives an example which is generalized.[12] It is this same semantic difference which marks the distinction between marked and unmarked articles in all uses, although it is not always the semantic distinction which determines article choice. Indeed, the cases where the two articles can alternate are rare, since article choice is usually determined by the same semantic-syntactic criteria necessary for pronominalization.

Generic nouns, which do offer choice between marked and unmarked in certain environments, cannot be isolated from generic sentences. An explanation of generic article use awaits an adequate treatment of generic sentences. A few remarks on the use of generic nouns will indicate the complexity of the issue. The generic indefinite is usually found in subject position (23), and is more constrained with regard to tense and aspect than the definite.

(24) J'aime beaucoup le café.
   'I like coffee very much.'
(25) *J'aime beaucoup un café. J'aime beaucoup un café le matin.
   'I really like a coffee. I really like a coffee in the morning.'

Repetition of nouns in generic sentences is not parallel to that in existential sentences, since type repetition is possible with either definite or indefinite generic nouns: (26) could follow from (22) or (23).

(26) J'en ai vu un hier.
   'I saw one yesterday.'

The use of the article in generic sentences is not predictable according to the same criteria used for existential sentences.

The analysis I have presented proposes a classification of articles based on semantic features and syntactic behavior, not on the distinction between definite and indefinite. The semantic opposition embodied in the definite/indefinite alternation (characterized perhaps as kineticism) is best described as markedness, since the specific semantic reading of the article depends on its function and the referential status of the noun modified. It is referentiality which predicts for the class of non-generic nouns the correct form of the article according to the same criteria necessary for pronominalization. Moreover, the underlying structure of the determiner node correctly accounts for variation in article choice due to quantification. Given this classification and these criteria for predictability, it is possible to describe the distribution of definite and indefinite articles and to understand their semantic and syntactic role in a grammar of French.

NOTES

1. A third account is that of Postal, who says that pronouns and articles are alternate realizations of the same bundles of semantic features, so 'I one, he one, we ones, them ones, etc. underlie the surface elements I, he, we, them, etc.' (p. 219). Delorme and Dougherty present arguments against his position.

2. Cf. Rivero: 'I have argued that the notion of referentiality associated with definite NPs and that of specificity in connection with indefinite NPs should be combined into one unique aspect of NPs in general' (p. 200). This study of French bears out the conclusion she has reached for Spanish. According to my terminology, referential NPs are specific; whether they are accompanied by definite or indefinite articles depends on their markedness.

3. Referentiality corresponds to what Cole terms 'anaphoricity'.

4. Guillaume (1919) uses this example, saying that anaphoric demonstration 's'applique a tout ce qui, dans le moment ou l'on parle, fait déjà partie, à un titre quelconque, de la représentation existante dans l'esprit, c'est-à-dire (1) aux choses déjà nommées (...) (2) aux choses dont le discours a suggéré le sentiment (les arbres, par example, en parlant de la forêt)' (p. 16).

5. Type and token generally correspond to identity of sense and identity of reference respectively.

6. The difference can show up syntactically in a relative clause.
    (i) Je cherche un homme qui sait jouer du piano.
        (referential)
        'I am looking for a certain man who plays the piano.'

(ii) Je cherche un homme qui sache jouer du
     piano. (nonreferential)
     'I am looking for some man who might play
     the piano.'

7. Cf. Givon (1975:73). 'If the corresponding affirmative involves the likelihood of performing the action with respect to "any member of the type x", then the noun x appears in the negative with a "nonreferential" interpretation. On the other hand, if the corresponding affirmative involves the likelihood of performing the action with respect to a "specific token of the type x", then the noun x appears in the negative as definite. One way or another, a referential-indefinite interpretation of a previously mentioned noun is clearly inappropriate.'

8. Kayne agrees that partitives are a class of nouns, not prepositional phrases: 'There are several reasons for believing that "partitives", such as <u>des soeurs</u>, are dominated by the node NP, that is _{NP}[des soeurs], despite their initial preposition. These reasons are, first, their appearing with verbs subcategorized for "___NP"; second, their filling other typical NP positions such as that of subject and of object of a preposition; third, their being passivizable; and fourth, their occurring in the detachment construction to the left, as in <u>Des soeurs, il en a</u> (pure PPs do not readily so occur)' (p. 117).

9. Hofman et al. suggest a derivation for a class of partitive nouns, but do not describe the criteria for determining that class. Their treatment is neither clear nor consistent, but it does touch on many of the significant characteristics of article use in French. Their distinction between substantial and referential corresponds to the functional distinction I draw between generic and referential. Their difference between 'de reprise' and 'de position' is the marked/unmarked distinction. The categorization and derivation I propose adequately handle all the problems they present, and go beyond their treatment in range of applicability.

10. Kayne (p. 29) suggests that some quantifying adverbs (as in (i)) should be generated as are adverbs (as in (ii)), not as noun modifiers.
  (i) elle a trop mangé de carrottes cette année
    'she has eaten too many carrots this year'
 (ii) elle a trop applaudi
    'she applauded too much'
My analysis excludes this possibility, since at some point <u>de</u> instead of <u>des</u> must be derived in article position (Kayne proposes <u>de</u> + bare NP). Since the <u>de</u> reduction rule and the underlying structure proposed in this paper are motivated and broadly applicable, they are preferable to Kayne's adverbial solution, and point rather to his alternate movement solution: 'some rule moving <u>trop</u> and <u>très peu</u> out of the object NP and across the past participle' (p. 29).

11. This same group of plural quantifiers can usually occur as adjectives of marked referential nouns: <u>les dix/quelques étudiants</u>. This is not true of <u>un</u> and <u>plusieurs</u>, however: *<u>l'un/les plusieurs étudiants</u>.

12. Burton-Roberts draws this distinction in slightly different terms. 'Among generic articles, the definite vs. indefinite distinction is merely a surface function of a deeper semantic distinction: that between the objective class itself (say, <u>the class whale</u>) and what constitutes membership of that class ('whaleness'). These two notions are quite distinct' (p. 432).

REFERENCES

Baker, C. L. 1973. Definiteness and indefiniteness in English. Indiana University Linguistics Club reprint.
Burton-Roberts, Noel. 1976. On the generic indefinite article. Language 42.427.
Cole, Peter. 1974. Indefiniteness and anaphoricity. Language 40.665.
Coursaget-Colmerauer, Colette. 1973. Les déterminants de la nominalisation. Cahiers de linguistique 3.38.

Cushing, Steve. 1972. The semantics of sentence pronominalization. Foundations of Language 9.186.
Delorme, Evelyne, and Ray C. Dougherty. 1972. Appositive NP constructions: We, the men; we men; I, a man. Foundations of Language 8.2.
Donnellan, Keith. 1971. Reference and definite descriptions. In: Semantics. Edited by Danny and Leon Jakobovits. London: Cambridge University Press. 100.
Dubois, Jean and Françoise Dubois-Charlier. 1970. Eléments de linguistique française: Syntaxe. Paris: Larousse.
Givon, Talmy. 1975. Negation in language: Pragmatics, function, ontology. Working Papers on Language Universals. Department of Linguistics. Stanford, Calif.: Stanford University.
Grevisse, Maurice. 1961. Le bon usage. Librairie Orientaliste Paul Geuthner, Paris.
Guillaume, Gustave. 1919. Le problème de l'article et sa solution dans la langue française. Paris: Librairie Hachette.
Guillaume, Gustave. 1964. Particularisation et généralisation dans le système des articles français. In: Langage et science du langage. Paris: Nizet. 143.
Hewson, John. 1972. Article and noun in English. The Hague: Mouton.
Hofmann, T. R., Judith McA'Nulty, and Jean-Pierre Paillet. 1972. Les partitifs et la syntaxe du groupe nominal. Cahiers de linguistique 1.33.
Jackendoff, Ray. 1968. Speculations on pre-sentences and determiners. Indiana University Linguistics Club reprint.
Kayne, Richard. 1975. French syntax: The transformational cycle. Cambridge, Mass.: MIT Press.
Partee, Barbara Hall. 1972. Opacity, coreference, and pronouns. In: Semantics of natural language. Edited by D. Davidson and G. Harman. Dordrecht, Holland: Reidel.
Perlmutter, David. 1970. On the article in English. In: Progress in linguistics. Edited by Manfred Bierwisch and Karl Heidolph. The Hague: Mouton. 233.

Postal, Paul. 1969. On so-called pronouns in English. In: Modern studies in English. Edited by David Reibel and Sanford Schane. Englewood Cliffs, N.J.: Prentice-Hall. 201.
Querido, Antonio A.M. 1969. Anaphore et deixis. The Canadian Journal of Linguistics 14.91.
Rivero, María-Luisa. 1974. Definite and indefinite NPs in Spanish. In: Linguistic studies in Romance languages. Washington, D.C.: Georgetown University Press. 189.
Wagner, Robert-Leon, and Jacqueline Pinchon. 1962. Grammaire du français classique et moderne. Paris: Librairie Hachette.
Wartburg, Walther von, and Paul Zumthor. 1958. Précis de syntaxe du français contemporain. Berne: Francke.

THE VARIABLE CONSTRAINTS ON MOOD IN PUERTO RICAN-AMERICAN SPANISH

JAMES P. LANTOLF
University of Texas at San Antonio

This paper reports and discusses the findings of a questionnaire on the selection of verbal mood in embedded clauses in Spanish. The questionnaire was administered to 188 informants from the Puerto Rican community of Rochester, New York during the summer of 1976.[1]
The overwhelming majority of studies on the varieties of Spanish spoken in the United States have centered on the Spanish dialects of the Southwest, Texas, and the West Coast. To be sure, a number of excellent studies have been conducted on the Spanish communities (largely Puerto Rican and Cuban) of the East Coast. Most of these studies, however, have been descriptive and have dealt primarily with lexical borrowing, phonology, and sporadic morphological phenomena. To my knowledge, none of these investigations has attempted to draw theoretical conclusions from their empirical findings. Moreover, the East Coast studies have concentrated on the large urban centers, including New York City, Boston, and Miami. As far as I am able to discern, prior to my work, no one had previously undertaken any extensive research on the Spanish-speaking community of Rochester.[2]

Rochester is a medium-size urban center with an approximate population of 290,000 inhabitants.[3] The Hispanic community represents 8 percent (23,000) of the city's total population.[4] By far the largest element of the Hispanic community is comprised of Puerto Ricans.[5] The majority of Puerto Ricans have migrated to Rochester directly from the island and not as one may suspect, from New York City. Furthermore, the Rochester community is primarily comprised of people from areas other than San Juan. Of those responding to the questionnaire, not a single informant listed San Juan as his point of origin.[6] The majority of the informants, if not native Rochesterians, were born in Ponce, Guayama, Cayey, Mayagüez, or the small villages of the interior.[7]

There may be some who are suspicious of the validity of data gleaned from questionnaires in this day of extensive personal interviews and data gathering with the aid of tape recorders. Nevertheless, I believe that a questionnaire continues to serve as a valid means of data gathering. I do not claim that because an individual selects one variant over another on a questionnaire, he will always use that form in speech. People are usually on their best linguistic behavior when they recognize that their language skills are being probed by an outsider. I do claim, on the other hand, that if an informant chooses a particular variant on a questionnaire, he at the very least possesses knowledge of that variant in his linguistic competence. Therefore, I do not pretend to be discussing in this paper current and consistent usage in Puerto Rican Spanish; rather, I take the position that the selected forms reflect a continued awareness, or lack thereof, of mood contrast in the linguistic knowledge of the informants.

As part of the study, the informants were asked to complete the biographical data sheet given in (1). A summary of the demographic data is presented in (2).

(1)

Edad:
Sexo:
Lugar de nacimiento:
Lugar de nacimiento de sus padres:
País de sus antepasados:
Tiempo pasado en los Estados Unidos:
Su primera lengua hablada:
Lengua hablada en casa:
Lenguas estudiadas en la escuela:
Empleo:
Empleo de sus padres:
Empleo de su cónyuge:
Educación:
  Primaria: 1 2 3 4 5 6
  Secundaria: 7 8 9 10 11 12
  Universidad: 1 2 3 4 5 6 7 8

(2)

Age 12-19:	76	41%	Sex M:	54	29%
20-40:	55	29%	F:	133	71%
40-67:	57	30%			

Residency in the United States
  6 mo.-1 year 10 mo.:   30   16%
  2 years-18 years: 158   84%
Language spoken at home
  Spanish: 145   77%
  Spanish and English: 43   23%
Social Class*
  Middle: 62   33%
  Lower: 126   67%

*Social class was computed on the basis of education and occupation or of parents' occupation if the informant was a student.

One of the concerns of linguists over the past decade has been the investigation of mood contrast in Spanish in light of the generative paradigm (see Hadlich 1971, Rivero 1972, Lozano 1972, Hooper and Terrell 1974, Hooper 1974, Kline 1974, Terrell 1976).[8] The studies cited here are largely theoretical in nature without much attention given to empirical verification in the speech community.

Recently, however, García and Terrell (1974) conducted an investigation of mood in the Spanish of Mexican and Mexican-American school children of El Paso, Texas and Ciudad Juárez, Mexico. Their intent was to verify whether or not the choice of mood in Spanish is subject to linguistic and extra-linguistic constraints and whether or not the constraints correlated with the semantic notions of assertion, presupposition, doubt, and command.

García and Terrell limited their work to one segment of the speech community: school children between the ages of 13 and 19. Although the present study is similar to that of García and Terrell in that it considers the selection of mood within a semantic framework, it is broader in its scope of extra-linguistic constraints on mood selection. Additionally, we are able to undertake a comparative analysis of the two dialects, which, though geographically divergent, share an important common feature: the omnipresence of English and the American culture. The comparison of data is an essential step toward the development of a unified dialectology of the varieties of Spanish spoken in the United States called for by Ornstein and Valdés-Fallis (1976).

The most widely held theory of the subjunctive in Spanish is that put forth in works such as Ramsey (1956) and which is frequently used in pedagogical explanations of mood. This theory is predicated on the notion that the mood of an embedded verb is syntactically determined by the features of the verb in the matrix S of a sentence.[9] The lesser known theory, at least outside of linguistic circles, is that proposed by Lenz (1944) and discussed by Gili y Gaya (1969) and more recently by Hooper and Terrell (1974). This theory contends that the use of subjunctive or indicative mood 'is correlated with what the sentence as a whole expresses about the truth of a proposition included in the sentence' (Hooper and Terrell 1974:484).

Hooper and Terrell (1974) classify sentence types into the semantic categories given in (3):

(3)

Assertion	
Assertion:	Juan viene
	'John is coming'
	Creo que Juan viene
	'I think John is coming'
Reporting:	José dice que Juan viene
	'Joe says John is coming'
Presupposition	
Mental act:	Me doy cuenta de que Juan viene
	'I realize that John is coming'
Comment:	Me alegro de que Juan venga
	'I am happy John is coming'
Doubt	Dudo que Juan venga
	'I doubt John is coming'
Volition	Quiero que Juan venga
	'I want John to come'

For each item on the questionnaire the informants were asked to circle the verb form which they believed to be the most natural or which they would be likely to use.[10] What follows is an analysis of the results as well as a comparison of the Puerto Rican-American data, where possible, with the data uncovered by García and Terrell (1974). To be sure, we cannot make a point by point comparison of the two studies, since in the present study, the informants were to make a choice between two variants, while in the García-Terrell project, the informants were to judge the acceptability of a particular utterance which contained a verb form in either the indicative or subjunctive mood. Any conclusions will therefore be based on overall trends uncovered by the two studies.[11]

In (4) we see the average rate of selection of indicative mood in embedded verbs by the Puerto Rican-American informants accompanied by the average acceptance rates of indicative discovered by García and Terrell.[12] I include the PR-A (12-19) group in (4) for two reasons: this group is the most directly comparable to the García-Terrell study, and as we shall discuss, age is an important

(4)

	PR-A*	PR-A (12-19)	M	M-A
Volition	4%	9%	8%	26%
Doubt	14%	20%	25%	47%
Presupposition	25%	36%	48%	56%

*PR-A = Puerto Rican American; PR-A (12-19) = Puerto Rican American ages 12-19; M = Mexican; M-A = Mexican American

extra-linguistic constraint on the selection of mood.

As is readily apparent in (4), the volitional sentences represent the least favored class with respect to the acceptability of the indicative mood. Proceeding down the list, we note a marked increase in the percentages favoring the indicative. On the basis of (4), we conclude that a weakening in mood contrast is underway in the Puerto Rican-American dialect the further one advances from the semantic category of volition. This also is the case for the Mexican dialects, although the loss of contrast seems to be more intense in Mexican-American Spanish.

Volition. Within the class of volition, the tendency, as has been mentioned, is to maintain the subjunctive mood in embedded verbs. This, in all likelihood, is due to the fact that volition is closely related to the category of 'imperative', the bastion of the subjunctive mood (García and Terrell 1974). Ramsey (1956:415) remarks that 'the principal use of the subjunctive is after verbs expressing an action calculated to cause another person or thing to act'.

While there is not a great deal of difference in the percentages of indicative selection for volitional sentences, it is worth pointing out that some sentences may have been seen as more strongly volitional than others (i.e. closer to the notion of imperative). This may account for the slightly higher percentages favoring the indicative in sentences (5) and (6).

(5) Piden que lo pagamos ahora mismo 'They ask that we pay for it right away'	10%	14%
(6) Sugiero que lo haces mañana 'I suggest that you do it tomorrow'	7%	11%
(7) Es necesario que llegas antes de las ocho 'It is necessary that you arrive before eight'	0%	0%
(8) Quiero que me lo pagas 'I want you to pay me'	1%	4%

Note: The percentages to the right indicate the rate of selection of indicative by the Puerto Rican group as a whole and by the younger members of the community, i.e. PR-A (12-19).

García and Terrell uncovered a similar trend in this semantic category. That is, slightly more than an average of 41 percent of the Mexican Americans accepted (5) and (6), while only 17 percent and 27 percent of this group approved of sentences (7) and (8) respectively.

To assess more accurately the condition of the mood system in Puerto Rican-American Spanish, the questionnaire was administered to 20 natives of Seville, Spain, all of whom were associated with the University either as students or faculty members, and all of whom were under the age of 30. The Spanish informants consistently selected the subjunctive mood for each sentence in the volitional category. We conclude that overall for volitional sentences the Puerto Rican Americans show a strong tendency to preserve the use of subjunctive as do the Mexican Americans. However, the Puerto Rican group appears to be somewhat more consistent in rejecting the indicative for these sentences than do the Mexican-American speakers.

Doubt. There is a relationship between doubt sentences and assertions which shows up under negation. Sentences pertaining to one semantic class can switch categories under the influence of negation, as illustrated in (9) and (10).

(9a) Es seguro que irán
'It is certain they will go'
(9b) No es seguro que vayan
'It is not certain they will go'
(10a) Dudo que vengan mañana
'I doubt they are coming tomorrow'
(10b) No dudo que vendrán mañana
'I do not doubt they will come tomorrow'

Sentence (9a) switches from an assertion with the embedded verb in the indicative to a doubt type sentence (9b) with the embedded verb in the subjunctive mood. In the sentences of (10), the opposite effect is achieved under the influence of negation. That is, (10a), a doubt sentence in the affirmative, becomes an assertion (10b) in the negative.

Terrell (1976) points out, however, that negation does not a priori cause a sentence to switch semantic classes. The negation of (11a), an assertive proposition, does not cause the embedded verb to change mood.

(11a) Juan cree que fueron
'John believes they went'
(11b) Juan no cree que fueron
'John does not believe they went'

According to Terrell (1976:230), in sentence (11b) the speaker is affirming as true a proposition which another speaker has doubted. Hence, the sentence remains as an assertion and the embedded verb remains in the indicative, even though the matrix verb has been negated.

As can be observed on the basis of (4) above, the indicative is more vibrant in the doubt class of sentences than it is in the volitional types. García and Terrell attribute this phenomenon to the fact that some of the sentences of the doubt category which prescriptively call for subjunctive are

in reality more affirmative than doubtful. In the
absence of normative pressure, speakers are freer
to react to the partially assertive nature of such
sentences and choose the indicative mood.[13]

Sentences (12) and (13) present an interesting
display of percentages.

(12) Es muy dudoso que voy con Uds. esta noche 'It is very doubtful that I am going with you tonight'	8%	30%
(13) Dudo que van a estar muy felices con este regalo 'I doubt that they are going to be very happy with this gift'	30%	37%

For the community as a whole, (12) expresses a
higher degree of doubt than does (13), which was
apparently felt to impart some degree of assertion. The younger speakers, on the other hand,
seemingly detected some assertion in both sentences. For the Mexican Americans, 54 percent
accepted (13) with the indicative, while 24 percent preferred (12) in the indicative mood. Thus,
although the percentages of the two groups differ,
the respective relationship between the two sentences is consistent for both dialects.

In sentences like (14), the embedded verb frequently appears in the indicative mood (Ramsey
1956:414).

    (14) Espero que acabas   1%   7%
          'I hope you finish'

As the evidence indicates, however, the Puerto
Rican informants reacted strongly to the doubt expressed by the sentence, and to no significant degree did they respond to any assertive properties
present.[14] All 20 Spanish informants likewise
viewed the sentence as conveying uncertainty toward
the proposition in question and chose the subjunctive mood.

From the comparative standpoint, the most noteworthy feature of the doubt sentences is illustrated by sentence (15).

(15) Es posible que comprarán una   14%   19%
     televisión a colores
     'It is possible that they will
     buy a color television'

According to the findings of García and Terrell, 43 percent of the Mexicans and 60 percent of the Mexican Americans accepted (15) as it stands, with the embedded verb marked for subsequence. García and Terrell conclude that the high rate favoring the indicative points to a linguistic constraint on the choice of mood at work in the Mexican-American dialect especially. In this dialect, subsequence exerts a much stronger influence than does subjunctive, which has no formal marking for future. This is clearly not the case for Puerto Rican-American Spanish, as is illustrated by the low percentages favoring indicative mood. In the Puerto Rican dialect, the subjunctive form more than likely plays a dual role, conveying both mood and subsequence.

For the same sentence (15) all 20 Spanish informants selected the subjunctive option. The Puerto Rican-American variety of Spanish is closer to Iberian Spanish in not being constrained in mood selection by subsequence than it is to its American sister, the dialect of the Mexican Americans.

Presupposition. Of the three semantic categories calling for subjunctive, presupposition is the closest to assertion. It is important, however, that we distinguish between what Hooper (1974) refers to as weak and strong presupposition. Without such a distinction, there appear to be some exceptions to the generalization made by Hooper and Terrell (1974) to the effect that indicative forms are used in assertions and subjunctive forms in all other types of propositions. According to Hooper, sentences of strong presupposition contain a complement which is always accepted as true, as in (16):

(16) Es triste que se vaya tan pronto
     'It is sad that you are going so early'

In weak presuppositions, on the other hand, the subordinate clause need not be presupposed to be true, as in (17).

(17) ¿Supiste que no habías dicho la verdad?
     'Did you find out that you hadn't told the truth?'

On one reading, (17) questions the matrix and the complement is presupposed to be true. On another reading, the speaker questions the truth of the complement clause itself (Terrell 1976). Hooper concludes that sentences containing weak presuppositions (mental acts) are assertions and therefore favor the indicative mood in embedded clauses.

Assuming that Hooper's conclusion is accurate, we would expect the greatest degree of variation in the selection of mood to occur in presuppositional sentences, since within this category there is already some instability. Hooper and Terrell (1974) go so far as to predict that if the mood system in Spanish begins to break down, it will originate in the presupposition class. The result of such a change would be a bipartite system in which the indicative would be used for conveying facts, with the subjunctive reserved for everything else. The percentages given in (4) tend to substantiate the fact that a change is indeed underway in the presuppositional class in favor of the indicative. To be sure, there is some degree of variation as we will point out in the following discussion.

Sentence (18) with the indicative option was the least favored by the Puerto Rican community in general. This is probably because the sentence has a connotation which could place it in the volitional category.

    (18) Es inútil que yo te contesta   6%   18%
        'It is useless for me to answer
          you'

The informants may have been reacting to the volitional quality in choosing such a low percentage of indicative.

  Sentences (19)-(21) express a good deal of emotional involvement on the part of the speaker (i.e. strong presupposition) and consequently the informants preferred the subjunctive mood over the indicative.[15]

    (19) ¡Qué ridículo que se acuesta tan   7%   15%
          temprano!
        'How ridiculous that he goes to
          bed so early'
    (20) Es triste que se va tan pronto   8%   18%
        'It is sad that he is going so
          soon'
    (21) Me preocupa el que estamos los   11%   11%
          dos solos
        'The fact that the two of us
          are alone worries me'

  Sentences (22) and (23) are somewhat enigmatic regarding the respective percentages of indicative selection.

    (22) ¡Qué bueno que te quedas con   54%   46%
          nosotros!
        'How good that you are remain-
          ing with us'
    (23) Es bueno que Uds. han llegado a   15%   30%
          tiempo
        'It is good that you have
          arrived on time'

One would expect (22) to impart a stronger comment than (23) and therefore favor the subjunctive to a higher degree.

If we consider the entire age gradient for sentence (22) we find that a greater percentage of the older age groups preferred the indicative than did the younger speakers. For the 20-40 group, 56 percent chose the indicative, while 63 percent of the over 40 age group selected the indicative mood. We would have predicted the lower percentages of indicative selection to have correlated with the higher age levels and the higher percentages to have done the same with the lower age group. The facts do not show this to be the case. All 20 Spanish informants chose the subjunctive for both (22) and (23). I am obliged to leave this rather curious turn of events unresolved for the time being.

The sentences which display the highest frequency of indicative selection are those which have an embedded verb marked for preterite tense, as can be seen in the following sentences.

(24) Me sorprendió que ustedes no   34%   50%
     pudieron ayudarnos con el plan
     'It surprised me that you could
     not help us with our plan'
(25) Se alegró de que no llovió   38%   57%
     'He was happy that it didn't
     rain'
(26) El que se negó a comentar prueba 72%   82%
     que sabe algo
     'The fact that he refused to com-
     ment proves that he knows
     something'

García and Terrell similarly discovered high rates of acceptability for sentences with the embedded verb in the preterite rather than imperfect subjunctive.[16] They contend this is because the subjunctive has no formal marking for preterite just as it has no formal indicator of subsequence. Moreover, presuppositions deal with facts, just as assertions do, and the factual nature of sentences (24) to (26) is further underscored by the past tense marking. With the exception of (26), the

Spanish informants unanimously preferred the verb form in the imperfect subjunctive.

For (26) both Puerto Rican groups favored the indicative to an overwhelming degree. On the other hand, for sentence (21), which also contains <u>el que</u>, both groups strongly favored the subjunctive. Although the rate of indicative selection for sentence (27) is between that found for (21) and (26), it is noticeably closer to the former than it is to the latter.

> (27) Siempre me sorprende el hecho de   18%   48%
>   que Juan trabaja
>   'The fact that John works always
>   surprises me'

We attribute the differences among the three sentences to two factors: (26) contains an embedded verb in the preterite and (21) and (27) impart stronger comments which are primarily carried by their respective matrix verbs, <u>preocuparse</u> and <u>sorprender</u>. If this is true, then <u>el que</u> is not used by itself in sentences in which the speaker wishes to make a strong comment about a particular proposition, and therefore, such sentences are seen as weak presuppositions.[17] This viewpoint gains support from the fact that seven of the 20 Spaniards opted for the indicative form <u>negó</u> in (26), while all 20 chose the subjunctive for both (21) and (27). It is also likely that for Puerto Rican-Americans and perhaps for other speakers as well, <u>el que</u> and <u>el hecho de que</u> do not occur regularly in normal discourse. When these expressions do appear, unless they cooccur with some other expression which indicates strong comment, it is in sentences containing weak presuppositions, which call for the indicative.

We conclude for this section that Puerto Rican-American Spanish shares the linguistic constraint on the selection of mood imposed by preterite with the Mexican-American dialect discussed by García and Terrell. What is more, the subjunctive is substantially diminished in frequency of occurrence in the presuppositional category more than in any other semantic class.

Assertion. A brief look at assertion reveals that as in the case of the Mexican-American dialect, Puerto Rican-American Spanish consistently uses the indicative in dependent clauses. The average rate of preference is given in (28).

(28)			
PR-A	PR-A (12-19)	M	M-A
10%	14%	19%	29%

The discrepancies in percentages, though relatively slight, nevertheless may provide a further indication of the more advanced state of the breakdown in mood contrast in the Mexican dialects.

Extra-linguistic constraint. In addition to the linguistic constraint on the selection of mood discussed above, the present study also uncovered an important extra-linguistic constraint: age.[18] In (29) we observe the average percentages of selection of indicative for each semantic category correlated with the three age groups utilized in the study.

(29)		Presupposition	Doubt	Volition
I	12-19	36%	20%	9%
II	20-40	20%	10%	2%
III	40-67	22%	7%	1%

As can be seen, group I consistently chose the indicative with the greatest frequency.

While we will not consider each semantic class in detail, as we have done in the previous section, there are several sentences which clearly illustrate the potency of the age constraint. Sentence (27), repeated here as (30), shows a marked difference between groups II and III on the one hand and group I on the other.

(30) Siempre me sorprende el hecho   I   II   III
     de que Juan trabaja   48% 12%   6%

The reasons for the disparity have already been examined in our discussion of presupposition.

For presuppositional sentences containing an embedded verb in the preterite aspect, the range of percentages given in (31) discloses that while preterite is an important constraint on the choice of mood for the Puerto Rican-American dialect as a whole, it is much more influential in the language of the younger segment of the community.

(31) Se alegró de que no llovió   57% 33% 30%
     Me sorprendió que ustedes no   50% 29% 32%
        pudieron ayudarnos con el plan
     El que se negó a comentar prueba   82% 67% 65%
        que sabe algo

Sentence (18) repeated here as (32) also provides a significant series of percentages.

(32) Es inútil que yo te contesta   18%   0%   0%

Apparently, the older informants (II and III) reacted more strongly to the volitional quality of (32) than did the younger group I, which saw the sentence as somewhat closer to the notion of assertion than to volition.

Within the category of doubt, the sentence for which we note the greatest discrepancy between I, and II and III is (33).

(33) Es muy dudoso que voy con   30%   0%   0%
     ustedes esta noche

Group I did not vary as sharply in its attitude toward sentences that supposedly express doubt as did the other age groups, as is illustrated by comparing (33) with (34).

(34) Dudo que van a estar muy   37% 30% 22%
     felices con este regalo

Group I viewed both sentences as more assertive than did either of the other groups, which considered only (34) as having any assertive properties.

One of the primary motives for conducting research into the mood system of Puerto Rican-American Spanish was to empirically test a hypothesis on syntactic change in natural language. The hypothesis was predicated on the notion that the mood of an embedded verb in a subordinate clause is morphologically predictable from the features of the matrix verb.

If indeed mood were syntactically determined by the matrix verb of a sentence, then in volitional constructions especially, the subjunctive would be redundant (i.e. carry no meaning), since its appearance could be expected with reasonable certainty each time a verb like _querer_, _preferir_, or _pedir_ occurred in the independent clause. Bull (1965:175) remarks that indicative and subjunctive moods can be in functional opposition only when both may appear in the same syntactic pattern. When only one mood is permissible, the moods are in complementary distribution, and therefore, the modal suffix does not perform a contrastive function. Its usage in this case depends entirely on arbitrary conventions. Green (1972:82) argues that according to the axiom of information theory which presupposes that a unit has a certain freedom of occurrence, the subjunctive mood in most instances carries no meaning whatsoever, since its appearance is almost always predetermined by the matrix verb.[19]

In this paper, we hold the view that language comprises not only the linguistic system utilized by a speech community, but also the linguistic norm of the community, which consists of language customs and traditions and which is determined by historical, political, and sociological factors (Coseriu 1958). Linguistic norm is as integral an aspect of an individual's competence as is system and must be learned along with the system.[20]

If the members of a speech community lose contact with the norm of their language over an extended period of time, we would expect the nonfunctional aspects of the language to begin to change. It was postulated that the variety of Spanish spoken in Rochester, New York was rife for change, because its speakers are immersed in an English-dominant society and, therefore, experience less intense normative pressures than those speakers who are in a Spanish-dominant society.

Given the above sociological setting, we would expect a syntactically generated mood system to begin to weaken noticeably in the area where contrast is virtually nonexistent, volitional sentences. On the other hand, we would not look for the contrast to blur in sentences like (35) where the contrast is supposedly functional.[21]

(35) Mamá se alegra de que papá vuelva-vuelve
'Mom is happy that dad is returning'

The evidence clearly indicates, however, that change is underway in precisely the area where the syntactic-based theory claims that contrast should be maintained. Furthermore, the area in which the subjunctive mood is most vibrant is where there is a minimum of contrast. This situation seemingly disproves the widely held notion that language tends to change in those areas where segments have become nonfunctional. The difficulty here, however, is not with the functional yield theory, but with the theory of mood. If mood is not syntactically determined by the matrix verb but is dependent upon the type of information the speaker desires to convey about a specific proposition, then mood is meaningful even in sentences of the volitional category.

We contend that the evidence presented in this paper provides significant empirical support for the semantic theory of mood.

Conclusions.
(1) The evidence empirically supports the semantic theory of mood as proposed by Lenz, and Hooper and Terrell.

(2) The selection of mood in Puerto Rican-American Spanish is subject to variable constraints. With one notable exception (subsequence) the linguistic constraints coincide with those of Mexican-American Spanish. The indicative mood is preferred most often in assertive propositions and least often in volitional constructions. In the doubt category, the indicative is favored more than in volitional types but less than in presuppositions.

(3) Within the volitional category, the closer one approaches to the notion of imperative, the less likely the indicative is to be chosen. In doubt constructions, some sentences express propositions which are closer to the notion of assertion and therefore contain an embedded verb in the indicative. Other sentences are seen as truly dubitative, and the subjunctive mood is preferred. In the presuppositional classification, the choice of mood is correlated with the relative intensity of the comment made about each proposition.

(4) There are similarities and differences regarding the linguistic constraints on mood selection between Puerto Rican-American Spanish on the one hand, and Mexican-American Spanish on the other. While preterite constrains the preference for subjunctive in both dialects, subsequence operates as a constraint in the Mexican-American dialect only.

(5) Age functions as an extra-linguistic constraint on the choice of mood in Puerto Rican-American Spanish. In each semantic class, the younger speakers consistently prefer the indicative to a greater extent than the older members of the speech community.

(6) García and Terrell raise the issue of whether or not we are dealing with an instance of linguistic change: 'Either mood system is variable at certain points but usually static for Mexican speakers while Mexican Americans are losing the mood contrast. Or the mood system is variable for all speakers and Mexican Americans being least subject to normative pressure represent the most advanced

state of these tendencies'. As is apparent from the above discussion, we contend that the mood system of Spanish is in the process of change in Puerto Rican and Mexican dialects of the United States. There is evidence to sustain this position.

Lorenzo (1966:123) discusses what he calls <u>la decadencia del subjunctivo</u> in the Spanish of Madrid. He points out that when speakers have an option of using a construction with the subjunctive or one without, they most frequently choose the latter alternative. Instead of using the more literary <u>acaso vaya</u> 'maybe I will go' <u>madrileños</u> prefer <u>a lo mejor voy</u>. In place of <u>Cuando tenga tiempo, te escribiré</u> 'When I have time, I will write to you' they use <u>Si tengo tiempo, te escribo</u> 'If I have time, I'll write to you'. According to Lorenzo, a great many cases in which the subjunctive had been preferred in older forms of the language are no longer acceptable today, largely because the subjunctive constructions have been supplanted by alternate means of expression.

If the subjunctive mood is giving way to alternate forms with the indicative in places like Madrid, it would not be at all surprising to discover that mood contrast is weakening in areas where Spanish-speaking communities are besieged by the dominant English-speaking culture of the United States. We conclude that Puerto Rican-American Spanish and its Mexican-American sister dialect are in the process of losing mood contrast in favor of the indicative. The change is more intense in the Mexican-American dialect than in the Puerto Rican variety, because Mexican Americans have coexisted for a much longer period of time with the English-speaking communities of the United States, and therefore, no doubt experience a substantially diminished degree of normative pressure.

NOTES

1. This paper represents one aspect of a larger project on the Spanish of Rochester, New York. In addition to mood contrast, the project investigates

preterite--present perfect contrast, S V versus
V S word order in questions, focus and free word
order, <u>tú</u> versus <u>usted</u>, and the <u>se me</u> construction.
Research for this study was sponsored by a fellowship and grant-in-aid from the Research Foundation
of the State University of New York. I would like
to thank Professor Tracy Terrell whose insightful
comments have effectively contributed to the final
form of this paper.

2. The remarks on the studies of Spanish in the
United States are based upon Teschner et al. (1975).

3. U.S. Bureau of the Census. Census of population: 1970. Vol. 1, Characteristics of the
population. Part 34, New York. Washington, D.C.:
United States Printing Office, 1973.

4. Morton Hoffman and Company. An analysis of
the housing assistance needs of lower income households and characteristics of selected other households groups city of Rochester as of October 1975.
Prepared for Bureau of Planning, Rochester Department of Community Development.

5. Other groups represented in the community of
Rochester include Cubans, Dominicans, and Chileans.
These groups, however, are widely dispersed throughout the region and were difficult to contact in
sufficiently large numbers within the time allotted for the completion of the study.

6. This is a significant point, because speakers from San Juan have a higher probability of having been influenced by English prior to arriving on
the Mainland than do those from other regions of
Puerto Rico (see Pérez Sala 1973 and Granda
Gutiérrez 1968).

7. In addition to the data obtained from the
biographical section of the questionnaire, more
general demographic and sociological data were obtained from interviews with political, social, educational, and religious leaders of the community.
I would like to single out for their special
assistance Rev. Laurence Tracy, Ms. Ursula Piñero,
and Mr. Julio Vásquez.

8. The recent interest in mood in Spanish seems
to have been stimulated by Lakoff's (1968) work on
abstract verbs and the subjunctive mood in Latin.

9. The subjunctive mood is largely restricted to use in embedded clauses which function as noun phrases, adverb phrases, or adjective phrases. The subjunctive does, of course, appear in independent sentences, as in commands ¡Venga acá! 'Come here!' or in sentences that express doubt, such as Tal vez vaya con nosotros 'Perhaps he is going with us'.

Analyses like those of Lakoff (1968), Hadlich (1971), and Rivero (1972) derive independent sentences from underlying subordinating constructions using abstract verbs or some sort of abstract feature akin to Hadlich's C feature for commands.

10. Although the questionnaire contains several sentences with adjectival or adverbial phrases, these sentences present some special problems which we cannot consider in the present paper.

11. García and Terrell include a greater number of sentences in their research than does the present study.

12. The Mexicans in the García and Terrell study were school-age students from Ciudad Juárez who would likely feel more pressure from English influence than would their peers in Mexico City.

13. We will again raise the issue of norm in more detail.

14. Gili y Gaya (1969) includes sentences such as (14) in the category which he labels as 'potencial', because they do not affirm the reality of an event or fact.

15. The remarks on the emotive quality of comment are based on information imparted to me by my native assistant who contributed to the formulation of the questionnaire. The assistant was a 27-year-old native-born Cuban who has lived in the United States for 10 years.

16. I do not include the García and Terrell sentences here because they utilize different sentences in their study, with the exception of (24).

17. According to Ramsey (1956:446), when el que and que function as subject of a sentence, the embedded verb generally appears in the indicative

mood. That is, the sentence is seen as making a comment on a proposition taken to be true.

18. Other extra-linguistic factors such as language spoken at home, and years of residency in the United States did not productively correlate with the choice of mood. Nevertheless, these extra-linguistic variables were found to relate to data uncovered in other sections of the questionnaire, such as tú versus usted.

19. Green contends that the subjunctive, although redundant, functions as a reminder of the type of clause we are treating.

20. The Spanish phonological system will tolerate such verb form as *andé and *sabo. The norm for the Spanish-speaking world, on the other hand, dictates that the 1st per sg pret of andar appear as anduve and the 1st per sg pres form of saber appear as sé. Spanish children, as can be expected, analogize on the basis of the vast number of regular verbs in the language and therefore, tend to produce the phonologically possible, but unacceptable forms cited. They must then somehow acquire the correct forms of the verbs. This process can take place through parental correction, schooling, or more importantly, peer-group pressure.

21. Bull (1965) maintains that variation in sentences like (35) is due to idiolectal differences, in which some speakers are committed to the indicative and others to the subjunctive. He believes that the subjunctive is especially common in literary language.

REFERENCES

Bull, William E. 1965. Spanish for teachers. New York: Ronald Press.
Coseriu, Eugenio. 1958. Sincronía, diacronía e historia: el problema del cambio lingüístico. Montevideo: Universidad de la República.
García, M. E., and T. Terrell. 1974. Is the use of mood in Spanish subject to variable constraints? Paper presented at the Fifth Annual

Symposium on Romance Linguistics. Ann Arbor: University of Michigan.

Garner, R. 1971. Presupposition in philosophy and linguistics. In: Studies in linguistic semantics. Edited by C. Fillmore and D. T. Langendoen. New York: Holt, Rinehart and Winston. 23-44.

Gili y Gaya, S. 1969. Curso superior de sintaxis española. Barcelona: Bibliograf.

Granda Gutiérrez, G. de. 1968. Transculturación e interferencia lingüística en el Puerto Rico contemporáneo. Bogotá: Instituto Caro y Cuervo.

Green, J. N. 1972. Spanish conditionals: Systems or rules? Archivum Linguisticum 3.75-85.

Hadlich, R. 1971. A transformational grammar of Spanish. Englewood Cliffs, N.J.: Prentice-Hall.

Hooper, J. 1974. On assertive predicates. Syntax and semantics IV. New York: Seminar Press.

Hooper, J., and T. Terrell. 1974. A semantic based analysis of mood in Spanish. Hispania 57.484-494.

Klein, P. 1974. Observations on the semantics of mood in Spanish. Unpublished dissertation. University of Washington.

Lakoff, R. 1968. Abstract syntax and Latin complementation. Cambridge, Mass.: MIT Press.

Lenz, R. 1944. La oración y sus partes; estudios de gramática general y castellana. 4th ed. Madrid: Revista de filología española.

Lorenzo, E. 1966. El español de hoy, lengua en ebullición. Madrid: Gredos.

Lozano, A. G. 1972. Subjunctives, transformations, and features. Hispania 55.76-90.

Ornstein, J., and G. Valdés-Fallis. 1976. On defining and describing U.S. varieties of Spanish: Implications of dialect contact. Paper presented at the Third Annual Colloquium on Hispanic and Luso-Brazilian Linguistics. Oswego, New York.

Pérez Sala, P. 1973. Interferencia lingüística del inglés en el español hablado en Puerto Rico: Un estudio sobre la sintaxis de los puertorriqueños. Hato Rey: Inter-American University Press.

Ramsey, M. A. 1956. A textbook of modern Spanish. Revised by R. Spaulding. New York: Holt, Rinehart and Winston.

Rivero, M. L. 1972. La concepción de los modos en la *Gramática* de Andrés Bello y los verbos abstractos en la gramática generativa. Revista de lingüística teórica y aplicada 9.

Terrell, T. 1976. Assertion and presupposition in Spanish. In: Current studies in Romance linguistics. Edited by M. Luján and F. Hensey. Washington, D.C.: Georgetown University Press. 221-245.

Teschner, R. V., G. D. Bills, and J. R. Craddock. 1975. Spanish and English of the United States Hispanos: A critical, annotated, linguistic bibliography. Arlington, Va.: Center for Applied Linguistics.

MORPHOLOGICAL REGULARIZATION
IN THE VERBAL PARADIGM
OF MODERN FRENCH

YVES-CHARLES MORIN
Université de Montréal

1. Introduction. We observe in modern French alternations between fleeting œ̇ (in French 'œ muet') and ε, where fleeting œ̇ is an abstract element which may be realized as œ or have no phonetic manifestation, depending partly upon the context, and partly upon stylistic conditions. This alternation is observed both in the derivational morphology, e.g. hotel [otεl]/hotelier [otœlye] 'inn/inn-keeper', bonnet [bɔnε]/bonnetier [bɔnœtye] 'cap/hosier', and in the inflectional morphology, e.g. je jette [žœžεt]/vous jetez [vušte]/vous le jetez [vulžœte] 'I throw/you throw/you throw it'.
We shall not be concerned mainly here with the conditions which account for the realization of fleeting œ̇; we shall instead analyze only the alternations between œ̇ and ε. Even though Selkirk (1972) and Dell (1973) analyze it as a phonological rule, we shall show that it should be more accurately described as a morphological process. This process, as we shall show, involves several morphophonological rules, one of which is a variable rule which shares the same properties of variability as have been observed with (natural) phonological rules. This contradicts directly a claim made by Stampe (1973), and accepted by most tenants of natural

generative phonology, e.g. Hooper (1975:544), that
morphophonological rules (or 'acquired' phonological rules) cannot be optional.

2. On the nature of fleeting œ̇. In this section
we shall be concerned briefly with the phonological
identity of fleeting œ̇. The traditional definition
of fleeting œ̇ is historical: it is the modern reflex of a former shwa. We know that in the historical evolution of French, some unstressed vowels disappeared completely, e.g. Lat. tabula > F. table,
whereas some were reduced first and then subjected
to various syncopes and apocopes, e.g. Lat. *veracu
(*verariu ?) > O.F. verai > F. vrai 'true'. In
modern French historical shwas may have three
states.

(a) They have completely disappeared, e.g. verai > vrai, peluche 'plush' which is pronounced [pluš] in every context by most speakers.

(b) They have been reanalyzed as one of the regular vowels œ, e, ɛ, or ø̸, e.g. quenouille [kœnuy] 'distaff', guenon [gœnɔ̃] 'she-ape', béton [betɔ̃] 'concrete', séjour [sežur] 'stay', cresson [krœsɔ̃/krɛsɔ̃] 'water-cress', prend-le [prãlø̸] (or [prãle] in some dialects, e.g. in Québec).

(c) They are the modern fleeting œ̇, which can delete in certain cases, e.g. the e in je: je le vois [žœlvwa] 'I see him'/je levais [žlœvɛ] 'I lifted'.

The rules which account for the deletion of such
fleeting œ̇ are the modern counterparts of the historical rules of syncope which affected the shwas.
At first these rules must have been true phonological rules. Most historians assume, cf. Fouché
(1969:508-527), that shwa although phonetically
close to e had a quality which made it phonetically
different from all the other vowels. It became
progressively rounded, first in the environments
of labial consonants, e.g. femier > fumier 'manure',
in the 12th century, but began to be phonetically œ
in the other environments in the 15th-16th centuries. Some time later, the rules which condition the realization of fleeting œ̇ are

approximately the rules that we observe in modern French. At this moment œ̇-deletion can no longer be a phonological rule: it must distinguish between two kinds of segments which are both phonetically œ, one which is subject to the rule, and one which is not, as for instance in modern French: le melon [lmoelɔ̃]/un melon [m̃lɔ̃] 'the/one melon' vs. le meulon [lmœlɔ̃]/un meulon [m̃œlɔ̃] 'the/one small stack'. This can be done by postulating an abstract shwa /ə/ subject to shwa deletion rules, and then a rule of absolute neutralization which converts all the shwas which have not been deleted to [œ]. Another less abstract solution, along the lines suggested by Kiparsky (1968) would be to mark diacritically the underlying œ's which are subject to the deletion rule. This is the solution that we shall adopt tentatively in this paper; when we use the symbol œ̇, it shall be implicit that it is a œ lexically marked for œ̇-deletion rules.[1]

3. The historical sources for the alternation œ̇-ɛ. Romance e and ɛ in stressed syllables became ɛ, yɛ, or ey (later oy) depending upon the environment; in unstressed open syllables they became shwa. This difference of treatment depending upon the stress thus lead to the following alternations:

ə - ɛ   péditat   > pɛtə (il pète) 'he farts'
         pēditáre > pətér (peter) 'to fart'
ə - yɛ lévat   > lyɛv (il lève) 'he raises'
         levāre   > ləvér (lever) 'to raise'
ə - oy pésat   > poyzə (il pèse) 'he weighs'
         pesáre   > pəzér (peser) 'to weigh'

It is possible also that there was a secondary alternating stress phenomenon at some time in the evolution of French to account for the fact that we do not find sequences of two shwas in French (there are a few exceptions in modern French, e.g. (res-)semeler 'to sole anew', Geneviève (proper noun), Genevois 'Genevan', but their historical evolution is difficult to establish). For instance in the development of chènevière 'hemp-field',

chénevis 'hemp-seed', and chènevotte 'stalk of
hemp', all derived from canapu-, both a's should
have become shwa, but the first one never reduced,
presumably because it received a secondary stress.
The alternating stress accounts for the fact that
in words such as hôtellerie 'inn', pètera '(he)
will fart' the two e's should have reduced to shwa,
but only the second appears as a fleeting œ̇, the
first one being ɛ. This secondary stress does not
seem to have had any effect on the other processes
that affected the vowels, and in particular had no
effect on diphthongization. This means that the
future of verbs such as lever and peser must have
been [lɛvəra] and [pɛzəra]. On the other hand, in
verbs where the thematic vowel had been deleted by
the regular processes of syncope in the future
tenses had no secondary stress, thus the future for
tenir and devoir was ten(d)ra and devra (the form
tiendra for tendra is analogical and introduced in
middle French) with a e which reduced to shwa when
it was in an open syllable.

The alternations ə-yɛ and ə-oy have all disappeared in the verbs of the first group, which is
the productive class for the verbs of modern
French. They can still be found in some verbs of
the nonproductive classes, e.g. je tiens/nous
tenons, je dois/nous devons. Verbs of the first
group which participated in the alternations ə-yɛ
and ə-oy have been reanalyzed and participate now
in the alternation ə-ɛ, as is the case for lever
and peser, or in the alternation e-ɛ, as is the
case for espérer. The alternation ə-ɛ, as a rule
is more stable, but in many cases there has been a
regularization in favor of the alternation e-ɛ, as
is the case for péter.

In some dialects, where shwa is phonetically œ
as in standard French, we observe a further development, in which the stressed alternant becomes
œ instead of ɛ. Thus we have in the Western French
dialect of Vendée described by Svenson (1959), the
following regularization: crever: [krœvey] 'to
burst'/ je crève: [ikrœv] 'I burst', lever: [lœvey]
'to lift'/ je lève: [ilœv] 'I lift'. It is not

simply a case where fleeting œ̇ has been replaced by a regular œ as it happens in some dialects, because they have not been reintroduced in the environments which allowed syncopation, <u>atteler</u>: [atley] 'to harness'/ <u>j'attèle</u>: [yatœl] 'I harness', <u>acheter</u>: [aštey] 'to buy'/ <u>j'achète</u>: [yašœt] 'I buy'.[2]

4. Generative treatments of the alternation œ̇-ε. Selkirk proposes an analysis which reflects the history of the development of shwa in standard French. In her analysis, the vowels underlying œ may be ε, yε, and (although she does not mention it explicitly) wa. She postulates a rule which reduces ε, yε (and wa?) to œ̇ when it is in prestressed position. Thus she accounts for the alternations shown below in (1) and (2).

(1) chanter /šãt + εr/ > [šãte] 'to sing'
    chanterai/šãt + εr + ε/ > sãtœ̇rε > [sãtrε]
    '(I) will sing'
(2) lève /lεv + œ̇/ > [lεv] '(I) lift'
    lever /lεv + εr/ > [lœve] 'to lift'
    lèverai /lεv + εr + ε/ > lεvœ̇rε > [lεvrε]
    '(I) will lift'

This way Selkirk can account easily for the alternating stress phenomenon which we observe in the future of verbs such as <u>lever</u>. This solution, however, has the disadvantage that it requires two different kinds of ε's in the phonology of French.[3] There would be one ε which undergoes a reduction to œ̇, as in <u>lever</u> [lœve]/<u>je lève</u> [žlεv], and one ε which does not, as in <u>rêver</u> [rεve] 'to dream'/ <u>je rêve</u> [žrεv] 'I dream'. We cannot even hypothesize that one of these ε's is actually an underlying e, as there are verbs in which e does not reduce, e.g. <u>sécher</u> [seše] 'to dry'/ <u>je sèche</u> [žšεš] 'I dry'.

This appears to be the nature of the objection given by Dell (1973:209) to Selkirk's analysis. He proposes instead an analysis in which the alternation is carried by a rule which is the reverse of the historical rule. Instead of deriving œ̇ from

underlying ε, yε, or wa, he proposes to derive ε in
the alternations œ̇-ε from an underlying œ̇, and
handle the variations œ̇-yε and œ̇-wa as morphological alternations. His implicit argument is that
his analysis requires only one lexically marked segment œ̇, whereas Selkirk's analysis would have re-
quired two such segments, œ̇ and $\dot{\varepsilon}$ (which becomes œ̇
in prestressed position, and contrasts with regular
ε which does not). It cannot be an accident that
the exceptional segment œ̇ is involved in two independent phenomena: œ̇-deletion, and œ̇-conversion
(to ε). This in a sense appears to be a further
justification for the diacritical analysis of shwa
in French: it is the same segment which both deletes and becomes ε in different contexts. Thus
œ̇ in the radical of the verb geler 'to freeze' may
delete in an open syllable, as in de geler [džœle]/
à geler [ažle], or becomes ε in a closed syllable,
as in je gèle [žžɛl] 'I freeze', je gèlerai [žžɛlrɛ]
'I will freeze'. On the other hand œ in gueuler 'to
yell' neither deletes, cf. gueuler [gœle/*gle], nor
becomes ε, cf. je gueule [žgoel/*zgɛl] 'I yell', je
gueulerai [žgœlrɛ/*žgɛlrɛ] 'I will yell'. Dell's
analysis also seems to receive some confirmation
from the morphological regularization that we observed in the history of French. If the alternations œ̇-yε and œ̇-wa are now morphological, then
the radical of verbs such as lever and peser must
have had at one time in their development two
allomorphs, /lyɛv-/ and /lœ̇v-/ for lever, and
/pwaz-/ and /pœ̇z-/ for peser. If the second allo-
morph is chosen as the new unique radical in the
regularization process, then we can account automatically for its new alternation œ̇-ε as the result
of the application of this phonological rule.[4]

Dell's rule of œ̇-conversion (to ε) has the
following form:[5]

(3) a.
    b. œ → ε / ___ $C_1 \begin{Bmatrix} \# \\ C \\ \text{œ̇} \end{Bmatrix}$
    c.

Rule (3) says that fleeting œ̇ is realized as ɛ when it is in a closed syllable, e.g. je lève [žlɛv] 'I lift', or when the next syllable contains another fleeting œ̇, e.g. nous lèverions /lœ̇v+œ̇+r+yɔ̃/ > [lɛvœryɔ̃] 'we would lift', but not when it is in an open syllable and followed by any other vowel, e.g. levons /lœ̇v+ɔ̃/ > [lœvɔ̃] '(we) lift', leveur /lœ̇v+œr/ > [lœvœr] 'lifter'.

5. Fleeting œ̇ in word-internal position. Dell's (implicit) thesis, as we have seen, was in favor of a diacritic analysis of fleeting œ̇. One of his arguments was that it was the same lexically marked segment that was subject to two complementary rules: œ̇-conversion and œ̇-deletion. This claim could be falsified if we could find œ's which alternate with ɛ, as predicted by rule (3) but fail to delete, or conversely. But this depends on the form which we will give to the rule of œ̇-deletion. Most linguists agree that the rule of œ̇-deletion has the following general form (4), to which we must add some restrictions, and in particular the restriction (5).

(4) œ̇ → ∅ / VC ___
(5) first restriction on œ̇-deletion: / ___ Ly

Rule (4) says that a fleeting œ̇ may delete when it is preceded by a single consonant, thus œ̇ may delete in il levait /i+lœ̇v+ɛ/ > [ilvɛ] 'he lifted' but not in il se levait /i+s+lœ̇v+ɛ/ > [islœvɛ/ *islvɛ] 'he got up'. Restriction (5) says that a fleeting œ̇ may not delete, even in the context described in (5), if it is followed by a group ry or ly; thus œ̇ deletes in vous appelez/vuz+apœ̇l+e/ > [vuzaple] 'you call', but not in vous appeliez /vuz+apœ̇l+ye/ > [vuzapœlye /*vuzaplye] 'you called'. If œ̇-deletion is defined by (4) and (5), then the fact that œ̇ never deletes in all the occurrences of the radical of crever [krœve] 'to burst' but still becomes ɛ in a closed syllable, e.g. il crève [ikrɛv] 'he bursts' cannot be taken as an evidence against the claim that the same

segment is involved in both processes. The œ in
<u>crever</u> never deletes because it is always preceded
by a cluster of two consonants. Therefore, before
we can assess Dell's claim, we should discover the
principles which govern œ̇-deletion, and particularly
in word-internal position. We know that in most
dialects of French œ̇-deletion has different characteristics in word-internal position. For instance
œ̇ does not delete after a group 'liquid+consonant'
in word-internal position, e.g. <u>fermeté</u> [fɛrmœte/
*fɛrmte] 'firmness', <u>départemental</u> [departœmãtal/
*departmãtal]. It is possible, however, in a phono-
logical word, e.g. in the expressions (<u>je ne suis
pas venu</u>) <u>pour me taire</u> [purmœtɛr/purmtɛr] '(I did
not come) to shut up', <u>pour te mentir</u> [purtœmãtir/
purtmãtir]. In this section we shall examine some
of the characteristics that œ̇-deletion should have
to be compatible with Dell's hypothesis.

It appears first that we should add the following
restrictions:

(6) Second restriction on œ̇-deletion: / $\begin{Bmatrix} s \\ š \end{Bmatrix}$ ___ vL

(7) Third restriction on œ̇-deletion: / $\begin{Bmatrix} p \\ b \end{Bmatrix}$ ___ $\begin{Bmatrix} s \\ z \end{Bmatrix}$

The second restriction appears to be necessary to
account for the fact that œ̇ does not delete in
words such as <u>sevrer</u> 'to wean' in contexts where it
should normally delete as in <u>tu l'as sevré</u>
[tülasœvre/*tülasvre] 'you weaned her'. In these
words, however, œ̇ still changes to ɛ in closed
syllables, e.g. <u>tu la sèvres</u> [tülasɛvr] 'you wean
her'. The third restriction appears to be necessary to account for the fact that œ̇ does not delete
in words such as <u>dépecer</u> [depœse/*depse] 'to carve'
where they also should delete if rule (4) were
applicable. In these words also, œ̇ still changes
to ɛ in closed syllable, e.g. <u>je le dépèce</u> [žœldepɛs]
'I carve it'. We can, however, cast serious doubts
about these second and third restrictions. They
might have been historical restrictions which account for the reanalysis of historical shwas as œ

in the following words: chevrette 'small goat', chevron 'rafter', chevreau 'kid', besoin 'need', besace 'wallet'. But it could also be an accident that the reanalysis has taken place in these words. For instance, it also took place in the words levraut 'leveret', levrette 'grey-hound', but as we shall see later in more detail, œ̇ may still delete in the future of je me leverai [ʒmœlvrɛ] 'I will get up' for some speakers, even though it is in the environment l—vr. Furthermore we observe the pronunciation [œ̃šfrø] for un chevreuil 'a deer' in the speech of some Quebecois, even though the second restriction seems to apply everywhere else. Finally œ̇ may delete in the verb décevoir 'to deceive', not only in the weak tenses (present, imperfect, subjunctive), but also in the strong tenses (future and conditional) where œ̇ is followed by a sequence vr, thus we may hear vous le décevez [vuldezve] 'you deceive him', and vous le decevrez [vuldezvre] 'you'll deceive him', although the pronunciation with a œ is more common both in the weak and the strong tenses: [vuldesœve] and [vuldesœvre]. Actually the second and third restrictions are needed in a synchronic description of French only in these cases where œ undergoing œ-conversion fails to undergo œ-deletion, i.e. in the verbs sevrer, dépecer, and peser. It would be at least as natural to consider the underlying œ's converting to ɛ in these verbs as nonfleeting œ's, i.e. reject Dell's hypothesis that there is a perfect coincidence between the two abstract segments.

Another piece of evidence is provided by the verb peler 'to peel'. For most speakers of French, historical shwas in the initial syllable of a word have been reanalyzed, specially when these shwas are preceded by a plosive p, or b or a fricative v and followed by a liquid. In some cases, the historical shwa has simply disappeared from the underlying lexical representation, e.g. verai > vrai 'true', pelote 'ball', pelure 'rind', peluche 'plush', pelouse 'lawn'. In some other cases the historical shwa has been reanalyzed as a regular œ, which appears in every environment, e.g. belette

'weasel', belotte (name of a card game), velu
'hairy', velouté 'velvety'. (The only exception in
my own speech of historical shwas that have not
been reanalyzed in these environments is velours
'velvet' where it is still a fleeting œ̈: du
velours [duvlur] 'some velvet'/ (je ne tiens pas)
à ce velours [asvœlur/*asvlur] '(I don't care) for
this velvet'). It is difficult then to maintain
that the historical shwa in peler which never deletes in most speakers' speech is not an underlying
regular œ̈. Still it converts to ɛ in closed syllables, as in je pèle [špɛl] 'I peel'.⁶

6. Thematic œ. In the previous section we have
purposely avoided mentioning another variable œ
which appears in the strong tenses (future and conditional) of some verbs, and which we shall refer
to as thematic œ. This thematic œ is also the
modern counterpart of a former shwa and shares
some, but not all, of the properties of word-
internal fleeting œ̈'s. In this section we shall
describe some of the characteristics of thematic œ
which will become pertinent in the next sections.

We may distinguish in the future and the conditional tenses two historical verbal paradigms, one
in which there used to be a thematic shwa, and a
second one without it, as exemplified in (8).

(8a) thematic paradigm 'to found'
je fonderais   [žəfɔ̃dərɛ] (Modern Fr.) [šfɔ̃drɛ]
tu fonderais   [tüfɔ̃dərɛ]   [tüfɔ̃drɛ]
il fonderais   [ifɔ̃dərɛ]   [ifɔ̃drɛ]
nous fonderions [nufɔ̃dəryɔ̃]   [nufɔ̃dœryɔ̃]
vous fonderiez [vufɔ̃dərye]   [vufɔ̃dœrye]
ils fonderaient [ifɔ̃dərɛə]   [ifɔ̃drɛ]

(8b) athematic paradigm 'to melt'
je fondrais   [žəfɔ̃drɛ]   [šfɔ̃drɛ]
tu fondrais   [tüfɔ̃drɛ]   [tufɔ̃drɛ]
il fondrait   [ifɔ̃drɛ]   [ifɔ̃drɛ]
nous fondrions [nufɔ̃dryɔ̃]   [nufɔ̃driyɔ̃]
vous fondriez   [vufɔ̃drye]   [vufɔ̃driye]
ils fondraient [ifɔ̃drɛ]   [ifɔ̃drɛ]

We can see that in modern French the only difference is now found in the first and second persons plural of the conditional. Historical shwa has deleted in these verbs as predicted by rules (4) or (5) (observe too that shwa-deletion remained optional in word-initial syllable, but it is obligatory in the other syllables), except in the first and second persons plural of the conditional where it was followed by a cluster <u>ry</u>. The question we may ask is whether the thematic œ̇ is a fleeting œ̇ which appears underlyingly in the whole paradigm of thematic verbs, or whether it is a regular œ which appears only in the first and second persons plural of the conditional. A test case should be given by verbs whose radical end with two consonants, where œ̇-deletion does not normally occur in word-internal position. But here we observe that all historically thematic verbs with a radical ending with two consonants do not behave the same way. Thus we observe three paradigms which we will call paradigms I, II, and III.[7]

(9)

Paradigm I	Paradigm II	Paradigm III
perdre	garder	darder
'to lose'	'to keep'	'to hurl'
špɛrdrɛ	žgardrɛ	ždardœrɛ
tüpɛrdrɛ	tügardrɛ	tüdardœrɛ
ipɛrdrɛ	igardrɛ	idardœrɛ
nupɛrdriyɔ̃	nugardœryɔ̃	nudardœryɔ̃
vupɛrdriye	vugardœrye	vudardœrye
ipɛrdrɛ	igardrɛ	idardœrɛ

Paradigm I corresponds to the former athematic paradigm. Paradigm II corresponds to the former thematic paradigm; observe that a thematic œ appears in the first and second persons plural of the conditional, exactly as is the case for radicals which end with a single consonant. In Paradigm III, however, thematic œ appears everywhere. The distinction between paradigms I, II, and III is not strict. We may observe variations both between speakers and within a speaker's own speech. Thus

verbs of the paradigm I may follow paradigm II,
<u>vous perdriez</u> being pronounced as though it were
<u>vous perderiez</u>, or conversely vous <u>garderiez</u> as if
it were <u>vous gardriez</u>. This variation depends
partly on the phonetical shape of the radical; most
verbs ending with a <u>v</u> tend to follow paradigm II,
e.g. <u>vivre</u> 'to live': <u>vous viveriez</u>, <u>suivre</u> 'to
follow': <u>vous suiveriez</u>, <u>écrire</u> 'to write': <u>vous
écriveriez</u> (next to regular <u>écririez</u>). Verbs which
historically should follow the paradigm II or III
may follow paradigm I when they end with a plosive
(but I have also observed the pronunciation
[vunɛmriye] in <u>vous n'aimeriez</u> (<u>mieux pas partir</u>?),
although this seems to be less frequent). Verbs
following paradigm III appear to be verbs that are
less commonly used than the verbs following paradigm II, both deriving from a former thematic paradigm. There is frequent variation between paradigm
II and III. Traditional descriptions for these
paradigms have postulated a ∅-theme for paradigm I,
and a theme œ̇ for paradigm II and III, œ̇ in paradigm
II being deleted by a special rule of œ̇-deletion
(10) which is restricted to verbs of paradigm II.

(10) thematic-œ̇-deletion:
œ → ∅ with restriction (5) in paradigm II.

Another solution would be simply to consider that
paradigm II has a theme œ in the first and second
persons plural of the conditional, whereas paradigm
III has a theme œ everywhere in the future and the
conditional. If this is the solution adopted, then
simplicity requires that verbs ending with a single
consonant follow paradigm II.

7. Complete regularization of the alternation
<u>œ-ɛ</u>. It has been observed for quite a long time
that some verbs which historically exhibit the
alternation <u>œ-ɛ</u> have been regularized. If we
examine the paradigm of a verb like <u>empaqueter</u> 'to
pack', we observe that in this paradigm the underlying shwa is deleted by rule (4) whenever it is
not realized as <u>ɛ</u>. This implies that this paradigm

is almost identical to the paradigm of a verb like
<u>contracter</u> [kɔ̃trakte] 'to contract', the only difference appearing in the present singular and in
the third person plural of the present indicative
and subjunctive, as well as in all the persons of
the future and conditional:

(11)

žãpakɛt	škɔ̃trakt	j'empaquete je contracte
nuzãpaktɔ̃	nukɔ̃traktɔ̃	nous empaquetons nous contractons
žãpaktɛ	škɔ̃traktɛ	j'empaquetais je contractais
ãpakte	kɔ̃trakte	empaqueté contracté
ãpaktã	kɔ̃traktã	empaquetant contractant

In the regularization that takes place, <u>empaqueter</u>
now follows the paradigm of <u>contracter</u>. This means
that the underlying œ̇ is now deleted everywhere,
even when it should normally be changed to ɛ through
the morphophonological rule of œ̇-conversion (3). In
other words, the regularization is lexical in
nature, the underlying form of the radical for
<u>empaqueter</u> being changed from /ãpakœ̇t-/ to /ãpakt-/.
This regularization has been first observed (to my
knowledge) by Pelletier in 1549 (cf. Fouché 1969:
524) who writes <u>déchicte</u> as the normal form for the
verb <u>déchiqueter</u> 'to slash'. Speakers of the language who use the regularized form are normally
aware of it, and it is rather frequent in all
varieties of French. If we examine the verbs which
undergo the complete regularization of the alternation œ-ɛ, they all share the property that the
last two consonants constitute a permissible word-final cluster, as we observe in (12).

(12) a. kt: déchiqueter, empaqueter, étiqueter, becqueter
     b. št: cacheter
     c. rt: fureter
     d. lt: se colleter, décolleter,␣pelleter
     e. yt: feuilleter

This regularization never occurs in radicals which
end with a cluster which is not possible word-
finally, as in ressemeler, the only exception being the verb feuilleter 'to peruse', which I have
often heard without final vowel as in je feuillete
[šfœyt]. The cluster yt is not a normal word-final
cluster in French; we must then assume that its absence elsewhere in the phonotactics of French must
be a historical gap.[8]

The clusters 'obstruent+liquid', as in je râcle
[žrakl] 'to scrape', are permissible. However, we
never find any case of complete regularization in
connection with verbs such as craqueler [krakle]
'to crackle'. Dell (1973:208) thinks that this is
a historical accident, and that such regularizations will eventually occur. Actually there are
strong arguments to the contrary. As we know this
process of regularization is very old (over 400
years) and there are still no such regularizations.
Clusters 'obstruent+liquid' in word-final position
are highly marked, and in most varieties of French
they are simply reduced by deleting the final
liquid, thus je lui montre [žẅimɔ̃t]/nous lui
montrons [nulẅimɔ̃trɔ̃] 'I/we show him'. This being
the case, we should not expect verbs such as
craqueler to undergo complete regularization,
since this would lead to the creation of marked
clusters. If we observe the Picard dialect described by Cochet (1932), we actually find that
the contrary is taking place. In this dialect,
the verb redoubler [œrduble] has been reanalyzed
as having an underlying œ̇, as exemplified by the
alternation redoubler [œrduble], il redouble
[irdubɛl] (next to [irdub]).[9]

8. Partial regularization of the alternation
œ̇-ɛ. In contrast with the complete regularization
described in the previous section, there is another
regularization which we can observe both in France
and in Québec. In this case, the underlying form
is not reanalyzed, rather the domain of application
of the rule changing œ̇ to ɛ is restricted. If we
take acheter 'to buy' as an example of this kind

of verb, we observe that the underlying shwa is
always realized as ε, when it is in a closed syllable, thus j'achète 'I buy' is pronounced [žašεt]
and not [žašt] (unlike cacheter 'to seal' which can
be completely regularized as in je cach'te ([škašt]).
On the other hand in the future œ̇ may remain non-
converted, thus next to the regular pronunciation
j'achèterai [žasεtrε], 'I will buy' we may hear
j'achetrai [žaštrε].

How can we account for this phenomenon? Recall
how traditional analyses propose the underlying
form /ašœ̇t+œ̇+rε/ for achèterai where there are two
underlying œ̇'s, one in the radical /ašœ̇t-/, which
we shall refer to as the radical œ̇, and one thematic
œ̇. In these analyses rule (3) of œ̇-conversion applies first and changes the radical œ̇ to ε; then
rule (4) applies and deletes the thematic œ̇, unless
the restriction (5) applies. Thus we have the
following derivation:

(13) underlying form: /ašœ̇t+œ̇+rε/
    œ̇-conversion   ε
    œ̇-deletion   ∅
    phonetic form   [ašεtrε]

We may account simply for the realization [žaštrε]
if we adopt the solution that thematic œ̇ is restricted to the first and second persons plural of
the conditional as we suggested before. Thus rule
(3) of œ̇-conversion would still be responsible for
the change of œ to ε in j'achète, but would not apply in the derivation (14) because the radical œ̇ is
no longer followed by the thematic œ̇, which was
necessary for rule (3c) to apply.

(14) underlying form: /ašœ̇t+rε/
    œ̇-conversion   -
    œ̇-deletion   ∅
    phonetic form   [aštrε]

If we turn to the conditional, we can see that
this cannot be the proper explanation. We observe
that there cannot be any correlation between œ̇-
conversion and the presence of a thematic œ̇. We

observe four main paradigms for the strong tenses
(future and conditional); paradigm A: there is a
thematic œ̇ in the first and second persons plural
of the conditional and œ̇-conversion occurs everywhere; paradigm B: there is a thematic œ̇ in the
first and second persons plural of the conditional
but there is no œ̇-conversion; paradigm C: there
is no thematic vowel but there is œ̇-conversion
everywhere; and finally paradigm D: there is no
thematic vowel and no œ̇-conversion. These four
paradigms are exemplified in Table 1.

Table 1.

Theme œ̇	Theme ∅
(a) œ̇ converts to ɛ:	
Paradigm A:	Paradigm B:
j'achèterai	j'achètrai
[žašɛtrɛ]	[žašɛtrɛ]
vous achèteriez	vous achètriez
[vuzašɛtœrye]	[vuzašɛtriye]
(b) No conversion:	
Paradigm C:	Paradigm D:
j'acheterai	j'achetrai
[žaštrɛ]	[žaštrɛ]
vous acheteriez	vous achetriez
[vuzaštœrye]	[vuzaštriye]

It is clear that attempts such as Dell's or Selkirk's to write a phonological rule to account for
œ̇-conversion cannot represent true generalizations
about the language. Instead there appears to be
at most one phonological rule, i.e. rule (15) which
corresponds to subrule (3a), and converts œ to ɛ
in a closed syllable, and which is therefore restricted to the present of the indicative and of
the subjunctive, because it is only in these tenses
that a radical œ̇ may be in a closed syllable. This
rule accounts for the alternation in j'achète and
vous achetez. We must also posit a morphophonological rule (16) which holds only for paradigms A
and B and applies independently of any theme. It
is clear for paradigm B that there cannot be any

phonological factors conditioning the change from
œ̇ to ɛ; speakers using paradigm B will convert the
radical œ̇ of a verb such as <u>lever</u> 'to lift' in the
strong tenses, e.g. <u>je lèvrai</u> [žlɛvrɛ] 'I will lift',
<u>vous lèvriez</u> [vulɛvriye] 'you would lift', but not
in the weak tenses of verbs such as <u>sevrer</u> 'to
wean', even though the radical œ̇ appears in similar
phonological environments, e.g. <u>je sevrais</u> [šsœ̌vrɛ/
*šsɛvrɛ] 'I weaned', <u>vous sevriez</u> [vusœvriye/
*vusɛvriye] 'you weaned'.

(15) œ̇ → ɛ / — C_1 #
(16) œ̇ → ɛ / — X $]_{\text{future,conditional}}$

Actually we observe a fifth paradigm, which is
half-way between paradigm A and paradigm C, and
which we shall refer to as paradigm AC. In this
paradigm, the theme œ̇ appears in the first and
second plural persons of the conditional; there is
no conversion of œ̇ to ɛ except when the theme is
phonetically present, thus <u>j'achetrai</u> [žašt̆rɛ]
'I will buy', <u>vous acheteriez</u> [vuzašɛtœrye] 'you
would buy'. To account for this paradigm we must
posit a weaker version of rule (16) which may take
the two forms (17a) or (17b).

(17) a. œ → ɛ / — C_1 œ̇
     b. œ → ɛ / — X $]_{1,2 \text{ pers. pl. conditional}}$

Rule (17a) corresponds to subrule (3c) and says
that the conversion of œ̇ to ɛ is conditioned by the
phonological environment. Note, however, the presence of an abstract element œ̇ in the definition of
this environment. Actually rule (17a) will apply
only in the first and second persons plural of the
conditional, and I see no reason why it should not
be represented as a morphophonological rule (17b).

We have just described five paradigms for these
verbs. It must be clear now how these paradigms
are used. Paradigm A is the nonregularized conservative paradigm, the other paradigms are innovative paradigms. All speakers of French may use

the conservative paradigm A; some will claim that
they use only the conservative paradigm, although
they may unknowingly use another one some of the
time. Most speakers will use next to the conservative paradigm A one (and usually only one) of the
innovative paradigms. I have observed some speakers who use two innovative paradigms, but this is
not the rule. Thus a given speaker can be characterized by his innovative paradigm. Thus we will
have the following characterization:[10]

Speakers A (no innovative paradigm):
  obligatory theme, rule (16) obligatory
Speakers B (paradigms A and B):
  optional theme, rule (16) obligatory
Speakers C (paradigms A and C):
  obligatory theme, rule (16) optional
Speakers AC (paradigms A and AC):
  obligatory theme, rule (17), rule (16) optional
Speakers D (paradigms A and D):
  optional theme, rule (16) optional (but some
    restrictions must be added).

In the last part of this section we shall examine
what are the factors which allow the optionality of
rule (16). We observe three contexts which favor
the optionality:
  (a) The radical œ̇ does not delete, either because
it is an 'exception' to rule (4): dépecer 'to
carve', peser 'to weigh', or because rule (4) is
not applicable: surmener 'to overdrive', ensorceler
'to bewitch', marteler 'to hammer', morceler 'to cut
up', parsemer 'to strew', harceler 'to hassle'.
  (b) When œ̇ is followed by an obstruent: achever
'to finish', acheter 'to buy', crocheter 'to
crochet', jeter 'to throw', rejeter 'to reject'.
  (c) When œ̇ is in the environment v--l: renouveler
'to renew': je renouvelerai [žrœnuvlœrɛ].
We observe that the innovation is possible whenever the syllabic structure of French can be preserved, in all other cases--i.e. when the radical œ̇
is fleeting and followed by a sonorant which, unlike
in case (c) above, cannot constitute with the

preceding consonant a permissible syllable initial cluster--the innovation is impossible, e.g. <u>geler</u> 'to freeze', <u>dégeler</u> 'to defreeze', <u>ciseler</u> 'to chisel', <u>chanceler</u> 'to stagger', <u>ressemeler</u> 'to sole anew'. The only exception is <u>semer</u> 'to seed' which may give in the future <u>vous semerez</u> [vusœmre] 'you will seed'; we see in that case, however, that the radical e̊ is in the initial syllable of the verb, and we know that in this position e̊ tends to be reanalyzed as regular œ.

The fact that this innovation affects specially the e̊ which is not fleeting, as in <u>dépecer</u> 'to carve', <u>peser</u> 'to weigh', etc. may be an indication that these are indeed regularized as regular œ, not as fleeting e̊ which somehow would fail to be subject to e̊-deletion rules.11

9. The status of optional morphophonological rules. If we turn our attention to speakers A and AC, rule (16) is clearly for them a variable rule. It is clearly a morphophonological rule since it applies only to specific tenses. It shares the same properties of variability as have been observed with (natural) phonological rules. In particular, most speakers are unaware that there is a variation in their speech. Its application also depends on prosodic factors, thus the rule will fail to apply more frequently when e̊ is further away from the end of the utterance, e.g. more frequently in <u>j'en acheterai deux</u> 'I'll buy two' than in <u>j'en acheterai</u> 'I'll buy some'.

There is a fundamental difference between a variable (natural) phonological rule and a variable morphophonological rule. If a speaker is unaware of his having a variable phonological rule in his grammar, he will claim that the rule does not exist (i.e. in French as in English word-final <u>t</u> deletes variably after <u>s</u>, but many speakers will claim that they never do it 'je pronounce toujours le <u>t</u> final dans le mot [artis]'). When speakers of French are unaware that rule (16) is optional, they will claim that it is obligatory.12

NOTES

I would like to thank here my students in my phonology classes at the Université de Montréal who have provided me with much of the data that I used for this analysis. For the varieties of French spoken in France, I have relied upon my students who come from France, and my friends, and their family to whom I apologize for having listened a little too much to how they spoke, rather than to what they said.

1. We note that similar processes are found in other dialects of northern French, but the modern reflex of shwa is not always [œ]; it may be [e] as in the Picard dialect described by Cochet (1932); thus il jette [ižɛt], il jetait [ištóa], elle jetait [alžetóa]; it may be [ü] or [i] in Wallon.

2. This phenomenon should be distinguished from another phenomenon in which ɛ becomes œ̇ when it is close to a labial consonant, as is the case frequently in some varieties of Québec and Acadian French, cf. Lucci (1972:55), where we find je me lève [žmœlœv], but also une lèvre [œnlœv], une fève [œnfœv]. In this variety of Vendéen, the change from ɛ to œ appears only in regularized verbs and in all phonological contexts.

3. Besides the fact that it cannot explain why the future forms of verbs such as tenir have been regularized from tendra to tiendra unlike the other forms where œ remains as in tenir, nous tenons, il tenait. Dell (1973:208-209) also observed that this solution could not account for some neologisms. Actually, if we accept some kind of cyclic application of the rules, we could dismiss his objections, thus hotelierisme could be derived from [#[otɛl+yɛr]ₙ#ism]ₙ giving [otœlyɛrism].

4. Actually these verbs had three variants /lyɛv-/, /lœv-/, and in the future and conditional /lɛv-/, and we could also claim that the variant /lɛv-/ has been extended.

5. Actually Dell's rule is more complex. Rule (3) will wrongly apply to the first fleeting œ̇ in

revenir /rœ̇+vœ̇nir/, which leads him to require that the first consonant following œ̇ be in the same morpheme for this œ̇ to convert to ɛ. Rule (3) will also wrongly apply to the initial œ of Genevois, or the second œ of ressemeler, which leads him to require that œ in the context of application (c) be followed by a nonsegmental element. The version of rule (3) as given by Dell will be as follows:

(i) œ̇ → ɛ / ___ C̑₁ { # / C / œ[-seg] }

The symbol C̑₁ is here to indicate that the consonant(s) C₁ must be part of the same morpheme as what precedes. This requirement is a direct violation of a putative universal proposed by Chomsky and Halle (1968:364) which says: 'Any rule which applies to a string of the form XYZ also applies to strings of the form X+Y+Z, XY+Z, X+YZ, where X, Y, Z stand for sequences of zero or more units and + represents formative boundary' (convention 105). Actually words such as Genevois and ressemeler are few in number (I know of only two other cases: Genevièvre, échevellé); in these words the pronunciation where the first œ is deleted is impossible: *[žnœvwa], *[rœšmœle], *[žnœvyɛv], *[ešfœle]. We can propose then that the first œ in these words is then a regular œ and not a fleeting œ̇: /zœnœ̇v+wa/ (for many speakers this is also true of Genève where the initial œ is not fleeting), /rœ=sœmœl+e/, /zœnvyɛv/, and /ešœvle/. As for the prefixes re-, de-, we may suggest in the framework of Chomsky and Halle (1968) a different boundary, e.g. revenir /rœ=vœnir/, devenir /dœ=vœnir/, which would make the initial œ̇ ineligible to rule (3). Therefore we cannot say that Dell's analysis is a true counterexample to Chomsky and Halle's putative universal. Rule (3), as it is expressed here, is perfectly legitimate within the framework used by Dell, without having to complicate it as (i).

6. The restrictions on rule (4) are valid for the varieties of French spoken in and around Paris (which have been the object of the traditional descriptions) and in Québec. They are not

necessarily valid for other varieties of French.
For instance in the français régional de Saint-
Etienne (France) word-internal œ̇ may delete after
a group 'liquid+consonant', thus: <u>fortement</u>
[fɔrtmã], <u>bord de mer</u> [bɔrdmɛr], <u>marguerite</u>
[margrit], <u>tourterelle</u> [turtrɛl]. In this same
variety of French, I also observed that historical
shwas have not been reanalyzed in words such as
<u>belote</u>: <u>la belotte</u> [lablɔt], <u>une belotte</u> [unbœlɔt],
<u>belette</u>: <u>la belette</u> [lablɛt], <u>une belette</u> [unbœlɛt],
<u>peler</u>: <u>à peler</u> [aple], <u>je veux le peler</u> [žvǿlpœle],
etc. Speakers of this variety of French are un-
aware that they may delete œ̇ in these words, and may
very sincerely say, as I have observed, that they
cannot say [margrit], [lablɛt] a few seconds after
they just said them. In this case they claim that
there is a [œ] in their speech, just as in Parisian
French.

7. In Québec French, the future is said to be
replaced by the periphrastic expression <u>aller+Vinf</u>,
e.g. <u>je vais acheter</u>, actually, it is not so infrequent, especially in the negative, e.g. <u>j'en
acheterai pas</u>. Most speakers have only paradigm
I and II, but not III. The vowel œ still appears
after a group 'obstruent+liquid' as in all varieties
of French, e.g. <u>je soufflerai</u> [ššuflœre/*ššuflre].
In this case the œ should not be analyzed as a
theme, but perhaps as an epenthesis(?).

8. There appears to be another phonotactic gap
in French; it involves word-final <u>lv</u>. There does
not appear to have been any regularization, how-
ever, of the words <u>élever</u>, <u>relever</u>, <u>unlever</u>,
<u>soulever</u>, etc.

9. I must admit that regularization such as
<u>ça craqu'le</u>, <u>je le nick'le</u>, all seem very bad to
me. The only exception is <u>renouveler</u>, as in <u>je le
renouvle</u>, where the reanalysis does not seem so bad
to me, although I have never heard it.

10. I have observed speakers D only in Québec;
I have observed speakers B, C, and AC, both in
France and in Québec.

11. Many speakers in Montréal have completely
regularized the verb <u>dépecer</u>: <u>je dépeuce</u> [ždepœs].

Some of my informants also told me that they have heard pronunciations such as <u>je jeute</u> (instead of <u>je jette</u>) <u>enleuve</u>! (instead of <u>enlève</u>!), but that it sounded like only old people could say that. It could be the same phenomenon as the one we mentioned in note 2.

12. I had the occasion of catching several of my friends saying <u>j'en achetrai</u> [žãnaštrɛ], who later claimed that they certainly could not say such awful things.

REFERENCES

Chomsky, Noam, and Morris Halle. 1968. The sound pattern of English. New York: Harper and Row.
Cochet, E. 1932. Le patois de Gondecourt. Paris: Droz.
Dell, François. 1973. Les règles et les sons. Paris: Hermann.
Fouché, Pierre. 1969. Phonétique historique du français. Volume 2: Les voyelles. Paris: Klincksieck.
Hooper, Joan. 1975. The archi-segment in natural generative phonology. Language 51.536-560.
Kiparsky, Paul. 1968. How abstract is phonology? In: Three dimensions of linguistic theory. 1973. Edited by O. Fujimara. Tokyo: TEC Company. 5-56.
Lucci, Vincent. 1972. Phonologie de l'acadien. Montreal: Didier.
Selkirk, Elisabeth. 1972. The phrase phonology of English and French. Unpublished Ph.D. dissertation. MIT.
Stampe, David. 1973. A dissertation on natural phonology. Unpublished Ph.D. dissertation. University of Chicago.

A SEMANTIC ANALYSIS
OF THE DIFFERENCE BETWEEN el/la AND lo[1]

RICARDO OTHEGUY
Rutgers University

The Spanish forms el, la, and lo, which I refer to as the l-forms, have traditionally been considered as all sharing the category of gender, lo being the neuter and el and la masculine and feminine respectively.

While the terms masculine, feminine, and neuter remain current in many treatments of these forms, many linguists have pointed out that the term 'neuter' is highly misleading and in no way contributes to our understanding of the distribution of these forms (cf. Hall 1965, Luján 1972, Manoliu 1970). This understanding, I suggest, will come only if we abandon the notion that lo is somehow the same as el and la except for being different in gender. Instead, we should look at el and la as having a different meaning from lo, this difference in meaning having nothing to do with being 'neuter' to the masculine vs. feminine distinction.

Here I propose to look at the l-forms, in general, within the broad theoretical tradition that views the postulation of signals and meanings as the central task of linguistics and, in particular, within the theoretical orientation of Form-Content analysis.[2] Thus, a meaning here is a hypothesis about the constant, invariable contribution that is made

241

to the process of inferring messages every time a signal is used. These meaning hypotheses thus enable us to explain the distribution of the signals.

The Spanish *l*-forms have traditionally been analyzed either as articles or as weak deictics, akin to the demonstratives *este*, *ese*, etc.[3] Here I will accept the deictic analysis and will consider that the *l*-forms, like the demonstratives, are used to point out, and to direct and concentrate the hearer's attention. In this analysis, *el/la* and *lo* share the same degree of deixis, in opposition to the higher degree of deixis of the demonstratives, as shown in (1).[4]

(1) Traditional analysis of the Spanish *l*-forms as deictics.

este	ese	aquel	el
esta ...	... esa ...	... aquella ...	... la
esto	eso	aquello	lo
Higher deixis		Lower deixis	→

Thus, for example, the difference between (2) and (3), and (4) and (5), is one of force or degree of the pointing.

(2a) Dame *esa* libreta.
 'Give me that notebook'
(2b) Dame *esa* que te compré.
 'Give me that (one) I bought you'
(3a) Dame *la* libreta.
 'Give me the notebook'
(3b) Dame *la* que te compré.
 'Give me the (one) I bought you'
(4a) Dame *eso* grande.
 'Give me that which is big'
(4b) Dame *eso* que te compré.
 'Give me that which I bought you'
(5a) Dame *lo* grande.
 'Give me that which is big'
(5b) Dame *lo* que te compré.
 'Give me that which I bought you'

In (2) <u>libreta</u> and <u>que te compré</u> are pointed out more strongly than in (3), and in (4) <u>grande</u> and <u>que te compré</u> are pointed out more strongly than in (5).

I will propose here that, in addition to sharing the same value in the semantic substance of Deixis, the forms <u>el/la</u> and <u>lo</u> enter into an opposition in another semantic substance. That is, I am proposing that <u>el/la</u> and <u>lo</u> have a meaning in which they are the same (the deictic one) and one in which they differ.

The semantic substance in which <u>el/la</u> and <u>lo</u> enter into an opposition is fundamentally concerned with the clarity and distinctness of what is pointed out by the deictic <u>l</u>-forms: <u>el/la</u> convey the meaning of clear, well-delineated boundaries; <u>lo</u> conveys the meaning of unclear, diffuse, and not well-delineated boundaries.

While it is very difficult to settle on a single word or set of words that will convey the nature of the semantic substance, I find that the word 'Discreteness' best captures what <u>el/la</u> and <u>lo</u> have in common. As shown in (6), I propose, then, that the forms <u>el</u> and <u>la</u> mean 'Discrete', and the form <u>lo</u> 'Nondiscrete'.

(6) Proposed meanings for <u>el/la</u> and <u>lo</u>

Discreteness $\begin{cases} \text{Discrete el/la} \\ \text{Nondiscrete lo} \end{cases}$

The relevant contrast is thus between utterances like (7) and utterances like (8).

(7a) Dame <u>el/la</u> bueno/a.
 'Give me the good (one)'
(7b) Dame <u>el/la</u> que te compré.
 'Give me the (one) I bought you'
(8a) Dame <u>lo</u> bueno.
 'Give me that which is good'
(8b) Dame <u>lo</u> que te compré.
 'Give me what I bought you'

The proposal about this semantic substance that I am calling 'Discreteness' is best understood if we remember that, as we just mentioned, the <u>l</u>-forms are weak demonstratives or deictics. The substance of 'Deixis' is purely and exclusively directional. It is used for the purpose of directing attention toward something, but without indicating in any way the nature of that something. This task is carried out by the signals that follow the deictic <u>l</u>-form. For instance, in (7) the <u>el/la</u> simply points and concentrates attention, while <u>bueno/a</u> and <u>que te compré</u> tell us the nature of what our attention is concentrated on.

I am proposing here that the task of telling us what the deictic is pointing to is carried out, not only by the material that follows the <u>l</u>-form, but by a semantic substance right in the <u>l</u>-form. The meanings of Discrete and Nondiscrete are interlocked with the deictic meaning and provide information about that which is pointed out. The meaning of Discrete tells us that what is pointed out by the <u>l</u>-form has well-defined, clear boundaries, which allow us to see it as a sharply delineated entity, while the meaning of Nondiscrete tells us that it has less well-defined, unclear boundaries.

So, for instance, the <u>bueno/a</u> and <u>que te compré</u> are perceived as having sharper and clearer boundaries in (7) than in (8). In (7) we are talking about a well-defined and clearly delineated good object or object that I bought, while in (8) we are talking about an unspecified number of things that have the property of being good or that I have bought. The <u>l</u>-forms thus contain a meaning that points, and one that comments on the distinctness of what is pointed to.

Thus, whether a speaker uses <u>el/la</u> or <u>lo</u> is not a matter of gender, but of the greater appropriateness of one or the other meaning to the messages that the speaker is trying to communicate.

While the meanings of the forms are always the same, the reason one meaning is more appropriate than the other is different from occasion to occasion depending on the intended message. That is, while el/la always signals 'Discrete' and lo 'Nondiscrete', the motivation for choosing a 'Discrete' or a 'Nondiscrete' deictic is different in the different contexts in which the l-forms are found. Thus while the explanation for the difference in the distribution of el/la and lo is always the same--namely, the hypothesized meanings--the validation of the explanation, of the meanings, requires that we look at a large array of different contextual factors.

One such factor is the lexical meaning of the verbs involved, as for instance, pasar 'pass', 'overtake', 'happen' and hacer 'make', 'do'. The lexical meaning of these verbs is such that the inferences we make on the basis of their meaning can range from very specific events to very general, unspecified events, as in (9) and (10).

(9a) Ese coche amarillo le pasó al de Andretti en la vuelta anterior.
'That yellow car overtook Andretti's in the previous lap'
(9b) ¿Qué le pasó a Carlos que ya no viene a las reuniones del club?
'What happened to Carlos that he no longer comes to the club's meetings?'
(10a) ¿Cuándo hizo Carlos esa casa?
'When did Carlos build that house?'
(11b) ¿Qué hizo Carlos cuando se enteró de la noticia?
'What did Carlos do when he heard the news?'

In both cases it is contextual factors that condition the different inferences that we make from the lexical meaning of the verbs: pasar in the specific sense of 'overtake' or in the general sense of 'happen'; hacer in the specific sense of 'build' or in the general sense of 'do'. So for instance in (10a) it is the presence of esa casa 'that house' that contributes to our inference of 'build' for the verb hacer, since building is what one does to houses. We thus see that verbs like pasar and hacer force an inferential decision that can be affected by the meaning of other signals. The signals that affect the interpretation of pasar and hacer can be lexical signals, as in the case of esa casa that we just saw, or can also be grammatical signals such as the l-forms that we are discussing in this paper. The effect that the choice of a 'Discrete' or a 'Nondiscrete' l-form has on the message we get out of verbs like hacer and pasar will be the first piece of evidence in favor of the 'Discreteness' hypothesis.

The difference between the two interpretations of hacer resides in whether the object of hacer is a tangible, physical object (the 'make' or 'build' sense) or an abstract occurrence (the 'do' sense). I propose that the meaning 'Discrete' suggests more readily a physical object than an abstract occurrence, and that the opposite is true of the meaning 'Nondiscrete'. This is so because the boundaries of a physical object are clearer than those of an occurrence, that is, the distinction between one physical object and another is sharper, more apparent to the senses, than that between one occurrence and another.

It follows from the postulated meanings of the l-forms, then, that when combined with a 'Discrete' l-form from which we infer a physical object, hacer will be interpreted in the concrete sense of (11).

   (11) Me parece mejor el que Carlos hizo.
        'I like better the one Carlos made.'

When combined with a 'Nondiscrete' l-form from which we infer an occurrence, hacer will be interpreted in the more general sense of (12).

   (12) Me parece mejor lo que Carlos hizo.
        'I like better what Carlos did.'

The same considerations apply to the different interpretations of pasar in (13) and (14), where el leads us to infer pasar in the concrete sense of motion and lo in the more general sense of 'happened'.[5]

(13) No me gustó el que pasó.
    'I didn't like the one that passed by.'
(14) No me gustó lo que pasó.
    'I didn't like what happened.'

But note that 'object' versus 'occurrence' are not the meanings of el/la and lo, but inferences drawn from their meanings of 'Discrete' and 'Nondiscrete' respectively, in conjunction with the lexical meaning of the verbs involved. Where different verbs are involved, there are different inferential possibilities and the range of interpretations from 'Discrete' and 'Nondiscrete' accordingly is different. For example, consider the different interpretations of (15) and (16).

(15) Alcánzame ese diccionario. A ver, aquí
    está la que quiere decir 'serendipity'.
    'Hand me that dictionary. Let's see, here
    is the (one) that means "serendipity"'.
(16) Alcánzame ese diccionario. A ver, aquí
    está lo que quiere decir 'serendipity'.
    'Hand me that dictionary. Let's see, here
    is the meaning of "serendipity"'.

The context indicates quite clearly that 'object' versus 'activity' is not what is at issue here, where dictionaries and translations are being discussed. The verb quiere decir suggests either a dictionary entry or its definition. Dictionary entries differ from their definitions in that dictionary entries are single, well-defined words, while their definitions are of variable nature and length. Given this alternative, I propose that the different messages we get with el/la and lo are consistent with the meaning hypothesis. The 'Discrete' meaning of el/la more plausibly suggests the single dictionary entry while the 'Nondiscrete' meaning of lo more plausibly suggests the less tangible notion of a concept or a definition.

In addition to allowing the speaker to refer to different kinds of entities in the nonlinguistic context, the meanings of 'Discrete' and 'Nondiscrete'

allow him to associate the l-form with different
linguistic antecedents. As is well-known, el/la
is used to pick out animate antecedents, as in
(17), and lo is used to pick out infinitives and
entire sentences, as in (18) and (19).

(17) Lola era la que mejor podía opinar sobre
eso.
'Lola was the one who could best have an
opinion on that.'
(18) Adelgazar es lo que deberías de hacer antes
del verano.
'Lose weight is what you ought to do before
the summer.'
(19) "¡Que se vayan!" fue lo que le oí decir yo.
'"Let them go!" was what I heard him say.'

This seems to follow from the postulated meanings
in a straightforward fashion, since animates have
clearer boundaries and are better delineated than
the names of occurrences and entire propositions.

In (17) through (19) the linguistic context provided only one alternative to associate with the
l-form and thus only one or the other l-form was
possible. In many cases, however, the speaker can
associate the l-form with different aspects of the
context depending on whether he uses a form meaning 'Discrete' or one meaning 'Nondiscrete', as
illustrated in (20) and (21).

(20) Carlos tiene una mujer ambiciosa, por la que
hace los más grandes sacrificios.
'Carlos has an ambitious wife, for whom he
makes the greatest of sacrifices.'
(21) Carlos tiene una mujer ambiciosa, por lo que
hace los más grandes sacrificios.
'Carlos has an ambitious wife, for which
reason he makes the greatest of sacrifices.'

Given this sort of a context, we may want to say
that Carlos made sacrifices because of his ambitious
wife or because of the fact of having an ambitious
wife. I propose that, given these alternatives, a

form meaning 'Discrete' is more appropriate for associating the l-form with the ambitious wife and one meaning 'Nondiscrete' is more appropriate for associating the l-form with the fact or circumstance of having an ambitious wife, since a set of circumstances is less tangible, has less clear boundaries, than a person. Thus with el/la we interpret the utterance, as in (20), as 'for whom he made the greatest sacrifices', and with lo we interpret it, as in (21), as 'for which reason he made the greatest of sacrifices'.

What we see, then, is that the choice of one l-form or the other responds, in every case, to the appropriateness of the meanings to the intended message. Still, we should not assume that we can establish absolute, formal criteria for when one or the other meaning will be appropriate. This is always a matter of context. Thus we find that while certain factors favor or disfavor one or the other meaning, there is not always a sharp line between the cases when one or the other form can be used. So, for instance, in (22) we find that when valor 'courage' appears by itself it is very difficult to refer to it with anything other than a form meaning 'Nondiscrete'.

(22a) *Valor es el que nos permite enfrentarnos a las dificultades de la vida.
(22b) Valor es lo que nos permite enfrentarnos a las dificultades de la vida.
'Courage is what allows us to face the difficulties of life.'

But as we see in (23) and (24) with el valor and ese valor, the more that we specify the kind of courage, the more it now becomes possible to present it, depending on the intended message, as either a 'Discrete' or a 'Nondiscrete' entity.

(23a) El valor es el que nos permite enfrentarnos a las dificultades de la vida. (??)
'Courage is the one thing that allows us to face the difficulties of life.'

(23b) El valor es lo que nos permite enfrentarnos
a las dificultades de la vida.
'Courage is what allows us to face the
difficulties of life.'
(24a) Ese valor es el que nos permite enfrentarnos
a las dificultades de la vida.
'That courage is the one that allows us to
face the difficulties of life.'
(24b) Ese valor es lo que nos permite enfrentarnos
a las dificultades de la vida.
'That courage is what allows us to face the
difficulties of life.'

The possibility of using el with el valor and ese valor but not when valor appears alone is supporting evidence for the meaning of 'Discrete'. Because of the higher deictic force of ese over el (see (1)) valor is pointed out more in (24) than in (23). The more valor is pointed out by el and ese, the more prominence it acquires, the more delineated it becomes. As a result of this, the form meaning 'Discrete' can now be associated with valor more coherently in (23) than in (22) and more in (24) than in (23).

Further support for the hypothesized meanings can be found in cases like (25) and (26).

(25a) La que compró Carlos fue la casa del suegro,
no la casa de María.
'The one that Carlos bought was the father-
in-law's house, not Maria's house.'
(25b) Lo que compró Carlos fue la casa del suegro,
no la casa de María.
'What Carlos bought was the father-in-law's
house, not Maria's house.'
(26a) *La que compró Carlos fue la casa del
suegro, no la finca de María.
(26b) Lo que compró Carlos fue la casa del suegro,
no la finca de María.
'What Carlos bought was the father-in-law's
house, not Maria's farm.'

In (25) we can say, again depending on the intended
message, either la or lo, while in (26) the only
alternative is lo.
  The difference between (25) and (26), quite obviously, is that in (25) que compró Carlos is associated with a homogeneous set (house and house), the
'father-in-law's house' and 'María's house'. On
the other hand in (26) the association of que
compró Carlos is with a heterogeneous set (house
and farm), the 'father-in-law's house' and 'María's
farm'. I propose that the distributional facts
shown in (25) and (26) are explained by, and provide evidence for, the postulated meanings because
it is more coherent to associate clear and well-
delineated boundaries with a homogeneous set than
with a heterogeneous one. Like objects are more
easily encompassed within clear boundaries than unlike objects. Thus for the homogeneous casa-casa
of (25) we can use 'Discrete' la, but not so for
the heterogeneous casa-finca of (26).
  Finally, I would like to consider a different
type of evidence in favor of the hypothesized meanings. We have been looking at distributional evidence in terms of qualitative skewings of occurrences, nonoccurrences, and selection of forms as
a response to the intended message. But we can
also look for evidence in support of a meaning
hypothesis in terms of quantitative skewings. In
other words, on the basis of the postulated meanings we can make statistical predictions about the
distribution of the forms in texts.[6] Because of
space limitations, we will look at only one such
prediction based on the meanings of 'Discrete' and
'Nondiscrete'.
  The l-forms in Spanish can occur in connection
with lexical items, as in (27), with de phrases,
as in (28), and with que phrases, as in (29).

   (27) Pintó la casa.
        'He painted the house.'
   (28) Pintó la de Pedro.
        'He painted Peter's (one).'

(29) Pintó la que te compré.
    'He painted the (one) I bought you.'

I suggest that lexical items, de phrases, and que phrases are in a scale of greater diffuseness and lack of delineation. Single words provide less varied information than de phrases, and de phrases provide less varied information than que phrases. A phrase with a de and a lexical item, such as (28), provides more information than one consisting of just the lexical item, as in (27), since the de phrase consists of the information of the lexical item plus the information provided by the de. And a que clause containing a verb provides more varied information than a lexical item or a de plus lexical item because, unlike these two, it contains a verb that describes an event or an occurrence.

Or, looking at it another way, we can say that of the three types of phrases, que clauses provide the least delineated and more diffuse type of information, while lexical items alone provide the most delineated information. De phrases are somewhere in between the two, providing less delineated information than a single, precise lexical item, but more delineated information than a que clause containing verbs.

Now, if this is the case, the meaning hypothesis predicts that there is greater coherence between the meaning of lo and que clauses than between the meaning of lo and de phrases and lexical items. The hypothesis also predicts that there is greater coherence between the 'Discrete' forms el/la and lexical items than between these forms and de and que phrases. If these predictions—which are based on the postulated meanings—are correct, we should find that counts performed on actual texts will show more instances of the more coherent messages than of the less coherent ones.

In (30) we see the results of a count that included sequences of l+word, l+de phrases, and l+que phrases.[7] We find that the count supports the hypothesis because the statistical prediction based on the postulated meanings is borne out. The

(30) Correlation between choice of <u>l</u>-form and
type of associated material.

	l+que+Vb		l+de+word		l+word	
<u>el/la</u>	65	35%	34	71%	83	94%
<u>lo</u>	119	65%	14	29%	5	6%
	184	100%	48	100%	88	100%

<u>l+que</u>/<u>l+de</u>, X^2 = 19.6, p < .001
<u>l+de</u>/<u>l+word</u>, X^2 = 14.3, p < .001

affinity between <u>lo</u> and the following material is much greater on the left-most column, the <u>que</u> clauses, and decreases as we move to the right one on the table, and the reverse is true of <u>el/la</u>. The more delineated the associated material, the more 'Discrete' <u>l</u>-forms, the less delineated, the more 'Nondiscrete' ones.

The evidence that we have presented here points to the validity of the 'Discreteness' hypothesis and confirms the need to abandon the concept of gender as an explanation of the differences between <u>el/la</u> and <u>lo</u>. In this regard, we should note that the data presented here in support of the meaning hypothesis is well beyond any analysis using the notion of gender.

In the <u>valor</u> examples in (22) to (24), for instance, the word <u>valor</u> is as 'masculine' when it has an <u>el</u> or an <u>ese</u> as when it does not; and yet when it appears alone it cannot be referred to by the masculine and we must go to <u>lo</u>. This makes sense if we think of <u>lo</u> as 'Nondiscrete', but not if we think of it as a neuter. Likewise, in the examples with <u>casa</u> and <u>casa</u>, and <u>casa</u> and <u>finca</u> in (25) and (26), the words <u>casa</u> and <u>casa</u> are a combination of feminine and feminine as much as <u>casa</u> and <u>finca</u>. In terms of gender, both are the same: <u>casa-casa</u> is feminine-feminine and <u>casa-finca</u> is feminine-feminine. The possibility of using <u>la</u> in one case but not in the other, therefore, cannot be explained in terms of femininity and must be explained in terms of the substance of 'Discreteness' that distinguishes <u>el/la</u> and <u>lo</u>.

NOTES

1. This paper is based on work that appears in less abbreviated form in Otheguy (1977). The forms el/la and lo are considered here both in what I call their prelexical environment and their pivot environment (el muchacho 'the boy', el que te presenté 'the one I introduced you to'). Since no evidence has ever been presented for the separation of these forms into 'articles' and 'relatives' (as in, for instance, Academia 1973:213-226) they are treated here as a single form.

2. For a discussion of the theoretical orientation of Form-Content analysis, see Diver (1975) and García (1975:38-58). For examples of work in Form-Content analysis, see, besides García (1975), Klein (1975, 1976), Reid (1977), and Zubin (1975), among others.

3. Grammarians have not always been as clear as one would like on the difference between viewing the l-forms as articles and viewing them as deictics. A discussion of this point, however, is beyond the scope of this paper, as is a discussion of the evidence in favor of the deictic analysis. See Otheguy (1977) for details. The hypothesis that the l-forms are deictics similar in meaning to the traditional demonstratives has been advanced by Alonso (1933:132) and by Bello (1847:202), Bull (1965:242), and, although with considerably less clarity as to what is meant by Deixis, by Gili y Gaya (1969:239-242), and Academia (1973:214).

4. The question of the place of él, ella, and ello in a scale such as (1) is beyond the scope of this paper, as is the question of whether él and el are one and the same signal. Also beyond the scope of this paper is whether the prelexical and pivot la and lo are the same as the clitics with the same phonological shape.

5. Actually, this is an oversimplification of the facts of interpretation. In utterances in isolation such as (11) and (12) we could get a 'make' or 'build' interpretation out of lo in cases like (12). In such a case (12) would translate as 'I

like better what Carlos made' as opposed to (11)
'I like better the one Carlos made'. The English
translation here captures the fact that the referent of (12), even if we give hacer a concrete,
'make' interpretation, would still be less clear
and specific than that of (11), thus conforming to
the meaning hypothesis.

6. For a discussion of the rationale for quantitative evidence of the sort we are about to present, see Reid (1977).

7. This count was based on a corpus of between 45,000 and 50,000 words, consisting of the following texts (see list of texts in the references for full citations): Short stories: Cela, García Velasco, Goytisolo, Mellizo, Mojica, Moreno, Sanz, and Vidal. Commentary: Areíto Editorial and Villalón. Novel: Perera. Due to the large number of prelexical 1-forms (1+word on the chart), Perera was excluded from this part of the count.

REFERENCES

Academia Española. 1973. Esbozo de una nueva gramática de la lengua española. Madrid: Espasa-Calpe.

Alonso, A. 1933. Estilística y gramática del artículo en español. Volkstum und Kultur der Romanem 6.189-200. Reprinted in: Alonso 1967.

Alonso, A. 1967. Estudios lingüísticos: Temas españoles. Madrid: Gredos.

Bello, A. 1847. Gramática de la lengua castellana. Buenos Aires: Sopena. Seventh Edition, 1964.

Bull, W. 1965. Spanish for teachers. New York: Ronald.

Casagrande, J. and B. Saciuk, eds. 1972. Generative studies in Romance linguistics. Rowley, Mass.: Newbury.

Diver, W. 1975. Introduction. Columbia University Working Papers in Linguistics 2.1-26.

García, E. 1975. The role of theory in linguistic analysis: The Spanish pronoun system. Amsterdam: North-Holland.

Gili y Gaya, S. 1969. Curso superior de sintaxis española. Barcelona: Bibliograf.
Hall, R. 1965. The 'neuter' in Romance: A pseudo problem. Word 21.421-428.
Klein, F. 1975. Pragmatic constraints on distribution: The Spanish subjunctive. CLS 11.353-366.
Klein, F. 1976. 'Same' vs. 'different' crosslinguistically: The 'articles' in English and Spanish. CLS 12.413-424.
Luján, M. 1972. On the so-called neuter article in Spanish. In: Casagrande and Saciuk, 1972.
Manoliu, M. 1970. ¿Qué es el neutro español? Revue Roumaine de Linguistique 15.241-246.
Otheguy, R. 1977. The meaning of Spanish el, la, and lo. Unpublished Ph.D. dissertation. Graduate School of the City University of New York.
Reid, W. 1977. The quantitative validation of a grammatical hypothesis: The 'passé simple' and the 'imparfait'. NELS 7.315-333.
Zubin, D. 1975. On the distributional properties of surface morphology and their consequences for semantic analysis. Columbia University Working Papers in Linguistics 2.189-218.

Texts Used

Areíto Editorial. Revista Areíto. Box 1124. Peter Stuyvesant Station, New York, NY 10009.
Cela, C. Sansón García, fotógrafo ambulante. In: Cuentos Españoles. Angel Flores, ed. Bantam Dual Language Books, 1960.
García Velasco, A. Ociosos y peregrinos. Revista Insula, No. 347, p. 16, 1975.
Goytisolo, J. El Guardia. In: Cuentos Españoles. Angel Flores, ed. Bantam Dual Language Books, 1960.
Mellizo, C. Prólogo. Revista Insula, No. 344-345, p. 32, 1975.
Mojica, V. Como si hubiera sido ayer. Revista Insula, No. 347, 16, 1975.
Moreno, G. Jota. Revista Insula, No. 343, 16, 1975.
Perera, H. El sitio de nadie. Barcelona: Editorial Planeta. 1972.

Vidal, C. El empleo. Revista Insula, No. 341, 16, 1975.
Villalón, J. El exilio y el liberalismo. In: Areíto 2.4-7.

PORTUGUESE VOWEL HARMONY AND THE 'ELSEWHERE CONDITION'

WAYNE J. REDENBARGER
The Ohio State University

In a 1972 LSA paper later published in <u>Linguistic Inquiry</u> (1974:61-80) James Harris presents a detailed argument to the effect that Portuguese phonology--and specifically its vowel harmony process--requires Kiparsky's 'Elsewhere Condition' (EC) on rule application for an adequate formulation. Harris presents a set of Portuguese phonological and morphophonological data; he next argues for a set of rules to describe the data, and then observes that Kiparsky's 'EC' is required to resolve an application problem with two of the rules. His argument is, therefore, of the following syllogistic form: the data is a given; solution 'x' is the best codification of the data; principle 'y' is necessary to be able to formulate solution 'x'; therefore, principle 'y' must exist.

Without question, this is a totally cogent syllogism. In addition, the data cited by Harris is not obscure or dialectal but rather is mainstream, prestige Brazilian Portuguese and is certainly correct.

Harris elected, however, to redefine the [e]-[ɛ] and [o]-[ɔ] contrasts not as a tense/lax contrast but rather as a primary height contrast. As Halle notes in his response to Ladefoged (1973:930) the Sound Pattern of English (SPE) feature framework specifies the [e]-[ɛ] contrast not as a height contrast but rather as a tense/lax contrast. We therefore have the following discrepancy between Harris' distinctive feature (DF) specifications and those used by Halle (see (1)).

(1) Harris (1974:66)   Halle (1973:930)

	/i/	/e/	/ɛ/		/i/	/e/	/ɛ/
high	+	–	–	high	+	–	–
low	–	–	+	low	–	–	–
				tense	+	+	–

The theoretical purpose of this present paper is to demonstrate that Harris' decision to change the SPE specification for [ɛ] and [ɔ] from [-low] to [+low] and ignore [±tense] in the formulation of his 'Lowering' and 'Harmony' rules is of the greatest consequence. I shall, by employing the DF [±tense],[1] reformulate both of the rules in question so that they can not only be made simpler formally, but can be made to apply to a wider range of data and in so doing eliminate entirely the rule application problems which demand the 'EC'. Obviously, if I can present a better analysis covering the same Portuguese data, and if I do not require any special metatheoretical principle of rule application such as Kiparsky's 'EC' to do so, it cannot be maintained that there exists any evidence from Portuguese for the Elsewhere Condition.

Analysis: Phonetics. Let us examine the specific differences between the two frameworks (the feature [c.p.] ≡ the SPE feature [low] for present purposes ... v. Perkell 1971):

(2)

	Harris			Halle		[-round]
+high}	i	u	+high}	i	u	vowels to the left of
-high) -low)	e	o	-high) -c.p.)	e-ɛ	o-ɔ	the slash; [+tense] vowels to
+low}	ɛ	a/ɔ	+c.p.}	a		the left of the hyphen.

In Redenbarger 1977 I noted that the F_2 of Portuguese [a] lies right along the 1.5 kHz natural resonance frequency demonstrating that it is definitely not a [+back] vowel ... in the modified feature framework used in Harris' analysis it must be a [+back] vowel to distinguish it from [ε]; this is a direct result of his having elected to change the specification of [ε] to [+low]. I noted there that the [ε] is right at the neutral F_1 natural resonance of 0.5 kHz showing it is not a [+low] vowel but merely [-high]. Those acoustic plots are discussed in detail in Redenbarger (1977) and will not be repeated here. One should, however, remember that there are good, a priori phonetic reasons for not changing the specification of [ε] to [+low] and of [a] to [+back].

Phonology. Let us then examine the data in Table 1. As these forms illustrate, the stem vowels in a related noun and 3rd person present indicative verb form always match if that stem vowel is an [i], [u], or [a]. In DF terms, the [+high] and the [+c.p.] stem vowels do not undergo any alternation between nouns and verbs.

If the underlying stem vowel is spelled 'e' or 'o', however, there does occur an alternation between related nouns and verbs. In fact, the stressed tense vowels [é] and [ó] are not found in 3sg. or 3pl. present indicative verb stems, even in the 'irregular' verbs. As Table 1 clearly illustrates, the underlying vowel is unaffected in nouns--one finds both stressed [é] and stressed [ɛ́] as in s[é]lo and regr[ɛ́]ssa; one finds both [ó] and [ɔ́] in f[ó]rça and n[ɔ́]ta. In the verb forms, however, there is only the lax vowel, i.e. only [ɛ́] and [ɔ́] as in s[ɛ́]la and f[ɔ́]rça.

One possible explanation is that there exist only [ε] and [ɔ] underlyingly in both the noun and verb forms, i.e. there is some larger restriction on the lexicon that all nonhigh vowels are lax. This analysis would require that the existence of the many stressed tense vowels in the noun forms be tensed by rule. Several previous studies have

Table 1.

Noun	3s.pr.ind.	3p.pr.ind.	gloss	alternation
t[í]ro	t[í]ra	t[í]ram	'shot'	[í]
fig[ú]ra	fig[ú]ra	fig[ú]ram	'draw'	[ú]
c[á]ça	c[á]ça	c[á]çam	'hunt'	[á]
esc[ó]va	esc[ó]va	esc[ɔ́]vam	'brush'	[ó]–[ɔ́]
f[ó]rça	f[ɔ́]rça	f[ɔ́]rçam	'force'	[ó]–[ɔ́]
p[ɔ́]rte	p[ɔ́]rta	p[ɔ́]rtam	'carry'	[ɔ́]
n[ɔ́]ta	n[ɔ́]ta	n[ɔ́]tam	'note'	[ɔ́]
inter[é]sse	inter[ɛ́]ssa	inter[ɛ́]ssam	'interest'	[é]–[ɛ́]
s[é]lo	s[ɛ́]la	s[ɛ́]lam	'seal'	[é]–[ɛ́]
conv[ɛ́]rsa	conv[ɛ́]rsa	conv[ɛ́]rsam	'converse'	[ɛ́]
regr[ɛ́]sso	regr[ɛ́]ssa	regr[ɛ́]ssam	'return'	[ɛ́]

attempted this, for example, Mattoso Câmara (1972) who relied on a rule of vowel harmony in nouns, and Hensey (1974) who does likewise. In such a formulation the change from [ɛ] and [ɔ] to [e] and [o] is due to a tendency on the part of the stem vowel to harmonize with the final -o of the masculine singular.

Whatever the possible historical validity of that hypothesis such synchronic forms as regr[ɛ́]sso (m.), p[ɔ́]rte (m.), esc[ó]va (f.), f[ó]rça (f.) (v. Table 1) and many more illustrate unambiguously that it is neither gender nor the final vowel which governs the tensing of nonhigh vowels in nouns. One must therefore reject that approach and posit the [ɛ]-[e] and [ɔ]-[o] stem vowel difference as an underlying difference.

In positing underlying /e/ and /o/ in such stems as:

/eskov+/   /foɾs+/   /inteɾes+/   /sel+/

one necessarily makes the claim that the lax vowel in:

esc[ɔ́]va   f[ɔ́]rça   inter[ɛ́]sse   s[ɛ́]la

is derived via a process restricted to verbs alone; if not the [é]/[ɛ́], and [ó]/[ɔ́] contrasts in nouns would be neutralized.

This process employs grammatical information and is codified as in (3).

(3)   V $C_0 + X]_{vb}$
        [-hi]
          ↓
        [-tense]

Since its effect is to lax the last vowel in verb stems I shall refer to this exceptionless morphological process as VbStmLxg (Verb Stem Laxing).
It accounts for the skewed distribution in Table 1.

Note that the ability to predict the tongue body height on the basis of universal physiological principles (v. Perkell 1971) and thus the ability to write this rule as a 'laxing' rule rather than a 'lowering' is much to be preferred over the formulation required by Harris' revised features specifications. Harris' rule is reproduced in (4).

(4) Harris 1974 rule 22: $V \atop [-hi]$ $C_0 +]_{vb}$
$\downarrow$
$[+low]$

In comparing these rules note first that there is a clear restriction against [+high,-tense] vowels in Brazilian Portuguese. Formulated as a change to [-tense] as I have it, the exclusion of the [+high] vowels is an absolute necessity; formulated as a lowering rule as Harris sees it, the exclusion of one end of a 3-ary height continuum from moving down to the bottom slot is purely arbitrary.

Also, the fact that [a] is unchanged by the VbStmLxg rule (and also that [ε] does not 'lower' to [a]) fits very naturally into a DF system which separates the pharynx constricting gesture [c.p.] from the true tense/lax pairs (v. fn. 1). In a framework using [c.p.] the segment [a] is already [-tense] and therefore the VbStmLxg rule operates vacuously; likewise, [ε] being the paradigmatic neutral vowel--[-tense,-c.p.,-back,...]--it is unaffected by a rule assigning [-tense] to vowels.

In his 1974 study, Harris assists the reader with a mnemonic chart of which rules produce each particular Portuguese stem vowel. It is most important to observe that his chart, which I reproduce in (5), is not of the phonetic data but instead is of the 'rules' for which he argues. Harris uses an 'L' to indicate a stem vowel lowered by his Lowering rule, an 'H' to indicate one changed by his Harmony rule, and a 'U' to indicate a vowel showing its Underlying quality on the surface.

I, on the other hand, should prefer to emphasize the unity of all three conjugations. Clearly, if a pattern can be found which holds without restriction across all conjugations that pattern is by

(5) (Harris 1974:62)

	-a- themes		-e-&-i- themes	
Pres. Ind.	L U L U L L		H H L U L L	
Pres. Subj.	L U L U L L		H H H H H H	
Imperative	L	U	L	U

definition more explanatory than a hypothesized pattern holding only in two conjugations and not in the other. It is this notion of maximal application with minimal ad hoc restriction which underlies every scientific argument of increased explanation. In search of such maximal patterns I thus propose the following chart of my own (Table 2) based on the following facts which hold across all three conjugations:

Columns 1--The stem vowels in the PresIndic 2sg, 3sg, 3pl forms all match the Imperative singular.

Columns 2--The stem vowels in the Pres Indic 1pl, 2pl, and the Imperative plural forms always match.

Columns 3--The stem vowel in the Pres Indic 1sg matches the PresSubj 1sg, 2sg, 3sg, and 3pl forms.

Columns 4--The stem vowels in the PresSubj 1pl and 2pl forms always match.

I have included in Table 2 samples for an underlying /o/ or /ɔ/ in all three conjugations, viz. morar 'to dwell', mover 'to move', and dormir 'to sleep'. This is precisely the same surface data cited by Prof. Harris; I have merely arranged it to emphasize different regularities.

While for reasons of exposition I have been referring primarily to back vowels in Table 2, the processes in question apply equally to front vowels as well; therefore the distribution of [ɛ]/[e]/[i] in verbs like secar, dever, and servir corresponds exactly with the distribution of [ɔ]/[o]/[i] in the table.

Table 2.

	1 2 3 4	1 2 3 4	1 2 3 4			
Pres Indic	1sg	ɔ́				m[ɔ́]ro	m[ó]vo	d[ú]rmo
	2sg	ɔ́	ɔ́	ɔ́		m[ɔ́]ras	m[ɔ́]ves	d[ɔ́]rmes
	3sg	ɔ́	ɔ́	ɔ́		m[ɔ́]ra	m[ɔ́]ve	d[ɔ́]rme
	1pl	o	o	o		m[o]ramos	m[o]vemos	d[o]rmimos
	2pl	o	o	o		m[o]rais	m[o]veis	d[o]rmis
	3pl	ɔ́		ó		m[ɔ́]ram	m[ɔ́]vem	d[ɔ́]rmem
Pres Subj	1sg	ɔ́	ɔ́	ó	ú	m[ɔ́]re	m[ó]va	d[ú]rma
	2sg	ɔ́	ɔ́	ó	ú	m[ɔ́]res	m[ó]vas	d[ú]rmas
	3sg	ɔ́	ɔ́	ó	ú	m[ɔ́]re	m[ó]va	d[ú]rma
	1pl	o	o	o	u	m[o]remos	m[o]vamos	d[u]rmamos
	2pl	o	o	o	u	m[o]reis	m[o]vais	d[u]rmais
	3pl	ɔ́	ɔ́	ó	ú	m[ɔ́]rem	m[ó]vam	d[ú]rmam
Imprtv	sg	ɔ́	ɔ́	ɔ́		m[ɔ́]ra	m[ɔ́]ve	d[ɔ́]rme
	pl	o	o	o		m[o]rai	m[o]vei	d[o]rmi

In Redenbarger (1977) I formalized a rule of Unstressed Vowel Tensing (abbreviated UnStrTnsg). This rule does what Harris' 'Neutralization' rule does and is not in dispute. I repeat it here in (6) for reference:

(6) UnStrTnsg   V̆
                [-c.p.]
                ↓
              [+tense]

If one correlates the -a-, -e-, and -i- columns in Table 2 in light of the effect of the UnStrTnsg rule, the table can be collapsed immediately. Specifically, column 2 is column 1 when unstressed; likewise, column 4 is the same as column 3 unstressed. In other words, if columns 1 and 3 are known, columns 2 and 4 can be derived by a single rule--UnStrTnsg.

Second, observe that the stressed vowel [ɔ] in column 1 runs across all conjugations. I have already demonstrated that VbStmLxg is a morphological rule which must be restricted to operate only on verbs; it is also evident from this distribution that it applies in -a- themes, -e- themes, and -i- themes. In short, VbStmLxg generates column 1.

Since with VbStmLxg we have column 1 and therefore, via UnStrTnsg, column 2 as well, the codification of column 3 will complete the picture. To do that one must look beyond the surface phonetic forms to the underlying forms.

Reanalysis of vowel harmony. The 'unmarked' mood in any Romance language is the indicative, in the same sense that 'present' is the unmarked tense. The Portuguese subjunctive has an explicit marker: the vowel -a- in the 2nd and 3rd conjugations, and the vowel -e- in the 1st conjugation. The indicative is characterized by the absence of that subjunctive marker, i.e. Jakobson's <u>signe zéro</u> (Jakobson 1939). Hence:

2sg PresIndic /moɾ+a+∅+s/ vs.
2sg PresSubj /moɾ+a+e+s/

What all the present subjunctive forms have in common with the 1sg Pres Indic is the presence of a vowel immediately following the conjugation's characteristic theme vowel. With a form like <u>moro</u> it is not a subjunctive marker, it is the person marker /+o/; in all seven forms of columns 3 and 4 there is an <u>underlying</u> /..+V+V../ sequence.

Portuguese has several ways of resolving such hiatus groups, but in the limited case under discussion the solution is to delete the first of the two vowels--which in all seven cases is the theme vowel. One, therefore, will never find the form *<u>morao</u> for 'I reside', only <u>moro</u>, never *<u>moraes</u>, only <u>mores</u>. The rule deleting this theme vowel was formulated as a separate morphological process by Harris, and labelled 'Truncation' (see (7)).

(7) (Harris 1974:65) Truncation: $X \; V + V \; Y]_{vb}$
$$\downarrow$$
$$\emptyset$$

We shall return to this rule directly.

Consider now the interesting phenomenon in the columns numbered 3 in Table 2--viz. the [ɔ]-[o]-[u] alternation. The key insight is that the stem vowels in the forms of column 3 harmonize in tenseness and height with the theme vowel iff the theme vowel is one of those deleted by the Truncation rule. The matrix in (8) summarizes the changes effected when the harmony rule operates:

(8)

		Stem Vwl		Theme	Conjuga-
		(before Harm)	(after Harm)	Vwl	tion
ɔ o u	a e i	/ɔ/ →	[ɔ]	a	1st
- - + high	- - +	/ɔ/ →	[o]	e	2nd
- + + tense	- + +	/ɔ/ →	[u]	i	3rd

Since only [-c.p.] stem vowels undergo harmony, the harmonizing process is limited to making the specifications for the features [high] and [tense] of the stem vowel match those of the theme vowel.

Employing the SPE 'α' notation invented solely for such assimilations (v. SPE Chapter 8) this can be formalized as in (9).

(9) Vowel Harmony
  (abb: VwlHarm)
$$\begin{bmatrix} V & C_0 + & V & + V \; .. \end{bmatrix}_{vb}$$
$$\begin{bmatrix} -high \\ -c.p. \end{bmatrix} \quad \begin{bmatrix} \alpha high \\ \beta tnse \end{bmatrix}$$
$$\downarrow$$
$$\begin{bmatrix} \alpha high \\ \beta tnse \end{bmatrix}$$

Note that VwlHarm, like VbStmLxg uses morphological information.

It should be emphasized that while I have been careful to argue against Harris' revision of the specifications for [ɛ] and [ɔ] by citing exactly the same Brazilian data he used, the VwlHarm rule works exactly the same in all dialects of Portuguese including Lusitanian.

According to my formulation, Vowel Harmony in Portuguese is a double assimilation process. There is a simultaneous and total assimilation in both tongue-body height and in tenseness; moreover, it applies in all three conjugations.

Harris' analysis is quite different from this one. In his formulation the Harmony rule operates only in the -e- and -i- theme conjugations. It is an easy matter to determine why Harris restricts his rule in this way ... he says so explicitly in his article:

> How then do we know that the low vowel of say first person singular indicative esc[ó]vo and subjunctive esc[ó]ve, of first conjugation escovar 'to brush' (cf. the noun escó[ó]va 'brush', which indicates nonlow /o/) is not produced by the Harmony rule? The answer is straightforward. It is not possible to formulate a reasonable Harmony rule that will cover the first conjugation as well as the second and third ... Barring some devious notational artifice I have overlooked, (18) [2nd/3rd conj. harmony] and (19) [1st conj. harmony] simply cannot be collapsed. (Harris 1974:70).

Harris has been trapped by the changes he has made to Halle's specifications. I suggest that the correct statement is, 'It is not possible to formulate a reasonable harmony rule that will cover all the conjugations when [ɛ] and [ɔ] are specified [+low]'. Thus, despite the fact that he retains the label, Harris must now settle not for a true harmony rule but for a raising rule (see (10)).

(10) (Harris 1974:69)

$$\begin{bmatrix} \alpha\text{round} \\ \alpha\text{back} \end{bmatrix} C_0 + \begin{bmatrix} V \\ -\text{low} \\ <+\text{high}> \end{bmatrix} + V ..]_{vb}$$
$$\downarrow$$
$$\begin{bmatrix} -\text{low} \\ <+\text{high}> \end{bmatrix}$$

First, note that Harris must resort to a common but highly dubious 'α,α' system not to codify an assimilation but solely to exclude [a] from undergoing his raising rule. Since Portuguese [a] is not actually a [+back] vowel to start with (v. Martins 1973) the intractable descriptive dilemma caused by relabeling [ɛ] and [ɔ] as [+low] is again apparent, since it is the presence of [ɛ] as a [-back +low -round] vowel that forced Harris to equate [a] with [ɑ], its slot having now been taken over by [ɛ].

Second, note that in Harris' rule the theme vowel is specified [-low]. Since the first conjugation is the only conjugation with a [+low] theme vowel, this specification is the functional equivalent of a restriction on the rule saying 'Condition--2nd and 3rd conjugations only'. Compare my VwlHarm rule using [tense] instead of [low] which requires no such restriction and predicts the distribution correctly for all three conjugations.

This problem is the direct result again of using [low] to distinguish the tense/lax pairs [ɛ]-[e] and [ɔ]-[o]. Viewed solely as a height change, the unity codified in my column 3 forms (Table 2) cannot be formalized. But, once we have only two heights to deal with, viz. [±high] instead of three [+high], [-high -low], [+low] the correct generalization is codifiable--the high vowels do not harmonize.

In summary: Harris (1) has written a raising rule and not a harmony rule, (2) has formal problems excluding [a] from undergoing the rule, and (3) must restrict his rule against operating in the first conjugation. In contrast, my VwlHarm rule is a true, full-assimilation harmony rule, needs no 'α,α' devices, and works in all three conjugations.

Indeed VwlHarm is actually simpler when it includes the first conjugation -a- themes than when they are excluded. If one wished to restrict Vwl Harm to just the -e- and -i- themes it would be necessary to change the [αtense] specification to [+tense] since both [e] and [i] are [+tense]. But according to the markedness conventions of SPE, an 'α' is less expensive since total assimilation is the most natural possible process. This principle would hold whether one is using a Stampian formulation for determining rule naturalness or a Prague School formulation. Thus, to try to exclude the -a- themes is to give up the most general possible formulation of the rule, in both the conceptual and formal senses.

This is an excellent case of a proposed change to a segment's specification being judged by the predictions it makes. The modification to the SPE features which Harris has made has forced him into a corner; the SPE specification plus the replacement of [low] by [c.p.], on the other hand, allows two extra generalizations to be captured and imposes a framework on the analyst which penalizes him if he tries to restrict the domain of application of VwlHarm.

There is, however, yet another very important generalization which one must forfeit in Harris' analysis, viz. 'the Portuguese forms which have harmonizing stem V's are a proper subset of those which lose their theme vowels by Truncation'.

In both Harris' analysis and mine the structural description for theme vowel truncation is in part identical to the SD for VwlHarm, viz. ...V C_0 + V ...]$_{vb}$. When using the SPE feature [low], however, one cannot write a harmony rule that will apply to all three conjugations as Harris has so accurately observed in the quote above. Harris' rule 5 (Truncation) and his rule 18 (Harmony) cannot, therefore, be collapsed since theme vowels truncate and stem vowels harmonize in all three conjugations.

Since I have written a true harmony rule which does apply in all conjugations it is eminently collapsable with the truncation rule by the use of a single parenthesis around the harmonizing vowel and the noting of the deletion of the theme vowel; i.e. whether there is a harmonizing stem vowel present or not, truncation takes place (see (11)).

(11) VHarm/Trn:

$$\ldots \begin{pmatrix} V \\ [-high] \\ [-c.p.] \end{pmatrix} C_0 + \begin{bmatrix} V \\ \alpha high \\ \beta tnse \end{bmatrix} + V \ldots]_{vb}$$
$$\downarrow \qquad\qquad \downarrow$$
$$\begin{bmatrix} \alpha high \\ \beta tnse \end{bmatrix} \qquad \emptyset$$

We thus capture the correct morphological generalization--'Though the conjugation class marker (the theme vowel) is lost when it is followed by another vowel, the conjugation class info is recoverable when you have a harmonizing stem vowel'. We, moreover, avoid having two separate morphological rules which can be ordered back-to-back and have highly similar SD's. The ability to now collapse VwlHarm and Truncation is then the fourth advantage to retaining the tense/lax contrast as the basis of the [ɛ]-[e] distinction.

VbStmLxg precedes VwlHarm and UnStrTnsg. Let us now consider what effect this reformulation has on

Harris' crucial example for his theoretical argument regarding the 'EC'.

It is central to my analysis that VbStmLxg apply before VHarm/Trn if the extreme generality of VbStmLxg is to be maintained. My view of the distribution is that the reason one finds [ɛ] only in stressed vowels is due to the effects of UnStrTnsg which tenses it to [e] in all unstressed environments. Although Harris also recognizes the need for UnStrTnsg (Harris 1974:66) he considers the above distribution to be due to a laxing process which operates only on stressed vowels; therefore, one finds [ɛ] only under stress (Harris 1974:75).

As an illustration of the importance of the rule order in my solution, in (12) are three sample derivations from <u>mover</u>.

(12)

	/mov+e+∅/	/mov+e+o/	/mov+e+muʃ/
VbStmLxg	ɔ	ɔ	ɔ
VHarm/Trn		o ∅	
Stress	ɔ́	ó	é
UnStrTnsg			o
	[mɔ́vi]	[móvu]	[movémuʃ]

The <u>fugir</u> class. Harris acknowledges that verbs like <u>discutir</u>, etc. in which the underlying stem vowel is a nonalternating [+high] [i] or [u] comprise 'the substantial majority of third conjugation verbs' (Harris 1974:73). However, there are a few 3rd conjugation verbs having an underlying stem [i] or [u] which changes to [ɛ] or [ɔ] in the column 1 forms (cf. Table 2) while maintaining the [i] or [u] quality elsewhere.

At the moment, my VbStmLxg rule has only one restriction on its input, viz. [-high]; let us consider for the moment the consequence of labeling these verbs 'Exceptional' (following Harris' [+E] diacritic suggestion) so that they undergo VbStmLxg (see (13)).

As I commented earlier, [ʊ] and [ɪ] are prohibited since in Portuguese all [-tense] vowels are [-high].

(13)

	/fuʒ+i+∅/	/fuʒ+i+o/	/fuʒ+i+muʃ/
VbStmLxg	o	o	o
VHrm/Trn		u ∅	
Stress	ó	ú	í
UnStrTnsg			u
	*[fóʒi]	[fúʒu]	[fuʒímuʃ]

Let us then put that descriptive statement into
productive rule form as in (14),

(14) $\begin{matrix} V \\ [-\text{tense}] \end{matrix} \rightarrow [-\text{high}]$

and apply it late in the rule sequence when we
apply the other surface-true phonological rules
such as UnStrTnsg. The result is: [fuʒu] and
[fuʒimuʃ] have no vowels which fit the SD, but
[foʒi] is changed to [fɔʒi] which is the correct
form.
   Note that this [+high] → [-high] lowering set
off by a laxing rule is identical to the laxing >
lowering well known from Old French; in OF all
prenasal vowels were changed to [-tense] vowels
and the [+high] vowels immediately became [-high]
(v. Redenbarger 1977). This evidence from another Romance language with a similar vowel system
is strong support for the present analysis of the
irregular fugir- class forms. Quite simply then,
the only odd thing about fugir is that it undergoes the VbStmLxg rule.
   Harris bases an involved theoretical argument
on his solution of the fugir forms which in turn
has a bearing on the need for Kiparsky's 'EC'.
There is no longer any need for us to go into
that, however, since as I have just shown, in my
solution: (1) the Harmony rule is not purely a
tongue-body raising phenomenon, (2) the order
VbStmLxg > VwlHarm is easy to maintain, and (3)
the exceptional class containing fugir can be pin-
pointed as to its exceptionality without affecting
the rest of the rule system.

In summary: by clinging to the uncontroversial specification of [ɛ]-[e] and [ɔ]-[o] as a tense/lax contrast and rejecting Harris' redefinition of these vowel pairs as a [±low] contrast we can codify the Portuguese Vowel Harmony process in such a way as to allow it to be stated as a natural full assimilation rule, i.e. a true Harmony rule, as a rule not needing 'α,α' devices, and as a rule which applies in all three conjugations. Since this last point permits VwlHarm to be collapsed with theme vowel Truncation, we also capture a previously uncodifiable morphological relationship between the deletion of the theme vowel and the harmonizing stem vowel. Finally, the codification of this unrestricted harmony rule eliminates a sticky rule application problem for which an extra metatheoretical condition had previously been needed, viz. the 'Elsewhere Condition'.

Theoretical implications. The universal measure of any scientific theory is the predictions which follow from its tenets. Thus, to have to go outside the holistic rule system and impose meta-theoretical constraints is something one does as a very last resort. One is properly wary when the rule system applies well in 99 percent of the cases but needs an outside function to patch up those cases when normal rule application generates incorrect outputs.

It is therefore understandable why from the moment of its formulation, Kiparsky's 'Elsewhere Condition' was seen as 'controversial' (Harris 1974:79). One skeptical of such metatheoretical intervention with the predictions of the grammar might paraphrase the 'EC' as: 'A rule always applies when its SD is met unless it knows that it would be messing up another rule's earlier effect, in which case it does not apply'.

Kiparsky uses such terms as 'incompatible' to describe when this must be done; he does not, unfortunately, formalize that notion so it can be tested scientifically. His only definition is to tell us that palatalization and voicing are not included in the definition (Kiparsky 1973:fn2) even if the structural description is met for both.

Combined with this one must consider the fact that Kiparsky's few segmental examples (the majority involve phenomena widely considered cyclic viz. stress and poetic metrics) seem to have alternative analyses available. Briefly, Kiparsky (1973:93) suggests that [ʃ] palatalization in Karok involves two <u>subcases</u> of the same rule applying conjunctively. But the crucial case [ʔíʃʃaha] can be got by applying Kiparsky's entire rule 6 iteratively to its own output--the result will be identical to applying both subcases on one application. Kiparsky's West Finnish example (1973:96) is indeed problematical if one insists on a synchronic underlying -k; but if we elect to specify the segment in question as underlying -h, then the deletion rule becomes -h → ∅ and is exceptionless; plus the crucial case involving the geminate is solved since as Trubetzkoy states, 'all Finnish consonants participate in the correlation of gemination (with the exception of j, v, d, <u>and h</u>)' (1969: 169). This is precisely the result predicted by applying the rules normally.

In short, Harris' 1974 article was not only the very first example of this supposedly universal principle to be seen in one of the widely known Western languages but, given the problems with Kiparsky's 1973 examples, Portuguese was frankly the first strong case in favor of 'EC'. But, as I have demonstrated at some length, if one uses Halle's DF specifications (1973:930) for [ɛ] and [ɔ], there is no evidence from Portuguese for the Elsewhere Condition.

Since Harris considers a rule which assigns the DF [-low] to be 'incompatible' with a rule later changing that specification to [+low] (1974:78) we have a concrete example of what might be encompassed under that definition if it were to be made explicit. But if that is truly an incompabible change, then my rules of VbStmLxg and VwlHarm or Harris' own rules of Harmony and Neutralization are counterexamples to the 'EC' since 'n forms

like /dev+e+o/ → [dɛv.. → [dev..., or
/moɾ+a+emoʃ/ → [mɔɾ.. → [moɾ.. first one specification for the feature [tense] (or [low] to Harris) is assigned and then the opposite 'contradictory' value routinely applies and overrides the earlier.

While the purpose of this paper is first to present a more elegant formulation of the phonological processes affecting the Portuguese vowel system and in so doing demonstrate that no metatheoretical condition such as 'EC' is needed for that codification, its second purpose is to point up that with Portuguese removed from the list of supporting languages, attention must be given by those who would maintain that 'EC' exists to promulgating several clear examples (not involving cyclic phenomena) and explaining the several counterexamples which--if Harris' definition of 'incompatible' is correct--abound in languages like Portuguese.

NOTES

The author is grateful to Professor James Harris for his immensely helpful comments on an earlier draft of this paper. This does not imply that we are in full agreement on the conclusions herein.

1. There exists a long history of differing approaches to defining tense/lax, e.g. physiological effect (Ladefoged 1971:75), acoustic effect (Wood 1975), causative muscle group (Perkell 1971), etc.--see Miller 1974 for a full history dating back to Sweet's 'shape of the vocal tract' definition. Thus, for two reasons: (1) most phoneticians and phonologists are already accustomed to the terms 'tense' and 'lax' and (2) to avoid making any definition-specific claims, I shall use [tense] to define the following tense/lax vowel pairs: [i]-[ɩ], [u]-[ɷ], [e]-[ɛ], and [o]-[ɔ]. These are universally stipulated to be tense/lax pairs by all partisans of whatever definition while the extension of this phonetic definition to include [a]-type vowels has little currency among phoneticians. In short we shall stay on absolutely

firm, uncontroversial ground. NB: With the advent of [c.p.] (v. Perkell 1971) to replace [low] the vowel [a] would no longer be specified [+tense] as in SPE.

2. For completeness one should note that there are two phonological rules which, being ordered after VbStmLxg, do produce systematic surface exceptions to this generalization. These rules, 'Pre-Nasal Tensing' and 'Pre-Palatal Tensing' are exceptionless, late rules and produce the tense vowels in [sóɲu] sonho 'dream', [xému] remo 'row', and [féʃə] fecha 'close' respectively. Clearly these forms do not disconfirm the generality of this distribution as stated. These rules are formalized in:

(PreNasTnsg)　　V　N　　(PrePalTnsg)　　V　　C
　　　　　　　　↓　　　　　　　　　　　[-c.p.] [+hi]
　　　　　　[+tense]　　　　　　　　　　[-back] [-back]
　　　　　　　　　　　　　　　　　　　　　　↓
　　　　　　　　　　　　　　　　　　　　[+tense]

REFERENCES

Chomsky, Noam and Morris Halle. 1968. The sound pattern of English. New York: Harper and Row.
Halle, Morris. 1973. Review of: Preliminaries to linguistic phonetics, by P. Ladefoged. Lg. 49.926-933.
Harris, James. 1974. Evidence from Portuguese for the 'Elsewhere Condition' in phonology. LI 5.61-80.
Hensey, Fritz. 1974. Portuguese vowel alternation. In: Generative studies in Romance languages. Edited by J. Casagrande and B. Saciuk. Rowley, Mass.: Newbury House. 285-292.
Jakobson, Roman. 1939. Signe zéro. Mélanges de linguistique, offerts à Charles Bally. 143-152.
Kiparsky, Paul. 1973. 'Elsewhere' in phonology. In: A Festschrift for Morris Halle. Edited by S. Anderson and P. Kiparsky. New York: Holt, Rinehart and Winston. 93-106.

Ladefoged, Peter. 1971. Preliminaries to linguistic phonetics. Chicago: University of Chicago Press.
Martins, M. Raquel Delgado. 1973. Análise acústica das vogais tónicas em português. BF 22.303-314.
Mattoso Câmara, Joaquim. 1972. The Portuguese language. Chicago: University of Chicago Press.
Miller, Patricia Donegan. 1974. A critical bibliography on the tense/lax distinction in vowels. Ohio State University, Working Papers in Linguistics 17.222-231.
Perkell, Joseph. 1971. A preliminary study of two suggested revisions of the features specifying vowels. Massachusetts Institute of Technology, Research Laboratory of Electronics, Quarterly progress report No. 102.123-139.
Redenbarger, Wayne. 1977. Portuguese [ɐ] as an advanced tongue root and constricted pharynx vowel. Proceedings of the 1975 linguistic symposium on Romance languages. Edited by M. P. Hagiwara.
Trubetzkoy, N. S. 1969. Principles of phonology. Berkeley: University of California Press.
Wood, Sidney. 1975. Tense and lax vowels. Lund University Phonetics Laboratory, Working Papers 11.109-113.

SENTENTIAL CLITICS
AND CLAUSE REDUCTION IN ITALIAN

MARIO SALTARELLI
University of Illinois

It is sometimes claimed that the infinitive in infinitival clauses like (1a) is an object nominal, which implies that the matrix verb 'want' functions transitively and is therefore not an auxiliary.

(1a) don't you want to go to Rome?
(1b) I want to, but I must put it off

Conversational responses like (1b) present serious problems for an homogeneous object nominal analysis of infinitival clauses. In particular, the <u>it</u> complement anaphor is not an appropriate response with the matrix verb 'want': <u>I want *it, but I must put it off</u>. Likewise, the zero complement anaphor is ungrammatical in the adversative phrase: <u>I want to, but I must put off</u> *(to). In general, this paper shows that the relational status of infinitival clauses derived through structure reducing rules like Equi-NP Deletion, Subject Raising or Verb Raising is revealed by the surface syntactic behavior of anaphoric phenomena like the <u>it</u>/zero alternation in (1). The appearance of <u>it</u> anaphors may indicate a noun phrase, a nominal, or a sentential complement (NP or S Pronominalization), whereas zero anaphors point out a verb phrase (VP Deletion). In languages which exhibit a greater variety of infinitival clauses, e.g. Italian, the anaphor test distinguishes surface infinitival constructions [X V-finite V-infinitive Y] into two separate types: Type I [X V-auxiliary V-main Y], Type II (X V-main Nominal Y]. Type I infinitival constructions are similar to simple verb constructions in that they define a similar range of syntactic phenomena: reflexivization, auxiliary selection, proclisis, etc. Type II infinitival constructions do not permit these phenomena. Where surface alternation can be observed, Type I can be said to be the output of Verb Raising, whereas Type II roughly defines the output of Equi-NP Deletion and Subject Raising.

The thesis which I attempt to demonstrate in this paper is that the phenomenon of proclitic placement of unstressed pronouns in Italian infinitival constructions is defined as taking place only in Type I constructions. Thus, the characterization of proclitic placement in a grammar of Italian needs no special syntactic rule; rather it is explained as the consequence of independently motivated rules of structure reduction. My proposal is the antithesis of a score of major solutions proposed in recent years, all within very similar theoretical frameworks: Clitic Placement (Kayne 1975) in French, Clitic Climbing (Roldán 1974) in Spanish, Verb Adjunction (Rivas 1974) in Spanish, Clause Reduction (Perlmutter and Aissen 1976) in Spanish, and Ristrutturazione (Rizzi 1976) in Italian. All of these studies suggest that the grammar of the language in question incorporates a special rule to account for the phenomenon, which is to be in addition to Verb Raising, Equi-NP Deletion and Subject Raising.

The arguments which will be presented in support of the claim made in this paper are based on the existence of surface syntactic evidence for a (so far unnoticed) negative correlation between the proclisis of unstressed object pronouns and 'sentential' pronominalization (and cliticization).
I will show, in other words, that in Italian there is a negative matching between infinitive constructions which permit the equivalent of *it* anaphors

discussed in relation to (1) and infinitive constructions which allow the unstressed object pronoun to appear after the infinitive as well as before the finite verb. By way of introduction, let us consider sentences (2) and (3).

(2a) Maria vuole chiamar<u>la</u>
 Mary wants to-callPRO
 (Mary wants to call her)
(2b) Maria <u>la</u> vuole chiamare   PROCLISIS
 Mary PRO wants to-call
 (Mary wants to call her)
(2c) *Maria <u>lo</u> vuole, ma non lo farà   S PRONOMIN
 Mary PRO wants, but NEG PRO will do
 *(Mary wants it, but won't do it)
(3a) Maria dice di aver<u>la</u> chiamata
 Mary says to-havePRO called
 (Mary says she called her)
(3b) *Maria <u>la</u> dice di aver chiamata   PROCLISIS
 Mary PRO says to-have called
 (Mary says she called her)
(3c) Maria <u>lo</u> dice, ma non è vero   S PRONOMIN
 Mary PRO says, but NEG is true
 (Mary says so/it, but it isn't true)

In (2) the unstressed object pronoun <u>la</u> may appear in enclitic position in (2a), as well as in proclitic position in (2b). On the other hand, in the same construction the infinitival clause <u>vuole chiamarla</u> may not be replaced by the anaphoric pronoun <u>lo</u> (2c). Conversely, in (3) the unstressed object pronoun <u>la</u> may appear in enclitic position in (3a) but not in proclitic position in (3b). On the other hand, in the same construction the infinitival clause <u>di averla chiamata</u> may be replaced by the anaphoric pronoun <u>lo</u> (3c). Thus, in (2) and (3) we have an example of the negative correlation between proclisis and sentential pronominalization; i.e. (2) allows proclisis but prohibits sentential pronominalization, whereas (3) prohibits proclisis but allows sentential pronominalization. What appears to determine the coefficients of the variable is the matrix verb. <u>Vuole</u> 'wants' governs proclisis

(thus preventing sentential pronominalization), and
dice 'says' accepts sentential pronominalization
(and disallows proclisis). We shall see that the
two lists of verbs do not consist of random lexical
items; rather, they consist of clear-cut semantic
subclasses of verbs.

In connection with (2) and (3) there are two
incidental facts which need to be mentioned at this
point. The pronoun lo in the adversative portion
of (2c) is a 'neuter' lo and not a result of S
Pronominalization. The antecedent of ma non lo farà
'but will not do it' is ma non la chiamerà 'but will
not call her'. The details of this type of anaphor
are not directly relevant to our discussion. Note,
furthermore, that the preposition di in (3a) is part
of the infinitival clause and not a particle of the
matrix verb. We shall see below that the choice of
di or a in infinitival clauses is to a large extent
predictable.

1. Noun Phrase Pronominalization and Cliticization. Under the analysis proposed in this paper
the conditions for proclisis of simple noun phrase
complements and sentential complements (including
their reduced forms) are essentially the same. A
pronominalized NP may appear in proclitic position
when it is the surface dependent (direct, indirect,
oblique) of the main verb. The condition is the
same for pronominalized nominals (including sentences) as exemplified below:

Type I: [Maria vuole chiamarla]   (2a)
Type II: [Maria dice [di averla chiamata]]   (3a)

In (2a) la, as the direct object of the main verb,
may be placed in proclitic position (2b). In (3a)
la is not the dependent of the main verb dice and
therefore cannot be placed in a proclitic position
(3b). The nominal di averla chiamata is the direct dependent of dice and can therefore be procliticized in the anaphoric form lo (3c). In this
section I discuss briefly the facts about NP

cliticization in Type I simple (noninfinitival) sentences.

(4) (a) Gianni chiama <u>Maria</u>
Gianni calls Mary
(Gianni calls Mary)
(a') Gianni <u>la</u> chiama
Gianni PRO calls
(Gianni calls her)
(b) Gianni scrive <u>a Maria</u>
Gianni writes to Mary
(b') Gianni <u>le</u> scrive
Gianni PRO-dative writes
(Gianni writes to her)
(c) Gianni manda <u>una lettera</u> <u>a Maria</u>
Gianni sends a letter to Mary
(c') Gianni <u>gliela</u> manda
Gianni PRO-dative PRO-acc sends
(Gianni sends it to her)
(d) Gianni va <u>al cinema</u>
Gianni goes to the cinema
(d') Gianni <u>ci</u> va
Gianni PRO-oblique goes
(Gianni goes there)
(e) Gianni ritorna <u>dal cinema</u>
Gianni returns from the cinema
(e') Gianni <u>ne</u> ritorna
Gianni PRO-oblique returns
(Gianni returns from there)
(f) Gianni fu colpito <u>dalla sua bellezza</u>
Gianni was stunned by her beauty
(f') Gianni <u>ne</u> fu colpito
Gianni PRO-oblique was stunned
(Gianni was stunned by it)
(g) Gianni ha due <u>macchine</u>
Gianni has two cars
(g') Gianni <u>ne</u> ha due
Gianni PRO-oblique has two
(Gianni has two of them)

In (4), sentence (a) represents the noun phrase form whereas (a') is the pronominalized and cliticized form. The same correspondence is kept for the other letters. (a') is an example of direct object, (b') indirect object, (c') direct and indirect object together. Note that in simple sentences the clitic pronoun must precede the verb. In modern Italian, enclitic position is not permitted with finite verbs. The only obligatorily enclitic position is required in affirmative commands and adverbial phrases like <u>avendola vista</u> 'having seen her' or <u>vistala</u> '(having) seen her'. (d', e', f', and g') are examples of oblique clitics: <u>ci</u> for 'motion to' in (d'), <u>ne</u> for 'motion from' in (e') as well as for 'cause or abstract agentive phrases' in (f') and partitive in (g'). The distinction between direct object <u>lo</u>/<u>la</u> and oblique <u>ci</u> is observed also in sentential cliticization, as we shall see in the next section.

2. Semantic classes and their syntactic inventory. As we mentioned in relation to (2) and (3) the determining factor in the correlation between proclisis and sentential pronominalization is the matrix verb. <u>Volere</u> 'to want' accepts proclisis but does not allow sentential pronominalization, whereas <u>dire</u> 'to say' accepts sentential pronominalization but does not allow proclisis. In (5) a summary is given of some 50 verbs and their syntactic behavior. Column 1 is proclisis, 2 is S pronominalization. In columns 3, 4, 5 an inventory of accepted complement types is given: sentential, accusative or dative with infinitive, simple infinitive. I would like to emphasize that the list of verbs which permit proclisis is not a random list of lexical items; rather, their syntactic behavior is exhibited on the basis of a strictly semantic classification. The negative correlation between proclisis and sentential pronominalization involves modal, aspectual, motion, causative, and perception verbs versus other classes of verbs. The former allow proclisis but no sentential pronominalization; the converse is the case for other classes of verbs. It should be noted that causatives (especially <u>fare</u>) prefer the proclitic position. Another class of verbs which includes verbs

(5)

	1 2 3 4 5	
MODAL	+ - - - +	1 Proclisis
ASPECTUAL	+ - - - +	2 S Pronomin
MOTION	+ - - - +	3 S-Complement
CAUSATIVE	+ - + - +	4 A/D Infinitive
PERCEPTION	+ - + + -	5 Infinitive
SAY KNOW BELIEVE	- + + - +	
COMMAND FORCE ADVISE	- + - + -	

like 'try' and 'attempt' seems to be moving toward the acceptance of proclisis. Speakers use the proclisis in unguarded conversation <u>ti provo a chiamare domani</u> 'I'll try to call you tomorrow'. When they are asked about it, however, they maintain that they must have made a mistake. A cursory look at the situation in Spanish indicates that these classes behave more or less as in Italian. French, on the other hand, differs considerably. It seems that only perception and causative (<u>laisser</u> in particular) verbs accept proclisis in a consistent way.

With regard to the types of complement (columns 3, 4, and 5) which each class accepts, notice that modal, aspectual, and motion verbs may appear on the surface only with an infinitival type of complement. There is, in other words, no distributional evidence for an underlying sentential source. Causative and perception verbs may appear either with a sentential complement or an infinitival complement. Perception verbs seem to allow in addition accusative with infinitive constructions. 'Say, know and believe' allow infinitival complements with equivalent subjects: <u>dice che è italiano</u> or <u>dice di essere italiano</u> 'he says he is Italian (or he says to be Italian)'. Finally, 'force, command, and advise' are found only in the accusative or dative with infinitive construction.

3. Proclisis and sentential pronominalization. In (6) through (16) I discuss verbs representative of

each class in (5), in an effort to substantiate the
negative correlation between proclisis and sentential pronominalization (both the direct and the
oblique type).

    (6a) può chiamar<u>la</u>, per favore?
           could-you callPRO, please?
           (could you call her, please?)
    (6b) <u>la</u> può chiamare, per favore?
           PRO could-you call, please?
           (could you call her, please?)
    (6c) no, non*<u>lo</u> posso
              NEG PRO I-can
          (no, I can't)

(6) is an example of the modal class which includes
<u>potere</u>, <u>volere</u>, <u>dovere</u>. Italian modals (as opposed
to English) are inflectionally the same as other
verbs. <u>Potere</u> accepts proclisis (6b) but prohibits
sentential pronominalization (6c).

    (7a) cominciò a scriver<u>la</u>
           he-began to-writePRO
           (he began to write it)
    (7b) <u>la</u> cominciò a scrivere
           PRO he-began to-write
           (he began to write it)
    (7c) *lo cominciò, ma non *lo finì
           PRO he-began, but NEG PRO he-finished
           (he began, but he didn't finish)

Aspectual verbs, exemplified in (7), include <u>finire</u>,
<u>cominciare</u>, and <u>continuare</u>. They differ superfici-
ally from modals in that they introduce the infinitival phrase with a preposition: <u>di</u> for the first
verb, <u>a</u> for the other two. Aspectual verbs behave
exactly like modals with respect to proclisis.
They allow proclisis (7b) and prohibit sentential
pronominalization (7c).

    (8a) andò a trovar<u>la</u>
           he-went to-visitPRO
           (he went to visit her)

(8b) la andò a trovare
     PRO he-went to-visit
     (he went to visit her)
(8c) *lo andò
     PRO-direct he-went
(8d) ci andò
     PRO-oblique he-went

Motion verbs like <u>andare</u> 'to go' in (8) allow proclisis (8b) of a direct object pronoun, but obviously they do not exhibit direct sentential pronominalization (8c). The entire infinitival phrase, however, may be pronominalized with the oblique anaphor <u>ci</u>. The oblique anaphor in (8d) should not be interpreted as meaning 'there', which is the normal interpretation given in noun phrase cliticization (4d'). Rather, it should be seen as referring to the entire infinitival phrase <u>a trovarla</u>. Note, in fact, that <u>ci</u> is also used as the anaphor in sentences where no motion or place is implied. For example, one might hear as a conversational response to <u>pensa a studiare</u> 'keep your mind on studying', <u>ci penso anche troppo</u> 'I keep my mind on it too much'. Observe, however, another fact about motion verbs exemplified in (9).

(9a) *andò a trovarla a Roma
     he-went to-visitPRO in Rome
     (he went to visit her in Rome)
(9b) *ci andò a trovarla
     PRO-oblique he-went to-visitPRO-direct
     (he went to visit her there)
(9c) ci andò
     PRO-oblique he-went

Notice in (9b) that <u>a Roma</u> may not be procliticized. Actually, it does not appear that it can be pronominalized at all, <u>andò a trovarcela</u>, even in enclitic position. Yet the entire infinitival clause may be represented with the anaphor <u>ci</u>. Such is the interpretation of (9c) in relation to (9a). Thus motion verbs are hybrid in the sense that they accept direct proclisis (8b). On the other hand, they prohibit oblique proclisis, but accept oblique sentential pronominalization.

(10a) fece scriver<u>la</u>
he-CAUSED to writePRO
(he had it written)
(10b) <u>la</u> fece scrivere
PRO he-CAUSED to-write
(he had it written)
(10c) *<u>lo</u> fece
PRO he-CAUSED

Causative verbs like <u>fare</u> and <u>lasciare</u> permit proclisis (10b) and prohibit sentential pronominalization (10c). These verbs (<u>fare</u> in particular) prefer the proclitic position to the enclitic position. (10a) sounds strange, although not necessarily ungrammatical. <u>Fare</u> means either 'coerce' or 'allow', whereas <u>lasciare</u> means only 'allow'. These verbs differ from modal, aspectual, and motion verbs in that one of them, <u>lasciare</u>, may take a sentential or infinitival complement. The reduced form is derived through the rule of Verb Raising or an equivalent formulation.

(11a) sentimmo cantar<u>la</u>
we-heard to-singPRO
(we heard it sung)
(11b) <u>la</u> sentimmo cantare
PRO we-heard to-sing
(we heard it sung)
(11c) *<u>lo</u> sentimmo
PRO we-heard

Perception verbs which may appear with a sentential complement include <u>sentire</u> 'hear, feel' and <u>vedere</u> 'see'. They allow proclisis (11b) and prohibit sentential pronominalization. Notice that (11b) is ambiguous. It may be interpreted also as 'we heard her sing' where <u>la</u> would be the logical subject of <u>cantare</u>. (11c) may also be viewed with a grammatical interpretation 'we heard it'. It seems clear on the basis of (11a,b,c) that perception verbs are

sensitive to Verb Raising as causative verbs are.
However, if we take into consideration (11d) and
(11e) we realize that perception verbs may enter
also into Type II infinitival constructions.

   (11d) lo sentimmo rimproverar<u>la</u>
         PRO-him we-heard to-scoldPRO-her
         (we heard him scold her)
   (11e) *<u>glie</u><u>la</u> sentimmo rimproverare
         PRO-dativePRO-accusative we-heard to-scold
         (we heard him scold her)

In (11e) we see that <u>la</u> of (11d) cannot be placed
in proclitic position, contrary to what we observed
in (11b). That (11d) is a Type II construction is
supported by the fact that two direct objects are
allowed on the surface: <u>lo</u> and <u>la</u>. In Type I constructions the logical subject of the lower verb
would be <u>la sentimmo cantare da Gianni</u> 'we heard it
sung by Gianni'. Whereas (11b) and (11a) are Type I
infinitival clauses derived through Verb Raising,
the probable derivation of (11d) is through Subject
Raising which would account for its Type II status.

   (12a) scrive di aver<u>la</u> vista
         he-writes to-havePRO seen
         (he writes that he saw her)
   (12b) *<u>la</u> scrive di aver visto
         PRO he-writes to-have seen
         (he writes that he saw her)
   (12c) lo scrive, ma non è vero
         PRO he-writes, but NEG is true
         (he writes it, but it isn't true)
   (13a) sa di aver<u>la</u> ricevuta
         he-knows to-have PRO received
         (he knows he received it)
   (13b) *<u>la</u> sa di aver ricevuto
         PRO he-knows to-have received
         (he knows he received it)
   (13c) <u>lo</u> sa, ma non <u>lo</u> ammette
         PRO he-knows, but NEG PRO he-admits
         (he knows it, but he doesn't admit it)

(14a) crede di aver<u>la</u> perduta
he-believes to-havePRO lost
(he believes he lost it)
(14b) *<u>la</u> crede di aver perduto
PRO he-believes to-have lost
(he believes he lost it)
(14c) <u>lo</u> crede, ma non <u>ne</u> è sicuro
PRO he-believes, but NEG PRO he-is sure
(he believes it, but he isn't sure of it)

In (12)-(14) we have examples of Type II infinitival constructions with the matrix verbs of 'say, know, and believe'. They allow sentential pronominalization (c) and prohibit proclisis (b). Let us now consider the last class of verbs, in particular 'advise' (15) and 'force' (16), which reject proclisis but accept sentential pronominalization.

(15a) consigliò a Gianni di denunciar<u>la</u>
he-advised to Gianni to-turn-in-PRO
(he advised Gianni to turn her in)
(15b) *<u>la</u> consigliò a Gianni di denunciare
PRO he-advised to Gianni to-turn-in
(he advised Gianni to turn her in)
(15c) <u>lo</u> consigliò a Gianni
PRO he-advised to Gianni
(he advised it to Gianni)
(15d) <u>glielo</u> consigliò
PRO-dative PRO-accusative he-advised
(he advised it to him)
(16a) forzò Gianni a denunciar<u>la</u>
he-forced Gianni to-turn-in-PRO
(he forced Gianni to turn her in)
(16b) *<u>la</u> forzò Gianni a denunciare
PRO he-forced Gianni to-turn-in
(he forced Gianni to turn her in)
(16c) <u>ci</u> forzò Gianni
PRO-oblique he-forced Gianni
(he forced Gianni to do it)
(16d) <u>ce lo</u> forzò
PRO-oblique PRO-accusative he-forced
(he forced him to do it)

Consigliare 'advise' (15) and forzare 'force' (16)
do not accept proclisis (b), but allow sentential
pronominalization (c). Note that these two verbs
differ from English in that 'advise' takes indirect
object for the person advised, whereas 'force' takes
direct object for the person forced. Thus, in keeping with the Relational Uniqueness Condition (only
one member for each functional slot), the infinitival
phrase will take direct object anaphor lo if the
matrix verb is 'advise' (15c), and if the matrix
verb is 'force' the infinitival phrase will pro-
nominalize to the oblique clitic ci (16c). Therefore, it seems that the selection of the surface
type of infinitival clause is made in terms of the
relational characteristics of the matrix verb. You
might have observed at this point a correlation between the prepositions introducing infinitival
phrases and their anaphors, namely, di is to lo
as a is to ci. This minor fact about the way the
nuts and bolts of Italian syntax fit together is an
unexpected bonus which follows from our type of
analysis. It casts a tiny beam of light onto the
mystery of Italian prepositions and their usage.
In concluding our discussion of 'advise' and 'force',
it seems clear that they may enter only into Type II
infinitival constructions. There is little distributional evidence for deriving (15) and (16) from
underlying sentential sources. An abstract derivational analysis would appeal to Subject Raising or
Equi, which predictably result in Type II infinitival constructions.

4. Five hypotheses pertaining to proclisis in
Romance. The development and placement of unstressed pronouns in Romance is certainly the most
intriguing phenomenon in the field from a theoretical point of view, as evidenced by a time-honored
tradition centering around Wachernagel's law of
accent for the Indo-European languages. The debate
persists in transformational grammar, where, in
total oblivion of the morphophonetic and syntactic attempts by earlier grammarians, we find at
least five major proposals claiming that an

independent rule of syntax controls the phenomenon in the grammars of the Romance languages. Although the five proposals suggest theoretically similar solutions, I shall discuss them briefly in view of the data and arguments presented in this paper.

4.1. The Clitic Placement hypothesis (Kayne 1975). Kayne (1975:65) argues in favor of a movement transformation, to be called 'Clitic Placement', which would prepose object pronouns to the verb under certain conditions to account for the following types of data in French: <u>Marie nous connaît</u>/*<u>Marie connaît nous</u> 'Mary knows us', <u>je ferai lire ce livre à Jean</u>/<u>je lui ferai lire ce livre</u> 'I will have John read that book/I will have him read it'. It is suggested that the preposed pronoun forms one constituent with the main verb as in (4a'). The proposal, as it stands, requires the rule to be obligatory for simple sentences. In infinitival clauses, however, the rule must be stated in such a way that the pronoun is obligatorily moved before the infinitive but only optionally before the finite verb <u>je peux le faire</u>/*<u>je le peux faire</u> 'I can do it' in a specified lexical subset.

4.2. The Clitic Climbing hypothesis (Roldán 1974). Roldán (1974:126) proposes a rule of 'Clitic Climbing' for Spanish which is claimed to account for all cases of clitic attachment including infinitival constructions (which were problematic for Kayne's French analysis). The generalization is the following: a clitic must be attached to the verb if the subject has been removed prior to the application of clitic attachment, and it is attached to the left of the verb if the sentence has a subject before the verb. In Roldán's analysis the grammar of Spanish has an optional transformation which moves clitics from a lower clause into a higher clause. The major criticism leveled against this hypothesis is that it requires a constraint to insure that clusters of clitics are moved together <u>quiero mostrártelo</u>/*<u>te quiero mostrarlo</u> 'I want to show it to you' (Perlmutter and Aissen 1976). This criticism is not valid if Clitic Climbing is defined on the node Clitic which subsumes one or more unstressed pronouns.

4.3. The Verb Adjunction hypothesis (Rivas 1974). Rivas (1974:18) proposes an abstract structure-changing transformation which takes the verb of the embedded clause and adjoins it to the verb of the matrix clause under the same node Verb. Rivas' proposal claims that the constituent structure of a sentence like <u>quiero presentártelo</u> 'I want to introduce him to you' is significantly different from the equivalent sentence with proclitic pronouns <u>te lo quiero presentar</u>. The claim is that in the latter, <u>quiero presentar</u> is one constituent V, whereas in the former, <u>quiero</u> and <u>presentar</u> form separate constituents. Verb Adjunction appeals to a more abstract syntactic analysis of the phenomenon in comparison with the Clitic Placement and Clitic Climbing rules. It claims that sentences with proclitic pronouns undergo a special rule, in addition to Equi-NP Deletion which yields the infinitival clause. Verb Adjunction has the same effect on the verb phrase as another independently motivated rule, namely Verb Raising, which is sensitive to a different set of verbs. Notwithstanding the resolution of the relation between Equi, Verb Raising, and Verb Adjunction, the evidence that proclitic and enclitic forms are structurally different is not supported by our study of the interaction between proclisis and sentential pronominalization, discussed in section 3. The Verb Adjunction hypothesis implies that the enclitic form of a sentence is a Type II infinitival construction, whereas the proclitic form is a Type I infinitival construction. In (6)-(16) I have established that the relational status of an infinitival clause is not affected by procliticization. In other words, sentential pronominalization is not possible in sentences like (7) in spite of the fact that both enclisis and proclisis are allowed.

4.4. The Clause Reduction hypothesis (Perlmutter
and Aissen 1976). Perlmutter and Aissen's proposal
is in essence identical to Rivas'. The rule, however, is formalized within a relational framework
which has distinct implications concerning the
organization of grammars and the universal nature
of language. The authors posit a rule of 'Clause
Reduction' for Spanish which makes dependents of a
complement verb dependents of the matrix verb (1976:
1). This proposal is of particular interest to the
subject matter of this paper because it claims that
analogous arguments can be made for Italian. Clause
Reduction is defined on networks of grammatical relations (subject, direct object, indirect object)
clustered around a verb. Relational networks may
contain more than one verb in hierarchical organization. Clause Reduction is, furthermore, sensitive to a lexical list of verbs functioning as
matrix verbs. By its effect, Clause Reduction
changes the dependency status of the network. Thus,
in quiero verla 'I want to see her' la is an object
pronoun dependent of the lower verb ver. After the
application of Clause Reduction we have la quiero
ver, where la has become the dependent of the matrix
verb quiero. Viewing proclisis in terms of relational dependency leads to some problems not posed
by Verb Adjunction or Clitic Climbing. The Clause
Reduction hypothesis implies that lo in the Spanish
sentence lo suele ver a las ocho 'she usually sees
him at eight' is the direct object of suele, which
is difficult to reconcile with the usual notion of
transitivity. Furthermore, there is no way to test
whether there has been, in fact, a change in dependency if we compare the sentence with its enclitic form suele verlo a las ocho. The only indication is the proclisis itself, the phenomenon which
the rule is supposed to explain. Assuming that these
credibility problems can be clarified or argued away,
there is one crucial fact about the behavior of
clitics which Clause Reduction is descriptively unable to handle, namely the perception verbs paradox
mentioned in connection with (11). Perception verbs
are sensitive to Verb Raising which results in a

Type I structure which permits proclisis (11b).
Perception verbs are also sensitive to Subject
Raising which results in a Type II structure which
does not permit proclisis (11e). Clause Reduction
is, in principle, incapable of resolving this paradox, since it is defined as either applying or not
applying. If it applies, as it should with the
matrix verb of perception, it would generate the
ungrammatical sentence (11*e). If we pull out perception verbs from the list which triggers Clause
Reduction, then the hypothesis wrongly defines
(11b) as ungrammatical.

4.5. The 'Ristrutturazione' hypothesis (Rizzi
1976). Rizzi (1976:2, 8) proposes that the grammar
of Italian has a transformational rule of 'Ristrutturazione' which optionally transforms a complex
underlying structure into a simplex one, creating
a single complex predicate out of the matrix and
subordinate verb. Ristrutturazione is sensitive to
modal, aspectual, and movement verbs. Accordingly,
<u>Piero vuole leggerlo attentamente</u>/<u>Piero lo vuole
leggere attentamente</u> 'Piero wants to read it carefully' are derived from the same underlying representation in which the infinitival clause is given
as a sentential object complement. The first
(enclitic) form of the sentence is derived through
the application of Equi-NP Deletion, whereas the
second (proclitic) form is derived through the
application of Equi-NP Deletion plus the proposed
rule of Ristrutturazione. As a result, in the first
(enclitic) form the infinitival clause retains its
independent complement status, whereas in the second
(proclitic) form the sentence is restructured as a
simple sentence. Ristrutturazione is identical to
Rivas' Spanish Verb Adjunction in that both capture
similar generalizations in the two languages.
Rizzi's line of reasoning focuses on the auxiliary
characteristics of the matrix verb.

Although I am in perfect agreement with the
'auxiliarity' focus of Rizzi's study, his conclusion in terms of an abstract rule raises questions
similar to those discussed in connection with Verb

Adjunction and Clause Reduction. In particular, the
Ristrutturazione hypothesis claims that the infinitival clause remains as an independent sentential complement if only Equi-NP Deletion is applied. The S
Pronominalization test discussed in section 3 shows
that this is not the case. The relational status of
the infinitival phrases where the matrix clause has
a modal, aspectual, motion, causative, or perception
verb remains constant in both the enclitic and proclitic forms of the sentences (6)-(11). It is only
in negative correlation with proclisis that we find
that infinitival clauses have a distinct relational
status (12)-(16).

5. The Auxiliarity hypothesis. In this section
I claim that the phenomenon of proclisis is properly
defined in the grammar of Italian without recourse
to additional rules such as we have seen in section
4. Proclisis is, in fact, only one conspicuous example of a variety of converging syntactic phenomena.
Our hypothesis is that this observed syntactic convergence is the direct result of a relational condition of 'auxiliarity', i.e. the more or less auxiliary function of certain classes of verbs in simple
and derived surface structures. The auxiliary status
of a particular matrix verb is empirically ascer-
tained through the transitivity test (4) and (6)-
(16). Derivationally, auxiliarity is a predictable
condition resulting from the interaction of general
semantic properties of verbs such as Modality,
Motion, Cause, Aspect, and Perception, with particular syntactic rules such as Verb Raising, Equi-
NP Deletion, and Subject Raising. Accordingly, in
Italian a causative matrix verb in a Verb Raised
construction functions uniformly as an auxiliary
(Type I infinitival construction), whereas a verb
of 'know' in an Equi construction will uniformly
behave as an intransitive verb (Type II infinitival
construction) as we have discussed at length in section 3. Formally, auxiliarity is characterized as a
general condition 'written into' the above mentioned
independently motivated rules of Italian, rather
than as an additional rule as proposed by the hypotheses discussed in section 4.

5.1. An empirical definition of auxiliarity. Of crucial importance for a nonabstract definition of auxiliarity is surface evidence which clearly distinguishes, on pretheoretical grounds, between Type I infinitival clauses and Type II infinitival clauses. As we have seen only Type I allows proclisis and its converging phenomena. Type I infinitival clauses are like simple sentences, where we find (obligatory) proclisis, reflexivization, relational uniqueness, and auxiliary selection conditions. Thus, an infinitival construction is classified as Type I if there is surface evidence for crucial behavioral properties. Otherwise, the infinitival construction is classified Type II. In (17) a list comprising a simple sentence (a) and the major types of infinitival clauses is given with their behavioral inventory and an auxiliarity index type.

		1	2	3	4	Type
(17) (a)	si è lavato	+	+	+	+	I
(b)	vuole lavarsi	+	+	+	+	I
(c)	comincia a lavarsi	+	+	+	+	I
(d)	si fece lavare	+	+	+	+	I
(e)	gliela sentimmo cantare	+	+	+	−	I
(f)	dice di essersi lavato	+	−	−	−	II
(g)	lo sentimmo rimproverarla	+	−	−	−	II
(h)	lo forzò a scrivergli	−	−	−	−	II

1 = Reflexivization; 2 = Proclisis; 3 = Relational Uniqueness Condition; 4 = Auxiliary Selection Condition

(17b-h) are examples of the major semantic classes given in (5): namely, modal (b), aspectual (c), causative (d), perception (e) and (g), say (f), force (h). Notice that auxiliarity is a squishy empirical concept. Only two discrete levels of clause reduction are needed to account for the phenomena discussed in this paper. Our clausal classification is based on the behavioral properties of proclisis, S pronominalization, and the relational uniqueness condition.

5.2. A derivational definition of auxiliarity. In keeping with a concrete derivational analysis, we distinguish between underlying and derived constructions of Type I and II. An infinitival complement is derived only if it appears as a sentential complement as well (cf. (5) columns 3, 4, 5), in accordance with a sort of syntactic 'alternation condition'. (17') is a derivational inventory of (17).

(17')				
(a)	SIMPLE S	I	Underlying	
(b)	MODAL	I	Underlying	
(c)	ASPECTUAL	I	Underlying	
(d)	CAUSATIVE	I	Derived:	Verb Raising
(e)	PERCEPTION	I	Derived:	Verb Raising
(f)	SAY	II	Derived:	Equi-NP Deletion
(g)	PERCEPTION	II	Derived:	Subject Raising, or Equi-NP Deletion
(h)	FORCE	II	Underlying	

5.3. Auxiliarity and the distribution of unstressed pronouns. The Auxiliarity hypothesis is not specifically about clitics as Clitic Climbing is (section 4.2), nor does it concern itself with dependency relations as Clause Reduction does (section 4.4). The hypothesis proposed in this paper is a definition of the degree of reduction brought about by syntactic rules such as Verb Raising, Equi-NP Deletion, and Subject Raising. The distribution of unstressed clitic pronouns is, however, crucially dependent on the auxiliarity status of the clause. An auxiliarity-based statement on the distribution of clitics is given in (18). For examples of (18) see (4a') for type (a), (4) for (b), (6) for (c), and (12) for (d). The distributional statement (18) is not sufficient to account for special tendencies in surface structure when we consider the examples in (19).

(18) (a) SIMPLE FINITE CLAUSES 　　　　[X PRO V-finite Y] 　　(b) SIMPLE NONFINITE CLAUSES 　　　　[X V-nonfinite PRO (V-nonfinite) Y] 　　(c) INFINITIVAL TYPE I 　　　　[X PRO V-finite (V-inf)$_1^n$ PRO Y] 　　(d) INFINITIVAL TYPE II 　　　　[X V-finite (V-inf)$_1^n$ PRO]

(19a)　(i)　 la fece scrivere (cf. also (10))
　　　 (ii)　?fece scriverla
(19b)　(i)　?ti provo a chiamare
　　　 (ii)　provo a chiamarti
(19c)　(i)　*voglio farti vederlo
　　　　　　'I want you to see it'
　　　 (ii)　voglio fartelo vedere
　　　(iii)　*ti voglio farlo vedere
　　　 (iv)　te lo voglio far vedere
(19d)　(i)　 sente cantarla
　　　　　　'she hears it sung'
　　　 (ii)　la sente cantare
　　　(iii)　*sente cantarla
　　　　　　'she hears her sing'
　　　 (iv)　la sente cantare

(18) must be supplemented by constraints which reveal certain shift tendencies in the present-day language and may have some implications for the underlying locus of object pronouns in Italian. In (19a), with causative as well as modal verbs, there seems to be a tendency to prefer the proclitic position, which can be interpreted as a tendency to make Type I infinitival clauses more like simple sentences. In (19b) we have a similar phenomenon: an indication that verbs like 'to try or attempt' are shifting or are in variation between Type II and Type I constructions. (19a) and (19b) give empirical evidence that clitics are 'leftbound' in Italian (as well as in Spanish, Saltarelli 1974) which accords with the recent history of the language. In (19d) we have an apparent paradox in the fact that the same type of

surface structure allows a distinct distribution of clitics. There are, in theory, different ways of handling this problem; the one we have considered is to invoke the leftbound criterion mentioned earlier: i.e. no clitic ever appears to the right of its underlying or 'logical' object position. The incorporation of this criterion in a derivational theory implies that the underlying position for pronouns is post-verbal, as it is for nouns. Accordingly, _la_ in (19diii) cannot appear in post-verbal position since it is the logical subject of _cantar_; it has become object through a structure reduction and relation-changing rule. (19c) involves two criteria. (19ci) is ungrammatical because causatives attract clitics, as discussed in (19a), which results in (19cii). (19ciii) shows that clusters of clitics form a unique constituent in surface structure; thus, the only possibility is (19civ). I would like to emphasize that surface structure constraints may tell us a lot about the social, historical, as well as internal organization of the grammar. In this function they have a legitimate place in the description of a language.

6. Summary and conclusions. The major issue in this paper has been to demonstrate that there are empirical indicators for distinguishing between two types of infinitival clauses. The strongest evidence is the discovery of a negative correlation between proclisis and sentential pronominalization, which helps us to establish, in a concrete manner, the constituency of infinitival clauses. Sentential pronominalization is, in other words, a transitivity test. If the infinitive clause can be replaced by an anaphor, then the matrix verb is transitive. If the test fails, the matrix verb is most likely to be an auxiliary. This negative correlation is in accord with a variety of converging phenomena, many of which were observed in earlier papers, notably Perlmutter and Aissen (1976) and Rizzi (1976). Auxiliarity/Transitivity as empirically and derivationally characterized in this paper

does not support an abstract rule account of the phenomena in question.

REFERENCES

Kayne, Richard. 1975. French syntax. Cambridge, Mass.: The MIT Press.
Perlmutter, David, and Judith Aissen. 1976. Clause reduction in Spanish. Mimeographed.
Rivas, Alberto. 1974. Verb adjunction in Spanish. Mimeographed.
Rizzi, Luigi. 1976. Ristrutturazione. Rivista di Grammatica Generativa 1(1).1-54.
Roldán, Mercedes. 1974. Constraints on clitic insertion in Spanish. In: Linguistic studies in Romance languages. Edited by Campbell, Goldin, and Wang. Washington, D.C.: Georgetown University Press. 124-138.
Saltarelli, Mario. 1974. Leftbound clitics in Spanish. Mimeographed.

SYLLABLE VERSUS WORD BOUNDARY IN FRENCH

SANFORD A. SCHANE
University of California, San Diego

The syllable has not played an explicit role in most descriptions within generative phonology. Within the last few years, however, there has been renewed interest in the syllable as a formal unit to be incorporated into phonological description. Hooper (1972) was one of the earliest, and certainly has been one of the strongest, advocates for the syllable; and, in fact, utilizing extensive data from Spanish, she has convincingly argued for the syllable boundary. She showed, for example, that several of the rules found in Harris (1969) can be considerably simplified if one has recourse to this special boundary. Walker (1973) has claimed that there are phonological processes in French whose description is also simplified if syllable boundaries are recognized.

I shall examine several phonological phenomena of French--in particular, vowel nasalization, consonant deletion, consonant devoicing, and open and closed syllable adjustment. The statement of these processes in the past has generally required reference to word boundaries. Then I want to see whether the description can be simplified (and become more insightful) by referring instead to syllable boundaries.

We shall see that the syllable boundary has an initial attraction, but that, by itself, it cannot

serve descriptively as an adequate device for dealing with most of these phonological processes. It is still necessary to identify where syntactic boundaries occur. This observation leads us to question whether the syllable boundary is needed for French and, if so, how it is to be amalgamated with the other types of boundaries.
First let us consider vowel nasalization.[1]

(1) (a) bonté [bɔ̃te] 'goodness'
    (b) bonifier [bɔnifie] 'to make good'
    (c) bon # garçon [bɔ̃ garsɔ̃] 'good boy'
    (d) bon # ami [bɔn ami] 'good friend'
    (e) bon ## à voir [bɔ̃ a vwar] 'good to see'
    (f) bon ## [bɔ̃] 'good'

The contexts for (a) and (b) are word internal--here nasalization occurs only when the nasal consonant is in turn followed by a consonant. Examples (c)-(e) represent external sandhi--(c) and (d) are liaison contexts and again nasalization takes place before a consonant, but not before a vowel; (e) is a nonliaison environment, so nasalization occurs even though there is a following vowel. A number of generative descriptions (Dell 1973, Milner 1967, Selkirk 1972, Schane 1974) have accounted for the contrast between (d) and (e) by postulating a different number of word boundaries--that is, words closely bound syntactically (i.e. in a liaison context) are separated by a single word boundary, whereas words more loosely connected have the normal double occurrence of the word boundary. Finally, (f) represents occurrence at the pause or at the end of a phrase--here too nasalization occurs and so the double word boundary is found.

The following rule (R1a) is a typical generative phonological formulation for accommodating the preceding data.

(R1a)   VN → Ṽ/___ $\begin{cases} (\#) C \\ \#\# \end{cases}$

The upper environment without the parenthesized boundary deals with case (a), the upper part with the boundary handles (c), whereas the lower context is for (e) and (f).

Hooper has proposed a set of universal principles for assigning syllable boundaries. Three of these are of immediate interest: (a) A syllable boundary occurs wherever there is a double word boundary, (b) within a word a single consonant between vowels belongs to the following syllable, and (c) within a word the syllable boundary falls between a sequence of two consonants.[2]

(2) $\emptyset \rightarrow \$ \begin{cases} \#\#\_\_\_ \\ V\_\_\_CV \\ VC\_\_\_CV \end{cases}$

These principles as presented are applicable to all forms of (1) except (c) and (d), where there is only a single occurrence of the word boundary. Leaving aside these two forms for the moment, we can see how the syllabification principles apply to the remaining forms.

(a) $bɔn$te$
(b) $bɔ$nifie$
(e) $bɔn$a$vwar$
(f) $bɔn$

It is clear that nasalization occurs whenever the nasal consonant is immediately followed by the syllable boundary.[3]

(R1b) VN → Ṽ/___$

Now how are we to handle forms (c) and (d), and, in particular, the latter? Syllabification here, where there is a single word boundary, cannot be the same as for the double word boundary, since the nasalization phenomenon for (d) is unlike that for (e). Rather (d) is similar to (b), the word internal situation. Hence, (c) and (d) require the following syllabification if R1b is to apply appropriately.

(c) $bɔn$gar$sɔn$
(d) $bɔ$nami

For French, then, where there is a liaison context (i.e. a single word boundary) the syllabification principles are similar to those internal to the word.[4]

Notice further that on the assumption that there are underlying final schwas (which may subsequently be deleted), both analyses will appropriately handle the feminine counterparts of (c) and (d).

(1) (g) bonne #fille [bɔn fiy] $bɔ$nəfiy^ə$
       'good girl'
   (h) bonne # amie [bɔn ami] $bɔ$nə$a$mi$ə$
       'good friend'

Having presented the relevant nasalization data, let us compare rules R1a and R1b. There can be no question but that R1b, utilizing the syllable boundary, is a superior formulation. Notationally, it is a simpler rule. Explanatorily, it characterizes succinctly the conditions under which nasalization occurs: it happens whenever the nasal consonant is syllable final. With the evidence thus far in favor of the syllable, we can ask whether other processes of French are equally more advantageously described by reference to this boundary.

There are several processes of French which traditionally refer to syllable structure. One such process concerns the vowels [ə] and [e]. These vowels only occur in open syllables; in closed syllables they both become [ɛ].

(3) geler [žəle] 'to freeze'
   (il) gèle [žɛl] '(it) freezes'
   (il) gèlera [žɛl(ə)ra] '(it) will freeze'
   gel [žɛl] 'freezing'
   gérer [žere] 'to manage'
   (il) gère [žɛr] '(he) manages'
   (il) gérera [žɛr(ə)ra] '(he) will manage'

The standard generative rule follows:

(R2a) ə,e → ɛ / ___ C $\begin{cases} C \\ \# \\ ə \end{cases}$

The first two environments typically are cases where the consonant following ə or e closes the syllable. By using the syllable boundary we can easily reformulate these two environments as a single one.

(R2b) ə,e → ɛ / ___ C$

This particular phonological process is peculiar in that a single consonant followed by schwa functions as a 'closed' syllable (i.e. the third part of R2a). This context could also be accommodated by R2b if we were to say that in French the sequence VCə is to be syllabified as VC$ə. Forms such as gèle and gèlera would then have the following syllabifications: $žèl$ə$ and $žèl$əra. The underlined schwas could then be appropriately converted to [ɛ]. As attractive as this solution may seem, this syllabification causes difficulties for the nasalization rule: a form such as the feminine bonne would be syllabified as $bɔn$ə$, causing the nasalization rule to apply incorrectly to produce *[bɔ̃].[5]

We must, therefore, reject a syllabification principle which allows a consonant followed by schwa to close the preceding syllable. In a syllable phonology, R2b will have to be expanded as R2b'.

(R2b') ə,e → ɛ / ___ $\begin{cases} C\$ \\ \$Cə \end{cases}$

It would appear that R2b could perhaps be salvaged by permitting schwa deletion to apply first. Then the ə or e would truly be in a closed syllable. This ploy is not really effective, for in those styles where schwas are preserved, it is still the case that ə and e become [ɛ]--[žɛləra], [žɛrəra].

If we compare rules R2a and R2b', we see that they are more or less equivalent in terms of notational complexity. However, one might still wish to argue that R2b' is more explanatory. It says that the relevant vowels become [ε] in a closed syllable or, exceptionally, in an open syllable when there is a following schwa, and it would be this second condition which is so peculiarly French. R2a, on the other hand, states that the change occurs whenever the consonant after the vowel is followed by another consonant, by a word boundary, or by a schwa. It is not so evident what the relationship is among these alternate contexts. So far the analyses encompassing the syllable boundary fare fairly well. However, difficulties begin to arise when we consider some additional processes.

Final consonant deletion in many ways is analogous to vowel nasalization. In instances of external sandhi the consonant is deleted precisely in those environments where nasalization would occur.

(4) (c) petit # garçon [pəti garsõ]
$pə$titgarsɔn$ 'little boy'
(d) petit # ami [pətit ami] $pə$titami$ 'little friend'
(e) (1e) petit ## arrive [pəti ariv]
$pə$tit$a$ri$və$ 'the little one arrives'
(f) petit ## [pəti] $pə$tit$ 'little'
(g) petite # fille [pətit fiy]
$pə$ti$tə$fi$yə$ 'little girl'
(h) petite # amie [pətit ami]
$pə$ti$tə$amiə$ 'little friend'

The following rule is a conceivable generative formulation of consonant deletion.

(R3a) $C \rightarrow \emptyset \: / \underline{} \# \begin{Bmatrix} C \\ \# \end{Bmatrix}$

The data of (4) reveal that the final consonant is deleted in (c), (e), and (f). These are precisely the environments where, in syllable phonology, the consonant would be immediately in front of a syllable boundary.

(R3b) C → ∅ / __$

Although there are similarities between the conditions where nasalization occurs and those where final consonant deletion is found, there is one important difference: nasalization takes place word internally; consonant deletion does not. It is for this reason that in R3a no word boundary is enclosed in parentheses (cf. R1a). This minor difference creates a major problem for an analysis with syllable boundaries. A word such as <u>acteur</u> would be syllabified as aktœr$, and according to R3b, the syllable-final <u>k</u> ought to be deleted.[6] I know of no way of constraining R3b so that it will not incorrectly apply internal to the word, except by stating that it does not apply word internally. But such statements are not available within a syllable phonology, for according to Hooper, morphological and syntactic boundaries are replaced (or, equivalently, they are deleted) whenever syllable boundaries are inserted. Hence, we have lost the information as to whether a consonant preceding a syllable boundary is word internal or not. In fact, any phonological process occurring uniquely at a syntactic boundary will be problematic for a syllable phonology. There are several other processes of this type within French.

One such phonological alternation is between [ɔ] and [o]--e.g. <u>sot ami</u> [sɔt ami] 'stupid friend', <u>sot garçon</u> [so garsɔ̃] 'stupid boy': the vowel <u>ɔ</u> is raised to [o] in final position.

(R4) ɔ → o / __#

(5)   sot ami   sot garçon
               sɔt#ami   sɔt#garsõ
    C → ∅   ---   sɔ#garsõ
    ɔ → o   ---   so#garsõ

But if R4 were to contain a syllable boundary instead of the word boundary, then the two situations could no longer be distinguished.

(6)   sɔt#ami   sɔt#garsõ
    ∅ → $ sɔtami   sɔtgarsõ
    C → ∅   ---   sɔgarsõ

After the deletion of t, sot ami becomes identical syllabically to sot garçon; in both cases the ɔ is found in an open syllable. But because the syllabification is different before the t is deleted, one might be tempted to raise ɔ to [o] first—that is, to claim that raising occurs in a closed syllable (before the t of sot garçon is deleted). Such a formulation is not only counterintuitive, but counterfactual as well. Examples such as métropolitain [metrɔpɔlitẽ], métro [metro] show that in any case a rule is required which raises ɔ to [o] in a final open syllable.

Another interesting process is the devoicing of word-final d in liaison. Consider the difference between grand ami [grãt ami] 'great friend (masc.)' and grande amie [grãd ami] (fem.).

(R5) d → t / __#

(7)   grand ami   grande amie
               grand#ami   grandə#amiə
    d → t   grant#ami   ---
    ə → ∅   ---   grand#ami

These examples, too, cause problems in a syllable phonology, for after the insertion of syllable boundaries, both forms have similar syllable division.

(8)   grand#ami   grándə#amiə
    ∅ → $ grandami   gran$də$amiə

Even processes which traditionally have been
described as pertaining to syllable structure still
require reference to word boundaries. A case in
point is the difference between <u>et les petites</u>
[e lɛ pətit] 'and the little ones' and <u>elle est
petite</u> [ɛl ɛ pətit] 'she is little'. The pronunciation is a conservative one, where the vowels of
the article <u>les</u>, verb <u>est</u>, and the pronoun <u>elle</u>
are all pronounced [ɛ]. Now there is a more casual
style where <u>ɛ</u> is raised to [e] in a final open
syllable. This raising affects the article <u>les</u>,
and verb <u>est</u>, but not the pronoun <u>elle</u>. For this
style, the first vowel then becomes the sole
differentiator of these two phrases--[elepətit] <u>et
les petites</u>, [ɛlepətit] <u>elle est petite</u>. Following are the rule and an illustration of its application. The first line of the derivation represents the stage at which consonant deletion and
schwa deletion have already applied.

(R6)   ɛ → e / __#

(9)   <u>et les petites</u>   <u>elle est petite</u>
                 e#lɛ#pətit   ɛl#ɛ#pətit
        ɛ → e   e#le#pətit   ɛl#e#pətit

If we just consider the syllabic structure of
these forms, again we find that they become identical and we can no longer differentiate the two
cases.

(10)   <u>et les petites</u>   <u>elle est petite</u>
                 e$lɛ$pə$tit   ɛ$lɛ$pə$tit
        ɛ → e   elepə$tit   *e$le$pə$tit

To be sure there is a tendency for certain vowels
to be raised in an open syllable, but only on
condition that the syllable boundary coincides with
the word boundary.
   We have seen that a system, such as Hooper's,
which inserts syllable boundaries both word internally and at syntactic boundaries, with consequent
loss of the latter, is incapable of treating certain

phonological processes within French--in particular, those occurring uniquely before the word boundary. Now, in all fairness to Hooper, it should be pointed out that within her framework of natural phonology she would not find acceptable all aspects of the analysis which I have given of the French data. One important difference is that Hooper (1976) distinguishes between phonological rules--those making valid generalizations about surface phonetic forms-- and morphophonemic rules, which primarily account for morphological alternations. Only the phonological rules would require in their statement strict reference to the syllable, whereas morphophonemic rules may refer to syntactic boundaries. Within Hooper's system, the rules of vowel nasalization, consonant deletion, and the devoicing of d would be morphophonemic ones. Here Hooper could legitimately make use of the word boundary. But the conversion of ə and e to [ɛ], the raising of ɔ, and the raising of ɛ must be phonological rules, as they state inviolable conditions on surface phonetic forms. Ideally they should be stateable uniquely with reference to the syllable. Yet the two raising rules definitely require word boundaries.

If syntactic boundaries were not eliminated, then it would certainly be possible to refer uniquely to those syllable boundaries which happen to coincide with word boundaries. This proposal is, of course, much weaker (and correspondingly much less attractive) than Hooper's because it requires phonological rules to be sensitive to both syllable and syntactic boundaries.

Let us see what happens if we incorporate a weaker version of syllable boundary placement. I shall assume that when there is a single occurrence of a word boundary coinciding with a syllable boundary (VC#CV), the syllable boundary is inserted after the word boundary (VC#$CV), but where there are two word boundaries (VC##V), the syllable boundary is inserted between them (VC#$#V). (The only raison d'être for this assumption is that it enables the rules to be easily stated.) Only in a

liaison context (VC#V) will the word boundary and
the syllable boundary not be in the same place
(V$C#V). Word-internal syllable boundaries will
be assigned as before. The following crucial
forms illustrate the proper placement of syllable
boundaries.

(11) (c) petit # garçon $pə$tit#garsɔn$
     (d) petit # ami $pə$ti$t#a$mi$
     (e) (le) petit ## arrive $pə$tit#$#a$ri$və$
     (f) petit ## $pə$tit#$#
     (i) acteur aktœr$

Recall that a final consonant is deleted at a
syllable boundary which coincides with a word boundary, but it is not deleted before a word-internal
syllable boundary.[7]

(R3b') C → ∅ / __#$

For the data in (11) the final consonant will be
deleted everywhere except in (d) and (i), for in
these forms the consonant is not immediately
followed by both a word boundary and a syllable
boundary.

The remaining three phonological processes--the
raising of ɔ to [o], the devoicing of d to [t],
and the raising of ɛ to [e]--all occur before the
word boundary (i.e. in the context __#). (See
rules R4, R5, and R6.) Since word boundaries now
occur in our revised formulation of syllable-
boundary placement, the standard generative phonological rules without modification are sufficient
to account for these data. In fact, any attempt
to incorporate the syllable boundary into these
rules either unduly complicates the rule or makes
it impossible to state.

These results are somewhat surprising, even para-
doxical. It has often been claimed for French
that at the phonetic level the word *qua* word does
not exist. Instead there are phonetic phrases and
sequences of syllables. It would seem then that
these processes ought to be stateable entirely

with syllable boundaries. Yet I have shown that
this type of description is not adequate for
French. Even if the word cannot be satisfactorily
defined phonetically, nonetheless the concept of
the word is indispensible for describing phonetic
processes frequently linked with the syllable.

The phonological rules we have examined fall into
three categories. Those, such as vowel nasalization and the change of ə and e to [ɛ], where the
most elegant statement refers uniquely to the syllable boundary; others, such as consonant deletion,
where the preferred formulation might contain a
combination of syllable and word boundaries; and
still others, such as the raising of ɔ, the devoicing of d, and the raising of ɛ, where reference has to be made uniquely to the word boundary.

Although the rules may not always be the most
elegant, it is certainly feasible to formulate all
phonological rules without reference to syllable
boundaries, as standard generative phonology has
always done. What is not possible, however, is to
state all rules without reference to syntactic
boundaries. Consequently, a strong version of
syllable phonology, without syntactic boundaries
at the point where phonological rules apply, fails.
What the French data seem to show is that the
optimal description may be the one which makes use
of both types of boundaries.

NOTES

1. Underlying representations are cited in the
standard orthography when there is no possibility
for confusion.
2. The syllabification principles cited in (2)
are by no means complete. For example, the syllable boundary will not always divide a sequence of
two consonants; it will precede the two consonants
if the first is an obstruent and the second is a
liquid or a glide--e.g. ta$bleau. The simplified
set presented here is adequate for the theoretical
points being made.

3. Rule R1b will not handle forms such as <u>bons</u> [bõ], <u>cinq</u> [sɛ̃k], etc., where in the same syllable, the nasal consonant is followed by another consonant. The rule should be modified as:
VN → Ṽ / ___C$_o$$.

4. It is not completely the case that where there is a single word boundary the syllabification principles are identical to what occurs word internally. For example, the sequence VC#LV (e.g. <u>petit # lapin</u> 'little rabbit') is syllabified as VC$LV ($pətitlapin) and not as a word-internal VCLV sequence would be syllabified--namely, V$CLV (see note 2). In fact, VC#CV is always syllabified as VC$CV, and VC#V as V$CV.

5. Vowel nasalization and ɛ-conversion could potentially affect the same vowel. Consider a form such as <u>(il) mène</u> [mɛn] '(he) leads', where the underlying representation is məne (cf. <u>mener</u> [məne]). For purposes of nasalization, the underlying initial schwa must be in an open syllable, so that nasalization does not occur, whereas for ɛ-conversion the initial schwa behaves as though it were in a closed syllable.

6. Walker notes the difficulty in the potential deletion of <u>k</u> with the syllabification aktœr$. To circumvent this problem he cites evidence in support of a tendency for open syllabification--e.g. $a$ktœr$, but he then points out that this solution engenders other complications.

7. We must assume that if a rule contains only the syllable boundary, then that rule is uniquely sensitive to syllable structure, and syntactic boundaries are not to be taken into consideration. Vowel nasalization is such a rule.

REFERENCES

Dell, François. 1973. Les règles et les sons. Paris: Hermann.
Harris, James W. 1969. Spanish phonology. Cambridge, Mass.: MIT Press.
Hooper, Joan B. 1972. The syllable in phonological theory. Language 48.525-540.

Hooper, Joan B. 1976. An introduction to natural generative phonology. New York: Academic Press.
Milner, Jean-Claude. 1967. French truncation rule. Quarterly progress report, MIT, 86.273-283.
Schane, Sanford A. 1974. There is no French truncation rule. In: Linguistic studies in Romance languages. Edited by R. J. Campbell, M. G. Goldin, and M. C. Wang. Washington, D.C.: Georgetown University Press.
Selkirk, Elizabeth O. 1972. The phrase phonology of English and French. Unpublished Ph.D. dissertation. MIT.
Walker, Douglas C. 1973. Syllabification and French phonology. Cahiers linguistiques d'Ottawa 3.

THE 'LOI DE POSITION' AND THE DIRECTION OF PHONOLOGICAL CHANGE IN THE FRENCH MID VOWEL SYSTEM

ALBERT VALDMAN
Indiana University, Bloomington

0. To resolve the vexing problems encountered in the analysis of the French mid vowel system linguists, from the turn of the century to today, have often resorted to the 'Loi de Position'. In its weaker form that generalization states that mid vowels are higher (or tenser) in free syllables and lower (or laxer) in checked syllables (see (1)).

$$(1) \quad V[mid] \rightarrow \begin{cases} V[high\text{-}mid]/\underline{}\begin{Bmatrix} \# \\ CV \end{Bmatrix} \\ V[low\text{-}mid]/\underline{}C \end{cases}$$

While the Loi de Position has undeniable utility as a pedagogical norm for French (Valdman 1972), as I will show, it is a grossly inaccurate observation about the distribution of the mid vowels in Standard French (SF). In its stronger form, the Loi de Position (LDP) implies a certain directionality of change in the mid vowel system. If, as is asserted, that generalization reflects inherent tendencies of the French language, it

should predict direction of variation and change as
one shifts from one style of SF to another or from
SF to nonstandard social and geographical varieties. In this paper, focusing on that aspect of
the LDP, I will test the strong form of the generalization against available empirical data. I will
conclude with remarks on the theoretical nature of
LDP and its place in a phonological description of
French.

1. On the observational adequacy of the Loi de
Position. As is well attested, in SF the low-mid
unrounded vowel [ɛ] occurs in final free syllables
and the rounded vowels [o] and [ø] are found in
final checked syllables (see (2)). In internal
syllables the facts are less clear. M. Grammont
(1914:40-42) indicated that, at least for the pair
[e] versus [ɛ], the vowel that occurred was conditioned by the immediate or more distant phonological context and by morphological factors. For instance, he asserted that a following r (tauto- or
heterosyllabic) tended to open the vowel. To account for such alternations as:

(3) presse [prɛs]   pressons [prɛsõ] vs.
    pressé [prese]
    bégaie [begɛ]   bégaiement [begɛmã] vs.
    bégayer [begeje]

he introduced the term vowel harmony (<u>harmonisation
vocalique</u>) to which he attributed a conditioning
effect strong enough to override morphological relations, as is shown by the examples in (3). Random inspection of the recently published <u>Diction-
naire de la Prononciation française dans son usage
réel</u> (Martinet and Walter 1973) suggests that these
three factors operate in a less than predictable
fashion and that it is difficult to rank them
hierarchically relative to each other (the figures
indicate the ratio of high-mid versus low-mid
vowels among the 17 representative speakers interviewed).[1] The claimed lowering effect of [R] is
shared by other consonants:

318 / ALBERT VALDMAN

(2) Distribution of the six mid vowel phonemes relative to word-final boundary and permissible final consonants.

Environment	Vowel e	ε	ɔ	o	œ	ø
–#	poignée	poignet	X	peau	X	peu
–C						
ž	(aurai-je)	aurai-je	loge	l'auge	X	(Mauberge)
t		sept	hotte	hôte	X	(meute)
z		pèse	X	pause	X	creuse
d		raide	rode	rôde	X	(Eudes)
l		sel	sol	saule	veulent	(veule)
n		benne	bonne	Beaune	jeune	(jeûne)
f		chef	étoffe	sauf	boeuf	X
v		lève	love	mauve	peuvent	X
r		serre	sort	X	soeur	X
j		oreille	X	X	feuille	X
p		guêpe	tope	taupe	X	X
b		plèbe	robe	aube	X	X
k		sec	roc	rauque	X	X
š		caisse	cosse	causse	X	X
s		pêche	poche	embauche	X	X
m		aime	homme	heaume	X	X
g		bègue	vogue	X	X	X
ñ		règne	grogne	X	X	X

(4) Phonological conditioning.
      horreur 0/17   honnête 0/17   Hollande 0/17

The tongue height of the vowel in a following syllable has uncertain effect:

(5) Vowel harmony.
      auto 13/4   autel 16/1   automne 13/3
      plaisir 8/9   plaisance 7/10   plaisantin 3/14
      plaider 8/9   plaideur 3/14

In none of the examples in (6) does the vowel of the stem appear regularly in the derived forms:

(6) Morphological analogy.
      nègre/négresse 17/0   négrier 17/0
      neige/neiger 14/3   neigeux 13/4
      bègue/bégayer 17/0

Malmberg (1941) underscored the influence of 'extra-phonic' factors such as the conventional spelling, but the direct effect of that factor is not apparent.

(7) laisser 11/6   léser 16/1
    aîné 9/8   aider 12/5
    lèche/allécher 16/1   allèchement 2/15
    léger/alléger 16/1   allègement 11/6

The presence of ai vs. è has a slight lowering effect, as does the graph aî vs. ai. The shift to the low-mid vowel in allèchement may also be attributed to the influences of the base form lèche. In allègement, in addition to the use of the grave accent, rhythmic features such as distance from the final syllable may be a significant factor in lowering the vowel. Compare:

(8) fosse 16/1   fossé 16/1   fossette 11/6
    fossoyeur 10/6
    cesser 15/2   cessant 7/10   cessation 9/8
    nécessaire 17/0   nécessairement 16/1

Overall, these data show that, given the low predictive power of LDP in internal syllables, phonemic status must be assigned to each member of the mid vowel pairs also in that environment and that the variation observed can only be accounted for by complex variable rules.

2. The directionality of the Loi de Position. Counterexamples to LDP are ascribed to 'extraphonological' factors. The following statement by B. Malmberg (1941:245) is characteristic of this point of view:

> La raison pour laquelle cette tendance [LDP] n'a pas aboutit est essentiellement de nature <u>extraphonique</u>. Ce sont des facteurs qui ne sont ni phonétiques ni phonologiques qui empêchent la langue de suivre son penchant naturel et qui maintient en partie un système qui ne correspond plus à son génie ... La véritable structure d'un système phonologique se manifeste parfois-- et c'est justement le cas en français--mieux dans ses tendances que dans une prononciation réglée et freinée par une tradition puissante et maintenue artificiellement par l'enseignement et par l'action des puristes.

If LDP is indeed an inherent tendency of the French phonological system, we should expect it to be more in evidence in informal and allegro styles, in the speech of the uneducated and untutored--varieties of French in use among the working and lower classes and in areas distant from the capital--and in speech forms having undergone rapid restructuring, such as the French-based creoles.

Hall (1948:9) and Politzer (1960:75) stated that contrasts between members of the mid vowel pairs are neutralized in fast colloquial speech. While it would not hold up in phonological phrase-final position, this observation accurately describes the behavior of mid vowels in internal syllables. But, as Politzer himself notes, the mid vowel that appears in internal free syllables where the contrast between high-mid and low-mid is suspended is phonetically closer to the low-mid member rather than the high-mid one predicted by the LDP.

(9) nécessité [nEsEsite] philosophie [filözöfi]
    heureuse [orøz]

In the examples of (9), [E] represents a mid-mid front unrounded vowel[2] and [ö] a slightly rounded centralized vowel. First noted by Martinet (1958), the second-level neutralization between a front and a back rounded mid vowel is becoming generalized in SF. Among Parisian speakers at least, the following pairs are indistinguishable:

(10) [lömönje] l'aumonier vs. le meunier
     [löfis]   l'office vs. le fils

Malmberg claimed that in final free syllables lower-class speakers evidenced the tendency to pronounce words containing the è-variable[3] with the high-mid alternant. This conclusion is not borne out by data collected recently by Léon (1972) according to the strictest canons of empirical research. That investigator interviewed 31 fourteen-year-old boys from working families in the Paris area. The subjects were asked to read sentences seeded with a wide range of key è-variable items (gai, quai, sais, billet, ticket, épais, serais, etc.). The responses were recorded and analyzed by a group of 13 judges, three of whom were trained phoneticians. The results showed the stable use of the low-mid member, not only for è-variable words, but also for items, such as the first person singular future ending, that have not traditionally been assigned to that variable (see (11)).

The striking difference between these recent observations and the testimony of traditional phoneticians of the period 1900-1940 does not reflect any significant change in the pronunciation habits of the Paris lower classes; rather, they cast doubt on the value of evidence unsupported by detailed specification of the social characteristics of

(11) Individual items:
quai 3/28   gai 3/28   balai 2/29
faudrait 1/30   pouvais 0/31
Minimal pairs:

	[e]	[ɛ]
clé	0	31
claie	14	17
épée	31	0
épais	5	26
prendrai	3	28
prendrais	2	29

subjects and of the circumstances surrounding the recording and the analysis of the data.[4] Deyhime's replication of Martinet's phonological questionnaire among university students also refutes Malmberg's claim about the directionality of the alternation [e] versus [ɛ] in final free syllables. In northern France and in Paris the percentage of high-mid vowel pronunciations among speakers who claim they contrast the two vowels has fallen in the space of one generation (see (12)).

(12)

	quai		les		serai	
	1941	1962	1941	1962	1941	1962
Northern France	42	23	59	47	53	42
Southern France	41	34	79	66	19	34
Paris	40	11	32	36	53	33

The fact that LDP generally operates in Occitan-speaking or Occitan-influenced areas of France cannot be adduced in support of it since this state of affairs appears to be traceable to the local substrate. Furthermore, here again the direction of change is the reverse of that predicted by LDP. I have investigated the distribution of mid vowels among teenagers (13 to 15 years of age) in an Occitan-speaking area (the department of Alpes Maritimes).[5] While the presence of the high-mid front vowel in final free syllables and of the

THE 'LOI DE POSITION' / 323

low-mid rounded vowels in final checked syllables
is nearly universal in guided conversation, vowels
constituting counterexamples occur in monitored
speech (13). Of particular significance were results obtained in an auditory questionnaire in
which subjects were asked to make various evalua-
tive judgments. They heard recorded sentences containing variable words produced with two alternative pronunciations: the local variant characterized by LDP and the Paris (normative) pronunciation.
Informants were asked to indicate (a) which variant
reflected their habitual pronunciation and (b) which
variant they preferred. In addition, they were
given a list of variable words (<u>billet</u>, <u>gauche</u>,
<u>feutre</u>) and asked to assess whether the pronunci-
ation was correct or incorrect, or whether the judgment was irrelevant. Several nonvariable items
were added as controls.[6]

(13)

	Variable		
	$\underline{\grave{e}}$ (billet)	$\underline{o}$ (gauche)	$\underline{eu}$ (feutre)
Directed conversation	362/2 (99%)	46/2 (96%)	13/5 (64%)
Sentence reading	288/38 (88%)	216/40 (84%)	212/30 (88%)
Habitual pronunciation	26/20 (57%)	29/16 (64%)	24/15 (86%)
Preferred pronunciation	19/12 (61%)	13/5 (72%)	15/18 (45%)
Correctness	24/5 (81%)	23/13 (64%)	8/10 (44%)

Finally, if LDP reflected the directionality of
change in the French mid vowel system, one might
expect it to surface in the French derived creole
dialects that show the amplification of other inherent tendencies of the language, for example, the
palatalization of dentals and velars and the analytic expression of tense and aspect categories. But
because of other changes, notably the loss of

postvocalic r, the distinction high-mid versus low-mid has become phonologized. In Haitian Creole this contrast appears in final free syllables.

(14) [mo] 'word' (mot) [mɔ] 'dead person' (mort)
     [bebe] 'baby' (bébé) [bɛbɛ] 'mute'

One does find lexically related pairs that exhibit low-mid/high-mid vowel alternations that suggest LDP (Tinelli 1978).

(15) [klɛ] 'light, clear' (clair) [klere] 'to light' (éclairer)
     [kɔz] 'cause' (cause) [koze] 'to cause' (causer)

But high-mid and low-mid vowels contrast in final closed syllables and there are numerous instances of low-mid vowels occurring in internal free syllables (Valdman 1977):

(16) [pa ret devãm] 'don't remain before me'
     [parɛt devãm] 'appear before me'
     [sot]/[soti] 'to go out' (sortir) [sɔt] 'stupid' (sot)
     [kɔkɔb] 'awkward' [kokobe] 'cripple'
     [kɔlɔkɔsɔ] 'miserly'

3. The Loi de Position and the French mid vowel system. In summary, there is little evidence in support of the claim that LDP is a productive rule of French. It is contradicted by easily observable facts in a broad spectrum of speech varieties and recent empirical studies indicate that it fails to account for the directionality of ongoing generation-to-generation changes. One wonders, then, why this spurious generalization held such attraction for several generations of French phonologists. It is no doubt mainly because it dovetails nicely with the widely accepted notion of the French midvowel system as a symmetrical 3x2:

(17) i   y   u
      e   ö   o
          a

Other surface distinctions are introduced by LDP and various lower-level rules accounting for environmentally conditioned vowel length.[7]

The symmetrical 2x3 midvowel subsystem implied by LDP fails to account for the interplay of length and vowel quality distinctions observable in all varieties of SF which, no doubt, provides the key to an understanding of the diachronic development of that language's vowel system. Indeed, precisely because it deals only with vowel quality LDP erroneously specifies parallel mappings of unrounded (front) e and rounded (front and back) ö and o. Whereas in final free syllables high-mid [e] contrasts with low-mid [ɛ], the rounded vowel contrasts in final checked syllables involve low-mid short phones vs. high-mid long (or half-long) phones: pomme [pɔm] vs. paume [po:m], jeune [žœn] vs. jeûne [zø:n].[8] In fact, these latter contrasts could be reanalyzed in terms of distinctive length oppositions and conditioned vowel quality differences: pomme /pom/ vs. paume /po:m/. In view of the role of length in effecting round vowel distinctions the contrast between [ɛ] and [ɛ:], (belle 'beautiful (f.)' vs. bêle 'he bleats') found widely in formal styles of SF, must be considered as part of a skewed seven-unit midvowel system:

(18)   e   ø   o
       ɛ   ɛ: œ   ɔ

In one of the few available detailed phonological descriptions of a regional variety of SF based on the speech of a clearly identified group of informants, Galand (1968) notes an ongoing shift from length to vowel quality as a distinctive feature. Some of the Burgundian speakers he observed differentiate pairs such as sot vs. saut, homophonous in SF, wholly by length: sot [so] vs. saut [śo:].

Others produce [ɔ] in final free syllables, a position from which that phone is excluded in SF, and effect a complex length plus vowel quality distinction: sot [sɔ] vs. saut [so:]. In the case of the front rounded vowels, contrasts occur only in final checked syllables, and while the opposition is more productive than in SF, the phonetic features involved are the same: short low-mid vs. long high-mid (fleuve [flœv] vs. neuve [nø:v]). In both varieties of Burgundian French a three-way distinction obtains among front unrounded phones in final free syllables and a two-way distinction in final checked syllables:[9]

(19)   belle   bêle   piquait   piqué   piquée
    System A   e   ɛ   e   e:
    System B   ɛ   ɛ: ɛ   e   ê

These facts point to a mid vowel system, more complex than that of present-day SF, containing two unrounded vowels and two rounded vowels occurring short or long:

(20)   e   e:
             ö   ö: o   o:
        ɛ   ɛ:

The facts brought to light by Galand suggest that the vowel system of SF does not reflect artificial elaboration and complexification through the influence of extralinguistic factors such as academic purism or the conventional orthography but, on the contrary, the leveling of a variety of clashing complex systems in flux. This view is consistent with the interpretation of SF as a koinè dialect in which highly divergent or localized features of provincial varieties are neutralized. If one interprets the term 'inherent tendency' to mean a state of equilibrium after extensive restructuring, LDP does not constitute such a tendency for French and its use as a heuristic device can only serve to mask facts and to miss significant generalizations.

NOTES

1. The speakers selected were representative of the widely traveled Paris upper middle class. The group is highly biased toward secondary and university teaching (10 speakers) and comprised 11 women and only six men.
2. In the literature this vowel is described as 'e moyen'. Another characteristic of the phonetic realization of the neutralized mid vowels is their relative shortness. In Occitan accented French, the mid vowels of internal syllables are indeed determined by the Loi de Position. The items in (9) would be pronounced [nesesite], [filozofi], and [ørœz]. However, there are few, if any, accessible empirical studies of that variety of Standard French and these observations remain unverified.
3. Words containing the è-variable are pronounced with [e] or [ɛ] and contrast with items always produced with [ɛ] (belle) or with [e] (fée).
4. Had Malmberg (1941) based his study on actual observation of Paris working class and lower class speakers, he would have obtained results similar to those of Léon. Where I was a schoolboy in a lower middle class and working class suburb of Paris (Rosay-sous-Bois), I recall our teacher correcting our 'erroneous' pronunciation of the first person singular future form with [ɛ] and drilling distinctions such as je prendrai vs. je prendrais.
5. The research, conducted in collaboration with Jean-Pierre Jardel, University of Nice, and with the assistance of Rosette Raynaud, also of that university, is supported by a research grant from the Centre National de la Recherche Scientifique of France (ATP Linguistique Générale D 1566: Facteurs ethnologiques et sociologiques dans la variation du français).
6. The o-variable refers to items containing [o] or [ɔ] in final checked syllable and the eu-variable to items containing [ø] or [œ] in the same environment.

7. Two rules specify length for mid vowels:
(1) a general rule lengthening all vowels followed by [r], [z], [ž], [v] in final syllables; (2) a restricted rule introducing length in final checked syllables containing [o] and [ø].

8. The recurrence of [o:] and [ø:] in final checked syllables in violation of LDP is explained by P. Delattre (1959:109) in a rather ingenious way: ' Ainsi l'[o] fermé de paume, afin de s'accorder avec la Loi de Position et les habitudes articulatoires du français, tend à se rendre "libre", à ouvrir la syllable, c'est à dire à repousser l'[m] vers une syllable suivante: [po-m]. C'est cela qui allonge la syllable'. This explanation requires one to posit a syllable boundary where length occurs (e.g. [po:$m]), an obviously ad hoc and untenable proposal.

9. The symbol [eˆ] denotes a vowel intermediate between [i] and [e].

REFERENCES

Delattre, Pierre. 1959. Rapports entre la durée vocalique, le timbre et la structure syllabique en français. French Review 32:547-552.

Deyhime, Guiti. 1967. Enquête sur la phonologie du français contemporain. La Linguistique 97-108, 57-84.

Galand, L. 1968. Timbre et longeur: les oppositions de voyelles dans une variété bourguignonne du français. Word 24.165-174 (A. Juilland, ed. Linguistic studies presented to André Martinet, Part II, Indo-European Linguistics).

Grammont, Maurice. 1914. La prononciation française. Paris: Delagrave.

Hall, Robert A., Jr. 1948. French (Language Monograph Series No. 24, Structural Sketch 1). Baltimore: Linguistic Society of America.

Léon, Pierre. 1972. Etude de la prononciation du 'e' accentué chez un groupe de jeunes Parisiens. In: Albert Valdman, ed. 302-312.

Malmberg, Bertil. 1941. Observations sur le système vocalique de français. Acta Linguistica 2.234-246.

Martinet, André. 1945, 1971. La prononciation du français contemporain. Paris-Geneva: Droz.
Martinet, André, and Henriette Walter. 1973. Dictionnaire de la prononciation du français dans son usage réel. Paris: France-Expansion.
Politzer, Robert. 1960. Teaching French: An introduction to applied linguistics. Boston: Ginn.
Tinelli, Henri. 1978. Open syllabicity versus morphosyntactic agglutination in French Creole. Orbis (forthcoming).
Valdman, Albert. 1972. La loi de position as a pedagogical norm. In: Albert Valdman, ed. 452-464.
Valdman, Albert, ed. 1972. Papers in linguistics and phonetics to the memory of Pierre Delattre. The Hague: Mouton.
Valdman, Albert. 1977. La structure phonologique des parlers franco-créoles de la zône caraïbe. Etudes Créoles. AUPELF, forthcoming.

LATINIST AND UNIVERSALIST MODELS IN SPANISH GRAMMAR

BARRY L. VELLEMAN
Marquette University

Just as the Romance languages derive from Latin, so their grammatical description was founded in Classical terms. The earliest full Romance grammar, that of Nebrija (1492), was substantially a translation of his earlier Latin grammar. Nebrija and his followers felt that a language could be made a vehicle for learned composition if it could be shown to be reducible to an 'art', exactly as Latin had been 'reduced'. In the four centuries after Nebrija, changing attitudes toward Latin and toward grammatical methodology resulted in a gradual weakening of the influence of the terms, concepts, and criteria of definition inherited from the analysis of the mother tongue, despite the presence of two separate conservative pressures. First, a pedagogical pressure encouraged the exploitation of parallels between Latin and Romance in order to teach the structure of each as a descriptive model of literary usage. A second, universalist pressure, seen especially during the seventeenth and eighteenth centuries and outside of Spain, was based on a developing philosophy of language according to which these parallelisms could somehow be 'explained' in mentalistic terms by abstracting their common elements, generally semantic.

In his introductory essay to his edition of Nebrija's Gramática, González-Llubera notes that the 'author's starting-point is Latin grammatical theory', and that all of the terminology and most of the definitions are reproduced from Nebrija's Latin grammar of 11 years earlier.[1] Nebrija follows Donatus, for example, in his distinctions of parts of speech, and his definition of the noun as a word 'declined for case, without tense, and meaning "body" or "object"' (p. 74). On the matter of nominal declension, Nebrija writes: 'The Castilian language has no declension of nouns, except for singular and plural; but it distinguishes the meaning of the cases by prepositions' (p. 88). However, he declines Spanish nouns in three declensions (-a, -o, others), and in five cases, omitting the ablative (p. 89). Spanish nouns have the same six features as Donatus' Latin nouns: quality, type, form, gender, number, and case.

Nebrija could find no Latin analogue for the non-inflected past participle of the perfect tenses, and postulated a new part of speech, the invariable participial noun (p. 105). This class is established solely on the basis of morphological invariability. However, greater consistency might have been achieved had Nebrija considered the formal and semantic relation of (adjectival) amado and (postauxiliary) amado, which differ only as the result of a neutralization of inflection in the latter environment. More significant is the fact that, in introducing the new term, Nebrija should write osemos 'let us dare'. Nebrija is wholly within the Donatus tradition, with occasional paraphrases of etymological definitions seen in Priscian (for example, the definition of the verb, p. 96). The Nebrija Gramática was the chief pedagogical text in Spain for centuries, partly as the result of its merits, and partly as the consequence of a law which prohibited the publication or use of any other grammar.[2]

In his 1558 Gramática castellana, Cristóbal de Villalón[3] recognizes Nebrija's Latinist tendencies, but realizes the difficulty he faces in avoiding

them: 'Although it is true that we claim to offer
a grammar of pure Castilian, to a high degree
divorced from Latin, we will be pardoned for avail-
ing ourselves of some of the names and terms of the
Latin language ... since they are terms which, in
their completeness and brevity, have great meaning'
(p. 11). After establishing a framework of the
three parts of speech postulated by Aristotle (p.
13), Villalón subdivides the 'article' into each of
Nebrija's classes save the gerund and the invariable
participial noun. Through one of a number of confusions of terminology, 'article' refers to non-
declinable forms (p. 12), demonstrative adjectives
(pp. 14, 19), subject pronouns and possessive adjectives (p. 34), and the intensifying adjective
mismo (p. 35); but the usual referent of the term
(el) is not classified. Included in the list of
verbal forms is el que ama, considered a 'present
participle' because it means amantem (p. 47). However, Villalón defines declension on formal, not
semantic grounds, and therefore rejects its presence in Spanish (pp. 15-16). Villalón's work can
be characterized as a carelessly written pedagogical grammar which exhibits occasional creativity.

In the early seventeenth century, to the question
of differences and similarities between Spanish and
Latin, was added a question of historical perspective. Nebrija had already realized that the state
in which his forefathers received their language
represented a 'corrupted' form of Latin (p. 5);
nevertheless, a minority view of this later period,
probably based on exaggerated nationalism and total
ignorance of the nature of linguistic change, held
that Latin was derived from Spanish. The foremost
exponent of this theory, Gregorio López Madera,
states in his Discursos (1601) that the similarities between the languages are the result of many
centuries of cultural contact between the Spanish
and Italian peninsulas.[4] Five years later, Bernardo J. Aldrete not only provided sound arguments
for a Vulgar Latin source, but also compared Italian, Portuguese, Catalan, and Castilian with the
mother tongue, and abstracted a number of early

'sound laws' for Castilian.5 López Madera's theory
was embraced, however, by Gonzalo Correas (1571-
1631) in his <u>Arte de la lengua española castellana</u>
(1626).6 Since the 'original' language was of divine origin, it must have been 'perfect', acoustically and structurally; Spanish, without the consonant clusters or complicated declensions of Latin,
must therefore be closer to the common source of
both (Correas, pp. 483-484; cf. Bahner, pp. 112-
113).

Despite confusions of chronology, Correas' <u>Arte</u>
continues to show the impact of the pedagogical and
universalist pressures. All languages coincide in
the 'general and substantial part of grammar', and
although 'their phrases and words may be different'
(p. 129); it is sound pedagogical theory to begin
with the student's own language, and, having
learned it, he is able to 'progress with greater
ease and rapidity in the grammar of the Classical
languages' (p. xviii). The art of grammar is that
which 'contains and teaches the general precepts
which suit all languages, and the particular ones
which pertain only to that one which it treats'
(p. 129).

Correas' originality resides principally in his
treatment of details, and not in his definitions or
theoretical pronouncements. While still within the
Classical mold (his three parts of speech parallel
those of Aristotle and Villalón), Correas' <u>Arte</u> is
characterized by a scepticism toward the wholesale
transference of concepts from one language to another. As Emilio Alarcos has observed, 'Correas is
not a passive receiver of the grammatical tradition.
He submits what he finds in grammars--ancient or
modern-- to the reagent of his linguistic experience' (in Correas, p. xxv).

In 1585, Francisco Sánchez de las Brozas published
his <u>Minerva</u>,7 a Latin grammar based on an hypothesis
of 'logical-grammatical parallelism' (Lázaro
Carreter, p. 133), a parallelism which moves away
from logical didactics and toward a rationalistic
position. Sánchez' theory of ellipsis, in particular, presupposes that mental structures somehow

underlie grammatical structures, and hints that the former are 'recoverable', independent of their presence in the latter. The work of Sánchez had a considerable influence on the Port-Royal <u>Grammar</u> of Lancelot and Arnauld (1660), as well as on a multitude of European 'general' grammars with the Port-Royal work as intermediary. These include the works of James Harris and William Ward in England, and, in France, those of Beauzée, Sacy, Condillac, Destutt-Tracy, and others. Nevertheless, the influence of Sánchez was imperceptible in Spain (Lázaro Carreter, p. 136). A few seventeenth-century grammars made reference to 'figurative syntax',[8] but the impact of Sánchez is seen most clearly in Benito de San Pedro's <u>Arte del romance castellano</u> (1769), modeled closely on Port-Royal. Here we begin to find generalist explanations, philosophical, historical, and logical. Thus gender was originated to 'distinguish, by means of expression, the sex of male or female' (p. 124). Although Romance has no declension by termination, the varieties of prepositions may be noted, 'and with this [may be kept] the analogy of the declensions of the Latins' (p. 143). As in syllogistic logic, the copula is the only 'pure' verb, latent in all other verbs (p. 3).

When Vicente Salvá questions the validity of such abstract statements in his 1830 <u>Gramática</u>,[9] he is in the position of a Villalón, who had earlier criticized excessive Latinization. The early decades of the nineteenth century witnessed Spanish decline and the independence of the Spanish-American nations. These factors fostered strong anti-Peninsular and anti-Classical sentiments among liberal Spaniards, many of whom fled to Paris and London. It was a period of experimentation in which the grammatical works produced show free thought and even open debate.[10] Vicente Salvá lived in London and published his grammar in Paris. The work is critical of grammars of the previous period, as was Villalón's, and is equally unable to provide an alternative. Salvá's definitions are curious blends of semantic, morphological, and syntactic criteria.

The article, for example, is 'a short word which, when placed before the noun or another part of speech in the noun's stead, indicates the type to which the object belongs, or serves to begin to determine the individual of which we are speaking, in addition to indicating always its number and gender' (p. 47).

Andrés Bello praises Salvá for his provision of both data and an anti-generalist viewpoint, but finds the latter's work asystematic.[11] Both Salvá and Bello consider themselves writers of grammars of a single language. For Bello, 'the speech of a people is an artificial system of signs' (p. 17). Language is chiefly arbitrary and conventional. Neither Latinist formulas, cross-language generalizations, nor historical explanations can describe the system of a language, since 'word classes do not differ from each other because of meaning, but because of their mutual connection and dependency in the language'.[12] Bello criticizes Salvá's semantic definition of the verb, stating that it is a list of varieties of verbs according to their meaning (pp. 47-48). The Spanish passive is not for Bello a separate (morphological) conjugation (as it was in Latin, or as accepted by the Spanish Academy), but rather the result of a (syntactic) operation undergone by the transitive-active sentence type (pp. 241, 250). The copula shares morphological features with other verbs, and cannot be considered latent or 'pure' simply because of meaning (p. 47). Bello attributes the 'cases' of Spanish to excessive Latinization in which the basis of analysis is translation (p. 111). The terms 'masculine' and 'feminine' refer, not to classes of objects, but to classes of nouns (p. 36). Bello's approach, while not entirely consistent, is theoretically that of the empiricist describing the data of the authors and his own, with few concessions to the Latinist and generalist pressures.

The relationship between Latinist and universalist grammar models in Europe has undergone several interpretations. One observer states that 'it is the Latinists [of the English tradition] who most easily believe that there are grammatical categories common to all languages', and calls the Port-Royal <u>Grammar</u> 'the traditional grammar of Latin generalised enough to accommodate French, with some reference to other modern languages'.[13] Noam Chomsky, on the other hand, has attacked what he considers the structuralist view that universal grammars were based on a Latin model.[14] Perhaps the truth lies between these views. The Renaissance pedagogical grammars which based single-language analyses on Latin formed a tradition from which the generalists drew. Proof is the fact that, while Chomsky is correct in pointing out instances in which the French generalists described structures with no Latin analogue, these were at times the object of decades of controversy (for example, the 'rule of Vaugelas').[15] However, points of coincidence were generalized in terms of categories derived from the study of Latin. The relation between Latinist and universalist models may be parallel to the distinction made between the pedagogical and the universalist pressures. Just as the structuralists have given data to their more mentalistic successors, so the followers of the pedagogical Latinist tradition provided analyzed data (not method) to the subsequent generalists. In the cases of Villalón and Correas we see that the duplication of Latinist terminology (and consequently that of grammatical characteristics, since classes such as 'neuter verbs' and 'present participles' had to be assigned referents) was an inevitable, if somehow undesirable, feature of early Romance grammars. The generalists added philosophical speculation in an attempt to 'explain', by abstraction, etymological theorizing, and postulates concerning the human mind and logic, the linguistic features deemed universal as the result of their presence in several languages, of which Latin had presented the clearest use of terms and the most widely accepted descriptions. Dwight Bolinger has written: 'Whether universal grammar would have been so generally accepted if Europe had been sharply divided, say, between two languages as unlike as French and Hungarian, no one can say.'16

On the whole, the pedagogical grammars were more 'prescriptive' than the general grammars, whose purpose was more the inquiry into causes than the clarification of usage. It is natural that grammars 'descriptive' of literary usage become increasingly 'prescriptive' as innovations of the spoken language create a widening divergence between the two levels. Prescriptivism, of course, is acceptable in the application of language descriptions to a pedagogy.

The analysis of nominal case affords a powerful example of the strong influence of the Latin tradition on subsequent developments in grammatical studies. The conflict between morphological and semantic definitions of 'case' reappears throughout general grammars in eighteenth-century France, and we have seen the difference between Nebrija and Villalón on this point. If the cases are defined morphologically, there are no cases in Spanish; if they are defined semantically, there are as many 'cases' as there are prepositions, and therefore case relations are reflected in the lexical meanings assigned to the prepositions, and are not inherent in the noun. Chomsky (<u>Cartesian Linguistics</u>, p. 45) has suggested that the Romance 'declensions' imply 'a belief in the uniformity of the grammatical relations involved, a belief that deep structures are fundamentally the same across languages'. One wonders, however, whether 'translatability' is evidence for the 'fundamental' identity of universal deep structure in grammars like Nebrija's. Neither the morphological nor the semantic interpretation of case leads to the conclusion that Spanish 'cases' are quantitively or qualitatively identical to those of Latin. The only support for such a conclusion comes from the influence of the Latin tradition.

In the Hispanic tradition, Nebrija and Villalón represent an era of Renaissance humanism, in which cultural and pedagogical pressures encouraged the use of the Latin framework. The works of Correas and San Pedro correspond to a period of scepticism and speculation. San Pedro is a transitional figure because his principal model was a Romance grammar, although one based on universalist precepts. The first half of the nineteenth century, during which were written the grammars of Salvá and Bello, marks the rise of Romanticism, and Spanish-American independence from European rule, political and intellectual. In Salvá we find an approach which leans less on Latinist formulas, and which consciously rejects generalist theory. Bello adds to this development the influence of British empiricism and the scientific method, foreshadowing later structuralist thought.[17] When the complete history of Hispanic grammatical thought is written, it may well provide insight into the relationships between linguistic thought and the history of ideas as a whole; for grammatical analysis is, as much as its subject matter, the expression of a culture.

NOTES

1. [Elio Antonio de] Nebrija, Gramática de la lengua castellana (Oxford University Press, 1926), p. xlii. All direct translations in this study are the responsibility of the author.
2. Fernando Lázaro Carreter, Las ideas lingüísticas en España durante el siglo XVIII (Madrid: Revista de filología española, Anejo XLVIII, 1949), p. 137.
3. Gramática castellana [1558] (Madrid: Consejo Superior de Investigaciones Científicas, 1971).
4. Conde de la Viñaza, Biblioteca de filología castellana (Madrid: Manuel Tello, 1893), p. 17. See also Werner Bahner, La lingüística española del siglo de oro, trans. Jesús Munárriz Peralta (Madrid: Ciencia Nueva, 1966), pp. 101-112.
5. Bernardo J. Aldrete, Del origen y principio de la lengua castellana o romance que hoy se usa en España [1606] (Madrid: Melchor Sánchez, 1647).
6. Arte de la lengua castellana [1626] (Madrid: Revista de filología española, Anejo LVI, 1954).

7. *Minerva, seu de Causis linguae Latinae Commentarius* [1585] (Lispsiae: Impensis Jo. Ambros. Barthii, 1793).
8. Juan Villar, *Arte de la lengua española* [1651]; quoted in Lázaro Carreter, pp. 134-135.
9. *Gramática de la lengua castellana* [1830] (Paris: Garnier Hermanos, n.d.).
10. See Vicente Lloréns-Castillo, *Liberales y románticos: una emigración española en Inglaterra (1823-1834)* (México: Fondo de Cultura Económica, 1954), pp. 145, 169-171; Dr. D. Antonio Puigblanch, *Opúsculos gramático-satíricos* (London, n.d.).
11. Andrés Bello and Rufino J. Cuervo, *Gramática de la lengua castellana* [1847] (Buenos Aires: Editorial Sopena Argentina, 1960), p. 20.
12. Bello, "Filosofía del entendimiento," in *Obras completas*, III (Caracas: Ministerio de Educación, 1951), 417.
13. Ian Michael, *English Grammatical Categories and the Tradition to 1800* (Cambridge University Press, 1970), pp. 165, 168.
14. *Language and Mind* (New York: Harcourt, Brace & World, Inc., 1968), p. 12; "The Current Scene in Linguistics: Present Directions," in *Modern Studies in English: Readings in Transformational Grammar*, ed. David A. Reibel and Sanford A. Schane (Englewood Cliffs, New Jersey: Prentice-Hall, Inc., 1969), p. 4.
15. See Chomsky's *Cartesian Linguistics* (New York: Harper & Row, 1966), pp. 56-57; *Language and Mind*, p. 13.
16. *Aspects of Language* (New York: Harcourt, Brace & World, Inc., 1968), p. 186.
17. See the author's "Structuralist Theory in the Bello *Gramática*," *Hispanic Review* (forthcoming).

WHAT IS A CREOLE?
THE EXAMPLE OF THE PORTUGUESE LANGUAGE OF TUGU, JAKARTA, INDONESIA

STEPHEN WALLACE
Cornell University

0. Introduction. Recent reports of nonstandard varieties of Portuguese spoken in Asia, for instance, that spoken in Malacca (Malaysia), have mentioned a further variety once spoken on the island of Java in Indonesia. This latter variety, often referred to as 'Java Creole', is best known through the work of Schuchardt, who, while never having visited the speakers of this language himself, had written texts sent from Indonesia to Europe. These texts were composed by several members of the village of Tugu near Jakarta (Batavia) under the supervision of the village pastor and forwarded by the Batavian Society of Arts and Sciences to Schuchardt (for samples of this text, see Appendix 2). These he put together with earlier data from the <u>Nieuwe Woordenschat</u> of 1780, an anonymous trilingual list of words and expressions in Dutch, 'common' Malay, and 'common' Portuguese (= 'Java Creole', sample in Appendix 1) and provided all with annotations in his 'Ueber das Malaioportugiesische von Batavia und Tugu' (Schuchardt 1890). Perhaps because there have been no later scholarly reports of this language, it is thought to have died out at the end of the nineteenth century (Hancock 1972:549; 1975:211).

The aim of this paper is two-fold. I would first like to present a summary of information which I collected in Indonesia in 1975 concerning the present status of 'Java Creole', its linguistic structure, and the sociocultural milieu in which it is spoken. The point, besides indicating that the language has not entirely disappeared, is to give the first direct linguistically oriented account of it. Secondly, I would like, using this language as an example, to discuss the use and usefulness of the term 'creole', which has in the recent literature concerning linguistic change and variation acquired a popularity far exceeding that of former times. But first, the language and its speakers.

1. Tugu and its people. The present home of 'Java Creole' is the village of Tugu, located within the boundaries of the Special Capital District of Jakarta. This district includes the city of Jakarta proper, the capital of the Republic of Indonesia, and a fair amount of land, once a rural agricultural or horticultural area, now increasingly used for industrial parks and suburban housing developments. The land which Tugu occupies belongs to the latter category. It is located just inside the northeast boundaries of the Capital District, approximately three kilometers southeast of Tanjung Priok, Jakarta's port on the Java Sea (see Noorduyn and Verstappen 1972 for maps showing the location of Tugu).

The traditional inhabitants of Tugu are descendants of the 'Portuguese' or 'Mardijkers' (freedmen), persons of almost exclusively Asian ancestry brought by the Dutch to Jakarta (then called Batavia) in the seventeenth century from former Portuguese colonies in South Asia (and Malacca?).[1] At the time, the Dutch were in conflict with various rulers on the island of Java itself, and thought it dangerous to populate their newly founded (1619) city of Batavia, established to be their administrative and commercial headquarters in the archipelago, with the surrounding Sundanese and Javanese. Large numbers of these 'Portuguese', as well as many other groups, such as Balinese, were thus brought in from long distances to be slaves and workers. The 'Portuguese', being Christians, were soon freed and became something of a petite bourgeoisie numbering over 5,000 in the first census of Jakarta in 1673. Many Dutch men took 'Portuguese' women as wives, since at that time practically no women went from Holland to the East Indies.

These 'Portuguese' people brought with them from abroad a form of Portuguese and possibly other languages as well. The evidence that we have indicates that in seventeenth-century Jakarta, the original migrants (probably) and their descendants (certainly) spoke Portuguese as a first language. In seventeenth- and eighteenth-century Jakarta, it appears, this Portuguese language even became the lingua franca of everyday discourse, especially in the European community, although most persons doubtless spoke Malay also. Towards the end of the eighteenth century, the use of Portuguese waned. As the city grew in numbers and diversity of its population, and as no more speakers of Portuguese came from abroad, Malay replaced it, and the 'Portuguese' people of central Jakarta, intermarrying extensively with members of other groups, disappeared themselves as a distinct group.

Around the years 1660-1670, however, some 150 of these 'Portuguese' people moved, or were moved, out of the city to an isolated rural area to the northeast--the present village of Tugu. There they lived as rice farmers, hunters, fishermen, and sometimes as small traders in the midst of an area, sparsely populated at the time, fairly heavily populated now, and inhabited by people of other groups. The traditional marks of Tuguers which distinguished them from their indigenous Indonesian neighbors were: their Christian religion (presently an Indonesian offshoot of Dutch Reformed Protestantism); their Portuguese language; their fondness for and cultivation of a type of music played on a <u>kroncong</u>, an instrument like a ukulele; and their relatively high social status as landowners and persons who could read and write.

Towards the end of the nineteenth century, Tugu began to lose its isolation. A railroad was constructed from the nearby port of Tanjung Priok to Jakarta and beyond, and the Tuguers began to exchange visits with and intermarry with members of the indigenous Indonesian Christian community at Depok, located to the south of Jakarta. (At the time, the churches in Depok and Tugu were served by the same Dutch minister.) Many Tuguers, possibly even from their earliest times in Tugu, also married Chinese or 'Malays' (as they refer to indigenous Islamic Indonesians). Before World War II, a number of Tuguers attended Dutch schools in Jakarta and found employment with the Dutch colonial administration or with Dutch businesses. During the confused and insecure aftermath of this war, as Indonesians fought against the Dutch for independence, some Tuguers left and settled first in New Guinea, then in Surinam, and finally in Holland. Presently about 300 persons reside in the village, many of whom are outsiders who have moved there from elsewhere.

Tugu in the 1970's, while still preserving many rural features, can no longer be called isolated. Asphalt roads and frequent bus service connect it, via Tanjung Priok or the bypass road system, with the center of Jakarta. The surrounding rice fields are being drained as land on which to build houses, factories, and warehouses. Many descendants of old Tugu families attend school, work, or live outside the community. Traditional village life is disappearing under the homogenizing onslaught of modernity.

2. The Portuguese language of Tugu.

2.1. General remarks. As mentioned, the Portuguese language of central Jakarta disappeared soon after 1800. It was maintained in a fairly complete state, as witnessed by the texts published by Schuchardt, until late in the nineteenth century. But in the 1970's the Tuguers are native speakers of the Jakarta variety of Malay.[2] Only a dozen or so of the oldest members of the community know much Portuguese at all, and that very fragmentary. They report that no one since their grandparents' generation has spoken Portuguese fluently. Evidently the social and physical opening up of Tugu towards the end of the nineteenth century made Malay a more useful and attractive form of speech for most purposes among succeeding generations of young people.

Even though Portuguese is no longer spoken as a first language in Tugu, it has not completely disappeared. The village musical group, the <u>Orkes Pusaka Kroncong Tugu</u>, besides singing songs in Malay and Dutch, sings four songs with Portuguese lyrics.[3] These four are: a lullaby, <u>Nina Bobo</u> 'Sleep, Little Girl', the text of which I have given in Appendix 3; and three others: <u>Yan Kaga Leti</u> 'Jan Has Diarrhea', <u>Bate-bate Porta</u> 'Knocking on the Door', and <u>Gatu Matu</u> 'Wildcat'. While the meaning of the forms in the first of these four is still known to the Tuguers, they are quite uncertain as to the significance of those of the last three--often the words themselves, sometimes in uncertain or distorted form, but not the meanings have been remembered from the past.[4]

Mr. Jacobus Quiko, the informal leader of the Tugu community, organized classes in the 1930's and again in 1972 and 1975 to teach Tugu Portuguese to the young people of the village who are, for the most part, completely ignorant of it. Older people in Tugu still use occasional words and phrases of Tugu Portuguese in greetings, leavetakings, and as a 'secret' language before outsiders. For instance, a common salutation is /ǰa kumi/ '(Have you) already eaten?'; a valediction, /anda kaǰu/ '(I/m) going home'. I was told that in a crowded public place where the presence of a pickpocket is suspected, one Tuguer might say to another: /ola, teŋ ladraŋ./ 'Look, there's a thief'. The range of vocabulary and constructions in such instances is, I think, quite limited; they seem to be for the most part fixed expressions included in conversations which are otherwise completely in Malay. In sum, Tugu Portuguese is not dead, but dying.

2.2. Linguistic structure. With this outline of the social history and setting of Tugu Portuguese, we now turn to the structure of the language as spoken in the 1970's. The following sketch is based on four sources. The first is the list of words and phrases printed in França (1970: 83-107) which I transcribed phonemically by using Mr. Jacobus Quiko as an informant. Mr. Quiko, who appears to know more Tugu Portuguese than other members of the community, has passive, but not active, recall of most of this material. The second is Mr. Quiko's dictation to me of the text of the lullaby Nina Bobo. The third is a list of 40 sentences composed in January, 1975, by Mr. Quiko for use in his language school for the village youth. The fourth is a small set of sentences, along with the numerals from one to fifteen, spontaneously tape-recorded by Mr. Quiko and transcribed by me. My phonemic transcriptions of these latter coherent texts are given in Appendix 3.

2.2.1. The structure of sound.

2.2.1.1. The phonology of the word. Distinctive contrasts of sound within words and the symbols used to represent these are given in Table 1.

2.2.1.1.1. Consonants. The voiceless stops are unaspirated. The resonant /r/ is a single tap, and /l/ is 'clear'. The glottal catch occurs only in a few forms taken from Malay, such as /bɔbɔʔ/ 'to sleep' (nursery word) and /kɔtɛʔ/ 'male genitalia'.

For contrasts of single consonants in word-initial position, compare: /pes/ 'fish', /tera/ 'land, country', /čua/ 'rain', /kere/ 'to want, be going to'; /bos/ 'you', /dedu/ 'finger, toe', /ǰa/ 'already', /gatu/ 'cat'; /fuma/ 'smoke', /subi/ 'to climb, enter'; /mao/ 'hand', /nobu/ 'new'; /riku/ 'rich', /leti/ 'milk'; /yo/ 'I'. The nasals /ñ/ and /ŋ/ and the glide /w/ do not occur in word-initial position. Possible word-initial consonant clusters are: (1) any obstruent (except /s/ and the laminals) plus /r/; (2) certain isolated sequences of

Table 1. The sounds of Tugu Portuguese.

Consonants:	Labial	Apical	Laminal	Dorsal	Laryngeal
Obstruents:					
Noncontinuants					
Voiceless:	p	t	č	k	
Voiced:	b	d	ǰ	g	(ʔ)
Continuants					
(Voiceless):	f	s			
Sonorants (voiced)					
Nasals:	m	n	ñ	ŋ	
Nonnasals					
Lateral:		l			
Tap:		r			
Glides:	w		y		

Vowels:	Front-unrounded	Central	Back-rounded
High:	i		u
Mid higher:	e	ə	o
lower:	(ɛ)	a	(ɔ)
Low:			
Other features:			
Accent:	´		

/s/ plus /k/ plus a possible /r/, for example: /pretu/ 'black', /tres/ 'three', /kria/ 'to care for, raise', /briŋka/ 'to play', /drumi/ 'to sleep', /grandi/ 'large', /friu/ 'cold', /skola/ 'school', /skrebe/ 'to write'.

Forms with word-initial vowels are, e.g. /ača/ 'to get, find', /ele/ 'he, she, it, they', /iste/ 'this', /ola/ 'to see, look', /uŋa/ 'one'.

In word-medial position, contrasting single consonants are all but /w/ (and /ʔ/). Besides the examples just cited, compare: /čupa/ 'to suck, smoke', /toka/ 'to hit', /faǰi/ 'to do, make', /čega/ 'to arrive, stop in'; /osu/ 'bone', /anoti/ '(at) night'/ /suña/ 'to dream', /gayola/ 'storage chest, trunk'. Word-medial consonant clusters are of the following general types: (1) nasal or liquid plus obstruent, (2) obstruent plus liquid, (3) /s/ plus nonlaminal voiceless stop, (4) liquid plus nasal, (5) stop plus /w/ or /y/. Examples are: /santa/ 'to sit', /limpa/ 'to clean', /siŋku/ 'five', /iñči/ 'full', /binsiŋku/ 'twenty-five', /oŋsoŋ/ 'by oneself, alone', /manda/ 'to order, send', /oñǰi/ 'eleven', /liŋgu/ 'tongue, language', /falta/ 'to be insufficient', /korpu/ 'body'; /pedra/ 'stone', /abri/ 'to open', /basta/ 'enough', /kaska/ 'peel, bark', /almiaŋ/ 'tomorrow', /karni/ 'meat', /gabyaŋ/ 'bird of prey', /nabyu/ 'ship'. Medial sequences of three consonants are nonlaminal stop preceded by a homorganic nasal and followed by /r/ or /w/, e.g. /lembra/ 'to remember', /kumpridu/ 'long', /mintroǰu/ 'to lie, prevaricate', /kaŋgreǰu/ 'crab', /siŋkwenta/ 'fifty'.

Consonants occurring in word-final position are normally only the apicals /s/, /r/, and /l/, and the velar nasal /ŋ/, e.g. /bos/ 'you', /aros/ 'cooked rice', /mar/ 'sea', /mal/ 'bad', /teŋ/ 'to be, have'. Final /n/ is rare, e.g. /saman/ 'week', /seren/ 'dew'. Other final consonants occur in forms taken from Malay or Dutch.

2.2.1.1.2. Vowels. Freely occurring vowels are /i/, /e/, /a/, /o/, and /u/, as in the examples cited above. The vowel /ə/ occurs before a

word-final /r/ or /l/, as in /otər/ 'other',
/polbər/ 'powder', /pastər/ 'bird', /betəl/ 'betel
nut'; in several words in the antepenult, such as
/əmpoku/ 'a little', /mənina/ 'girl'; and in derivatives such as /katərǰi/ 'fourteen' (from /katər/
'four'). Evidently under the influence of Malay,
which normally does not tolerate higher mid [e]
and [o] in closed syllables, the vowels /e/ and
/o/ are occasionally lowered in such positions,
e.g. /pes/ (pronounced [pes] or [pɛs]) 'fish',
/bos/ (pronounced [bos] or [bɔs]) 'you'. Nonvariable lower mid /ɛ/ and /ɔ/ occur only in a few
Malay words, such as /bɔbɔʔ/ 'to sleep' (nursery
word) and /kɔtɛʔ/ 'male genitalia'. Certain rarely
occurring complex syllabic nuclei may be conveniently analyzed as simple vowel plus /w/ or /y/,
e.g. /oytu/ 'eight', /kawdu/ 'turtle', /malay/
'Malay' (indigenous Indonesian). Sequences of two
nonidentical syllabics occur in forms such as:
/mao/ 'hand', /friu/ 'cold', /čua/ 'rain', /kria/
'to care for', and /seu/ 'sky, heaven'. There is
presently some hestitation as to whether /i/ or
/e/, /u/ or /o/ occur in several forms, e.g. /bonetu/
or /bunitu/ 'pretty', /miu/ or /mio/ 'half, middle'.

2.2.1.1.3. Accent. For most forms pronounced in
isolation, accent, consisting chiefly of a rise in
pitch, occurs on the penultimate syllabic nucleus
(in monosyllables on the only syllabic nucleus).
Certain forms are exceptional in taking final accent: /nalá/ 'there', /pontadór/ 'hunter'. The
form /kátərji/ 'fourteen' maintains the accent of
the simplex /katər/ 'four'. In this discussion, I
indicate such exceptional occurrences of accent
with an acute accent mark.

2.2.1.2. Phrasal phonology. While it is beyond
the scope of this paper to discuss in detail the
phonology of utterances longer than those cited, I
mention several prominent facts. One, word boundary is not audible; there is liaison between successive elements in phrases. Two, sequences of
sounds occur across word boundaries which do not

occur within words. Three, only the last word of
a phrase receives accent. A fuller account would
have to take these phenomena into account. For
the sake of clarity, I write word boundaries even
though there is nothing in the pronunciation
which marks them within phrases; and I use ordinary marks of punctuation to indicate the prosodic
division of speech into phrases, rather than attempting to describe the intonational contours.

2.2.2. The structure of meaning. This section
is a sketch of the ways in which smaller meaningful elements are combined to form larger meaningful
elements. In the current state of Tugu Portuguese
it is impossible to ascertain many details; one can
only report the few meager facts available.

2.2.2.1. Form classes. Without justification I
shall use generally accepted terms to refer to the
form classes of Tugu Portuguese. These classes can
be posited on the basis of the usual syntactic and
semantic criteria.

2.2.2.2. The structure of phrases.

2.2.2.2.1. The nominal phrase. The head of a
nominal phrase is a noun or pronoun. Such a form
may be either simple or doubled. Doubling a noun
indicates totality or collection, e.g. /filu/
'son(s), child(ren)' vs. /filu filu/ '(all the)
sons, children'. Doubling a pronoun indicates indefiniteness: /ki/ 'what' vs. /ki ki/ 'anything'.
Preceding a noun may be a quantifier, a demonstrative, or the form /otər/ 'other', e.g. /tantu
ǰenti/ 'many people', /dos prata/ 'two rupiahs
(unit of currency)', /iste kaǰu/ 'this house',
/aka bela/ 'that old woman', /otər waruŋ/ 'another
food stall'.[5] Also preceding a noun and allocating
it to a certain entity may be a pronoun plus the
possessive particle /sua/ or /su/, eg. /yo sua pai/
'my father', /bos sua olu/ 'your eyes', /ele su
nomi/ 'his name', /ki sua kabalu/ 'whose horse'.[6]
Following a noun may be an attribute. Such

attributes are of different sorts: (1) local deictic particles, e.g. /ǰenti nalá/ 'that person there', (2) a stative verb (adjective), e.g. /panu karu/ 'expensive cloth', (3) another nominal phrase, e.g. /kristaŋ otər nasaŋ/ 'Christians of other ethnic groups'. Two nouns may be joined in the serial construction by the particle /e/ 'and', e.g. /papel e tinta/ 'paper and ink'. A demonstrative may stand anaphorically for a nominal phrase: /iste/ 'this one'.

2.2.2.2.2. The prepositional phrase consists of a preposition plus a nominal phrase, e.g. /na greǰa/ 'in church', /na meǰa/ 'at the table', /ku yo sua kamradu/ 'to my friend', /ku gatu/ 'along with a cat, and a cat', /por yo/ 'for me', /koma ǰenti mal/ 'like a bad person'. A prepositional phrase may be followed and modified by the limiting particle /namás/ 'just, only' or by the intensive particle /dretu/ 'very, really'.

2.2.2.2.3. The verbal phrase centers around a verb. Morphologically, the verb may be simple, e.g. /anda/ 'to go'; or double, indicating iterated non-directed activity, e.g. /bate bate/ 'to knock (repeatedly)'. Semantically, verbs indicate states, e.g. /bormelu/ '(to be) red', or /teŋ/, 'to be, to have'; or actions, e.g. /kumi/ 'to eat'.

Various sorts of preverbal modifiers may precede the verb. These include: (1) quantifiers: /tantu kumi/ 'to eat a lot', (2) negatives: /nuŋku karu/ 'not expensive', /naŋ rikadu/ 'don't scold!', (3) modal and aspectual particles: /kere bisti/ 'want to get dressed', /ǰa kere drumi/ 'already wants to sleep'. Mr. Quiko reports the following order should all of these cooccur: 'aspect, negation, mode, and quantity', as in /ǰa nuŋku kere tantu kumi/ 'doesn't want to eat much any longer'.

Verbs of action occur with a nominal phrase as goal after them, e.g. /bisti panu karu/ 'wear expensive cloth', /kompra meǰina/ 'buy medicine'. The existential verb /teŋ/ 'to be, to have' and its negative form /nunte/ (contracted from /nuŋku teŋ/)

'not to be, not to have' may have a following
nominal complement indicating the entity whose
existence is asserted or which is said to be
possessed by some entity: e.g. /nunte doi/ 'not
to have any money'.

Following the verb, and usually following the
nominal complement, if any, various kinds of modifiers are possible. These include: (1) prepositional phrases, e.g. /kompra sigero por yo/ 'buy
cigarettes for me', /prende na skola domiŋgu/
'study in Sunday school', /anda na kota/ 'go to
town', (2) locative, temporal, or measuring expressions, e.g. /anda kaǰu/ 'go home', /anda agora/ 'go
now', /kompra tres prata miu/ 'but for three and
one-half rupiahs'. Also following the verb, and
evidently always final in the verbal phrase, are
possible modifiers /dretu/ 'very, really' and
/namás/ 'just, only': e.g. /sabroǰu dretu/ 'very
delicious', /anda kaǰu namás/ 'just go home'.

2.2.2.3. The structure of clauses. The following major types of clauses can be distinguished in
Tugu Portuguese. They are described first in the
neutral subject-predicate (or topic-comment) order,
and with full specification of clausal constituents.

2.2.2.3.1. The equational clause consists of two
nominal phrases: /ele ǰenti tatər/ 'he is a
Chinese'.

2.2.2.3.2. An existential clause consists of a
verbal phrase with an existential verb and its
complement, e.g. /teŋ ǰenti/ 'there are people'.
A possessive clause consists of a nominal phrase
indicating the possessor and an existential verbal
phrase, e.g. /yo nunte doi/ 'I don't have any
money'.

2.2.2.3.3. The narrative clause consists of a
nominal phrase indicating the agent, or entity to
which some state is ascribed, plus a verbal or
prepositional phrase as predicate (comment), e.g.
/iste kaǰu grandi/ 'this house is large', /ele

kumi na meǰa/ 'he eats at the table', /bos koma
ǰenti dodu namás/ 'you're just like a crazy person'.

2.2.2.3.4. For purposes of topicalization, a
locative or temporal expression may be separated
from a verbal phrase and preposed as first element
of a sentence (see examples in Appendix 3: B-39,
B-40, C-1, C-9). Similarly, the goal of a verb of
action or complement of an existential verb may be
preposed (examples in Appendix 3: B-26, B-29) in
order to topicalize it. In some of our sentences,
the order is predicate-subject (or comment-topic):
(see Appendix 3: B-3, C-10). Interrogative expressions are always preposed in the corpus: (see
Appendix 3: B-3, B-23, C-10).

2.2.2.3.5. Minor and reduced clauses. Salutations, responses, and the like constitute minor
clause types of their own, e.g. /boŋ dia/ 'good
day!', /seŋ/ 'yes'. Under appropriate circumstances
of discourse, the full clause types described above
may be reduced to only a predicate (or comment).
In imperative utterances, the agent /bos/ 'you' is
often unmentioned.

2.2.2.3.6. Complex constructions. Phrases and
clauses may be concatenated without any overt segmental marking into paratactic constructions. The
meaning is various: in Appendix 3 (C-1), elaboration; in B-31, alternative; in B-29, contrast; in
B-30, result. In C-9, the clause /bos kompra ele
sua binagər/ 'you buy their vinegar' is a subordinated complement of the verb /da/ 'to give, let,
allow'. Further possibilities of such constructions in present-day speech are unknown; a brief
perusal of the texts in the <u>Nieuwe Woordenschat</u> and
in Schuchardt (1890) will show that this point of
the present sketch especially would have to be
elaborated in a more complex description of extant
Jakarta Portuguese.

3. Tugu Portuguese: A moribund creole.

3.1. The forms cited in this paper, along with those from the other available sources, attest that the peculiar language of Tugu is by lexical classification a Romance language and specifically a variety of Portuguese. The distance from metropolitan Portuguese is, however, rather extreme. While I cannot here go into the many possible influences on the language before it reached Jakarta, it is clear from our earliest substantial evidence in Jakarta that the language has undergone considerable change, often change in the direction of Malay. Hancock (1975) contains a detailed analysis of various forms of Asian Portuguese and the many factors--African, South Asian, and Malay --which have influenced them. I mention below a few salient features of modern Tugu Portuguese for the purpose of the present discussion, with the provisional claim that earlier varieties of Portuguese spoken in Jakarta are little different.[7]

3.1.1. Phonology. The consonantal inventory of Tugu Portuguese (TP) is almost identical with that of Malay. One difference is that TP lacks the common Malay sound /h/, and has /ʔ/, frequent in Malay, only in a few forms. Another difference is the presence of /f/ in TP, which occurs in Malay only in loanwords such as /foto/ 'photograph'. We note in particular that TP, like Malay, has no voiced spirants, no /š/, and no palatal lateral, as does metropolitan Portuguese (MP).

Distinctive vocalic nasality is absent in TP (it is very marginal in Malay); a final nasalized vowel of MP usually corresponds in TP to /Vŋ/. The system of syllabic nuclei has been reduced, especially the number of possible diphthongs.

The possible consonant clusters of TP are more numerous than those of Malay; yet those which occur have been fairly readily accepted into Malay in numerous loans from Sanskrit, Arabic, Dutch, Portuguese, and English.

3.1.2. Morphology. There has been complete loss of the complex inflectional morphology of MP. There is no derivational morphology to speak of in TP, except isolated remnants like the relationships between, e.g. /dos/ 'two' and /doǰi/ 'twelve', /filu/ 'son' and /fila/ 'daughter', /ponta/ 'to shoot, hunt' and /pontadór/ 'hunter'. Like Malay, TP has doubling of stems: /filu filu/ 'children' like Malay /anak anak/; /bate bate/ 'to knock' like Malay /kətɔk kətɔk/.

3.1.3. Syntax. TP abounds in syntactical constructions untypical of the Romance languages spoken in Europe, e.g. the possessive construction of pronoun plus /su(a)/ plus noun. This construction is reminiscent of the use of the possessive particle /puña/ in 'bazaar' Malay forms such as /saya puña kawan/ (literally: 'I have friend') 'my friend' (cf. literary and standard Malay /kawan saya/). There is a noticeable tendency in TP to rely on unmarked juxtaposition rather than on marking by function words. Some present-day features of topicalization in TP, with associated features of intonation, strike one as peculiarly Malay.

3.1.4. Semantics. The semantic range of MP forms has often been changed, for the most part expanded, e.g. TP /albər/ 'plant (vine, shrub, tree)' like Malay /pɔhɔn/ and unlike MP árvore 'tree'; TP /čupa/ 'to suck (e.g. milk from the breasts); to smoke (e.g. a cigarette)', like the semantic range of Malay /isəp/ and different from that of MP chupar 'to suck, suck up, absorb'; TP /ku/ 'with, to, and', like colloquial Malay /sama/, and unlike MP com 'with'.[8]

3.1.5. Lexicon. Forms of non-Portuguese origin are not uncommon in the Portuguese of Jakarta and Tugu. Some are from Malay, e.g. /kampuŋ/ 'village' and /waruŋ/ 'food stall'; many are from Dutch, e.g. /kokis/ 'cookie' (see Hancock 1972 for a list of Dutch loanwords in Schuchardt's texts).[9]

3.2. In its pre-twentieth-century form as recorded in the <u>Nieuwe Woordenschat</u> of 1780 and in Schuchardt (1890), the Portuguese of Jakarta and Tugu doubtless deserves the appellation 'creole' in its classic sense: a reduced form of a language, at first spoken natively by no one and in limited social circumstances, but later adopted, with necessary expansion, as the native language of a community for the purpose of general communication. According to Hancock (1975:217-218), 'Java Creole' and its near relatives spoken in Malacca, Singapore, Macau, and Hong Kong are descendants of a Porguguese pidgin which developed in the early maritime contact between Portuguese and North and West Africans. As the Portuguese 'seaborne empire' spread, this language was taken to many ports, including those in South Asia, where it sometimes became the native language of groups closely associated with the Portuguese and their commercial activities. Historians (e.g. de Haan 1917:221) have traced the origin of the Jakarta 'Portuguese' people to Arakan and Bengal, and especially to the Malabar and Coromandel coasts of southern India; so we assume that it is here that the creolization of Tugu Portuguese took place before the ancestors of the Tuguers were brought to Jakarta in the seventeenth century. The status of Tugu Portuguese as a genuine creole in the nineteenth century is attested by the report of Beukhof, the Dutch pastor of the church in Tugu:

> The language of the Christians in Tugu in their mutual intercourse is Portuguese, or rather a patois of this language. The people of the present day can no longer understand a Portuguese book or the Bible in this language. They call this language high, and their own vernacular low Portuguese. Their love of this language is especially evident from the fact that they, in the midst of a Malay population, and after so many years of instruction in Malay in school and church, still always continue to use the Portuguese jargon. (Beukhof 1890:27; my translation)

Now, of course, what remains of the dying language is being maintained artificially. Yet in the last century and before, Tugu Portuguese was a paradigmatic instance of a creole and, besides that, a paradigmatic instance of a language maintained due to extreme group solidarity and abandoned due to integration into a larger speech community.

4. Pidgins and creoles.

4.1. To call older Tugu Portuguese a creole is to use the term 'creole' in a sense which would almost certainly disturb no one. The interest in sociolinguistics and ethnolinguistics during the last decade or so, however, has seen the term 'creole' and its partner 'pidgin' extended to situations quite different from those of Tugu Portuguese, Haitian French, or Melanesian English. It has indeed become fashionable to call any aberrant form of speech a pidgin or creole, and to refer to any relatively extreme process of linguistic change as pidginization or creolization.

In a recent study of language learning, for example, we are presented with the hypothesis that 'the learner language evolves from pidginization, to creolization, to eventual conformity with the target language norm' (Schumann 1974:151). This hypothesis was proposed on the basis of similarity between the first stages of a new language being learned by an adult and a (true) pidgin, and that between intermediate stages and a (true) creole. Pidgins and creoles are thus said to be models for the development of 'learner languages' (Schumann 1974:145, elaborated in Schumann 1976).

With respect to linguistic change, Le Page has remarked that 'many of the world's languages have probably undergone creolization at one time or another' (Le Page 1966:vii). For Bailey (1973:34), the phenomenon of creolization is even more pervasive: 'Creolization is normal; all languages have probably once been creoles'. Using the term 'creole' to refer to a mixture of linguistic systems spoken by native speakers, and allowing for different proportions of mixture, Bailey (1973:33, 134) applies the term 'creole' to Swahili and English.

The trend, then, has been to equate reduction with pidginization, expansion with creolization, or creolization with significant influence of one language or another. Such equations have been criticized by Hymes (1971:65-90), who has tried to extract the distinctive features which differentiate unusual forms of speech and make a taxonomy which shows both the similarities and the differences among them. Such forms of speech include not only pidgins and creoles, but also lingua francas, argots, koinés, foreigner talk, dying languages, and even baby talk and the likes of the Australian 'mother-in-law language'. Hymes's classificatory criteria are both linguistic--reduction and expansion, simplification and complication, degree of confluence of linguistic traditions--and social--communication within groups or between groups, primary or secondary means of communication, presence or absence of autonomous norms, relation to existing linguistic norms.

In this admirable attempt to achieve terminological clarity in a very complex situation, Hymes's concluding definitions of the terms 'pidgin', 'creole', 'pidginization', and 'creolization' are remarkably similar to, if somewhat more inclusive than, the traditional restricted definitions of these terms. According to Hall (1966:xii-xiii), for an instance of an earlier formulation, a 'true pidgin' is a language defined by the following characteristics: (1) sharp reduction of grammatical structure and vocabulary and (2) established existence as a secondary language native to no one and used by at least two different groups as a means of intergroup communication. A creole, on the other hand, is a language which has grown out of a pidgin to become the first language of a speech community, developed by expanding grammatical and lexical resources. While not part of the definitions per se, it is clear from Hall's later discussion that pidgins and creoles show 'extensive carryover patterns' from other languages (Hall 1966:86), and that they have structures 'complete in themselves' and 'amenable to formulation' (107). The crux of Hymes's (1971:83-84) reformulation of these definitions is to include the notion of extensive influence from another language ('convergence') into the definitions themselves, and to allow for instances in which creoles have arisen from 'pre-pidgin continua', that is, incipient pidgins which have not yet become fixed as full pidgins. Pidginization and creolization are then, according to Hymes, the processes of reduction, convergence, and restriction in use on the one hand, and of expansion, convergence, and extension in use on the other hand, which lead to established pidgins and creoles.

Whether one chooses the formulation of one or another of these investigators who have considered a wide variety of linguistic situations, or minor rewording or reformulation of either, is perhaps a matter of taste. And there will doubtless remain borderline cases which resist classification. Yet the important points are the following.

One, analytical clarity is promoted if most technical terms are confined in sense rather than extended. If there are similarities between a true pidgin and a person's attempts to speak a foreign language, it does not clarify the matter to use the term 'pidgin' for both. One should rather extract the features common to both, e.g. sharp reduction in grammatical and lexical possibilities. There are essential differences between the inadequate English speech of the individual Costa Rican migrant observed by Schumann (1976) and the English used among certain groups in Melanesia. The first has not achieved the status of an 'autonomous norm', to use Hymes's term, while the second has. It is this major difference in social use which makes a difference in terminology attractive: the first is unestablished, individualistic 'foreigner talk' (Ferguson's term cited by Hymes); the second, a socially established pidgin.

If, when investigating linguistic change, one sees similarities between the processes leading to true creoles and those occurring in ordinary situations, it would seem to be of little help to stretch the term 'creole' to refer to the resultant linguistic states in both circumstances. If every language is more or less a creole, then why do we need the term 'creole'? My answer is that this term is most useful to denote certain varieties of speech very near one end of a spectrum of possibilities, and not a wide range of the continuum.

Two, there is nothing magic about pidgins and creoles, or in the processes which lead to their development, as current fascination with these terms suggests. Hall (1966:122-123) is especially clear on this:

> All the evidence available so far indicates that the type of linguistic change and the mechanisms involved--sound-change, analogy, borrowing of various kinds--are the same for pidgins and creoles as they are for all other languages. The only difference lies in the rate of change --far faster for a pidgin (because of the drastic reduction of structure and lexicon) than for most languages. When a pidgin has become nativized, the history of the resultant creole is, in essence, similar to that of any other language.

Only if one starts from an extremely ethnocentric position (the only real French is that approved by the Académie); or from a view of language as a rigid system où tout se tient; or from an extremely individualistic and socially unrealistic position (e.g. Chomsky's famous dictum: 'Linguistic theory is concerned primarily with an ideal speaker-hearer, in a completely homogeneous speech-community ...')--only then is there anything particularly strange about pidgins and creoles. What these sorts of language show is that human linguistic activity, far from being confined to the ability to create an infinite set of determinably grammatical sentences (of the sterile kind: 'John and Mary and Sue and Bob ... were at the party'), is based on more

primary concerns. Above all is the desire and
necessity to communicate with other human beings.
In social situations such as those giving rise to
pidgins, much of the usual linguistic machinery is
discarded, ignored, or changed in order for human
beings to share essential information. When a
pidgin, or pidgin-like variety of speech, becomes
the native language of a community, speakers use
every human means of elaborating their speech in
order to be able efficiently to coordinate their
activities to a fine degree.

The lesson of the study of pidgins and creoles,
as both Hall (1966:107) and Hymes (1971:3-11) have
emphasized, is to have brought into one's very ears
the lengths to which human beings will go to create
and adapt speech, to cast off old patterns and
adopt new ones, in order to serve their changing
social needs.

5. Recapitulation. Summing up the linguistic
history of the people of Tugu in this light, we
see first of all the rise of a reduced form of
Portuguese in the early maritime contact between
Portuguese and Africans. This pidgin was then
taken to various Asian ports where the Portuguese
established themselves. Here, some groups of local
people found it convenient to adopt Portuguese as
a language of general communication. The language
was expanded in scope. When the Dutch wrenched
people away from South Asia and transported them
to Jakarta, the creolized Portuguese which they
spoke was further adapted to local conditions by
drawing on Dutch and especially Malay. While Jakarta Portuguese disappeared around 1800 in the
central city, its speakers in Tugu, while not remaining free from the influence of Malay, maintained Portuguese as one of the marks of difference
distinguishing them from their 'Malay' neighbors.
Finally, the Tuguers also became more integrated
into the wider community of Malay-speaking Jakarta
in the early twentieth century and abandoned their
distinctive variety of Portuguese for most purposes.

WHAT IS A CREOLE? / 361

This exposition will, I hope, make the following contributions: first, to present useful facts about a poorly known Romance language; second, to underline the need for restriction in the use of the terms 'pidgin' and 'creole'; and third, to show another example, in the rise and demise of the Portuguese spoken in Jakarta and Tugu, of human linguistic adaptability.

NOTES

The field research on which this report is based was done in Jakarta, Indonesia, from August to December, 1975, while I was collecting materials for a doctoral dissertation on Jakarta Malay. Financial support for my stay in Jakarta and for research expenses came from the Social Science Research Council and from the National Science Foundation. Local sponsors were the Indonesian Institute of Sciences and the National Center for Language Development. I am indebted to John Wolff of Cornell University for his encouragement of this study of Tugu Portuguese, and to Larry King, Marilyn Martin, and Ian Smith of Cornell for assistance at several points. I am deeply grateful to the Quiko family of Tugu, especially Mr. Jacobus Quiko (born 1920) and his household, for their help and interest. Without Mr. Quiko's lifelong devotion to the language of his ancestors, we would know much less about Tugu Portuguese than we do. The responsibility for the information contained herein is, of course, solely mine. This paper supersedes a previous unpublished description of the linguistic situation in Tugu, and is the first in a series of reports in which I hope to bring together and analyze in detail what is known about the Portuguese language in Jakarta.
    1. The historical information contained here in Section 2 is based on the following sources: Beukhof (1890), Boxer (1965, 1969), Castles (1967), de Haan (1917, 1935), de Water (1937), Huet (1909), Milone (1966), Schuchardt (1890), and interviews with the present inhabitants of Tugu. A modern

historical reevaluation of the primary sources of information on the 'Portuguese' of Jakarta would be highly desirable.

2. To be precise, the rural subvariety of Jakarta Malay. See Wallace (1976:7-40) for a general discussion of the linguistic situation in Jarkarta.

3. This music group consists of about a dozen male villagers who both play and sing, and one or two female singers. Occasionally friends from central Jakarta join in. Instruments are: (Western-style) cello, guitar, violin, mandolin, and triangle; two Indonesian instruments, the <u>rebana</u> (stringed) and the <u>kempul</u> (small percussion); and three sizes of <u>kroncong</u> instruments. These latter five-stringed instruments are called by the following names: /mačina/ (smallest), /pruŋa/ (middle-sized), and /bordaŋ/ (largest). For a description of <u>kroncong</u> instruments and the role of <u>kroncong</u> music in colonial Jakarta, see Manusama (1919). Besides playing for its own enjoyment, the group has performed on Indonesian radio and television, and at the Jakarta Art Center (Taman Ismail Marzuki). A phonographic recording of their music (regrettably not including any Portuguese songs) was published by Galloway Records (Paris) as the thirteenth in the series <u>Musique du Monde</u> (<u>Java</u>: <u>Kroncong de Tugu</u>; no. GB 600 532 B). This record is now evidently out of print.

4. The version of <u>Yan Kaga Leti</u> as presently sung by the villagers is essentially the same as that given by Schuchardt (1890:29-30; songs 16 and 17 combined). See also França (1970:104). The version of <u>Bate-bate Porta</u> is much as the last verse of the 'Cradle Song' combined with lines from the 'Kafrinju' printed in França (1970:103, 105). I was unable to obtain a written version of the lyrics of <u>Gatu Matu</u>. Because of the great philological problems in interpreting these songs, I include in this paper only the still transparent lullaby.

5. The postposed demonstratives of the texts in Schuchardt (1890) are untypical of either the language of the <u>Nieuwe Woordenschat</u> or the present

spoken language. Schuchardt (1890:23) suspects, and I am inclined to agree, that his texts from Tugu were first written in Malay and then translated into Tugu Portuguese. Standard written Malay (Indonesian) has postposed demonstratives; the colloquial Malay of Jakarta, preposed demonstratives.

6. In earlier texts, we sometimes find /miña/ or /me sua/ instead of /yo sua/ 'my' and /sua/ by itself indicating third person possessor. See examples in Appendix 1. Note the isolated expression /nos sior/ 'our Lord' in the modern texts (Appendix 3).

7. Strictly speaking, one should compare Tugu Portuguese with the metropolitan Portuguese of the fifteenth to sixteenth centuries. I am unable in this paper to go into the complex historical problems of this, however, and will use modern standard Iberian Portuguese instead (e.g. as described in Hills, Ford, and Coutinho 1944). A phonological description of Jakarta Malay is available in Wallace (1976:41-64), and a broader grammatical description in Ikranagara (1975).

8. In the texts in Schuchardt (1890) we also find /ku/ 'by' (with agent of the verb in a passive-like construction), and occasionally as a marker of the goal of a verb in an active-like construction. Jakarta Malay sama 'with, and, by, to' corresponds to standard Indonesian dengan 'with', dan 'and', oleh 'by', and kepada 'to'.

9. Schuchardt (1890:passim) points out occasional lexical borrowings into the Portuguese of Tugu and Jakarta from South Asian languages, e.g. /manduku/ 'frog' and /čunambu/ 'lime, calcium' (cf. Sanskrit /maṇḍūka-/, Hindi /maṇḍuk/ or /maṇḍak/ 'frog', and Tamil /cuṇṇāmpu/ 'lime, calcium'). While there are a fair number of South Asian (both Indo-European and Dravidian) loans in Malay, these two are to my knowledge unknown in that language (cf. Jakarta Malay /kɔdɔk/ 'frog' and /kapʊr/ 'lime, calcium').

APPENDIX 1. The Portuguese of Jakarta and Tugu:
            Eighteenth Century.

Source: <u>Nieuwe Woordenschat</u>, p. 106; reprinted in Schuchardt (1890:94). My provisional phonemic transcription, with interlinear gloss and translation. These sentences represent instructions to a servant.

(1) /anda ola kantu akel siñu teŋ kaẙu./
    go see if that gentleman be home
    'Go see if that gentleman is at home.'
(2) /fala yo manda miña rekadu./
    say I send my greeting
    'Say that I send my greetings.'
(3) /e manda pergunta k(i)lai teŋ kun sua saudi./
    and send ask how be with his health
    'And ask how his health is.'
(4) /kantu kere da akel ondra kun yo por čega
       miña ǰuntu./
    if want give that honor to me for stop-in
       my meeting(??)
    'And if he would do me the honor of stopping
       to visit me.'
(5) /yo lo manda miña kareta./
    I later send my carriage
    'I'll send my carriage.'
(6) /yo nunteŋ kontenti ki ile lo pasa peo./
    I not-be happy that he later walk foot
    'I wouldn't be happy if he walked.'

APPENDIX 2. The Portuguese of Jakarta and Tugu:
            Nineteenth Century.

Source: Schuchardt (1890:60-61). My provisional phonemic transcription, with interlinear gloss and translation. The paragraph concerns types of oil. Forms of Malay origin are indicated by <u>M</u> in the gloss; those of Dutch origin, by <u>D</u>.

(1) /aǰiti klapa bratu dretu./
    oil coconut(M) cheap very
    'Coconut oil is very cheap.'

(2) /uŋa takər ses rupia./
   one jar(M) six rupiah(M)
   'One jar costs six rupiahs.'
(3) /uŋa takər teŋ trintadós botel, uŋa botel
      teŋ siŋku peñči./
   one jar(M) have thirty-two bottle(D?)
      one bottle (D?) have five 'little-pint'(D)
   'One jar has thirty-two bottles, and one
      bottle has five measures.'
(4) /aǰiti bar brabu dretu, toka fogu uŋ tamimu./
   oil earth potent very, hit fire a little.
   'Petroleum is very potent, even if it comes
      in contact with a little fire (??).'
(5) /lantas sande, miste sirbis somproŋ
      na(ŋ) olu fika danu./
   then(M) light, should use lampshade(M)
      lest eye become damaged
   'When it is lit, one should use a lampshade
      lest one's eyes become damaged.'
(6) /nos ola kilei fuma na nos olu./
   we see how smoke in our eye
   'We see how much smoke is in our eyes.'
(7) /aǰiti lampu./
   oil lamp
   'Lamp oil.'
(8) /aǰiti ǰarak aka bunitu buat dəmpúl prau./
   oil castor(M) that good for(M) caulk(M)
      boat(M)
   'Castor oil is good for caulking boats.'
(9) /aǰiti largati aka ǰenti sirbis baŋ panu./
   oil crocodile that person use redden(M) cloth
   'Crocodile oil people use to redden cloth.'

APPENDIX 3. The Portuguese of Jakarta and Tugu:
            Twentieth Century.

Source: Mr. Jacobus Quiko of Tugu. My phonemic
transcription of 1975. Forms of Malay and Dutch
origin are indicated by M and D respectively.

A. Text of the lullaby <u>Nina Bobo</u>/nina bɔbɔʔ/.

Refrain:
/nina, bɔbɔʔ, o mənina bɔbɔʔ;/
/nina, bɔbɔʔ, o mənina bɔbɔʔ./
Verse:
/drumi, ya drumi,/
/fila bonitug/
/drumi namás,/
/y̌a nunte moskitu./
Verse:
/yo su fila/
/y̌a kere drumi;/
/y̌a tantu briŋka,/
/y̌a tantu kumi./

Gloss:
girl, sleep(M), o girl sleep (M);

"

sleep, yes(M) sleep,
daughter pretty:
sleep just,
already not-be mosquito

I's daughter
already want sleep;
already much play,
already much eat.

In English prose:
'Sleep, little girl, o sleep, little girl; sleep, little girl, o sleep, little girl. Sleep, yes sleep, pretty daughter; just sleep, since there are no longer mosquitoes. My daughter already wants to sleep; she has played a lot, she has eaten a lot!'

Note: This lullaby is sung in the same form to male children.

B. Sentences composed by Mr. Jacobus Quiko for his <u>Eskola Papia Christao</u> /(e)skola papia kristaŋ/ 'Christian Language School' in January, 1975. Transcribed from Mr. Quiko's typescript.

(1) /yo kere bebe agu./
I want drink water.
'I want to drink water.'
(2) /ele kere drumi./
he want sleep
'He wants to sleep.'
(3) /ki bos sua nomi?/
what you 's name?
'What is your name?'

(4) /ele kumi aros./
he eat rice
'He eats rice.'
(5) /iste kaǰu grandi./
this house big
'This house is large.'
(6) /ele prende skrebe./
he learn write
'He is learning to write.'
(7) /iste pedra bormelu./
this rock red
'This is a red rock.'
(8) /iste kalsaŋ bonetu./
this pants nice
'These are nice pants.'
(9) /anda kaǰu namás./
go home just
'Just go home.'
(10) /iste koba ǰa podər./
this onion already rotten
'This onion is already rotten.'
(11) /kompra sigero por yo./
buy cigarette for me
'Buy me some cigarettes.'
(12) /ele sua pai ǰa mure./
he 's father already dead
'His father is already dead.'
(13) /iste ləntera karu dretu./
this lantern expensive very
'This lantern is very expensive.'
(14) /bos kere na undi?/
you want to where?
'Where do you want to go?'
(15) /bos nuŋku limpa korpu./
you not wash body
'You didn't bathe.'
(16) /ǰa, na rio./
already, in river
'Yes I did, in the river.'
(17) /na rio teŋ tantu pes./
in river be many fish
'In the river there are many fish.'

(18) /bos koma ǰenti dodu namás./
you like person crazy just
'You're just like a crazy person.'

(19) /sior dios/
lord God
'Lord God'

(20) /nos sior/
our lord
'our Lord'

(21) /na mundu teŋ tantu ǰenti./
in world be many people
'In the world there are many people.'

(22) /ele ponta iste tigər./
he shoot this tiger
'He shot this tiger.'

(23) /ki sua kabalu aka?/
who 's horse that?
'Whose horse is that?'

(24) /yo sua pai bisti baniaŋ./
I 's father wear pajamas
'My father wears pajamas.'

(25) /nosotər bisti panu karu./
we wear cloth expensive
'We wear expensive sarongs.'

(26) /iste figura yo bende ku ele./
this picture I sell to him
'This picture I sold to him.'

(27) /ele kumi na meǰa./
he eat at table
'He eats at the table.'

(28) /toma alfada, yo kere drumi./
get pillow, I want sleep
'Get a pillow, I want to sleep.'

(29) /alfada teŋ, istera nunte./
pillow be, mat not-be
'There's a pillow, but there's not a mat.'

(30) /bos ǰa grandi, naŋ briŋka namas./
you already big, don't play just
'You're already big, so don't just play.'

(31) /bos kere serbis, nuŋku?/
you want work, not?
'Do you want to work or not?'

(32) /yo nunte doi, nunte ki ki./
    I not-have money, not-have anything
    'I don't have any money, don't have anything.'
(33) /tres prata mio./
    three rupiah half
    'Three and a half rupiahs.'
(34) /yo kere kaga./
    I want defecate
    'I want to defecate.'
(35) /naŋ miǰa nalá./
    don't urinate there
    'Don't urinate there.'
(36) /aka bela kumi betəl./
    that old-woman eat betel
    'That old woman chews betel nuts.'
(37) /bos sua olu bormelu./
    you 's eye red
    'Your eyes are red.'
(38) /seŋ, yo sua olu doenti./
    yes, I 's eye hurt
    'Yes, my eyes hurt.'
(39) /iste anoti čua kabrola./
    this night rain hard
    'Tonight there's a hard rain.'
(40) /iste dia čua piči piči./
    this day rain drizzle drizzle
    'Today it's drizzling.'

Isolated forms in the margins:
/kenti/ 'hot'
/braŋku/ 'white'
/pretu/ 'black'
/keŋ/ 'who' (but see sentence 23 above with /ki/ as 'who')

C. Utterances spontaneously tape-recorded by Mr. Jacobus Quiko, October, 1975. My transcription.

(1) /dia domiŋgu, tantu ǰenti kristaŋ, kristaŋ tugu,/
    day Sunday, many people Christian, Christian Tugu,
    'On Sunday, many Christians, Tugu Christians,'

/kristaŋ otər nasaŋ, faǰi orsaŋ na greǰa./
Christian other ethnos, make prayer at church.
'Christians of other ethnic groups, worship
   in church.'
/filu filu e fila fila prende na skola
   domiŋgu./
son son and daughter daughter study in school
   Sunday.
'The boys and girls study in Sunday school.'

(2) /laba naki yo sua sapatu./
bring here I 's shoe.
'Bring my shoes here.'
/yo kere bisti iste./
I want wear this.
'I want to wear them.'
/yo kere anda na kota agora./
I want go to town(M) now.
'I want to go to town now.'
/yo ķere kompra meǰina./
I want buy medicine.
'I want to buy medicine.'

(3) /bos sabe ǰenti nalá?/
you know person there?
'Do you know that person there?'
/ele su nomi?/
he 's name?
'His name?'
/ele su olu koma largati dretu./
he 's eye like crocodile really.
'His eyes are really like (those of) a
   crocodile.'

(4) /bos toma papel e tinta./
you get paper and ink.
'Get paper and ink.'
/yo kere skrebe ku yo sua kamradu./
I want write to I 's friend.
'I want to write to my friend.'

(5) /ele ǰenti boŋ dretu./
    he person good very
    'He is a very good person.'
    /ele ǰenti tatər./
    he person Chinese [babbler]
    'He is a Chinese.'

(6) /bos koma kačor ku gatu./
    you like dog and cat
    'You are like a dog and a cat.'
    /baklai namás./
    fight(M) just
    '(You) do nothing but fight.'

(7) /iste galiña piklinu./
    this hen small
    'This is a small hen.'
    /ǰa da siŋku obu siŋku dia./
    already give five egg five day
    'It has laid five eggs in five days.'

(8) /bos naŋ rikadu namás, koma ǰenti mal./
    you don't scold just, like person bad
    'Don't just scold, like a bad person.'
    /bergoña, teŋ ǰenti./
    ashamed, be person
    '(You ought to) be ashamed, there are people (here).'

(9) /anoti ǰenti malay nuŋku da bos kompra ele sua binagər./
    night person 'Malay' not let you buy they 's vinegar
    'At night Malay people won't let you buy their vinegar [referring to a local superstition called pamali].'

(10) /sabroǰu dretu iste kokis./
    delicious very this cookie(D)
    'These cookies are very delicious.'
    /na undi bos kompra iste?/
    at where you buy this?
    'Where did you buy them?'

/nalá./
there
'There.'
/nuŋku karu, dos prata./
not expensive, two rupiah.
'They weren't expensive, only two rupiahs.'
/podi dretu./
may very.
'That's not bad.'
/na otər waruŋ, bos kompra iste tres prata miu./
at other food-stall(M) you buy this three rupiah half
'At another food stall you pay three and a half rupiahs for them.'
/bos sabe?/
you know?
'You know?'

(11) /bos nuŋku medu?/
you not afraid?
'You're not afraid?'

(12) /agora yo anda oŋsoŋ namás./
now I go alone just
'I'll just go alone now.'

(13) Numerals:
/uŋa/ 'one'   /nobi/ 'nine'
/dos/ 'two'   /des/ 'ten'
/tres/ 'three'   /oñǰi/ 'eleven'
/katər/ 'four'   /doǰi/ 'twelve'
/siŋku/ 'five'   /treǰi/ 'thirteen'
/ses/ 'six'   /kátərǰi/ 'fourteen'
/seti/ 'seven'   /kiñǰi/ 'fifteen'
/oytu/ 'eight'

ANNOTATED BIBLIOGRAPHY

Bailey, Charles-James N. 1973. Variation and linguistic theory. Arlington, Virginia: Center for Applied Linguistics.

Beukhof, J. 1890. Eene verwaarloosde zuster. Aanteekeningen omtrent het verleden en heden van de kleine Christen-gemeente te Toegoe. Leiden: D. Donner. [A history of Tugu, with heavy emphasis on ecclesiastical matters. Considerable information about the community in the 1880's, when the author was pastor of the village church. Christmas greeting in Tugu Portuguese given on p. 28 (cf. the versions in Schuchardt 1890:31; França 1970:105).]

Boxer, C. R. 1965. The Dutch seaborne empire. 1600-1800. New York: Alfred A. Knopf.

Boxer, C. R. 1969. The Portuguese seaborne empire. 1415-1825. New York: Alfred A. Knopf.

Castles, Lance. 1967. The ethnic profile of Jakarta. Indonesia 3.153-204. [Useful general discussion of origins of Jakarta's population. Early migration, including that of Portuguese, pp. 155-162.]

de Haan, Frederik. 1917. De laatste der Mardijkers. Bijdragen tot de Taal-, Land- en Volkenkunde 73.219-254. [Concerns the person and family of Augustijn Michiels, a prominent Portuguese Mardijker in Jakarta around 1800. References to general history of Portuguese in Jakarta.]

de Haan, Frederik. 1935. Oud Batavia. Second edition. Bandung: A. C. Nix & Co. [The standard work on the history of early colonial Jakarta. Many references to Portuguese, Portuguese language, Mardijkers, etc., available by checking index.]

de Water, A. 1937. De Portugeesche gemeente van Toegoe. Algemeen Protestantsch Kerkblad (Weekblad voor de Protestantsche Kerk in Nederlandsch Indië) vol. 4, no. 27 (July 8, 1937). [Discussion of the situation in Tugu in the mid 1930's. History based on Beukhof (1890). I have seen only a typewritten copy of this article lent to me by Mr. Jacobus Quiko.]

França, Antonio Pinto da. 1970. Portuguese influence in Indonesia. Jakarta: Gunung Agung. [An amateurish account written by a former

Portuguese consul in Jakarta. Portuguese influence in Java, pp. 33-43. Appendix III (pp. 83-101) contains linguistic material from Tugu supplied by Mr. Jacobus Quiko and originating from the <u>Woordenlijst</u> (q.v.). Appendix IV (pp. 102-106) has music of two Tugu <u>kroncong</u> songs (from Manusama?) and lyrics of four. The lyrics of the <u>Moresco</u> (p. 106) probably originate from Manusama (1919:4). Many mistakes throughout, both in form of Tugu Portuguese and in English translations.]

Hall, Robert A., Jr. 1966. Pidgin and creole languages. Ithaca: Cornell University Press.

Hancock, Ian F. 1972. Some Dutch-derived items in Java Creole Portuguese. Orbis 21.549-554. [A list of Dutch loanwords in the Portuguese of Schuchardt's (1890) texts.]

Hancock, Ian F. 1975. Malacca Creole Portuguese. Asian, African, or European? Anthropological Linguistics 17.211-236. [Valuable comparison of several Portuguese-based pidgins and creoles, with particular attention to Malacca. References to Jakarta-Tugu Portuguese based on Schuchardt (1890). Useful bibliography of sources on Asian Portuguese.]

Hills, E. C., J. D. M. Ford, and J. de S. Coutinho. 1944. Portuguese grammar. Revised by L. G. Moffatt. Boston: D. C. Heath and Company.

Huet, G. 1909. La communauté portugaise de Batavia. Revista Lusitana 12.149-170. [Historical information on the Portuguese people of Jakarta, with references to Tugu.]

Hymes, Dell, ed. 1971. Pidginization and creolization of languages. Cambridge: Cambridge University Press. [Sections referred to are the editor's preface (pp. 3-11) and his introduction to Part III 'General Conceptions of Process' (pp. 65-90).]

Ikranagara, Kay Glassburner. 1975. Melayu Betawi grammar. Unpublished Univ. of Hawaii dissertation. [A grammatical description of a variety of Jakarta Malay in the framework of 'case grammar'. Useful for finding grammatical information about

Malay perhaps unavailable in works on standard varieties. For my interpretation of the phonology of Jakarta Malay, see Wallace (1976.)]

Kähler, Hans. 1966. Wörterverzeichnis des Omong Djakarta. Veröffentlichungen des Seminars für Indonesische und Südseesprachen der Universität Hamburg, Band 5. Berlin: Verlag von Dietrich Reimer. [Introduction is a sketch of phonology and morphology of Jakarta Malay (but see Wallace 1976 for another view of the phonology). Body of work is a glossary of Jakarta Malay, often containing forms and meanings unavailable in standard Malay or Indonesian dictionaries.]

Le Page, Robert B. 1966. Foreword to Jamaican creole syntax, by Beryl L. Bailey. Cambridge: Cambridge University Press.

Manusama, A. T. 1919. Krontjong. Als muziekinstrument, als melodie en als gezang. Batavia: G. Kolff & Co. [A discussion of kroncong and its role in colonial Jakarta. Page 4 has Portuguese lyrics of song Moresco. Music of Moresco and Prounga between pp. 5 and 6 (source of music in França?). References to kroncong in Tugu, pp. 6ff.]

Meister, Georg. 1692. Der orientalisch-indianische Kunst- und Lust-Gärtner. Dresden. [Report of a German traveler. Dialogue in Jakarta Portuguese (pp. 215-222) reprinted in Schuchardt (1890:11-14). Orthography difficult to interpret.]

Milone, Pauline Dublin. 1966. Queen city of the East. The metamorphosis of a colonial capital. Unpublished Univ. of California, Berkeley, dissertation. [History of colonial Jakarta as a city. Discussion of Portuguese-Mardijker component of the early city, pp. 174-182.]

Naro, Anthony. 1973. The origin of West African Pidgin. In: Papers from the Ninth Regional Meeting of the Chicago Linguistic Society. Edited by C. Corum, T. Smith-Stark, and A. Weiser. Chicago: Chicago Linguistic Society. 442-449. [Hypotheses concerning origins of Portuguese 'reconnaissance language.']

Nieuwe Woordenschat. Uyt het Nederduitsch in het gemeene Maleidsch en Portugeesch. Zeer gemakkelyk voor die eerst op Batavia komen. Te Batavia, by Lodewyk Dominicus, Stads-Drukker, op de Tygers-Gragt, aan de West-Zyde, 1780. [Anonymous extensive trilingual list of words and expressions in Dutch, colloquial Jakarta Malay, and Jakarta Portuguese. Dutch orthography variable. Reprinted in Schuchardt (1890:90-147).]

Noorduyn, J., and H. T. Verstappen. 1972. Pūrṇavarman's river-works near Tugu. Bijdragen tot de Taal-, Land- en Volkenkunde 128.298-307. [Reinterpretation of famous Sanskrit lithic inscription found in Tugu. Useful maps showing location of Tugu, pp. 301 and 303.]

Schuchardt, Hugo. 1890. Ueber das Malaioportugiesche von Batavia und Tugu. Kreolische Studien IX. Sitzungsberichte der k. u. k. Akademie der Wissenschaften zu Wien (Philosophisch-historische Klasse) 122.1-255. [Introduction (pp. 1-20) has early history of Portuguese in Jakarta, including Meister's (1692) dialogue. Pp. 20-90 contain materials from Tugu of 1880's. Parallel Tugu Portuguese and Malay texts in variable Dutch orthography composed by several inhabitants of Tugu, including a 'B. A. Quikoe' (p. 56), who is evidently the paternal grandfather (named Bernardus Albertus Quiko; died about 1910?) of Mr. Jacobus Quiko. Lyrics of songs from Tugu, pp. 24-42. Reprint of Nieuwe Woordenschat, in rearranged form, pp. 90-147. General discussion, pp. 147-255, but many explanatory notes throughout.]

Schumann, John H. 1974. The implications of interlanguage, pidginization, and creolization for the study of adult language acquisition. TESOL Quarterly 8.145-152.

Schumann, John H. 1976. Second language acquisition. The pidginization hypothesis. Language Learning 26.391-408.

Wallace, Stephen. 1976. Linguistic and social dimensions of phonological variation in Jakarta Malay. Unpublished Cornell Univ. dissertation.

[General sociolinguistic situation in Jakarta,
Chapter I. Phonological structure of Jakarta
Malay, Chapter II. Socially determined variation
and phonological history, Chapters III-V.]

Woordenlijst. 1937. [A trilingual list of about
1,000 forms in Dutch, Malay, and Tugu Portuguese.
Selections printed, but with little care for
accuracy, in Franca (1970:83-101). According to
Mr. Jacobus Quiko, the compiler was a Dutchman
from Bandung named Dr. H. H. Noosten who gathered
the Portuguese materials in Tugu from older
villagers. The format is evidently that of Dutch
dialect survey materials: typewritten Dutch and
Malay equivalents in first two columns, blank
third column. Tugu Portuguese forms in Dutch
orthography written by hand in third column by
Noosten's Sundanese clerk. I have photocopies
of the original (possessed by Mr. Quiko) which
I plan to make generally available.]

RULE REORDERING IN THE
PHONOLOGICAL HISTORY OF SPANISH
(O SEA, ¿TIENE EL IDIOMA UN ESPÍRITU?)

STANLEY WHITLEY
West Virginia University

Western Romance lects agree in palatalizing Proto-Romance /lj/ to /ʎ/. Old Castilian, however, from its beginnings shows the further evolution ʎ → ž. Then, during the great consonantal shifts of Early Modern Spanish, this [ž] devoiced to [š] (which eventually made its way to the velum). Thus, we posit two ordered rules for the history of Castilian.[1]

(1) ʎ → ž
(2) ž → š

Now, after (1) had applied, geminate /ll/ palatalized in all Spanish dialects, as shown in (3); this gives, in the synchronic grammar of Old Castilian, a /ž/ from earlier /lj/, /ʎ/ from earlier /ll/.

(3) ll → ʎ

Interestingly, in many dialects of modern Spanish this new [ʎ] has now passed on to [ž] also, and even to [š].

(4) ʎ → ž

Question: has there been rule-addition of two fortuitously similar rules (1, 4), or has (1) been reordered (=(4)) to apply to the output of rule (3)?

This question is a crucial one, as rule-addition and rule-reordering are both recognized today as important mechanisms in language change, but with different implications. Rule-addition makes the weaker claim in simply observing what seems to be a remarkable coincidence but nothing more. The two spirantizations of $ƛ$ are merely accidents, and have nothing to do with each other. One who makes such an observation might point to the facts that (1) and (4) are centuries apart and that they probably originated in different parts of Spain (northern for (1), southern for (4)). But the 'coincidence' is truly remarkable; indeed, it is extraordinarily suspicious.

The rule-reordering answer makes the stronger, and more interesting, claim that (1) and (4) are the same rule, applying before (3) at one stage and after it at a later stage. Rule-reordering is a concept developed most notably by Kiparsky (1968, 1971) and King (1969), who illustrate it with convincing examples from Finnish, Swiss, and German dialects. They also attempt an explanation in terms of child language acquisition. Two rules are perceived by the LAD-equipped language learner to operate inefficiently, i.e. in 'marked' order—one rule $\underline{A}$ generates an output which fails to feed, or even bleeds, a subsequent rule $\underline{B}$. The child, in order to maximize derivations, reorders them so that $\underline{B}$'s output now feeds into $\underline{A}$.

The child's contribution to this reordering remains hypothetical, but the Kiparsky/King analysis otherwise seems to be borne out in their examples, which show a clear trend towards a feeding order of rules. In fact, the above Spanish example readily conforms to their analysis of rule-reordering, as shown below.

nonfeeding	feeding
(1) $ƛ \to \check{z}$	(3) $ll \to ƛ$
(3) $ll \to ƛ$	(4) $ƛ \to \check{z}$

As will be shown in this paper, many other examples of rule-reordering rise to the surface in the phonological history of Spanish, and, as a descriptive term, 'rule-reordering' seems apt. But lurking behind the explanation for rule-reordering is a somewhat dubious assumption, namely that the child (or whoever has reordered the rules) finds evidence for reconstructing the original (1) in the first place. In fact, the original output of (1) has now passed on to /x/ (which has not happened yet in the case of the more modern (4)), without leaving behind any morphophonemic alternations. That is, when (3) was added to the grammar, (1) was already dead, synchronically speaking, and unrecoverable to the presumed reorderer of the rules. A strict adherence to the Kiparsky/King hypothesis would even imply that O. Cast. [mužér], [kabéʎo] both have [ž] (or [x]) now, which is not the case.

Another example from Spanish in which rule reordering seems, initially at least, the best explanation concerns 'shimmer'.[2] Latin /ŭ/ before a palatal yields two reflexes in Old Aragonese, depending on which rule--Raising (o → u) or Laxing (o → ɔ)--applies. Both apply to the same structural description, and therefore are mutually bleeding; this fact enables us to account for the different reflexes very handily by ordering Raising before Laxing in one case, and vice versa in the other.

(5)

	/mŭltu/	/kŭltĕllu/
(other rules):	mójto	kojtéʎo
RAISING	mújto	kujtéʎo
LAXING	-----	-------
	↓	↓
	[mújto]	[kujtjéʎo]
	'much'	'knife'

(6)

	/vúltŭre/	/adŭ́ktu/
(other rules)	bójtre	adójto
LAXING	bǒjtre	adǒjto
RAISING	------	------
	↓	↓
	[bwéjtre]	[adwéjto]
	'vulture'	'brought'

The same approach has been taken in the assignment of stress to *carácter* in Modern Spanish (Harris 1969, Whitley 1976), and, as a purely synchronic statement, it works. But diachronically, this use of rule-reordering again poses problems for the Kiparsky/King theory, although not for lack of morphophonemic alternations (cf. Arag. *muito* ~ *multitud*, *adweito* ~ *aducir*). Here the sticking point is the lack of any clear evidence that one ordering antedates the other; in fact, in chronicling the phonological rules which have applied to Aragonese through the centuries, I have discovered that the application of other rules indicates that Raising and Laxing were virtually adjacent in ordering, perhaps coetaneous additions to the grammar. If so, then it is extremely unclear what diachronic sense can be assigned to the notion of 'rule-reordering'.

Of course, shimmer such as that in Old Aragonese is exceedingly limited and almost word-specific. But it is rather more difficult to shove aside the problems of rule-reordering in cases such as (1), because there is an astonishing number of them. Regardless of how their reordering is to be explained, it is an observable fact that many rules of Spanish which applied long ago applied again later once new outputs were generated which could feed into them.

In the following sections we will examine recurrent, or 'recrudescent', rules in depth.[3] Two types will be distinguished, as defined below; as will be shown later, the two differ in how they might be explained in a theory of language change.

'More natural rules' are rules which are grounded in natural processes such as assimilation, with ample parallels outside Spanish and its sisters. 'Less natural rules' are rules which are difficult to characterize as 'natural', and relatively uncommon outside Spanish.

More Natural Rules.

(7) Nasal assimilation
Within Latin:
contemnere
computare
intendere
implere
Latin to Old Spanish:
amb(ĭ)tare → (amdar) → andar
comp(ŭ)tare → contar
somnium → sueño
ampliu → ancho
sem(ĭ)ta → senda
dominĭcu → domi[ŋ]go
Modern Spanish:
homerun → jonrón

Comment. Nasal assimilation has been a productive synchronic rule in the grammars of all three stages; as a tendency, it can be reckoned universal.

(8) nj → ɲ	
Latin to Old Spanish	Modern (nonstandard dialects)
Hispania → España	nieto → ñeto
ba(l)neu → baño	nieve → ñeve
tingere → teñir	junio → juño
seniore → señor	opinión → opiñón

Comment. Palatalization of alveolars in general is a well-attested process in many languages, and, in terms of distinctive features, is completely 'natural'.

(9) V → [-syll] / V
    ⎡-lo ⎤
    ⎣-str⎦

Latin to Old Castilian:
  e(g)o → yo
  bracchiu → *brakjo → braço
  crūdēle → cruel ([krw-])
  vadeat → vaya
  coag(ŭ)lare → cuajar ([kwa-])
  fidēle → fiel ([fje-])
  le(g)e → ley
Old Castilian to Modern Castilian:
  amades → (amaes) → amáis
Colloquial modern:
  real → [r̄jál]
  pasear → [pasjár]
  cohete → [kwéte]
  peor → [pjór]
  to(d)avía → [twaβía]
  la(d)o → [láw]
  maestro → [májstro]

Comment. The reduction of vowels to glides when contiguous to other vowels can be observed in many languages as a diachronic process. Note also that both Latin and Modern Spanish contain synchronic rules which generate glides from underlying high vowels (Latin: [i u] ~ [j w], Spanish: envío ~ enviar)

(10) j → ∅ / V
           [-bk]

Latin to Old Spanish	Modern (New Mexico, northern Mexico, Nicaragua, Asturias, Judaeo-spanish, et al.)
frigidu → frío	rodí(ll)as
legale → leal	estré(ll)a
pejōre → peor	sí(ll)a
jenĭperu → enebro	po(ll)íto
vagīna → vaína	cuchí(ll)o
fugīre → huir	bi(ll)éte
*jectare → echar	

Comment. Though not as common in other languages, the loss of [j] when adjacent to [i] or [e] does have precedents; cf. Eng. *east* for *yeast* in some dialects, Japanese *ye* → *e*. Note also the synchronic derivation of the verb form *rio* in modern Spanish: /r̄e+jó/ → r̄ijó → r̄ió.

(11) a → $\begin{bmatrix} -lo \\ -bk \end{bmatrix}$ / ___ j̃

Latin	
caelu → *kɛlu	-ariu → -e(i)ro
caecu → *kɛku	factu → feito, hecho
quaero → *kʷɛro	canta(v)i → canté(i)
Modern (all over, especially in Colombia, Chile)	
traído → tráido → treido	
baile → beile	

Comment. The second column mixes *e* < *ai* for several of Menendez Pidal's types of yod; if distinguished, each type would show further recurrences. The differences (*e*, *ei*) reflect Castilian as opposed to Leonese and Aragonese. This kind of change is a very natural and widespread process of umlaut (*metafonía*, *inflexión*), as are the following two.

(12) $\left.\begin{array}{l} ɔ → o \\ ɛ → e \\ e → i \\ o → u \end{array}\right\}$ / ___ $C_0 \begin{bmatrix} +sonor \\ +hi \end{bmatrix}$

Latin to Castilian (Aragonese)	Modern Asturian
fŏlia → hoja (fuella)	potro → potru → putru
fŏvea → hoya (fueva)	este → esti → isti
rĕg(u)la → reja (riella)	primero → primiru
cŭnea → *konja → cuña	techo → tichu
fŭgio → huyo (fuyo)	feo → fíu
vendemia → vendimia	tarde → terdi

Comment. The lefthand half of the rule has been left unformalized because the standard features for vowel height ([high], [low]) do not furnish a simple way to capture the general raising process.

RULE REORDERING / 385

(13) (al) → aw → o / ___ C

Comment. Many cases could be cited for aw → o
(audire → oír, causa → cosa, paupere → pobre) and
for al → aw. The following derivation shows that
the latter has applied at least twice in Castilian
(fauce → hoz 'ravine', falce → hoz 'sickle',
salice → sauce 'willow'; cf. Aragonese foz, but
falz, salz).

(14)

	/fáwke/	/fálke/	/sálike/
Preceding rules:	háwd^{z}e	hált^{s}e	sáled^{z}e
al → aw	------	háwt^{s}e	-------
aw → o	hód^{z}e	hót^{s}e	-------
syncope	-----	-----	sáld^{z}e
apocope	hod^z	hót^s	-------
final devoic.	hót^s	-----	-------
al → aw	-----	-----	sáwd^{z}e
O. Cast.:	hoz	hoz	sauze
	[hót^s]	[hót^s]	[sáwd^{z}e]
plur.:	hozes	hoces	
	[hód^{z}es]	[hót^{s}es]	

The processes in al → aw → o are paralleled in many
languages, including French (falsu → [fo], altru →
[otr]) and English (chalk → [čɔk], salt → [sɔt]).

(15) $\begin{bmatrix} -\text{sonor} \\ +\text{cor} \\ +\text{cont} \end{bmatrix}$ → [-vce] / ___ #

Old Spanish	Modern (Castilla la Vieja)
me[s], me[z]es	verda[θ], verda[ð]es
cru[t^s], cru[d^z]es	salu[θ], salu[ð]es
ha[t^s], ha[d^z]er	virtu[θ], virtu[ð]es
relo[š], relo[ž]es (?)	

Comment. The structural description is not
quite correct since [+continuant] is supposed to
do for affricates as well as fricatives; but I see
no other way to refer to coronal affricates and
fricatives, whether strident or not. Cf. final
devoicing rules of German and Russian.

386 / STANLEY WHITLEY

(16) r ~ l

Latin to Spanish	Modern (Andaluz, Ebro Valley, Chile, Caribbean, et al.)
miraculu → milagro	olol (pl.: olores)
Mercuris → miércoles	matal (fut.: mataré)
robur(e) → roble	ayel
marmore → mármol	porvo
parabola → palabra	gorpe
periculu → peligro	argo
pallidu → pardo	

Comment. Confusion of liquids is natural enough given their similar feature-composition. Of course, most of the earlier examples involve metathesis or dissimilation, rules whose environments (two liquids in different syllables) are unlike that of liquid neutralization in modern dialects (syllable-final position).

(17) w ~ v, β, b

Latin	Latin to Old Castilian
w → v	verrere → barrer
	vota → boda
	vermiculu → bermejo
	vivire → bivir
	-aba → -ava

Old Cast. to Modern	Modern (nonstandard)
b⎫ v⎭ → [b ~ β]	w → βw, ʸw (huevo)

Early Modern	Modern Aragonese
debda → deuda	clau (plur.: claves)
cibdad → ciudad	
cabdal → caudal	

Comment. These labials circle around in revolving-door fashion in many languages, though especially in Spanish. Yet their feature compositions are quite unlike in the Chomsky-Halle system (but see Campbell 1974 for a new feature [+labial]).

(18) [+del rel] → [-del rel]

Early Modern Spanish	Modern dialects (notably Andaluz)
t^s → s, θ	č → š (chico, charlar, pecho, tacha)

Comment. Deaffrication is probably a borderline case in this classification. Although it involves only one change in feature specifications (and is thus rather natural in generative phonology), and is well attested elsewhere (French and Portuguese č → š, t^s → s; East Franconian p^f → f; Greek d^z → z), it is hardly the predetermined fate of all affricates in all languages.

Less Natural Rules.

(19) ∅ → e / #___sC

Latin to Old Spanish	Medieval borrowings
scala → escala	sphera → esfera
statu → estado	studiare → estudiar
Stephanu → Estevan	speculativu → especulativo
strictu → estrecho	
speculu → espejo	spiritu → espíritu
scribere → escrivir	statua → estatua
sponsu → esposo	speciale → especial
Modern borrowings	
snob → esnob	
standard → estándar(d)	
sphygmo-manometros → esfigmomanómetro	

Comment. The earliest application of e-prothesis is attested in other varieties of Romance as well, e.g. French é(s)tat, é(s)troit, é(s)criver, etc.; but only in the Iberian languages did it become a permanent fixture that has continued to apply. This rule, unlike many others cited in this list, is still productive, as can be seen in the treatment of modern loanwords and in the synchronic derivation of estar, which still acts like /star(e)/ (Harris 1969:141). It could be interpreted as natural only in the sense that VCCV might be a less marked syllable structure than CCV; but many

if not most other languages (including modern
French) find initial sC tolerable in a way that
Spanish never has.

(20) d → ð → ∅ / V__V

Latin to Old Castilian	Modern (variable rule[4])
ridere → reír	solda(ð)o
tepidu → tibio	habla(ð)o
cadere → caer	esta(ð)o
radice → raíz	la(ð)o
pede → pie	vivi(ð)o

Comment. French, too, lost /d/ via the intermediate stage of [ð]; yet there is little evidence
for ð-deletion as a natural, panlinguistic tendency.
English, Greek, and Icelandic quite contentedly
maintain [ð], while in German it moved on to [d].

(21) VCjV → VjCV

Latin to Old Spanish	Modern Aragonese
capio → *kajpo → quepo	había → haiba
-ariu → *-ajro → -e(i)ro	
bassgu → *bajsso →	vulgarismo:
baxo (→ bajo)	nadie → naide

Comment: Yod metathesis is decidedly a rare
quirk, although it seems to have flourished in the
spoken Latin of several parts of the Empire. The
modern example from Aragonese is limited to this
one verb, and competes in some dialects with heba
(where a medieval metathesis occurred: aj → e).
The 'vulgarismo' is cited by Menéndez Pidal (1968:
147), but not localized.

(22) t → ∅ / n__#

Latin to Old Spanish	Within Old Spanish
amabant → amavan	(grand') → grant → gran
tenent → tienen	cuant → cuán
dant → dan	sant → san
sunt → son	
Modern Aragonese	
dien	
fuan	
mon	

Comment: While it occurred in a few other Romance languages, this deletion is difficult to explain as a general linguistic tendency in all languages. The Modern Aragonese examples could be explained as dating from the Old Spanish application of the rule, except that Old Aragonese tended to retain the t in dient, fuant, mont. At least in those dialects where 'mountains' is [monθ], the Aragonese t-deletion must have followed the early modern shift of [ts] to [θ], and is thus distinct from earlier applications of (22).

(23) m → n / __#

Latin to Old Spanish	Modern Spanish
tam → tan	ultimátu[n]
cum → con	álbu[n]
quem → quien	

Comment. The first version applied so early that it must be reckoned as a development in spoken Latin, and would be unremarkable but for the fact that Spanish still rules out final /m/.

(24) f → φ → h

Latin to Old Castilian	Modern (nonstandard)
faba → haba	[φ], [h] in fácil, feo, café
filiu → hijo	
fumu → humo	
fungu → hongo	
farina → harina	
ferru → hierro	
farctu → harto	
facere → hazer	

Comment. Since Menéndez Pidal, it has been customary to wrap up aspiración and file it away under 'Basque substratum', which is an interesting theory about what triggered it, but only a theory about what triggered it. At any rate, it is fascinating that the frequently postulated intermediate stage, [φ], has begun to eat away at modern [f] as well; and, at least for a few speakers an ocean away from downtown Pamplona and Bilbao, [ɸ] is starting to give way to [h] (Resnick 1975:25). Parallels for (24) are rare outside Spanish, though Japanese [ɸ] and [h] derive diachronically and synchronically from the same phoneme.

It is well known, of course, that the ultimate fate of the output of the original (24) is ∅ in most lects, by virtue of rule (25). To my knowledge, (25) has not reapplied in Modern Spanish--yet;[5] but the Early Modern Spanish elimination of /h/ has a predecessor within Latin, as shown. With analogs at least in Greek, French, and urban British English, (25) might be classified among the 'More Natural' rules; it is given here only as a follow-up of (24).

(25) h → ∅

Latin	Early Modern Spanish (except marginal dialects)
h̷ora	h̷aba
h̷abere	h̷ijo
h̷omine	h̷umo, etc.

(26) V $\begin{bmatrix} -sonor \\ -cont \end{bmatrix}$ C V → ∅   Condition: C ≠ liquid

  1   2   3 4   1 2 3 4

Latin to Old Spanish	Modern Spanish
aptare → atar	exacto → [esá(k)to]
captare → catar	extraño → [estráɲo]
ipse → [ese]	excepto → [esé(p)to]
fraxinu → [fresno]	directo → [diréto]
	séptimo → [sétimo]

Comment. <u>Grupos cultos</u>, as they are traditionally called, seem always to have been anathema to the phonological system of Spanish. By assimilation, Latin itself eliminated several non-homorganic clusters (<u>ad-cipio</u> → <u>accipio</u>, <u>ob-ferre</u> → <u>offerre</u>, etc.); by means of (27), the group <u>kt</u> in Romance found its own solution, which, like the outright dropping of the consonant in (26), likewise has its followers today.

(27) k → j / __ t

Latin to Old Castilian (Arag., Leon.)	Modern Andaluz, non-standard American
ŏcto → ocho (ueito)	efecto → efeito
nŏcte → noche (nueite)	carácter → caráiter
directu → derecho (dereito)	perfecto → perfeito
	seductor → seduitor
trūcta → trucha (truita)	
factu → hecho (feito)	

Comment. In Aragonese and Leonese--and, indeed, Portuguese, Catalan, and French--/kt/ yielded /jt/, which advanced one assimilatory step further in the Castilian affricate [č]. (27) has a modern equivalent, as shown, but here it competes with (26) and with the alternative solution [wt].

(28) r → s (→ ∅) / __ s

Latin to Old Spanish	Modern Aragonese
ŭrsu → osso	mullés 'mujeres'
travĕrsu → traviesso	primés 'primeros'
sursu → suso	
deorsu → yuso	
Santo Domingo	Asturian
isse 'irse'	isi 'irse'
	caesi 'caerse'

Comment. On the face of it, (28) seems a straightforward matter of assimilation. But for a 'natural' assimilatory process, it is somewhat complex in terms of changed feature specifications, and rather uncommon in the languages with which I am familiar (although rs may have become ss as early as Latin). Scholars who find (28) applying rampantly in other languages might wish to reclassify it under 'More Natural'.

(29) ʎ → j

(30) $j \rightarrow \hat{j} \rightarrow \begin{Bmatrix} \check{z} \\ \check{y} \\ \hat{j} \end{Bmatrix} / \begin{Bmatrix} \# \\ V \end{Bmatrix} \_\_ V$

Latin to Leon., Arag., and Cast.	Modern Yeísta Dialects[6]
mul̯ier → muller, mujer aurīc(u)la → oreilla, oreja cīli̯a → cella, ceja meli̯ōre → mellor, mejor	ella, llama, pollo, calle = [j ɟ̂ ž y̌]
Latin to Old Spanish	Urban Castilian
jŏcu → juego jammagis → jamás jŭvene → joven jŏvis → jueves	yo, yeso, ya, mayo = [y̌, ɟ̂]

Comment. (29) and (30) together bring us back to the first case cited, which is one of the most complex congeries of rules as well as one of the most interesting. (30) is probably as old as Proto-Romance; all of the Western Romance languages and their dialects attest to the spirantization, and even affrication, of /j/ in the positions indicated: jŏcu gives [ž], in Fr. jeu, [y̌] in It. giuoco, [ž] in Port. jūgo, [ž] in Cat. joc. In Old Spanish dialects, both [y̌] and [ž] emerged, with the former predominating word-initially and the latter elsewhere. Castilian later extended the allophone [ž] to all positions (cf. rule (18)), but Aragonese shows the original affricate in its <u>choven</u> 'joven' (where i̯, like other medieval sibilants, has devoiced by (31)).

Thus spirantization, or <u>rehilamiento</u>, of /j/ applied even in early Romance; but it also applied later to a delateralized Castilian [ʎ] (< medial /lj/, /kl/, /gl/), whence O. Cast. [mužér] as opposed to Leonese and Aragonese [muʎér]. So much for application two of (30) and application one of (29).

A new [ʎ] arose in Old Spanish from /ll/ and initial /pl kl fl/. But from the seventeenth century on, this new [ʎ] has in turn delateralized in <u>yeísta</u> dialects, with the output merging with Spanish [j] (hence, application two of (29)).

Presently, most dialects of Spanish apply some
degree of <u>rehilamiento</u> to Spanish [j] (=/ʎ/ and
/j/ in <u>yeísta</u> dialects, /j/ in <u>lleísta</u> dialects),
ranging from a voiced palatal fricative [ɉ] to an
affricate [ǰ] or--coming full circle once again--
[ž]. Thus, in summary, (29) has applied twice in
the history of Spanish, and (30) has applied three
times, as shown graphically in (31).

(31)
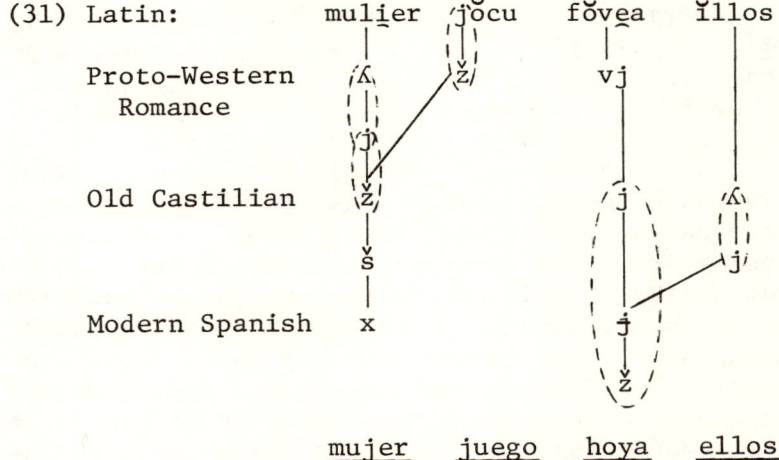

Then, to complete the picture, we have only to bring
in the general sibilant devoicing rule (32).

(32) $\begin{bmatrix} +\text{strid} \\ +\text{cor} \end{bmatrix} \rightarrow [-\text{vce}]$

Comment. This rule applied once in Early Modern
Spanish to [dᶻ z ž ǰ]. Intriguingly, many <u>Porteños</u>
are now devoicing the [ž] generated by the <u>re-
hilamiento</u> of ɉ < j, ʎ: [póšo], [káše], [pláša],
'pollo, calle, playa'.

Rule addition and readdition, or rule reordering
and reordering?

Toward a theory of recrudescent rules. The examples presented copiously demonstrate that some rules
in the history of Spanish have applied again and
again. We can return now to the question posed

earlier, which, simply put, is why? I believe that
the sheer number of recrudescent rules and their
striking similarity in input and output rules out
an answer in terms of repeated rule-addition.
Given the plethora of possible phonological rules
now catalogued from the study of many languages, it
would seem somewhat myopic to insist that ʎ → j
(→ ɟ) was added twice, and merely as a coincidence.
One immediately wishes to know why [ʎ] again gave
way to [j] (and not, for example, to [l], [ç], [ḍ],
[l̡], or just [l]⁷), and indeed, why it changed
again at all.

Yet in many cases an answer in terms of rule-
reordering will also be improbable, as argued
earlier. The sample reorderings adduced by Kiparsky and King were still reflected in synchronic
alternations; following their theory, one might
easily imagine a perceptive LAD which reverses two
rules already existent in the grammar to maximize
their applications. To explain all of the above
Spanish examples in the same way would require un-
assailable evidence that rule A was still present
in the grammar and applying before rule B prior to
its 'reordering' after B. But while the more ingenious and more intrepid abstract phonologists
may still perceive alternations in lácteo ~
leche (whence a (27) which is still in the grammar) and auditivo ~ oír (whence (13) and (20)), I
am unable to find any convincing evidence within
Old Spanish grammar for the original delaterali-
zation and rehilamiento prior to their 'reordering'
in yeísmo. The same holds for the earliest applications of, for example, rules (11), (12), (15),
(16), (21), (22), (23), (25), (26), (28), and (30).

Let us cast about for a different explanation of
recrudescent rules. Traditional Hispanic linguists
themselves have been struck by the fact that modern
processes reflect those of bygone eras, delaterali-
zation and rehilamiento above all. Though most
(e.g. Spaulding 1943) content themselves with
merely observing the parallel, some strike out
more boldly in search of an explanation. Generally, these explanations sort out into two groups,

which I will call 'natural process' and 'specific tendency'.

Those who interpret recrudescent processes as natural processes which can be expected to apply maximally in all languages have a point. At least 11 of the 24 rules above have some grounding in general processes encountered in many languages; and most can easily be expressed with distinctive features to show 'marked' segments becoming 'unmarked'. That they apply again and again may not be due to any special property of Spanish phonology or to any internal determinism in its history, but simply because, after all, nasals do tend to assimilate, liquids are periodically interchanged, and so on. Such processes are to be explained as part of general, universal grammar.

But the rules listed as 'less natural' resist such an interpretation, although Alonso (1967:161) has attempted this in connection with yeísmo. In a well-documented treatment of the chronology and mechanics of this process, he avers that [ʎ] is a rather unstable phone prone to delateralize, and finds parallel evolutions in dialects of French, Italian, Catalan, Rumanian, Hungarian, and Brazilian Portuguese. But this generalization does not take into account the facts (1) that [ʎ] remained stable in those lects for a long time, (2) that [ʎ] survives in many nonstandard French dialects and Italian, Catalan, and Portuguese dialects, (3) that other evolutions of [ʎ] are possible, and (4) that many languages[8] preserve [ʎ] while readily engaging in truly natural processes such as nasal assimilation. Like the Neogrammarians' notion of 'ease of articulation', Alonso's account cannot explain why one language rids itself of a phoneme that flourishes in another language.

Certain proposals by Prague-inspired devotees of économie also fall into the natural-process category. Alarcos Llorach (1950:154), for example, describes as 'transfonologización' the intrasystemic dynamics whereby phonemes are introduced, shifted, and lost. In Early Modern Spanish, [ž → š → x], [j] becomes a fricative, certain affricates become fricatives, and /h/ drops out in order to maximize and regularize the overall system of correlations. In some respects, this resembles generative notions of markedness and the elimination of redundancy, whence 'naturalness'; but diagrams of phonemes scattering about in search of better-positioned casillas libres bear on the phonemes themselves, and not on the question of why the rules involved were 'recrudescent'. The problem remains.

Let us consider the other approach, 'specific tendency', according to which recrudescent rules (especially the 'less natural' ones) represent inherent and permanent tendencies in the language itself. For example, Zamora Vicente (1967:79) observes $\underline{\Lambda} \rightarrow \underline{\check{z}} \rightarrow \underline{\check{s}}$ in Argentina and judges it a 'tendencia al ensordecimiento, viva y actuante en la lengua' ('tendency toward devoicing, alive and operative in the language'); Entwhistle (1936:221) finds here a 'general tendency of the Spanish language'; Alonso (1967:207-208), taking another tack, brings several repeated processes together as part and parcel of a continuing 'marcha general de la lengua', whose method is ablandamiento ('lenition', or even vaguer, 'softening') and whose distant goal (meta lejana) is an open syllable. Martinet (1955: 322) agrees that certain recurrent processes of Spanish may be specific tendencies in the language.[9]

'Tendency' is an apposite term in this regard, and seems quite attractive until it is examined more closely. What is a 'tendency'? How does it become a part of a language, and where is it stated in the series of rules that makes up the phonological history of a language? How, precisely, does it constrain its evolution? Such questions are highly important. If recrudescent rules are to be attributed to language-specific tendencies, then somewhere one must formulate a general mechanism that (1) constrains the number of possible changes to a specified group of rules and (2) is activated in a well-defined way when a representation appears that could feed into those rules.

Otherwise, 'tendency' becomes a nebulous black
box of causal energy tantamount to a <u>genio</u> or
<u>espíritu</u> which guides the language as it sees
fit.

The latter alternative was taken up enthusiastically in early comparative linguistics, notably in Grimm's notions of <u>Sprachgeist</u> and <u>Kreislauf</u>,[10] but linguistics has since abandoned the mystical in favor of the empirical; no one today would seriously postulate spirits in language. Even so, no less sober a linguist than E. Sapir (1921:154) has discerned a definite 'drift' in the evolution of English case endings, and asks:

> ... if [some] variations are born only to die
> without trace, while the equally minute, or
> even minuter, changes that make up the drift
> are forever imprinted on the history of the
> language, are we not imputing to this history
> a certain mystical quality?

Attempting to answer Sapir's question, R. Lakoff (1972) suggests that tendencies in the evolution of a language are governed by a general constraint on possible changes which she calls a 'metacondition'. She exemplifies one such metacondition in the drift toward analytical grammar in the Indo-European languages. Such a constraint is significant because it makes a general statement about disparate individual developments which are not necessarily due to universal natural processes. Yet she, too, sees little provision in linguistic theory for formalizing such a condition (1972:179):

> I do not at present see any way of characterizing
> this metacondition formally. Nor can I imagine
> how it could be considered as part of a synchronic description of a language. I cannot
> imagine how it could have been learned by a
> speaker, if it is part of his linguistic knowledge at all.

My own view, after surveying the remarkable number of recrudescent rules in Spanish, is that diachrony may be governed by constraints akin to the derivational constraints which have recently been posited for synchrony.[11] While the synchronic constraints recognized so far have been exceedingly diverse (grammatical 'conspiracies' against certain rule applications, general constraints governing underlying, intermediate, and surface-phonetic representations, rules which hark back to underlying representations, and so on), all share the common denominator of global application; that is, they are relevant to several stages in derivation and not just to the particular input and output of a particular rule.

Compare the diachronic situation in Spanish. During the history of Spanish, [d] has passed into the language twice; in each case, the further evolution of the [d] has been determined, so to speak, by a constraint such that it fricativizes and then drops. The segment [ʎ] has been generated twice; at least in some dialects, this phone has in both cases met a constraint such that a palatal lateral delateralizes, if it changes at all, and then joins the evolution of [j]. The latter in turn is fed into a globally applying rule which fricativizes it. Where they change at all, [f] and [kt] are constrained to undergo specific rules. And so on. Positing a global constraint on the universe of possible changes in Spanish would greatly simplify an overall account of its history.

Yet, like Lakoff I am at a loss in characterizing diachronic constraints and theorizing where they should be stated in a series of diachronic rules, or, even worse, in the synchronic rules of the native speaker. Such are the problems with derivational constraints, in fact, that Kiparsky (1972:224) views them as ad hoc (i.e. nongeneral) 'functional' explanations which slide into ghastly shades of teleology. He instead suggests

    a way in which the concept of a 'tendency',
    which lends functionalist discussions their

characteristic fuzziness, can be made more precise in terms of hierarchies of optimality, which predict specific consequences for linguistic change, language acquisition, and universal grammar.

But 'hierarchies of optimality' (themselves rather 'fuzzily' defined and formulated in Kiparsky's article) will not suffice to explain all diachronic tendencies. They are based on the linguist's panlinguistic, universalistic projections of natural changes, and, as has been maintained throughout this paper, a goodly number of the recrudescent rules of Spanish are neither 'natural' nor 'universal'. Why should [ð] drop in Spanish but remain in other languages or convert into a stop? Why should [kt] repeatedly undergo a rule yielding [jt] in Spanish but change into [pt] in Rumanian and stay as is in many languages? Why whould [j] undergo <u>rehilamiento</u> three times in Spanish but never in English? Such changes do not obey universal, language-independent laws or hierarchies, but pertain directly and specifically to the continuing evolution of Spanish. They are integrally and peculiarly as much a part of its diachronic description as well-known constraints on stress, initial clusters, vowels, and vibrants are a part of its synchronic description.

In summary, it appears to me that diachronic derivational constraints are the only adequate explanation for recrudescent rules, at least the less natural ones. A literal interpretation of reordering shipwrecks on those cases where there is little or no evidence for actual reordering by the LAD; natural explanations, including Kiparsky's hierarchies, work very well with nasal assimilation but not ð-deletion, <u>f</u>-aspiration, or <u>rehilamiento</u> and <u>yeísmo</u>; and while people have <u>espíritu</u>, languages—however we may reify them—do not. Globally applying derivational constraints may still be quite fuzzy, but I suggest that there is strong evidence for them in the phonological history of Spanish.

NOTES

1. Rule (1) has been simplified for purposes of illustration. As shown by rules (29) and (30), the actual process had intermediate stages.
2. 'Shimmer' refers to cases in which the expected reflex of a proto-unit varies inexplicably. Cf. Agard 1971:10.
3. Otero (1971:52) uses the term 'recurrent' ('ciertos procesos pueden resultar "recurrentes" y repetirse si las condiciones son propicias'). However, aside from a reference to Anderson, he gives little further attention to procesos recurrentes, although his glossary of phonological rules contains three which are 'fuera de serie'.
4. (20) today applies virtually everywhere in the Spanish-speaking world, with the extent of deletion tied to social class, style, and phonological environment.
5. Nevertheless, in the case of the aspiration of syllable-final -s, (25) is applying in some dialects.
6. The distribution of lleísmo/yeísmo is currently too complex to give here. For detailed information, see Canfield 1962, Zamora Vicente 1967, Alonso 1967, and Resnick 1975.
7. In fact, Alonso (1967:167-168) has unearthed a statement by one Gonzalo Correas, who observed in 1626 that in Extremadura [ʎ] was becoming [l]. At this time, there were as yet few indications of the second round of ʎ → j, so this extremeño rule represented a completely new Spanish rule, ʎ → l. Yet today Extremadura is yeísta; the old rule reasserted itself.
8. Ruhlen 1975 lists a sizeable number of languages with /ʎ/.
9. According to Martinet, these--and not just f → h--are due to the Basques, which is not only overgeneralized speculation, but only begs further questions.
10. Kreislauf does seem seductive here; recrudescent rules give a strong impression of a language developing cyclically.

11. Lakoff herself notices the similarity between her metaconditions governing diachronic derivation and certain synchronic derivational constraints.

REFERENCES

Agard, F. B. 1971. Language and dialect: Some tentative postulates. Linguistics 65.5-24.

Alarcos Llorach, Emilio. 1950. Fonología española. Madrid: Editorial Gredos.

Alonso, Amado. 1967. Estudios lingüísticos: temas hispanoamericanos. Madrid: Editorial Gredos.

Campbell, Lyle. 1974. Phonological features: Problems and proposals. Language 50.52-65.

Canfield, Delos Lincoln. 1962. La pronunciación del español en América. Bogotá: Instituto Caro y Cuervo.

Entwhistle, W. J. 1936, 1969. The Spanish language. London: Faber & Faber.

Harris, James. 1969. Spanish phonology. Cambridge: MIT Press.

King, Robert D. 1969. Historical linguistics and generative grammar. Englewood Cliffs: Prentice-Hall, Inc.

Kiparsky, Paul. 1968. Linguistic universals and linguistic change. In: Universals in linguistic theory. Edited by E. Bach and R. T. Harms. New York: Holt, Rinehart and Winston, Inc.

Kiparsky, Paul. 1971. Phonological change. Reproduced by Indiana University Linguistics Club.

Kiparsky, Paul. 1972. Explanation in phonology. In: Goals of linguistic theory. Edited by S. Peters. Englewood Cliffs, N.J.: Prentice-Hall, Inc.

Lakoff, Robin. 1972. Another look at drift. In: Linguistic change and generative theory. Edited by R. P. Stockwell and R. Macaulay. Bloomington: Indiana University Press.

Martinet, André. 1955, 1970. Économie des changements phonétiques. Bern: Francke.

Menéndez Pidal, Ramón. 1904, 1968. Manual de gramática histórica española. Madrid: Espasa-Calpe.
Otero, Carlos-P. 1971. Evolución y revolución en Romance. Barcelona: Seix Barral.
Resnick, Melvyn. 1975. Phonological variants. The Hague: Mouton.
Ruhlen, Merritt. 1975. A guide to the languages of the world. Language Universals Project, Stanford University.
Sapir, Edward. 1921, 1949. Language. New York: Harcourt, Brace and World, Inc.
Spaulding, Robert K. 1943, 1971. How Spanish grew. Berkeley: University of California Press.
Whitley, M. Stanley. 1976. Stress in Spanish: Two approaches. Lingua 39:301-332.
Zamora Vicente, Alonso. 1967. Dialectología española. Madrid: Editorial Gredos.